Fighting with the Eighteenth Massachusetts

The Civil War Memoir of Thomas H. Mann

Edited by
John J. Hennessy

LOUISIANA STATE UNIVERSITY PRESS
BATON ROUGE
MM

Copyright © 2000 by Louisiana State University Press
All rights reserved
Manufactured in the United States of America
First printing
10 09 08 07 06 05 04 03 02 01 00
5 4 3 2 1

Designer: Barbara Neely Bourgoyne
Typeface: Sabon and Copperplate
Typesetter: Coghill Composition, Inc.
Printer and binder: Thomson-Shore, Inc.

Library of Congress Cataloging-in-Publication Data:

Mann, Thomas H., 1843–1916.
 Fighting with the Eighteenth Massachusetts : the Civil War memoir of Thomas H. Mann / edited by John J. Hennessy.
   p.   cm.
 Includes bibliographical references and index.
   ISBN 0-8071-2577-6 (alk. paper)
 1. Mann, Thomas H., 1843–1916. 2. United States—History—Civil War, 1861–1865—Personal narratives. 3. United States. Army. Massachusetts Infantry Regiment, 18th (1861–1864) 4. Massachusetts—History—Civil War, 1861–1865. 5. Soldiers—Massachusetts—Biography. I. Hennessy, John J. II. Title.
 E513.5 18th .M36 2000
 973.7′4444—dc21
                                          00-008371

The paper in this book meets the guidelines for permanence and durability of the Committee on Production Guidelines for Book Longevity of the Council on Library Resources. ∞

Contents

Preface ix
Abbreviations xix

ONE   To War: "Only Cogs in the Wheel"   1
TWO   "The Sacred Soil of Virginia"   20
THREE   Yorktown: "Chase them up some more!"   43
FOUR   Peninsula Campaign: "Next Door to Defeat"   59
FIVE   Second Manassas and Antietam   85
SIX   Fredericksburg: "Wicked and Murderous"   108
SEVEN   Mud and Renewal   127
EIGHT   Chancellorsville: "The Most Desponding Hours of My Life"   150
NINE   Gettysburg: "One Continuous Roar"   166
TEN   Respite, Recruits, and Politics   186
ELEVEN Fall 1863: Swift Victory and Numbing Stalemate   204
TWELVE The Wilderness: "Beginning of the End"   224

Epilogue: Long Journey Home   239
Appendix A: A Treatise on Army Mules   241
Appendix B: Journey to Mine Run   246
Bibliography   253
Index   259

Illustrations

Photographs

following page 143

Mann in Zoave-style uniform

Mann in regulation Union uniform

1870s tintype of Mann

View of Mann family homestead

1880s portrait of Mann

Maps

Eighteenth's roundabout to Harrison's Landing   77

Northern Virginia and Maryland: Eighteenth's operation, August–September 1862   88

Eighteenth Massachusetts at Fredericksburg   117

Eighteenth's route to Chancellorsville   154

Eighteenth Massachusetts on Story Hill, Gettysburg   177

PREFACE

For 230 years, citizen-soldiers have been the hallmark of America's great armies and navies. In times of national crisis, volunteers have flocked to the military banner—schoolmates and business partners and teachers and students marched off together, to serve together, to die together. They have brought to the armed forces a wisdom, irreverence, and naiveté that has driven professional military men to distraction. The underlying tension between a youthful upbringing based on the relentless exercise of personal freedom and the strict necessities of soldiering has been one of the defining aspects of the American military experience.

In turn, the wartime experience of these citizen-soldiers often became the central epoch in their lives. Many (like Thomas Mann) would rise to prominence in their communities after the war, forging careers as doctors, writers, industrialists, and politicians. But when these community patriarchs died, they often elected to have themselves identified on their tombstones as soldiers (probably the most menial and lowest-paying job many of them ever had). And because these young men would rise to dominate industry, media, and politics, they ensured that their military experience became not just central to their own lives, but to the national life. It is in part because of this that our nation—while proudly proclaiming its non-militarism—is dotted with more preserved acres of hallowed ground, manicured national cemeteries, and gleaming martial memorials than probably any nation in the world.

The memoirs and letters of Thomas Mann reflect many things. They are, fundamentally, a marvelous recounting of a common soldier's experience in the Civil War. Mann was literate, well-read, perceptive, and witty—suited to offer us one of the better records of wartime trials. His is a marvelous testament to that age-old American struggle between volunteer soldiers and the officers charged with turning them into efficient fighting men. The memoirs also reflect the attempt by Mann's generation to enshrine their wartime experiences in the nation's memory (judging from the modern industry that surrounds the Civil War, Mann and his cohorts succeeded spectacularly). Most importantly, Mann's recollections and wartime writings reveal the underlying struggle that served as the backdrop for his military experiences. To a greater degree than most, Mann's memoir illustrates the personal, social, and intellectual upheaval that accompanied—and ultimately defined—America's most momentous epoch.

When eighteen-year-old Thomas Mann marched off to war from his home in North Wrentham, Massachusetts, in the summer of 1861, he faithfully reflected the perspective of an entire generation. He went, he would say two years later, "purely out of love for adventure and the excitement of this kind of life." He recognized that war would require energy, enthusiasm, confidence, and perhaps some courage—for those were the qualities required to ensure the quick restoration of the Union (and no one doubted that outcome in mid-1861). But he had little concept of the one quality this war would demand above all others from him and his nation: determination.[1]

The Civil War in America during the summer of 1861 was a vastly different affair than it would become two years later. Most Northerners, including the soldiers, saw the war then as a straightforward, precise effort to reattach the wayward South to the Union—much as a surgeon today would reattach a severed finger or toe. The object seemed to be to bring the Confederacy back by doing as little damage as possible; the South's armies would be destroyed, to be sure, but the South at large and its institutions would be spared.

Defeat at First Bull Run did much to explode that illusion, but even more damaging to the illusion were the Union victories in the first year of war. Triumphs at Fort Donelson and Shiloh in Tennessee did nothing to bring the South magically back into the fold. Instead, they demonstrated that this war would require more than a single, surgical, military expedition. With stalemate, many in Washington advocated (successfully) that the restoration of the Union would require not just the military defeat of the South, but its complete subjugation—the wholesale demolition of a society built on a foundation of slavery.

The transformation of the American Civil War from a purely military exercise designed to restore the Union into a determined social, economic,

---

1. Mann to his mother, January 9, 1864, Thomas Mann Papers, Brown University.

and military crusade bent on demolishing and then transforming Southern society was no mere scholarly exercise. Thomas Mann—bright, aware, and literate—observed, experienced, and reacted to all of it.

Thomas Henry Mann was born April 8, 1843, the first son of the seventh generation of Manns in North Wrentham (now Norfolk), Massachusetts—about thirty-five miles southeast of Boston. His mother, Lydia, and father, Levi, operated a prosperous farm in Wrentham and toiled successfully to raise five sons.[2] Thomas Mann "early revealed unusual mental capacity," and he developed an especial interest in literature and language. As a teenager, he joined the local lyceum to discuss politics and current events. His parents charted for him an academic course designed to take him from Wrentham to Harvard and into the world.[3]

War, however, interrupted that idyllic journey to adulthood. In the wake of the firing on Fort Sumter in April 1861, Thomas Mann and much of the Wrentham militia determined to enlist to preserve the Union. These men became the corpus of what would be Company I of the Eighteenth Massachusetts Infantry. After training in Dedham and Readville (an experience wonderfully related by Mann in the memoir), the Eighteenth Massachusetts traveled by sail and rail to the front in the wake of the disaster at First Bull Run.

The Eighteenth joined the army that most everyone agreed would be the Republic's salvation: the Army of the Potomac. Commanded by Major General George B. McClellan, the Army of the Potomac would eventually grow to 130,000 men, accompanied by hundreds of cannon and miles of supply trains. McClellan would be widely recognized as a preeminent organizer and motivator. What he lacked, however, was the will to use his newly created army to its full potential. He stalled, complained, and overestimated the strength of his foe. Turgid progress punctuated by defeat would be the character of the war in Virginia during Mann's first two years of service.

Despite the lack of success in the field, McClellan, at least, forged in the Army of the Potomac a cohesive identity. Mann, along with much of the rest of the army, came to love his commander. Because of their devotion, the men in the ranks generally refused to accord blame for defeat on their beloved "Mac." Indeed, the Army of the Potomac would become expert at locating blame for failures elsewhere. The most common scapegoat: the

2. Levi Mann, obituary, clipping in the Mann Papers.
3. "Thomas Mann Deceased," clipping in the Mann Papers.

government in Washington, which Mann (as well as McClellan) saw as unsupportive of McClellan's ends.

Mann's oft-repeated resentment toward the government he served had its root in two factors. First, he saw the government's efforts to manage the war as mere interference in the prerogative of McClellan as commander. Second, as his months in service ticked away, Mann would see the Union war effort change in a way he thought both objectionable and unnecessary. The change culminated in September 1862 with Lincoln's issuance of the preliminary Emancipation Proclamation. Mann was no supporter of slavery, but he could not justify, as he wrote, "desolating the country for the sake of freeing the slaves." The army largely railed against the measure and all that accompanied it. The high command of the Army of the Potomac—led by McClellan—actively engaged in the tense debate over Union war aims (the last time in American history the military would so obviously throw itself into the debate over what were properly civil and political matters). Mann would have subscribed fully to the words of his corps commander, Fitz John Porter. The Emancipation Proclamation, Porter wrote, will "tend only to prolong the war by rousing bitter feelings of the south, and causing unity of action among them, while the reverse with us. Those who fight the battles of the country . . . wish to see [the war] ended honorably—by a restoration of the Union, not merely by a suppression of the rebellion, for there is a wide difference."[4]

Thomas Mann skirmished constantly—though always politely—with his abolitionist family at home over the great issues of the day. Over time, his views on slavery would become more muted as he recognized the military value of abolishing slave labor in the South (though even in his postwar writings, when time allowed for judicious reflection, he did not abdicate his deeply rooted stereotypes of Black Americans). He would not, however, mute his views on McClellan. He declared to his family in 1864, "As long as I . . . or any *intelligent* soldier of the 'Army of the Potomac' [lives] you will never hear the last of McCellan." Mann would be true to his word, remaining a devoted partisan long after most soldiers and veterans had recognized the general's considerable shortcomings.[5]

Mann's concerns about the direction of the Union war effort stopped well short of any perceptible lack of support for the war. He repeatedly

4. Mann to his father, November 15, 1862, Mann Papers; Fitz John Porter to Manton Marble, September 30, 1862, Manton Marble Papers, Library of Congress.

5. Mann to friends at home, March 14, 1864, Mann Papers.

rejected those who advocated "peace at any price"—a negotiated end to the war on the best terms available. In 1863, he even briefly decried McClellan for his association with Democrats who espoused a peace platform—Mann's only recorded displeasure with his old commander. (He later reasserted his devotion to the man, no matter his politics or his party.) When some of the members of the Wrentham Lyceum suggested Mann had Copperhead tendencies, he bristled in response and threatened to cut off all communication with his old debating adversaries. He chided those at home who chose not to join the war effort—the "young men of N. W[rentham] will be sorry that they have not had a hand in the vindication of the Old Flag," he wrote.[6] As the war progressed and as the toll in humanity and health mounted, Mann (like most Union soldiers) increasingly felt that the sacrifices of the men in the field could only be justified by unambiguous victory.

Thomas Mann was a classic example of a Conservative Patriot of the Civil War period. He, like so many members of the army, loved his country and fought desperately to preserve it, but disagreed with the political and social tack used to reunite it.

By 1864, the war that had started as an adventure had turned into a consuming, bloody, and cruel struggle of will and determination. Mann had by then experienced all the campaigns of the army, missing barely a day to sickness and suffering nary a scratch on eight battlefields (an uncommon feat given the frequency of illness and wounds). He had seen the impact of war in all its forms—horror on the battlefield, Southern civilians struggling amidst shortage and destruction, freed slaves flocking to the army by the hundreds. All this Mann noted and endured better than most. Still, the experience extracted a heavy toll. So severe were Mann's trials that they compelled him to decide not to reenlist at the conclusion of his term in August 1864—spurning a huge bounty or perhaps a commission in one of the new regiments of African-American troops. He made his choice to return home, he wrote, not out of a lack of commitment, but simply because of hardship: "If the Battles in which we have been engaged, or [are] likely to be, [were] all that induced men not to enlist again, I should not hesitate a moment but be only too glad to try three years longer. It is the long, dreary and tiresome marches that wear upon one's health, and the military discipline that one very much dislikes, who is as fond of freedom as myself."[7]

6. Mann to members of the lyceum, April 25, 1864, Mann Papers.
7. Ibid.

When the army marched out of its Culpeper County camps and into the Wilderness in May 1864, Thomas Mann stood just three months from discharge—certain that this would be his last campaign. But on May 5, 1864, misfortune finally found Thomas Mann. Late that afternoon, he fell into Confederate hands, a prisoner. His decision not to reenlist suddenly became moot. Though his wartime recollections end with his capture, his wartime ordeal would continue through ten months in Confederate prisons, including Andersonville.

The experience of war transformed Thomas Mann, as it did everyone who suffered it. Months before his capture he had warned his parents, "You will find me very much changed in everything but outside appearance when I come home."[8] We know little of Mann the prewar child, so gauging the change is impossible. But we do know that Mann the postwar adult became a serious student, physician, editor, father, and husband—indeed, a classic American success story of the Gilded Age. After recovering from his debilitating prison experience, Mann traveled to Albany to attend medical school. He received his degree, married Julia Backus, and in 1872 moved to Block Island, off the coast of Rhode Island. There he built an elegant home (later used as a hotel) and practiced medicine at modest profit until 1875—occasionally receiving payment in potatoes or even salvage from shipwrecks.

This sometimes harsh, isolated life took its toll, and in 1875 Mann and his wife moved to Woonsocket, Rhode Island, where the doctor delivered babies and carried on a healthy practice until the mid-1880s (having, along the way, four children of his own). Citing diminished health, he retired from medicine and moved to Milford, Massachusetts. In 1887, after a brief foray as a druggist, he founded and edited the *Milford Daily News*. Three years later he moved to Fitchburg—in central Massachusetts—where he took the editorial reins of the Fitchburg *Evening Mail*. Not surprisingly, he never wavered from the Democratic ideals he and George B. McClellan shared, and his paper became a bastion of Democratic thought.

In 1896, President Cleveland appointed Mann postmaster of Fitchburg, and he became, as the *Boston Herald* opined, "one of the best postmasters Fitchburg ever had." A few years later he left Fitchburg to live with his daughter in Connecticut. There Mann would die on March 2, 1916, hailed as a "brave soldier, a gentleman of refined instincts, with a heart that overflowed with the milk of human kindness.... In the death of Dr. Mann the

8. Mann to friends at home, March 14, 1864, Mann Papers.

country loses one of her best types of citizens . . . and it can be truly said that the world is a better place for his having lived in it."⁹

THE MEMOIR

From the beginning of his war experience, Thomas Mann seemed determined to record it. During the war, he wrote frequent letters home—some of them chatty, some of them detailed and descriptive, some of them opinionated. Immediately following the war, he sat down to record his prison experience (a period not covered by his letters). The result, finished in 1867, was, by Mann's own admission, bitter and opinionated. Having thus relieved his angst, Mann put the prison memoir (if not the memories) aside for more than twenty years and embarked on his medical practice.

Mann's 1887 entry into the newspaper business coincided with a renewed interest in his wartime memories. In 1890, he pulled out his old prison memoir, moderated the vitriol, opinion, and "explosive adjectives," and sent it to *Century Magazine,* then one of the most popular periodicals in the nation. In July and August 1890, *Century* published "A Yankee in Andersonville," and Thomas Mann became a minor literary celebrity. The memoir is gracefully and formally written, lacking the breezy informality of his later writings. But Mann did not extinguish all his bitterness; nor did he correct all his errors (some of them born of bitterness, no doubt). When the *Century Magazine* later collected the best of its wartime remembrances for consolidation into the now-famous *Battles and Leaders of the Civil War,* they elected not to include Mann's Andersonville article. That recollection sank into relative obscurity, and there it remains.

Perhaps the short-lived success of "A Yankee in Andersonville" inspired Mann to record his combat and field experiences, too, for the old soldier again set to writing. Drawing heavily on his wartime letters and on the recollections of his tent-mate and friend, Sergeant William S. Alderman ("Sergeant Bill" in the memoir), Mann reconstructed his wartime travels and trials. In doing so, he assumed the third person, referring to himself as "Corporal Tom" or, occasionally and humorously, "our hero." When the third person failed to suit him, he reverted to edited excerpts from his wartime letters or the postwar recollections of Alderman. The result is an historiographical panacea: memoir interwoven closely with, and supported by, wartime documents.

9. The details of Mann's postwar life are taken from a series of clippings found in the Mann Papers.

The memoir ends rather abruptly with Mann's capture in the Wilderness. Indeed, doubt whether Mann actually even finished the work remains. Surely he never progressed beyond the "first draft" of composition, for his writing lacked the careful editing and punctuation that characterized his Andersonville memoir and the other articles Mann published in the 1890s. The original draft of the memoir exhibited a mania for semicolons; he wrote sentences of a length to appall high school composition teachers; he occasionally mixed tenses and metaphors. Given his occupation as a newspaper editor at the time, it is hard to believe he went back and carefully read his work after he completed the narrative. He surely would have dismissed one of his reporters for writing so carelessly.

At the same time—grammar and punctuation aside—one can see a clever mind and the hand of a skilled writer in Mann's work. His word pictures and imagery are sometimes masterful. His rhythm matches the mood of the moment. At one point in the narrative, he uses toil and detail as a literary device calculated to convey the toil of endless, confusing countermarching. The reader leaves the section dazed and not a little confused—an intentional effect courtesy of Thomas Mann.

In editing Mann's memoir, I have sought to improve it as Thomas Mann the postwar newspaper editor likely would have. I have broken sentences and eliminated some of the endless repetition of semicolons. In a handful of places I have reordered the text or inserted or replaced words for clarity. Only rarely did Mann stray so severely that deletions from the text were in order. These few significant alterations and deletions—perhaps a half-dozen—are indicated in the footnotes.

A major feature of the memoir is Mann's excerpts from his wartime letters (and occasional excerpts from Sergeant Alderman's postwar memoirs). By inserting these excerpts, Mann was clearly seeking an opportunity to revert to the first-person to make the memoir more immediate and personal. The reader is cautioned to view the letters more as a literary device than as a literal recounting of his wartime missives, for Mann edited his letter excerpts heavily—polishing them considerably. I have generally opted not to undo Mann's revisions, for he occasionally added substantial detail and always made the wartime missives more readable. Perhaps the most extreme example of Mann's manipulation of his wartime letters comes in his recounting of the Mine Run Campaign. For comparative purposes, I have included the full text of his Mine Run letter as an appendix.

In a few places, I have added letter excerpts (unpolished) that Mann chose not to include. Most of these insertions reflect Mann's attitudes on the great issues of the day; a few add narrative detail not included in the memoir. In one instance (the Second Battle of Manassas), I have inserted an extensive letter excerpt in place of Mann's postwar text. In this instance, the contemporary letter (to which Mann may not have had access when he constructed his memoir) is vastly superior in content to the original memoir. In another place (his recounting of the Battle of the Wilderness), I have included passages from short articles that better recount his capture on May 5, 1864. All such insertions are indicated in the footnotes.

Apparently Thomas Mann made little or no attempt to get his memoir published during his lifetime. He certainly had ample opportunity. As a newspaper editor, he could have serialized it in a local newspaper (even his own), as hundreds of veterans did. Or he could have used publishing connections in New York or Philadelphia to bring it to the market. Instead, the draft of the memoir languished and eventually was forgotten. It resurfaced again in the early 1990s, when Thomas Mann's grandsons found it among the family's papers. They took the step Thomas Mann should have taken ten decades ago: they submitted it to a major publisher.

I am indebted to brothers Hank and Bill Mann for bringing the memoir to light and for sharing their extensive knowledge of their grandfather. I am also grateful for assistance from several others: Frank O'Reilly of Guinea, Virginia, who shared his exhaustive knowledge of the Battle of Fredericksburg; Noel Harrison of Fredericksburg, whose unparalleled knowledge of Civil War–era sites around Fredericksburg is matched only by his willingness to share it; Robert E. L. Krick, who answered queries about the Peninsula and Seven Days; Lindsay Batchelor of Fredericksburg, who helped to organize research materials; Dan Lorello of Albany, who provided research materials on short notice. And finally, I want to thank my daughter Caroline, whose joyous view of life inspires me in all that I do.

I send you into the memoir with the ruminations and rationale of Corporal Thomas Henry Mann, Eighteenth Massachusetts Infantry:

> History, as a rule, only takes cognizance of the movements and plans of commanders, the battles they won or lost and their political results, the rank and file receiving even less notice than is accorded to well running horses or the keen noses of a pack of hounds in a successful fox hunt. The late civil war, however, will be likely to go down into history somewhat modified in detail and narrative, differing from the stereotyped methods of the ancients by receiving the impress and certifications of thousands of the common sol-

diers who acted their part in it. As Sergeant Bill well says: "It happens sometimes, in narrating events, that the little incidents are quite as interesting to the reader or listener as are the recorded histories of great occurrences. Besides there are always great writers, and it is their peculiar province to write of great things, leaving the little things for the little fellows to tell."

Abbreviations

FSNPL   Fredericksburg and Spotsylvania National Military Park Library

O.R.   U.S. War Department, *Official Records of the War of the Rebellion*

USAMHI   U.S. Army Military History Institute, Carlisle, Penn.

FIGHTING WITH THE EIGHTEENTH MASSACHUSETTS

ONE

To War

"Only Cogs in the Wheel"

The ironic mania that surrounded civil war that summer of 1861 thoroughly infected Wrentham, Massachusetts. For decades, Americans had dreaded disunion and conflict. But now war had come, and the people of Wrentham and the rest of America heralded its arrival. Amidst the excitement, forty-three young men from Wrentham gathered with boyish excitement to fight what would be the nation's bloodiest war. These mechanics, clerks, jewelers, and even a "bonnet bleacher" would become the nucleus of Company I, Eighteenth Massachusetts. They were not boys, but men; they were men, but not dispossessed of boyish whims. They possessed physical vigor, but few were accomplished. Most met the prerequisite for good soldiering later described by a Michigan veteran: "A man can fight better if he has nothing else to live for. . . . The genuine soldier should have no thought or hope beyond success on the battlefield."[1] Few of the "Wrentham Company" who gathered that summer could envision that some of them would never return, and all who did would forever be changed.

The ritualistic transformation from citizen to soldier in times of crisis is a decidedly American process. It is (fortunately) a rare occurrence in American history—when entire communities nobly package up and send off their best young men to subdue an ignoble cause. When it has happened (during the Civil War and during World War II), it is hard to say which has affected the other more: the civilians the military, or the military the former civilians. That reciprocal effect is plainly evident in Mann's memoir, and no more so than in this first chapter.

The regiment's early experience would be dominated by a man who would largely shape Mann's view of the military and war: Colonel James

---

1. Stephen Sears, ed., *For Country, Cause, and Leader: The Civil War Journal of Charles B. Haydon* (New York), 112.

Barnes, commander of the Eighteenth Massachusetts. The sixty-year-old Barnes was a native of Boston who, despite a West Point education, had spent most of his prewar career as a civil engineer working for railroads all over the eastern half of the continent. One officer described him thus: "The colonel remarked that he was somewhat inclined to be fat, in which remark I entirely coincided with when I saw him. He seemed as if he might be a very smart officer, however, notwithstanding his size. I found him a regular specimen of a smart, good-natured Yankee, somewhat illiterate to be sure, as one could tell from his conversation. . . . Stockings, according to his dialect, is spelled 'storkings,' shoes 'shues.' However, he can make himself understood, I suppose, and that is the main thing." Mann's good friend William Alderman ("Sergeant Bill" in the memoir) called Barnes "one of those inflexible willed men that is bound to have his own way at all hazards." The process of turning bonnet bleachers, teachers, and mechanics into soldiers was uniquely suited to this man who had the instinct, bearing, and training of a soldier and a lifetime's experience as a civilian.[2]

Thomas Mann and the other members of the Wrentham Company followed a familiar path to the front that summer of 1861: from hometowns to training camp at Readville, down Broadway amid cheering crowds in New York City, and on to the burgeoning army in muddy, businesslike encampments around Washington, D.C. More important than the path, though, was the process. Mann's first months in service would introduce him to a new world of friends, comrades, and routines—many of them vividly chronicled here. They would be men with whom he would forge lifetime bonds or, in some cases, decades-long antipathy. This process of transformation is a familiar one—veterans of World War II will recognize the characters and the incidents—but rarely is it so well described as it is at Mann's hands.

The unit of an army is the regiment. Men only count as so many cogs in the wheel of a machine. In civil life a man is the unit, and must be counted as such, and reckoned with individually. In army life the regiment only is taken into consideration, and its individuality is pretty much fixed by its commander. The army commander decides the efficiency of seasoned

2. Stephen Minot Weld, *War Diaries and Letters of Stephen Minot Weld* (Reprint, Boston, 1978), 48. William Alderman, "Reminiscences of Gen. Barnes," unidentified clipping from the *Sunday Republican,* in the Alderman Papers, Fredericksburg and Spotsylvania National Military Park Library (hereinafter FSNMPL).

troops by the ability, dash, and cool-headedness of the colonel commanding the regiment. These preliminary statements will explain, between the lines, the difficulties encountered by the government of making the voluntary recruit into the fraction of the unit of an army.[3]

The duration of the late civil war—almost exactly four years—was very trying at the time, even to the final victors. The impatience exhibited by those who took no part in the battles that were fought, except to shout from behind the desks in their counting-rooms "why don't the army move!" was still more pronounced. Yet an army composed of a million men—fully a thousand regiments—was formed; the men were schooled into soldiers, taught to become parts of a great machine; officers were culled out of the unschooled mass and sifted, selected and rejected, and still others culled, drilled, and educated to command; the battle was forced, engaged and won, all in the same length of time a boy is required to spend in college. Since a generation has passed, looking back at the history of that war its duration seems incredibly short, and its results decisive and complete.

The formation of the volunteers into companies, and these into regiments, was very similar in a thousand instances, and of the 50 or more regiments sent from Massachusetts the preliminaries of each were so nearly like every other that a description of one will, in the main, practically cover all, so the writer will endeavor to picture the trials and troubles, the joys and glories of the 18th Massachusetts Volunteers, for two important reasons. First, because its history has never been written and, second, being a member of Company "I" of that regiment, for four years, its tribulations were a personal experience or observation.

"I" was known as the Wrentham company, and its nucleus was about 30 young men who formed the militia of that town between the 50s and 60s of the present [19th] century. During the latter part of April, 1861, these men went to Dedham, the shire town of the county and, joining with Company "F," the Dedham militia, camped in the agricultural building on the county fair grounds. Within a few days both companies had each their full compl[e]ment of 100 men and officers, in fact many more offered

---

3. To complete the organizational chain: ten companies (each commanded by a captain) composed a regiment; four to eight regiments (each commanded by a colonel) composed a brigade; three or four brigades (each commanded by a senior colonel or brigadier general) composed a division; three or four divisions (commanded each by a brigadier or major general) composed a corps; and at various times in its existence, from three to seven corps (each commanded by a major general) composed the Army of the Potomac.

themselves than could be accepted. "D" company from Middleboro, another from Plymouth, and six others from as many of the Cape [Cod] towns, soon joined, so that before the first of July the regiment of ten companies was full, and went into camp at Readville by the side of the 20th Massachusetts Vols.[4]

I, F, and D companies fraternized very closely all through the war, perhaps from the fact that all three were made up of distinctively country boys who had sympathies in common. Company "F" was assigned to the right of the regiment; "D" to the left, and "I" became the color company, occupying the centre. In other words, the ranking company or the one first commissioned as a company, took the right, the next in rank took the left, and the third the centre.

Of the Wrentham company, about 40 belonged to that town and represented the old families whose names are distinctive of the locality—such as the Blakes, Bonneys, Richardsons, Jordans, Manns, Morses, Bugbees, Hemenways, etc. The other half of the company was recruited from the adjoining towns of Franklin, Walpole, Foxboro, Medfield and Medway, with a scattering of men from more distant places in the state. The other companies similarly represented the old families of the towns from which they hailed.

In electing officers, the companies were only restricted, or rather cautioned, to select such as could pass a satisfactory examination before a commission appointed by Governor Andrew, and nearly all of the 500 companies raised throughout the state elected their commissioned and non-commissioned officers, each in its own way; though during the formation of a company its captain was practically settled upon before a dozen men had been gathered, as he was generally the leader in its formation. The lieutenants selected were also the men, next to the captain, most instrumental in getting the men together. The formation of the companies

---

4. Known as the "Harvard Regiment," the Twentieth Massachusetts included names representing the finest families of Massachusetts. Future supreme court justice Oliver Wendell Holmes Jr., future brigadier general William Francis Bartlett, Paul Revere descendant Paul J. Revere, and many others were among the notables in the Twentieth. Once in the field, the Eighteenth and Twentieth would never serve together and, indeed, would rarely encounter each other. The Twentieth served in the Second Corps, the Eighteenth in the Fifth. For an account of the Twentieth's stay at the camps at Readville, see George A. Bruce, *The Twentieth Regiment of Massachusetts Volunteer Infantry, 1861–1865* (Boston and New York, 1906), 2–9. See also Anthony J. Milano, "Letters from the Harvard Regiments," in *Civil War: The Magazine of the Civil War Society*, 13.

into a regiment was the prerogative of the governor, who also appointed the regimental officers.

The man[5] chosen to command "I" company proved to be only a holiday officer, at that time the most soldierly looking and best drilled one, but he showed the "white feather" when real trouble came a year later, and found it most convenient to resign altogether from further participation in the defence of the country. One of the lieutenants made a good officer, and continued until disabled, while another[6] foolishly filled up with whiskey— and it was said to have been a poor article at that—when about to be examined by the commission, and failed to pass. He was an Irishman, and showed both patriotism and pluck by taking his place in the ranks and fighting the war out as a private soldier. The man chosen in his place proved to be about the same caliber as the captain, and soon found business that required his presence away from the dangers of the front.

Of the five sergeants and eight corporals elected, nearly all earned officer's commissions before the war closed, and two of them became commanders of the company, one following the disabling of the other.

The casualties of battle and exigencies of war so changed the officers of the regiment that its colonel became a major-general, and men who went out as lieutenants became respectively colonel, lieutenant colonel, and major, either of the 18th or some other regiment organized later.

The three or four weeks during which "F" and "I" companies occupied the agricultural building was a picnic. But little effort was made toward discipline or drill that was taken seriously, yet no remarkable excesses were indulged, or serious mischief perpetrated, though the 200 occupants of that spacious building were having a rollicking good time. The state was furnishing rations and the respective towns the uniforms and clothing.

A majority of the boys were not far from home, and if the inspiration came over one, or a dozen, to spend a day or two among the early scenes of their childhood, they went and returned much as they pleased, regardless of the threats or reprimands of the newly fledged officers. Visitors were

---

5. Captain Frederick D. Forrest, a twenty-four-year-old shoemaker from Wrentham. Though Mann indicates Forrest resigned under a cloud, the records show that he was discharged for disability on October 24, 1862—six weeks after Antietam.

6. John McGinnis, twenty-six years old, a bootmaker from Walpole. This "quick-witted son of Erin" was, wrote Alderman, "a good, plucky man when it came to fighting" but "quite lawless and always being 'brought up' for some misdemeanor." McGinnis would serve the regiment's entire three-year term. William Alderman, "Reminiscences of Gen. Barnes," an unidentified clipping from the *Sunday Republican*, FSNMPL.

received and entertained, both with food and lodgings, and the fun of a soldier's life seemed so continuous that they begged to be allowed to enlist. Enough offered themselves to swell each company to 200 men instead of the 100 allowed.

Given the opportunity, a pillow fight is easily promoted, and is always a possibility among robust children, resulting in a few scattered feathers and a spanking here and there—a tame affair compared with a mattress fight participated in by 200 embryo soldiers. In a spacious hall and the darkness of night, with material handy, and more ludicrous if not serious results are apt to materialize. Such a fight did occur in this hall, and was indulged to that extreme which makes the place look as if a cyclone had scattered a haystack and the contents of a score of wash-day clothes-lines through it.

No one knew what started the melee, or why it stopped. Each man had for a mattress a bag loosely filled with straw, which made a very comfortable bed provided its occupant had the knack of properly arranging it. One night, after a general quiet had fallen over all, one of those mattresses came suddenly bounding the whole length of the hall, across a closely packed row of 60 or 70, as if propelled by a catapult, scattering loose straw from its open end to mark its track. It could hardly be expected that a room filled with men, spoiling for a rumpus, would allow that bag of straw to remain quietly where it lodged, and these were in the right humor, so back it bounded, and another and another followed.

In less time than it takes to tell it, every bag of straw in the hall was on the move, and were kept moving until, torn and twisted and flying through the thickening air, they were dissolved into empty bags and scattered straw. What little clothing the boys had retained upon retiring for the night, parted company with the wearers of it and joined the discarded jackets and trousers in mixing with the flying straw about the hall.

A sight! Well, it was. When several of the officers put in an appearance and dimly lighted up the scene with five or six tallow candles, one man could not be distinguished from any other. Nearly all were naked, with straw ground into the hair of their heads—and beards, if they had any—everything as badly mixed as it were possible to combine men, straw, empty sacks, and all kinds of wearing apparel. After all, the scrimmage was not so bad as the modern, closely contested foot-ball game, and the injuries were trifling—a few bloody noses and scratches, a few torn sacks, and a general mixing of clothing which required several days to sort to respective owners.

This is a sample of the manner in which soldiering started during May and June, 1861, but even it was a little rough for a few of the sensitive members of both "F" and "I," so when these companies were marched to an out-door camp in Readville that kind scattered homeward instead. Six weeks later, when the news of the battle of Bull Run, of July 21,[7] was fully comprehended—while the retreat from that battlefield was reaching even to Boston—quite a number more of the fiercest fire-eaters slunk out of the ranks and went home. Thus were the files well weeded until the ten full companies that left for the front, on August 26, were made up of men who meant business, and were somewhat seasoned to out-door camp life.

At this stage of the war—before there was any fighting except the bombardment and surrender of Sumter—men and boys did not enlist from quite the same motives as were exercised a year later when an urgent call was issued for 400,000 more, to assist in subduing the gigantic rebellion. The regiments formed prior to that little affair at Manassas were not made up of men who felt the necessity of becoming soldiers, but rather from the class who were inclined to like camp life and the comradeship it afforded. The respective companies of the Eighteenth secured many men who were better adapted for soldiers than anything else; they liked the kind of life that the army offered and, in many instances, made the reliable veterans who fought the war out, or were killed or disabled in the act. They were the kind of men who would have been first to enlist in a South Carolina regiment if born natives of that state.

William [Alderman][8] enlisted because his sweetheart's love was not strong enough to consent to marry him against her father's expressed wishes, and he saw the opportunity afforded by army life to escape from his sorrow while venting his anger upon the enemies of his country. Tom[9]

---

7. The First Battle of Bull Run, or Manassas—the first major battle of the Civil War. The battle was a decisive and shocking defeat for the Union. No doubt the defeat encouraged some to leave the ranks, as Mann relates, but the battle in fact stimulated both sides to intense recruiting and training. When again the armies took the field in Virginia the following year, they were many times larger, better equipped, better drilled, and capable of vastly more horrific slaughter, as will be seen.

8. Sergeant William Alderman, Mann's close friend and postwar correspondent. Alderman shared many of his recollections with Mann, who in turn quoted them in this memoir. Hereafter Alderman is generally referred to as "Sergeant William." Alderman's letters are privately owned and restricted, but copies of them and a handful of published reminiscences by Alderman can be found at the Fredericksburg and Spotsylvania National Military Park Library (FSNMPL).

9. "Tom" is Mann's reference to himself throughout the memoir.

was in much the same frame of mind, though the conditions were reversed. His father seriously objected to the girl of his choice, and the damsel was not well disposed toward entering a family that interposed such emphatic prohibitions upon young Tom. The call for soldiers gave him his opportunity to wipe out what he considered the disgrace of the thing.

Frank [Smith][10] had finished school and was undecided what work to engage in. As a school boy he enjoyed a rough and tumble scrap with another, and the associations of company "I" were just to his liking. He had a cousin of about the same age, born and brought up in South Carolina, who gave much the same reasons for fighting to a finish on the other side, and Frank said the thing ought to be evened up, so offered himself to help vindicate the civilization of old Massachusetts. If he had any special reasons for enlisting they never came to the surface.

In connection with this type of soldier, it may be affirmed that the rough-and-tumble boys, the overbearing, always-picking-a-fuss kind generally made rather indifferent soldiers. The quiet boy, edging away from a quarrel and shunning the bullying business, was the kind to depend upon for business in a tight place.

John [McGinnis] liked whiskey better than any other thing, judging from his record, though he never shirked a fight and was in his element during the carnage of a Bull Run, Fredericksburg, or Gettysburg. His very estimable wife could get along with John, but scorned John "corned," so John enlisted to find the opportunity to reform. This was the man elected for 1st lieutenant, and who failed of a commission from the examining board because material spirits had obtained control of the immaterial too early in the day.

Dennis [Short][11] had wandered down from his Canadian home several years before, worked for a farmer whose estate joined that of Tom's father, became the bosom friend of Tom in snaring, trapping, and fishing the farms over, and enlisted because Tom did.

James [Snow][12] was a model Sunday-school boy, meek and gentle as a lamb, the pet of all the lady Sunday-school teachers, and never had the op-

---

10. Private Frank G. Smith, a seventeen-year-old jeweler from North Attleborough, killed at Second Manassas, August 30, 1862.

11. Private Dennis Short from Wrentham, a nineteen-year-old "varnisher" who would serve out the regiment's term.

12. Private James B. Snow, eighteen years old, a paper maker from Franklin. He would be captured at the Wilderness in May 1864 and would survive ten months as a prisoner of war.

portunity to even see a circus. At the time he was turning his 18th year a change was becoming perceptible, and if it had not been for the war no doubt he would have grown into a bad man. The army took him in as naturally as water takes a duck, and he floated through it all, even to reenlisting, growling, grumbling, and the boss profane man of the company, though seldom shirking. It should be noted here, however, that at this writing he is a leading man in the town of his residence, and a prominent church worker.

So the whole roll could be sized up, but these are sufficient as samples. The boys gave as many different causes that acted as the deciding incentive for enlisting, as any vocabulary can furnish, while there were the silent ones who never unburdened to most intimate friends. It would be wrong, however, to ascribe any of the enumerated and outspoken reasons as the underlying motive in any but exceptional cases. A spirit of patriotism, a determination to vindicate free institutions, to preserve the Union, the legacy from their fathers, had settled deep into the life of New England, as represented by these young men, and they were in a state of mind to fight it out—most of them did.[13]

The few who were influenced by no deeper motives than of the character mentioned, never saw a battle, or even succeeded in crossing the Potomac into the hostile country.

Toward the last of June the companies began to gather at Readville for the formation of a regiment. Tents were provided; the regular uniform of the United States army was donned, and knapsacks, haversacks, canteens, cartridge-boxes, and the old Springfield musket became the equipment of the newly fledged soldiers. Colonel James Barnes was commissioned to command, with Lieut. Col. Timothy Ingraham[14] as second, and Major Jo-

---

13. For a complete and authoritative look at the motives of soldiers of the Civil War, see James M. McPherson, *For Cause and Comrades: Why Men Fought in the Civil War* (New York, 1997).

14. A Massachusetts native, the fifty-one-year-old Ingraham had seen prior service in the Third Massachusetts, a ninety-day regiment that saw no action. He would remain with the Eighteenth for a year, when he would assume a new position with the Thirty-eighth Massachusetts. His wartime service, including active campaigning in Louisiana under General Nathaniel Banks, would earn him a brevet (honorary) brigadier generalship for "brave and meritorious services." *Massachusetts in the Army and Navy during the War of 1861–65*, Vol. 2, 185; Roger D. Hunt and Jack R. Brown, *Brevet Brigadier Generals in Blue* (Gaithersburg, 1990), 308.

seph Hayes[15] third. Fisher A. Baker,[16] one of the lieutenants of "F" company, was selected by Colonel Barnes for adjutant, and he soon became very efficient, retaining that position for three years until promoted to the rank of Lieut. Colonel.

Colonel Barnes was a graduate of West Point—fifth in the class of 1829, in which Robert E. Lee was second and Joseph E. Johnston thirteenth—had seen service in the war with Mexico, and also as an engineer in the French service during the Crimean war. He was a regular martinet in discipline, and thoroughly hated by the rank and file for the first year, and as strongly loved and respected afterwards, the reasons why will appear as the history of the regiment grows. He rode a fiery steed that no other man could mount, but it could not throw the doughty Colonel, even when he—the colonel, not the horse—was too drunk to stand on his own feet.[17]

With the advent of "Jimmy Barnes" work commenced, the exasperating process of making soldiers was inaugurated, and men, platoons, companies, battalions, and the regiment, were taught to move on geometrical lines—no circular movements were allowed except the wheel—right angles were the thing; even the individual soldier was taught to form a right angle with the earth trod upon, and wear his cap with the visor at a right angle to his own face.

The making of a soldier from the raw recruit, of the man fresh from the shop, counting-room, farm, or of the boy from the village school, was no

15. The twenty-six-year-old Hayes would rise to become the longtime commander of the Eighteenth and then ascend further to brigadier general in 1864. He was a Harvard graduate and before the war practiced both banking and civil engineering. He would be wounded seriously in the Wilderness in May 1864, captured in August 1864, but returned soon enough to be with the Fifth Corps at Appomattox. No intact collection of his papers is known to exist, though substantial snippets of his memoirs can be found in the Joshua Chamberlain Papers at the Library of Congress. See Ezra Warner, *Generals in Blue* (Baton Rouge, 1964), 220–21.

16. The efficient Baker makes regular appearances in Mann's memoir. He was a twenty-four-year-old lawyer from New York City and would prove to be an outstanding military bureaucrat. Some of his writings can be found in the Amasa Guild Scrapbook at the Dedham Historical Society.

17. For more on Barnes see Weld, *War Diaries and Letters,* 48; Warner, *Generals in Blue,* 20–21; Alderman, "Reminiscences of Gen. Barnes," unidentified clipping, FSNMPL; William Alderman to his parents, October 1, 1862, William Alderman letters, FSNMPL. Allen Johnson, ed., *Dictionary of American Biography* (New York, 1928), Vol. 1, 630–31. No papers of Barnes's are known to exist, so he remains something of an enigma, though in the pages that follow Mann does an admirable job of revealing Barnes as he has never before been known to historians.

easy matter, and no one knew it better than "Jimmy Barnes." Making machines from live men, dictating how many buttons must work, and the exact angle of the tilt of the chin, was not taken to kindly by the very men who performed the best service one, two, and three years later. In less than a year, when the first shell from the rebel fort at Yorktown howled and sputtered close above the heads of this devoted regiment and, bursting, flung several panels of a Virginia fence into its ranks, the necessity of discipline became suddenly apparent.

It was roll-call at six in the morning, and every man not excused by the surgeon must be in his respective company's ranks to answer, rain or shine. Half an hour later, hard-tack, boiled salt junk, and coffee were announced, by fife and drum, and it must be gathered in then or go without, for those who wore shoulder straps were much given to standing around the coffee kettles to see that the company's cook issued no rations to tardy comers. The commissary department furnished rations, weighed to the fraction of an ounce, for every man. But if he was not on hand to take them his allowance was passed to the credit of a company fund—or the proceeds into the pockets of the quartermasters and cooks, and there was no mother's cupboard to sly into.

Guard mounting was at eight o'clock, another very exact affair. All good soldiers might be, in fact were, detailed for guard duty in their turn, but delinquents had police duty to perform instead. This meant to clean up the camp for the day. Guard duty was performed about each regiment, by posting a soldier every 60 feet and requiring him to walk that beat, back and forth, dressed in his best clothes, brasses polished, shoes and straps well blacked, and with musket so clean that it could be handled with the whitest of gloves without leaving a sign of dirt—for two hours on and four off during twenty-four. Then it was that the private must observe his angles, and the blessed privilege of bringing his musket to "present arms" whenever an officer loitered near his post. In fact it was an obligation rather than a privilege, liable to ignominious punishment if neglected.

James [Snow], though a fairly good soldier, was always inclined to drag a little behind his comrades, while William [Alderman] was always up and dressed, and took his rations and guard duty on time, believing that slackness never paid when the comforts of a soldier's life were under consideration. That inevitable guard-mounting was the bane of Jim's life, particularly when Sergt. William called out the detail of company "I." The[y] hastily swallowed coffee [so] that time might be gained for an hour's hard work upon the musket that Jim had allowed to rust while diligently engaged in his favorite game of "high-low-jack," the polishing of shoes, etc., to pass the inspection of Adjutant Baker; then to have the rammer withdrawn from the barrel of his musket to ruin the white gloves of the inspecting officer; to be sent to his quarters in disgrace, and made to perform the dirty police work of the camp, occurred many times with Jim, and others of his kind. Even the shirt collars of the boys did not escape inspection, and it was not unusual to have the "impertinent" question sharply put: "When was your shirt washed last?" followed by the brief order: "Go wash it!"

One hot day in July, while Tom was acting as corporal of the police force for the time, he found attached to it a comrade who was inclined to be a little shiftless—one George [Maintien],[18] who later died in Andersonville prison. He was a little older than Tom, one of the hectoring, teasing kind who delighted in tormenting those too small to whip him, sticking pins . . . where they did not properly belong which caused an uneasiness on Tom's part, so pronounced at times as to bring the schoolmaam's switch about his shoulders. That night Tom remarked: "Didn't I exercise the authority of a corporal, today, to the fullest extent, and keep George busy at the dirtiest work the camp afforded!" There is little question but he, George, put in a full day's duty. Tom was not particularly a revengeful boy, but George needed a little discipline smartly applied, and the former was not in a bad mood to make it count very effectually. Boys do even things up.

Another of those hot, July days saw Sergt. William detailed for a duty that was thoroughly relished, in one sense, though rather irksome in another. All companies had their typical lazy and shiftless character, and "I" was not an exception. Jordan [Hartley][19] was not only very derelict about washing his clothes but equally so in regard to his person. This day Adjutant Baker sharply reprimanded Orderly Sergeant [Preston] Soule[20] for allowing one of his men to appear for inspection in such a condition. Soule did not relish the rebuke and, turning to Sergt. William, ordered: "Take a file of men, march Jordan to the pond and see that he is scrubbed from hair to heels, like h—l!" When the squad reappeared, three hours later, the

18. Private George H. Maintien, twenty-five, a jeweler from Wrentham. Captured at the Wilderness on May 6, 1864, he would die at Andersonville Prison on July 16, 1864.

19. Private Hartley Jordan, nineteen years old, a mechanic from Wrentham. He would be discharged for disability in September 1863.

20. Preston Soule, twenty-seven, a "traveling clerk" from Middleboro, would die of disease May 14, 1862.

sergeant reported that the Orderly's commands had been strictly complied with. Jordan . . . probably never received so thorough a scrubbing, and judging from his appearance, as seen 25 years after, had not since.

The everlasting drilling by companies, battalions, squads, and in the manual of arms, wearied everybody; the boys did not realize at this time that, aside from its necessity as a matter of discipline and skill, the exercise thus afforded was essential to health and good spirits. For the first month regimental tactics were rarely attempted, but drilling by squads, platoons, and in the manual of arms commenced at nine o'clock; hour after hour, days succeeding the day and one week after another, it was this same motion and maneuver over and over again.

"Fall into two ranks! Right—dress! Attention! You, James, carry your head back and chest out! Now, right—dress! I say, you Inman, there, hav'nt you got any belly? If you have, bring it out in line. Front!"— accent always very pronounced on the last word of the command, with a long pause between it and the preceding.

"Company, present—arms! Carry—arms! Come, wake up there, David, get your gun into place before dinner-time! Order—arms!"

"Shoulder—arms! Charge—bayonets! Recover—arms! Right shoulder shift—arms! You, there, Dorethy and Ramsbottom, carry your bayonets higher, and not be thumping the brains out of the rear rank."

"Carry—arms! Order—arms! Why can't you bring them down together, and not sound like horses galloping across a forty foot bridge! Shoulder—arms! Company, right-face! Forward—march! Jordan can't you learn to step off with your left foot? Halt! Now try it again. Company, forward—march! Into four ranks—march! File left—march! Get round there, Maintien, we ai'nt going to a funeral!"

"Double-quick—march! Company—halt! Left—face! Don't you know left from right, Fuller? Right—dress! Front! Order—arms! Parade—rest!"—and so on for two hours, maybe three, and it must be well done else the slack and inattentive soldier was sentenced to an hour's extra drill in the "awkward squad."

At twelve o'clock the bugle call announced "roast beef," and most of the boys were ready for the soup, even if the cook, Tift,[21] did make it in the same kettle used for the week's washing. Tift positively denied using this kettle for all purposes, but many of the members of this company paid

---

21. Private Ransom Tifft, forty-four years old, a butcher from Franklin. One of the two oldest men in Company I, he would serve out his term of service.

him by the week to do their washing, and the most curious never could discover but one kettle in his possession, the regulation government affair for soup and coffee, and formed their conclusions accordingly. This Tift was a thrifty fellow, never caught at spending a cent, while making a little extra as cook for the company, and more by taking in washings.

"Assembly" sounded at two o'clock, and until four the field officers[22] generally took a hand in the maneuvers, directing their attention to showing the line officers their respective places in the machine. The boys usually enjoyed this better, while being taught to wheel by battalion and company front; to march by company front, break into platoons and reform the company from them. Later, the drill became still more complicated, taking the men away from camp where room was found for the maneuvering of the regiment, and the officers were put through their lessons.

The line officers showed the same stupidity . . . in handling their platoons and companies that the privates did in managing their paces and equipments, mixing them up in inextricable confusion—one company across another, the right of the line where the left belonged, and two companies trying to pass through the same gap at once where there was room for but one. Then the line officers had to catch it from the mounted ones; horses were unruly because the riders had not yet learned to manage both men and horses at the same moment—calling out explosive words with a vim and snap suggestive of profanity. The privates enjoyed these tangles, the hot words and uncomplimentary epithets that the company officers were made to swallow without the privilege of replying, remembering similar language that had been administered, ad liberum, when the elbow did not touch, by an inch, where it ought. It did serve to tone the commissioned ones down a little, but had no appreciable effect upon the noncoms.

The camp at Readville[23] was very finely located, about eight miles from Boston, occupying a level plain, of 40 or 50 acres, on the east of the Boston & Providence railway, at the foot of the Blue Hills, and bounded on the east and south by the Neponset River. At this time Blue Hill was not

---

22. Field officers consisted of the major, lieutenant colonel, and colonel; the line officers mentioned here were the company commanders.

23. Readville was one of Massachusetts's major camps of assembly and training for new regiments. Recently, it has gained fame by its portrayal in the movie *Glory*; it was here that, more than a year after the Eighteenth Massachusetts departed for the front, Massachusetts's first regiment of African-American soldiers, the Fifty-fourth Massachusetts, received its acculturation into the military life.

occupied by large, magnificent residential estates, while the surrounding country was sparsely populated, so that the opportunity for sham battles and charges was all that could be desired. No doubt the field officers enjoyed putting the regiment through the tactics of a charge upon an imaginary enemy as keenly as the true sporting man takes in a horse race—so the rank and file sized the business up at the time.

There were times, however, when [we men in the ranks] enjoyed it, particularly when the day was hot, and the charge was made by regimental front upon an enemy supposed to be located in the woods about the foot of Blue Hill. Then the men were likely to get well scattered before the wild, headlong rush could be stopped; and the line officers must be called together to receive a lesson from the colonel before the wandering pieces of the machine could be got into place. In several instances, squads from the charging column continued to the top of the hill, three miles away, before realizing that they were out of place. This kind of drilling was a diversion that broke the monotony and routine of soldier-making.

At five o'clock dress-parade occurred, to give the drum-major a chance to show off, and the colonel an opportunity to pose before the men he commanded—so those who carried muskets said. But it was a very precise affair, during which every man must appear in his best clothes and on his best behavior, with polished muskets and white gloves. What the gloves had to do with crushing the rebellion was always a puzzle to the ordinary private, though some no doubt believed that the showing made by the Eighteenth Massachusetts Volunteer regiment, 1000 strong, in a perfect line, clothed in white gloves and the regulation dress coat, able to "order arms" and "present arms" like automatons—when exhibited to the "rebel horde" would cause the greatest skedaddle on record, thus bringing the war to an immediate close.

Dress-parade was an affair of an hour's exhibition, the grand climax of every day except a chance one that was so stormy that the colonel did not like to soil his epaulets and silk sash. A regimental dress-parade, with a full brass band, is an inspiring sight and played its part well in producing that pride of regiment that served well, a year or two later, when there was serious work on all sides.

No more welcome sound was heard at Readville than the six o'clock call, announcing that it was time to pay another visit to the cook, and there were very few who did not quickly learn this peculiar call of the bugle for rations, no matter how poor the ear was for the other musical sounds blown from it.

At eight the fife and drum played a rattling bit of music to signify that the duties of the day were done, except for those who guarded the camp, and to bed was in order. At nine "curfew" rang, but it was from the bugle, or fife and drum, instead of convent bells; all the same, however, it meant "lights out."

This is a little sketch of the every-day work of camp life at Readville, but it reduced—or raised—the man to a soldier, and this regiment left that place for the seat of war August 26, 1861, as fine body of men as Massachusetts ever sent out to vindicate its patriotism and civilization, as the sequel proved.

"On to Richmond!" was a standing part of the head-lines of all the newspapers of the day, and was shouted from every street corner before the first three-year regiment reached the scene of action or crossed "Mason's and Dixon's line." The Eighteenth began to be impatient, and its officers, as well as the rank and file, were getting anxiously suspicious that the war would close, and the rebellion be ended, before it was afforded the opportunity to win any glory.[24]

Time changed that sentiment somewhat, particularly when the men began to smell the smoke of real battle, and in this the peculiarity of human nature was exhibited to a marked degree. Those who showed the greatest anxiety to meet the rebel host, who declaimed the loudest of the valor that possessed them, and of the ease with which all "Secesh" would succumb to it, were the ones who petered out soon as the first opportunity was afforded to engage the enemy.

The day came when Colonel Barnes concluded that his regiment was sufficiently drilled to go to the front and take further lessons in the immediate vicinity of the foe it was to meet. So during the afternoon of August 26, 1861, the camp equipage, officers, men, horses, and the brass band, were loaded or climbed on board a train drawn up by the side of the camp for the purpose, and started for Stonington to take one of the Sound steamers for New York. Though enumerated last, this brass band was the pet of the field officers, who carefully looked after the welfare and touchy sensibilities of its 26 members.[25]

---

24. In a letter on September 11, after the regiment had reached the front, Mann told his father, "It is the general belief that the 18th Regt. will eat a thanksgiving dinner at home without seeing much fighting." Mann to friends at home, September 11, 1861, Mann Papers.

25. Brass bands were a common appendage to regiments early in the war, when regiments often had audiences as they ground their way through training. But within a year, with

The breaking of this first camp was a serious business compared with some other moves made later, and the train, when loaded and ready to start, looked as if two or three hundred families had broken up housekeeping to emigrate. Each officer's possessions were equal to three privates, and each private took as much on board the train as any three cared to move from one battle-field to another, after the first year's experience. The tendency of raw soldiers to overload themselves is irresistible.

The outfit carried by Tom from this camp was a fair sample of all. It consisted of a musket; cartridge-box containing 40 rounds of ammunition; canteen holding three pints of water; haversack with three day's rations, though these rations can hardly be enumerated because they were not the regulation army allowance, as will appear later; and last, the knapsack, in which and upon it was loaded and strapped everything that Tom's individual ingenuity could cram and hang. The regulation straps and buckles were reinforced by rope and string, and when the finishing touches were bestowed, the last strap buckled, it was a marvelous thing. From the company's quarters to the train was less than 500 yards; had it been a mile a farm wheel-barrow would have been necessary for the knapsack alone.

Its contents and attachments were: Two pair of woolen drawers and shirts, three pairs of stockings, one pair shoes, one blouse and extra pair of trousers, six handkerchiefs, two pair white cotton gloves, hair brush and comb, looking-glass, razor, strop, soap, bag containing needles, thread, thimble, buttons, etc.; portfolio containing pens, ink, writing paper, envelopes, pencils and drawing paper, etc.; bible, two volumes of "Washington and his Generals," by Headley; pistol, dirk-knife, bunch of boneset herb furnished by his grandmother; a pair of heavy woolen blankets, one rubber blanket, and the army overcoat.

His haversack, like others, was well filled with home dainties for the occasion, such as mince-pie, cake, pot of butter, cheese, tea, coffee, sugar, condensed milk, and blackberry jam. Those who were so unfortunate as to have no mothers, sisters, or sweethearts at hand, with home fixings, were readily supplied by the more favored ones who had an abundance and to spare. Our hero succeeded in getting all this to Washington, to the rear of the Capitol building, but not across the Potomac. Such a feat was

---

the audiences gone and front ranks shrinking, most bands would vanish—either sent home or absorbed into the regimental ranks. See, for example, Eugene A. Nash, *A History of the Forty-fourth Regiment New York Infantry* (Reprint, Dayton, 1988), 94. Most men of the Eighteenth's band were discharged on August 7, 1862.

rendered possible because the only marching required was a mile or two in New York and another mile from the B & O depot to Capitol Hill [in Washington], and at this stage the regimental supply trains were utilized somewhat. Upon arriving in New York, on the morning of August 27, Colonel Barnes could not resist the temptation to show off his command, so it was marched up to and down Broadway, past the Astor House, and finally to the Elizabethport ferry boat. As it marched in ranks of twos and fours, and was maneuvered by platoons and company front, the ovation received was everything that officers or men could desire. Before reaching the Astor the band struck up "John Brown's body lies mouldering in the grave, etc.," and the thousand marching men joined in, as with one voice, at concert pitch. It did create a sensation that attracted crowds to every window and doorway, and filled the sidewalks.

The arrival of this body of troops in Washington, two days later, somehow did not attract the amount of attention it expected. Others had been there before, and the customary ovation that had been accorded en route was omitted here. So many troops had already gathered that the city had recovered from its scare, and the profuse welcome extended to earlier arrivals was an old story, so the Eighteenth crawled into some old barracks, under the darkness of night and during a drizzling, foggy rain, glad to be let alone in its disappointment.

On September 2d the march was to Capitol Hill, behind the Capitol of the nation, and the regiment occupied ground where the Congressional library now stands, being placed under the command of Gen. Benj. F. Butler.[26] This march through Pennsylvania avenue, although only a mile, was very severe on account of the unlimited mud which had been produced by recent rains, and the heavy loads carried by the men; its slough holes and putty-like consistency, which reached an unknown depth, had been caused by the parts of artillery and commissary trains that were so constantly moving through and churning it up. Hogs and pigs, singly, in twos and threes, and in droves, disputed the right of way.

An attempt was made to move this regiment up this avenue with something like the eclat of Broadway, but it was soon abandoned as one after another of the heavily loaded men reached to their waists in a slough hole

---

26. Benjamin F. Butler, one of the most prominent civilian soldiers of the war, a classic political general. His tenure in Washington at this time—and hence his association with the Eighteenth Massachusetts—would be exceedingly brief, and indeed Mann may be mistaken that Butler ever had command over the troops around the capitol at this time. See Benjamin F. Butler, *Butler's Book* (Boston, 1892), 287–88.

or, measuring their length, disappeared entirely for the instant beneath mud and slime, to be pulled out by more fortunate comrades. So the order was passed down the line: "Route step!" Then an opportunity was afforded the men to clear a way among the wallowing swine with clubbed muskets, and pick a footing along the edges of gullies of mud.

Pennsylvania Avenue of 1861 has ceased to exist. Then it was unpaved and a general rendezvous for the swine of the city, and this regiment met with no worse sloughs during its four years of service, "Burnside's Mud March" excepted, than along this mile of the "finest" avenue of the Capital of the Nation. One foot in depth to two in advance, was the average progress made; while coaxing one foot out the other was sinking into unknown abysses, and when drawn out it made a noise like a suction pump from which the water is about exhausted. Frequently a shoe or boot was left in the mud, and the fishing for the lost article was ludicrous to all but the fishermen. It was nasty mud as well as sticky. A shoe that went down into it a number seven was hauled out, to all appearances, a number 12. Some one dubbed these soil-excavators, "pontoons," a name that stuck throughout the war to many a pair of feet that were above the average size. It was four days after this "mud march" through the avenue before the boys could make a presentable appearance, then it was a failure compared with a Readville dress-parade. Washington was a disappointment in every particular.

TWO

"The Sacred Soil of Virginia"

The first months in the army, in college, in marriage, in the work world are always the most vivid. So it was for Thomas Mann. On September 6, Mann fired his musket for the first time. "It made me stagger back 6 feet, very near knocked me down," he told the folks at home.[1] *Days later, a member of the regiment suffered the Eighteenth's first wound—though inadvertently at his own hands. Mann wrote of the event with some excitement: "He was laying [sic] on the ground with his gun loaded (we all have our guns loaded the most of the time) and as he said dreamed that we were attacked by the rebels and that he fired at their head man and they returned the shot and hit him and he then waked up finding he had shot his own foot off about one half!"*[2] *On the heels of these experiences came the first brigade drills, the first sham battles, the first photographs, the first shots in anger, and the first holidays away from home.*

The fall and winter of 1861 to 1862 saw the Eighteenth Massachusetts assume its place in the army, both physically and organizationally. Physically, the Eighteenth spent its first weeks in Virginia just across the Potomac, working on and camping near Fort Corcoran—on the hills overlooking Georgetown. Later, the regiment and brigade would move westward to Hall's Hill. While there, Mann and the Eighteenth got their first glimpse of the army at large, its commander, and President Lincoln during the huge review at Bailey's Crossroads in November 1861. Then they settled into a wintertime routine that included picket duty, digging earthworks, and endless drill. Into this toil they injected as much levity, culture, and recreation as they could. Mann gives us a vivid look at these efforts.

1. Mann to "N. J. & E," no date (but shortly after their arrival in Washington), Mann Papers.

2. Mann to friends at home, September 11, 1861, Mann Papers.

Organizationally, the Eighteenth found itself in a brigade commanded by General John Martindale—a man with great oratorical (and even some musical) ability but little battlefield courage. Martindale's brigade proved to be a quibbling mosh of intrigue. The Thirteenth New York and Second Maine would teeter on the edge of mutiny during the fall of 1861; part of the Second Maine would mutiny altogether on the eve of Gettysburg. The Twenty-fifth New York, said one man, was "composed of New York roughs, Bowry boys, 'Dead Rabbits,' etc. Their colonel has been court-martialed on charge of treason...." The colonel of the Twenty-second Massachusetts—the closest thing the Eighteenth had to a "sister regiment"—was radical Republican Senator Henry Wilson. Wilson's presence, his close association with Martindale, and their mutual disdain for corps commander Fitz John Porter would help stimulate immense suspicion of Porter and McClellan among radical members of Congress and the administration. This would be the germ that would grow into complete mistrust of the army by the government and the government by the army (a phenomenon that would generate much comment from Mann). Indeed, of the six regiments in the brigade, only two—the Eighteenth Massachusetts and the First Michigan—escaped the barbs of gossips and intriguers. They were the calm siblings in a raucous family.

Early in September Colonel Barnes marched his regiment across Long Bridge,[3] which reached from the Capital to the enemy's country, to the "sacred soil of Virginia," and it was received with open arms by Brigadier General J. H. Martindale.[4] As the enthusiastic troops were about to climb the bluffs on the south side of the Potomac, he made a ringing speech from

---

3. Located approximately where the Fourteenth Street Bridge is today, just southeast of the Jefferson Memorial. Two other bridges linked Washington to Virginia: Aqueduct Bridge in Georgetown and Chain Bridge about four miles upstream from Aqueduct Bridge.

4. John H. Martindale, brigadier general and commander of the brigade to which the Eighteenth Massachusetts was assigned. A West Point graduate, Martindale eschewed the military before the war and took up the bar. Spare, shrill, and politically well-connected, Martindale had received his commission as brigadier general just a month before Mann and the Eighteenth Massachusetts arrived at the front. Corps commander Fitz John Porter described Martindale as "intelligent and active and attentive to his duties when they did not clash with his interests or safety." Porter added that Martindale was "vain, ambitious of advancement and unscrupulous in his means of attaining his ends." Nonetheless, Martindale was a powerful public speaker and would be popular with his men—a central figure in the Eighteenth's first year of toil at the front. Warner, *Generals in Blue*, 312–13; Undated memorandum by Fitz John Porter, Porter Papers, Reel 3 (container 7), Library of Congress; Wil-

the back of the magnificent black stallion that he strode, which stirred this enthusiasm to its profoundest depths. It was like touching a match to a sky-rocket, till there was not a man who doubted his own individual ability to cope with any five that the Confederacy could produce. With such a brigade commander the Eighteenth figured that it would take about six months to preserve the Union—some were fully persuaded it would take only three.[5]

The march was along these bluffs . . . past Arlington, the ancestral home of General Robert E. Lee, to Fort Corcoran, opposite Georgetown, where the camp was pitched and occupied nearly a month. From "Camp near Fort Corcoran, Va." the Eighteenth conducted its voluminous correspondence with home friends, in that exuberance of spirits born of an optimistic view which thus far had received no drawback and—throwing the "sacred soil" of Virginia into formidable earth-works, with pick and shovel.

The view from the camp was fine, covering the cities of Washington and Georgetown, the Potomac river for five or six miles, and the three bridges—Chain, Aqueduct, and Long—that crossed it. The objects of interest to these newly-fledged defenders of the Union were: the . . . line of earth-forts along the bluffs, from above Chain bridge on the north to Alexandria in the south, a distance of fifteen or more miles, for the defence of the National Capital, and mounting them with hundreds of heavy cannon; and the abandoned residence of Gen. Lee on Arlington Heights,[6] which was directly across the Potomac from the "White House."

The peculiar spirit, call it revenge, anger, or spite, that dominated the Federal as well as the Confederate soldiers at this stage of the war, was illustrated by the persistent and repeated attempts to destroy this magnifi-

---

liam Alderman, "The 18th Regiment's Glee Club," unidentified clipping from the *Sunday Republican*, FSNMPL; John Berry, Diary, July 4, 1862, *Civil War Times Illustrated* Collection, USAMHI; Unsigned letter from a member of the Thirteenth New York in the *Rochester Democrat and American*, July 15, 1862.

5. Another member of the Eighteenth commented rather optimistically during this period, "We are closing in fast on the rebels, and hope soon to make them surrender." Letter of C. H. S., *Cambridge Chronicle*, October 19, 1861.

6. Today preserved as the Custis-Lee Mansion, a National Park Service site. The home sits directly above the grave of President John F. Kennedy. Around it is the compelling landscape of Arlington National Cemetery. Behind the house are buried the remains of nearly two thousand Union soldiers taken off the fields of Manassas. Included among these souls are undoubtedly one or more members of the Eighteenth Massachusetts, and perhaps of Company I.

cent mansion. Happily all these efforts were frustrated, though it required a strong and vigilant guard of regular soldiers from the old standing army. The grounds, gardens, and parks filled with stately old forest trees, were leveled and ruined by throwing up unsightly earth-works over all parts of this princely property, so that the mansion stood alone as barren as a barn.

Tom, who it must be remembered was an 18 year old boy at this time, in writing to his father from this place, under date of September 6, says: "North Carolina and Georgia have withdrawn their troops from the war, and we have surrounded all the secesh army in Virginia. We have about 10,000 troops on this side of them, besides several companies of artillery and six forts with heavy mounted cannon; and in Western Virginia we have a large army driving them toward us. Also, on the southern side we have artillery and troops sufficient to hold them; and they have no escape." And he adds the very sanguinary statement: "We all expect to eat a Thanksgiving dinner at home."

During the month the Eighteenth was largely occupied in throwing up the formidable earth-work known as Fort Corcoran, and in building a road toward Chain Bridge, which crosses the Potomac above Georgetown.[7]

During the early days of October the defensive line of Washington was pushed farther out, to the ridge of hills, the most prominent of which is Munson's, Upton's, and Hall's. The Eighteenth, in taking its position on the latter hill, was brigaded with the 2d Maine, 13th New York, 22d Mass., and 25th New York regiments.[8] These five, under the command of Gen. Martindale, ultimately became the 1st brigade, 1st division of the 5th army corps; the division being under the command of Gen. Morell,[9] and

---

7. Fort Corcoran sat atop the heights at the western end of Aqueduct Bridge, which linked Georgetown with Arlington. Today "Key Bridge" stands near the site of Aqueduct Bridge. Fort Corcoran was one of more than sixty-five forts built to defend Washington during the first year of the war, completely ringing the city. The best work on the Washington defenses is Benjamin F. Cooling, *Symbol, Sword, and Shield: Defending Washington during the Civil War* (Reprint, Shippensburg, 1991).

8. The brigade would later be joined by the First Michigan.

9. Mann is incorrect in according Morell a division command at this time. He would continue to command a brigade until the spring of 1862, when he rose to divisional command. Brigadier General George Morell ranked first in the West Point class of 1835. Before the war, he pursued a career in law, but returned to military service at the outbreak of the hostilities. Almost unknown today, Morell was a mainstay of the army's Fifth Corps for the first year of the war. His obscurity is attributable to his personality. A staff officer said of him, "Morell was not a dashing officer and he had so little idea of making an effect, that he missed favorable opportunities." Porter, a close confidant of Morell's, assessed him to be "of

the corps under Gen. Fitz John Porter.[10] Hall's Hill, which was nine miles from Washington, was near the center of the new line of defences established; the right of the line reaching well toward Harper's Ferry, and the left covering Alexandria on the south.

This camp was a sightly place, overlooking a large extent of country in the direction of Manassas, Centreville, Fairfax, and Bull Run, where the enemy from 50,000 to 100,000 was supposed to be waiting impatiently for a fight. To the rear the unfinished dome of the Capitol could be seen. During October and a part of November more or less drilling was exacted of the troops, though much of the time was occupied in leveling the magnificent forests of chestnut and pine for several miles in front of this range of hills. Details that constituted the greater part of the regiment were sent out every day, with axes, till more than 30 square miles of forest were leveled with the ground. It was the harvest time for chestnuts, and as the large old trees were brought to the ground the nuts were thrashed out by the bushel. Thousands of bushels were thus gathered by the army so that they were a drug in the camps of the men who munched them all winter, roasted, raw and boiled.

Persimmons were plenty, and soon as the men learned at what stage of ripeness they could be eaten this favorite food of the opossum was quickly appropriated. It is a peculiar fruit, and until apparently well advanced toward the stage of decay can no more be eaten than a piece of alum. When decay is marked and its fair plumpness has collapsed into the condition of a very rotten apple, then the persimmon is delicious, though thou-

---

bright, clear mind, familiar with his duties and always true to them, though not initially very active or pressing." A civilian observer called him "an interesting man; he looks like a dear father, but wears a long white beard." Warner, *Generals in Blue,* 330–31; Richard T. Auchmuty (Fifth Corps staff) to Carswell McClellan, January 12, 1892, Porter Papers, reel 31 (container 63), frames 88–89; undated memorandum by Fitz John Porter, reel 3 (container 7), Porter Papers; Katherine Prescott Wormley, *The Other Side of War: With the Army of the Potomac* (Boston, 1889), 52–53.

10. Porter would not assume corps command until May 1862 and until then commanded the division in which the Eighteenth served. Called by one man the "most magnificent soldier in the army," Fitz John Porter was army commander George B. McClellan's friend, confidant and, at times, sycophant. McClellan called him "probably the best general officer I had under me." History has judged Porter less charitably, recognizing his penchant for intrigue and his active disagreement with the policies of the government he served. George B. McClellan, *McClellan's Own Story* (New York, 1887), 139; Stephen W. Sears, ed., *The Civil War Papers of George B. McClellan* (New York, 1989), 340–41; A. K. McClure, *Abraham Lincoln and Men of War-Times* (Philadelphia, 1892), 371–72.

sands entirely ruined their appetites for this fruit by biting it too soon. [Private John] McGinnis said: "savin ye prissence, if this be the kind of frut Ave presinted to Adam for to ate, be jabbers, he ought to hav' squealed on her soon as the A'mighty lave him open his jaw!" This remark was made as soon as this Irish Wit of the company could control his organs of speech after taking a bite from an unusually fine looking specimen.

When the country was properly cleared, to give full range for the artillery of the army, drilling commenced again in dead earnest; the bayonet, skirmish, squad, battalion, company, regimental and brigade drill. It was the unanimous and profane opinion of the whole army that it was being drilled like h—l. The only respite was the detail for picket duty, which was hailed with delight by the Eighteenth when its turn came.

The advance of the picket line from four to six miles in front of the army, the detail being made up for three days at a time, during the fall and winter of 1861, afforded a decided and welcomed break in the camp and drill monotony. It also afforded opportunities to gather in some fresh pork, chickens, sweet potatoes, tobacco, et cetera, which, on the quiet, were considered a picket's perquisites, though strictly forbidden by the different division commanders. Picket duty was not governed by prescribed rules and regulations or, to be more exact, it had but two rules, namely: keep wide awake and allow of no passing in or out of the lines without the countersign. At this stage, however, few cared to venture into the vicinity of the picket line, even with the countersign.

The earlier picket service was not dangerous, but toward the Spring of 1862 the lines were advanced so that occasionally a little excitement was raised that was thoroughly enjoyed. The order to "allow no living thing to pass the lines," was interpreted literally, and many an unlucky pig or stray calf or sheep was added to the regular rations because they did not give the countersign, or persisted in passing the lines.

Our heroes, Sergt. Bill and Corporal Tom, each tell of their first experience on the picket line; both literally true though from different standpoints of the same line. In their own words, Sergt. Bill says:

> A march of three or four miles perhaps, toward Fall's Church, and that part of the picket line which we were to occupy was reached, and noiselessly as possible we filed to the relief of the old guard. I remember that the men we relieved were not over communicative, but they did give us to understand that their experience had been such that constant vigilance had been the price of their safety, and that there had been a good deal of firing along the ·picket line during the previous night.

Clearly they had not crushed the rebellion, and there remained for us to take up that job just where they left it. I recall that our orders were, "not to fire unless we saw something to fire at." "Something," I suppose was intended to mean the enemy, but as it proved it was perhaps rather too broad. Perhaps the officers commanding the guard were a trifle nervous themselves, otherwise the order might have been more explicit. However, the men had hardly been posted when the "stilly night" was vexed by the sharp report of a musket.

Ah! It had come at last. We had been expecting it for weeks. The ball had opened, and the expected time when we should stand up to be shot at had arrived. That the enemy was in front of us there was no doubt at all, and quite probably in force. Eyes were strained to the utmost peering into the uncertain light in front of us. Every stump and stone began to take on human shape, and each gently waving bough or bush assumed the attitude of a stealthily approaching form. The report of another musket in the opposite direction up the line proved too much for the nerves of several, and resulted in quite a fusillade.

The reserve guard was ordered to fall in. Officers were running up and down the line trying to find out the cause of the rattling fire. The guards who were responsible for all the noise and excitement felt sure they had seen something suspicious, but under close questioning failed to give that something any tangible shape. Every few minutes the crack of a rifle on some part of the line kept expectation on tiptop, and vigilance from subsiding. Singularly enough, the rebs failed to return our fire. Not a single shot answered to our angry rattle. And so the night wore on, with every now and again a renewal of hostilities, until at last, greatly to our relief, the first tints of color in the east heralded the approach of day. Whether the enemy withdrew as the darkness gave place to the sun's cheerful rays, or whether there had been no enemy to withdraw, was a question over which was had many lively disputations.

Corporal Tom says:

One incident in my first experience upon the picket line is well remembered, because I was the unintentional instigator of considerable excitement. It was early in October and the post, which I was one of the four to occupy, was somewhat advanced beyond adjoining ones on account of the nature of the ground in its vicinity, and the parting caution of the officer who located its position was, "keep a sharp lookout." The first night was a very dark one, and we four were thoroughly alive to the duty imposed upon this particular post, realizing that the whole rebel army might steal past and take the sleeping Union forces by surprise.

About midnight a faint glimmering light was discovered in our front, and one proposed in a subdued whisper to fire at it. The bare suggestion was all that was needed, acting like a spark to gunpowder. Besides, only a few days before our regiment had been provided with new Springfield rifles which we were impatient to test. It instantly became the unanimous opinion of all four that it was our duty to raise an alarm and put the sleeping army on the alert.

The noise of the shot, its echo and re-echo in the dead of night, excited us wonderfully so that the remaining three fired as if panic-stricken, and we loaded and fired again and again. Still the light glimmered. The nearest post took up the refrain and passed it along to the next, and the next, till the whole picket line extending over a mile or more was firing at some imaginary enemy.

In a few minutes the commanding officer, with the whole reserve of fifty or sixty men, came hastening to our excited post, ready for fight. We pointed to the light and he, quickly drawing his three inch revolver, discharged the whole six barrels in quick succession in the direction of it. Then he ordered the reserve to fire. Still the light glimmered.

It began to look like war in earnest and it was improved to the extent of our ability. The light had no business there and meant mischief to the great army behind us, so the fusillade was kept up at intervals till daylight. As the grey streaks of dawn began to show in the east, the field officer who commanded the picket line in front of Porter's division, arrived upon the ground with the greater part of two regiments at his back.

Of course the glimmering light faded with the appearance of daylight, and much of the excitement had subsided, but it was thought best to send out a scouting party to investigate the strength and character of the enemy we had so gallantly held at bay the livelong night, and forty volunteers were called to act in that capacity. Two hours later they returned, and reported that the light was from a tallow dip, shining from the attic window of a negro cabin, about 500 yards in front of our post; the cabin not being visible by daylight because there was just enough brush between it and our post to hide it, but at night the light glimmered through.

The cabin was occupied by an old and deaf negro wench, and the candle was burned all night because, as she said: "Deed, massa, I was afeared to sleep in de dark." All our vigorous firing had not awakened her, and not a single mark of a bullet could be found about the hut. Our shots had fallen at least a hundred yards short, and it was learned a month later that the nearest rebel who bore arms was not within fifteen miles of our picket post that night.[11]

11. Unlike most first-person quotations in the memoir, this one is not found in Mann's letters. Instead, he apparently chose to relate these events more personally and constructed his memoir in the first person.

This was some of the training received by the "Army of the Potomac," but its engagements were not always so bloodless or ridiculous as this, and this regiment marched and countermarched, bivouacked and fought in Virginia till not a fence rail with which to build a camp-fire, not a sheep, pig, chicken, or anything eatable or burnable was left south of the Blue Ridge or north of the James; and every acre was barren as if swept by fire—while 100,000 men were being killed or crippled. As Sergt. Bill said: "By the Lord Harry, Sir, these first duties in the enemy's country are not to be disparaged. The veteran 'Army of the Potomac' that forced Gen. Lee to finally surrender at Appomattox was not the creation of a day. It was the result of much discipline, through toil, hardship and danger."

Somehow wine, women and song have always been intimately associated, but the army sadly lacked the principal deity of the three. The appearance of a woman within the lines of the Eighteenth was so rare that they were angels indeed. In a few instances, during the four years, one or another of the officer's wives visited her respective husband's quarters, when they were established for the winter, but the non-coms and privates had to content themselves with the facilities afforded by the post office department for any kind of communication with mothers, wives, sisters, or the other fellow's sister. Of song and music there was plenty, and wine was not altogether an unknown quantity.

In the matter of women and correspondence, probably no two men in the whole regiment were better posted than Sergt. Bill and Corporal Tom. This is all the more remarkable because both were very modest young men and not much given to courting the favor of the other sex; their early experience, as already noted, seemed to bar them out. But these two were pounced upon by the whole of company "I," and to a considerable extent by the regiment, in whom to repose their tender, and otherwise, secrets. Bill must have been quite adept at writing love-letters before the war, and Tom was not long in learning how after camp life commenced. Anyhow, between the two they had more or less to do with most of the epistles of that nature which left, or were received by, the company, as well as with others more serious or pertaining to plain, prosy business.

Some dozen or more members of this company, not to mention others of the regiment, could not write, or were very indifferent hands at managing some of the details such as orthography, posology, syntax, or the art of satisfactorily expressing one's feelings in plain, every-day English, and these "experts" were pressed into the service of helping out. The less able a man is, or feels himself, regarding English composition, the more he wants to clothe his thoughts in the choicest of language to his best girl, and both our heroes usually enjoyed the fun while furnishing expressions for all conditions and stages of feeling.

The long winter evenings while in camp upon Hall's Hill were pregnant with much letter writing, and those who left no particular sweetheart behind soon found one, or more, with which to open a correspondence. Somebody's sister was willing to cheer a soldier's life by dainty, effusive, sentimental, or plain womanly and sisterly letters. If the soldier could not write, or was a very indifferent writer, it was all the same—Bill or Tom was at hand to supply the deficiency.

Some of this letter-writing resulted in happy marriages, more in pleasant friendships, but most was only a passing, grateful shadow and about as tangible. In one instance, with which Tom was somewhat concerned, a curious train of circumstances developed, which he relates in a serio-comic vein, though its parallel might be duplicated many times. It commenced about Christmas time by Sergt. Henry [Davis][12] applying to our hero for assistance in writing a letter to a lady, a sister of one of his comrades, to open a correspondence. Tom was willing and a strong, pathetic letter, slightly tinged with a hint of sentiment, was produced and sent to the lady who lived in central New York. Sergt. H. was a good penman but that was the full extent of his abilities with the English language, so far as a pen was concerned, so Tom scribbled a proper introductory letter, in pencil, punctuated and phrased it, which the sergeant carefully copied upon approved paper, in his graceful, flowing hand.

An answer came, the lady was agreeable and the correspondence was entered upon with ardent zest; was voluminous, frequent, and continued so long as the sergeant remained with the regiment. He never dared to trust his own abilities alone, so Tom read all the missives received in order to assist properly in composing those sent. It is but justice to the sergeant to say that he soon found enough to say without Tom's assistance, though the latter was still considered necessary to put the ideas furnished into presentable shape. To make this part of the story short, [Henry] re-enlisted in the winter of '63–'64, enjoyed a furlough of 30 days, which he improved to visit his lady-by-correspondence-love, engaged her to marry him when the "cruel war was over," returned to the regiment and was then lost sight of by Tom for nearly two years.[13]

12. Sergeant Henry C. Davis, twenty-three, a farmer from Brattleboro, Vermont.

13. The records show that Sergeant Davis did not reenlist, but was discharged at the expiration of the regiment's term of enlistment on September 2, 1864.

The sequel was developed to the narrator of this story on his visit, during the winter of '65–'66, to central New York, where the attractions were such that he remained to teach at the village school. During one of Tom's long Saturday drives through the country, with a Miss T, one of the few toll-gates still left in those parts was met, and a prepossessing young lady appeared to collect the customary toll. Her countenance appeared so familiar to Tom that the gaze or stare he bestowed upon it attracted the attention of the lady by his side.

"What possesses you to flirt so earnestly with that Miss K," asked Miss T.

"I was not flirting," replied Tom, "but I have seen her somewhere before this, and I would like to place her."

"No you haven't, because she has never been a hundred miles from home, for I have known her all my life," said Miss T.

Questions and explanations followed until Tom was able to trace his previous knowledge of Miss K to the picture possessed by Sergt. Henry, two years previous. The team was shortly turned about, the toll-gate soon reached again where introductions followed. Of course our hero did not give away his part of the assistance rendered to Sergt. Henry, but took the occasion to heartily congratulate Miss K upon her approaching marriage with the ex-soldier.

The most astonishing coincidence in relation to this case was developed during the drive home. Tom told of his instrumentality in aiding Sergt. Henry; was gently chided by Miss T, though with a curiously quizzical tone, which ended in a confession. The lady by Tom's side, that he was so assiduously waiting upon, had performed the same offices for Miss K that he had been rendering to Sergt. Henry. "Well," said Tom, with a deep drawn sigh of relief, "then they are well matched, and I will borrow no further trouble over the matter."

Wine was more or less plenty, though usually found in the shape of raw, fiery whiskey recently distilled, and which was kept in stock by the brigade commissary for emergencies. Occasionally a soldier would make an emergency, and the chances were more than even that the guard house soon gathered him in.

During the day following the release from guard duty of the preceding twenty-four hours, the 30 or 40 men of a regiment thus relieved were excused from all duty, except in an emergency, and a large share of them were readily granted passes, good for 24 hours, to visit other parts of the army. For a time, two men from each company, each day, were granted leave to visit Washington or Alexandria, and advantage was taken of these passes to procure intoxicants, bring them to camp by the canteen-full, until the privilege was so badly abused that the returning soldier was thoroughly searched, and relieved at Long Bridge by the provost guard. The word "contraband" had not then been applied to the negroes, but to smuggled whiskey, and a soldier found intoxicated was accused of having taken too much "contraband goods" aboard.

The sale or possession of liquors were strictly prohibited, though on occasions of unusual moment or after some extra hardship and exposure, rations of raw whiskey were dealt to the soldiers in limited quantities—even though there were enough who refused such a ration to supply the lovers of it with sufficient to make crawling on all fours the only safe method of locomotion.

General Blenker's division,[14] which at this time was located to the south of Hall's Hill and nearer Alexandria, was a peculiar one and made up of nearly all nationalities, though the Germans and Bohemians predominated. Its officers were men who had served in some capacity or other in the different European armies, and the previous career of most of them would not bear close inquiry. That of Colonel D'Utassy, commanding the Garibaldi regiment, is a sample. He was a Hungarian and a rider in Franconi's circus, but his American career terminated in the Albany penitentiary.[15] In this division were Zouaves from Algiers, men of the "Foreign Legion," Cossacks, Garibaldians, English deserters, Sepoys, Groats, Swiss, beer drinkers from Bavaria, men from North Germany, and whole detachments from the army of the Grand Duchess of Gerolstein. Blenker himself had been an officer under King Otho of Greece. Gen. McClellan said of this division: "Their drill and bearing was good, for all the officers, and probably all the men, had served in Europe, and I could control them as no one else could."

14. Brigadier General Louis Blenker, a native of Germany, commanded a division that would eventually become part of the Eleventh Corps of the Army of the Potomac.

15. Colonel Frederick D'Utassy commanded the Thirty-ninth New York Infantry. D'Utassy and the Thirty-ninth stimulated some of the most flowering jingoistic prose of the Civil War era. Mann's description reflects these prejudices. A man in the Twentieth Massachusetts similarly called the Thirty-ninth New York "a beastly set of Dutch boors, Maccaronis, & Frogratecs, in short the rag tag & bobtail of all creation, little short beastly fellows with big beards and more stupid than it is possible for an American . . . to conceive of." Robert Garth Scott, ed., *Fallen Leaves: The Civil War Letters of Major Henry Livermore Abbott* (Kent, Ohio, 1991), 237. See also Michael Bacarella, *Lincoln's Foreign Legion: The 39th New York Infantry, the Garibaldi Guard* (Shippensburg, 1996), 18–19.

The rank and file of the other divisions composing the army knew this one as the one place, within the lines, where lager flowed as freely as water, and liquors of all kinds were dispensed as openly by the sutler as if running a saloon in the New York Bowery. Blenker's division was the attractive point of all who hankered after something stronger than coffee, and passes were utilized to make friendly calls upon congenial spirits here.

As if to corroborate the astuteness of the combination "Wine, Women, and Song," wine and song were thoroughly blended in this division, and the lack of the regulating element of the three was simply a necessity incidental to war. The assertion of Gen. Blenker that upon a half hour's notice he could collect as fine an orchestra, quartette, vocal or instrumental soloist, or chorus, as the country could produce, seemed warranted by the facts. Certainly it was a thrilling and inspiring treat to listen to the singing of the German Choral songs by the combined voices of several regiments, when accompanied by their full brass bands. In fact Blenker's division afforded the opera of the army as well as its beer garden.

It should not be inferred from these little digressions that the army was addicted to liquor drinking. Of company "I," more than half absolutely refused whiskey when offered as a ration by the Commissary. Half of the remainder accepted it because recommended by the surgeons in charge, and the remaining one-fourth could not be classed as drinking men; and this company presented a fair average of the New England soldier, at least. There was less drinking and drunkenness in the "Army of the Potomac" than in any section of country that contained within its borders 100,000 people.[16]

The Eighteenth furnished a glee club of singers whose fame extended throughout the army corps, and whose singing was so inspiring that their less talented comrades cheerfully accorded them the many respites from regular duty, and other favors, shown by the officers of the corps, from Gen. Porter down through the brigade, regimental and company com-

---

16. The abstemiousness of the army was no doubt attributable in part to the scarcity of alcohol. On occasions when alcohol was available—New Year's, for example—the army surely reflected the tendencies of the general population. The officer corps, which had regular access to alcohol, certainly and regularly consumed its rightly proportion of spirits as the war progressed. See Bell I. Wiley, *The Life of Billy Yank* (Reprint, New York, 1971), 252–54. Perhaps the most vivid chronicle of the use of alcohol in the Army of the Potomac is Thomas Francis Galwey's memoir, *The Valiant Hours,* edited by Wilbur S. Nye (Harrisburg, 1961). See especially 75–76. For more commentary see "From Captain Weidman," *Lebanon* [Pa.] *Advertiser,* August 6, 1862.

manders. This club was organized at Hall's Hill and continued for nearly three years, until broken up by the exigencies of vigorous campaigning. Sergt. Bill was one of the prime movers and the baritone of the club; [Frederick] McAvoy,[17] since of minstrel fame, was soprano; Maintien, who died at Andersonville, was first tenor, and Sergt. [Ezra] Bly[18] second tenor, all of company "I." Corporal Jones, of "D," was a bass or baritone singer, and another member of company "I," Corporal [George] Alfred,[19] could rattle the bones or pick the banjo to perfection. Many was the rare treat furnished by this musical club, and the remembrance of it constitutes one of the pleasant memories of the war, of the thousands who heard it.[20]

Their repertory included all the popular music of the day, from "John Brown's Body"[21] and "Louisiana low-lands" to one of Mozart's anthems. On one piece of music, however, they had a copy-right, by common consent. It was written especially for this club by Gen. Martindale, sprang immediately into enthusiastic popularity, and held it for years. It is reproduced here for it can hardly be found elsewhere.

SONG

When battle's music greets our ear,
Our guns are sighted at the foe,
Then nerve the hand, and banish fear
And comrades, touch the elbow.

Chorus: Touch the elbow, comrades elbow,
Elbow comrades, touch the elbow.
Nerve the hand, banish fear
Comrades, touch the elbow.

17. Private Frederick McAvoy, a nineteen-year-old upholsterer from Fall River. Wounded at Second Manassas, he would be discharged in December 1862.

18. Ezra K. Bly, a twenty-one-year-old "tinman" from New Bedford. He would be wounded at Fredericksburg, but would reenlist and serve out the war.

19. George H. T. Alfred, a hatter from Walpole. Discharged in November 1862 as a result of wounds received at Second Manassas.

20. William Alderman called the Eighteenth "an exceptionally musical regiment." "From the very first," wrote Alderman, ". . . the boys who were musical began to 'find each other out' and lively song relieved man an hour that otherwise would have been dreary enough." Alderman noted with some glee that Colonel Barnes, though "no musician at all," gave the glee club broad freedom to move about the camp, "wherever our fancy led us." William Alderman, "The 18th Regiment's Glee Club," unidentified clipping from the *Sunday Republican*, Fredericksburg and Spotsylvania National Military Park Library (FSNMPL).

21. In 1861, Julia Ward Howe composed new lyrics for this song, and it is best known today as the "Battle Hymn of the Republic."

Home and country, patriots, fire,
Kindle our souls with fervid glow,
And Southern traitors shall retire
When Northmen touch the elbow.

Chorus: Touch the elbow, comrades elbow,
Elbow comrades, touch the elbow.
Southern traitors shall retire,
Northmen, touch the elbow.

A cannon shot may plow the rank
And through us strike a deadly blow,
Close up the space the ball made blank,
And comrades, touch the elbow.

Chorus: Touch the elbow, comrades elbow,
Elbow comrades, touch the elbow.
Close up the space the ball made blank,
And comrades, touch the elbow.

Though many brave men bite the sod,
And crimson heart's-blood freely flow,
Shout, as their spirits soar to God,
On, Comrades, touch the elbow!

Chorus: Touch the elbow, comrades elbow,
Elbow comrades, touch the elbow.
Shout, as their spirits soar to God,
On, Comrades, touch the elbow!

Now show the rocks of which you're made,
The Gen'ral signals,—"March, Hallo!
Double the quick-step, First Brigade!
Charge! Comrades, touch the elbow!"

Chorus: Touch the elbow, comrades elbow,
Elbow comrades, touch the elbow.
"Double the quick-step, First Brigade!
Charge! Comrades, touch the elbow!"

Sergt. Bill says, quite modestly, that General Martindale having done his part well in giving the club a Brigade song, what were we to do about the music? "Not one of us had ever been guilty of unloading such a thing as a musical composition, but we had to act or forever hang our heads in shame. Some one suggested the bandmaster, and to the bandmaster we went, suggesting that he lay his head alongside ours and see what could be produced. If I remember rightly the product was principally due to the head of the bandmaster; at any rate I make no claim."

Corporal Tom's remembrance of this production corroborates the Sergeant, except, as he says, "Bill always had the credit of the composition, while the bandmaster furnished the technique and adaptation to the different voices." The verdict in regard to the fitting of the music to the words, was instantly attested by the universal popularity accorded to it by the whole brigade, and even at the headquarters of the army.[22]

In speaking further of this club, of which he was the moving spirit as well as the balance-wheel, the sergeant says:

> Many and various were the experiences of our glee club during the winter of '61 and '62 while encamped at Hall's Hill, and many the generals we serenaded from General McClellan down. Whether we really sang well, or whether in the absence of anything better our music passed muster, is not for me to decide, but we were always applauded to the echo, and enjoyed the hospitality of all we sang to. The opening campaign of spring restricted our musical efforts to a large extent, though not altogether. The last time I recollect singing to General Martindale was the night of the 5th of July, 1862. It was just after the Seven Day's fighting before Richmond when the army, defeated, fell back to Harrison's Landing on the James River, and we were encamped near the famous "Westover mansion," which was occupied as headquarters for our corps by General Porter.
>
> I remember that night well for General Martindale was depressed and sorrowful. We sang "Touch the Elbow," of course, as we always did to him. He called us in and talked to us in his dramatic way. Referring in his talk to the lines in his song—"a cannon shot may plow the rank, and through us strike a deadly blow. Close up the space the ball made blank, and comrades, touch the elbow"—he said: "Ah, yes! I've seen it. Within the past few days I've seen a cannon ball strike down in the ranks—and kill a man! Perhaps several men; the ranks close up, touch the elbow and press on. And the tears ran down his cheeks and his voice was tremulous with emotion.

---

22. This passage on Martindale's songwriting and Alderman's composing is lifted largely from Alderman, "The 18th Regiment's Glee Club," unidentified clipping from the *Sunday Republican*, FSNMPL. Brigadier General Daniel Butterfield, one of Martindale's fellow brigade commanders, also had a penchant for composing. He developed a distinctive bugle call for his brigade and then wrote the melody for "Taps" at Harrison's Landing in July 1862. See Oliver W. Norton, *Army Letters, 1861–1865* (Reprint, Dayton, 1990), 323–27.

Speaking further of General Martindale, the sergeant pays him this well deserved tribute while telling of his characteristics:

> General Martindale, who commanded our brigade and who among our officers was the best loved of them all, came to us when we crossed the Potomac and made our first encampment just opposite Georgetown, where we spent many days building an earthwork, which was named Fort Corcoran. He was a New York man, from Rochester, a celebrated criminal lawyer. I remember him as the most eloquent speaker I heard while in the army, and I doubt if I ever heard his superior anywhere. He was magnetic, full of fire, and carried everything before him, seemingly. He was, besides, dramatic. Every gesture, every attitude, had the grace and finish of the most studied stage production, and it all seemed to come naturally, there being no posing or apparent effort. About the first taste we had of his mettle was when we raised the stars and stripes over Fort Corcoran. The Eighteenth was formed for the occasion so as to represent three sides of a square; when the general, mounted on his black stallion, a superb specimen of equine beauty, rode in beside the flag-pole, and the colors were hoisted and floated gracefully in the breeze. The general removed his hat, and sitting his horse with unconscious grace, began to talk to us.
>
> He said it was the emblem of freedom upon which the eyes of the whole civilized world were turned; that the oppressed and downtrodden of every land were gazing upon it as the one beacon of promise, even as the wise men of the East looked upon the Star of Bethlehem; that we were there to defend its honor, and make it supreme in every part and section of our beloved land. And, he continued, pointing upward to it with outstretched arm: "Men of Massachusetts! Will you stand by that flag?" The boys with deafening shouts cried: "We will! We will!" And with upturned face and hand still pointing heavenward he cried: "By the help of Almighty God, so will I!" Wheeling his horse, he galloped well away before we recovered the use of our voices, but not out of hearing before the cheers both long and loud followed him. It was all so unpremeditated, so natural, so spontaneous, and withal so inspiring, it captured the regiment away down to the most insignificant private, and made the timid brave for the moment at least.[23]

General Martindale left the army on July 11, 1862, on sick leave, and somewhat under a cloud that has never been explained, never to return. So did most of the men, sooner or later, that the army had learned to love and trust; McClellan, Porter, Hooker, and Warren among the number. Some

23. Quoted from Alderman, "The 18th Regiment's Glee Club." For more commentary on Martindale, see John Berry, Diary (Sixteenth Michigan), July 4, 1862, *Civil War Times Illustrated* Collection, USAMHI.

for political reasons; others with charges preferred by inferior officers that have since been disproved.[24]

It is little that the rank and file of an army could not be expected to know of its formation, destination or plans, and any inquisitiveness shown by a private with such turn of mind was very sure to result in confusion worse confounded. Army officers were not in the habit of communicating information to any part of the machine they were trying to maneuver. On the contrary it was a part of the drill to stamp out all the reasoning faculties a private might try to exercise.

Tom illustrates this phase of army life very accurately by a little occurrence that came under his observation. W, a comrade of his, thought he was being drilled by Sergt. [Henry] Davis [more] severely than there was any call for, and consequently gave the drill-sergeant some back talk that was not relished. The sergeant swore roundly at W and put him through the steps, manual, and facings with prolonged and increased vigor. Knowing that swearing was contrary to army regulations, soon as the latter was dismissed he waited upon the colonel to complain of the sergeant for this breach of discipline. After the usual salute, W opened his complaint by saying: "Colonel, Mr. D has——" The colonel interrupted him angrily, and with fire in his eye exclaimed: "*Mister*? There *are* no misters in the army." "I thought, sir—" he began again, apologetically. "Think? think?" cried the colonel. "What right have *you* to think? *I* do the thinking for this regiment! Go to your quarters!"

True, at this stage of the game, and during the following year, the politicians . . . insisted upon receiving a detail of the plans of the commanding general from day to day. And they also exercised the same military acumen in divulging and criticizing those plans to the newspapers and country. Al-

---

24. Alderman's description of Martindale after the Seven Days battles as "depressed and sorrowful" is unsurprising. What Alderman did not know was that on the evening of July 1, after Malvern Hill, Martindale had panicked and proposed to several of his fellow officers that the entire army be surrendered. He then left the field ahead of his brigade and retired to Harrison's Landing (by some accounts, he was the first Union officer to arrive there). General Porter would prefer charges, and Martindale would be subject to a court of inquiry. The court found Martindale's conduct "reprehensible," but recommended that no action be taken against the general. Martindale would never return to the Army of the Potomac, though he would hold a significant command in the Army of the James in 1864. See the Court of Inquiry for John H. Martindale, Record Group 153, Court Martial Case File KK298, National Archives; George H. Lyman to Porter, December 10, 1862, Porter Papers, reel 2, frames 457–59, Library of Congress.

though two hostile armies, of 100,000 men each, occupied the ground between Washington and Richmond, and the peremptory order was to allow no living thing to pass between, still McClellan's plans were common property at Richmond as in Washington. The privates were readers, and the newspapers that were freely admitted within the lines gave away many an important move and dished up for the Rebels . . . the political bickerings and exigencies of the occasion.[25]

The army, to the last man, soon learned to love McClellan, and to impose implicit confidence in his commanding abilities.[26] To him the revered Lincoln trusted the task of creating the "Army of the Potomac." McClellan was the most youthful appearing officer of all the generals, so that he was quickly hailed as a "Young Napoleon," and being under average size, was affectionately christened "Little Mac." The estimate of him, written several years after the close of the war by the Comte de Paris,[27] voices well the feelings of the magnificent army he organized and commanded. The Comte says: "His military bearing breathed a spirit of frankness, benevolence, and firmness. His look was piercing, his voice gentle, his temper equable, his word of command clear and definite. His encouragement was most affectionate, his reprimand couched in terms of perfect politeness.

25. Railing against the press—though viewed today largely as a modern phenomenon—was nearly an art form during the Civil War. Virtually every prominent officer of the army complained in some form about press coverage; some worked actively to limit or stymie it altogether. Just before Fredericksburg, for example, General Hooker (then a grand division commander) beseeched the secretary of war: "I wish you could choke the newspapers. They are a nuisance in their effect on certain minds." General Carl Schurz wrote similarly to Senator Charles Sumner: "Whatever you can do to induce the authorities in Washington to stop the circulation of disloyal newspapers in the army, do it. It is necessary. This source of demoralization must be stopped." Joseph Hooker to Edwin Stanton, December 4, 1862, Stanton Papers, Library of Congress; Carl Schurz to Charles Sumner, February 13, 1863, Schurz Papers, Library of Congress.

26. George Brinton McClellan, thirty-five years old, was the commander of the Army of the Potomac for fifteen months, beginning in August 1861. McClellan's persona, personality, foibles, and virtues are well documented and need not be recounted here. Suffice to say that Mann's impression of McClellan was typical, though in no way universal. See Stephen W. Sears, *George B. McClellan: The Young Napoleon* (New York, 1988) and Sears, ed., *Papers of George B. McClellan*.

27. Captain Louis Phillipe, the Comte de Paris, was one of three French noblemen who volunteered on McClellan's staff during the Peninsula Campaign. After the war, the Comte became something of a "talking head," offering well-respected commentary on the war in many articles and a massive four-volume work, *History of the Civil War in America* (Philadelphia, 1875–1878). See William H. Powell, ed., *Officers of the Army and Navy (Volunteer) Who Served in the Civil War* (Philadelphia, 1893), 144.

Discreet, as a military or political chief should be, he was slow in bestowing his confidence; but once given it was never withdrawn. Himself perfectly loyal to his friends, he knew how to inspire others with an absolute devotion. Unfortunately for himself, McClellan succeeded too quickly and too soon to the command of the principal army of the Republic."

On November 20, in a cold, drizzling rain, occurred the grand review of this army at "Bailey's Cross Roads," extending to the south from Munson's Hill. No such display had ever been witnessed in the United States, the novelty of the spectacle attracting all the dignitaries of the nation from Washington. President Lincoln with his entire Cabinet rode at the head of McClellan's brilliant military family, down the long lines of troops, to the music of hundreds of regimental bands, accompanied by a thousand rattling drums and screaming fifes. Sixty thousand men were drawn up on these plains, armed and equipped, for the President's inspection. Soon as the troops had been thus reviewed the long lines began to wheel into regimental or company front and, with the step and alignment of veterans, marched by the reviewing stand—proud to show the President and the country the perfection of that drill which for months previous had only been tolerated because it must. . . .[28]

Sergt. Bill writes:[29]

> The day appointed for the review came at last, and glad enough were our boys to have it come, for Col. Barnes had for some time been giving us unheard-of doses of drill. . . . The army was formed in column of brigades . . . As Col. Barnes was the ranking colonel of the brigade, we occupied the front line, and therefore enjoyed an unobstructed view of the president and the grand cavalcade as it swept by in front of us. The president rode by the side of Gen. McClellan as they made the round of the army, passing every [command] . . . They necessarily had to ride fast in order to accomplish the

---

28. Deleted here are two paragraphs describing new uniforms received shortly after the Bailey's Crossroads review—uniforms that were a gift from American residents in France and offered as a "prize" to the three regiments at the review adjudged to be the best drilled. Neither men nor officers liked the uniform, and the regiment wore it for a short time only, retrieving their regulation army outfits in March 1862. See also William Alderman, "President Lincoln's Review," unidentified clipping from the *Sunday Republican*, FSNMPL.

29. This passage does not appear in the original memoir, but has been added by the editor. It is from William Alderman, "President Lincoln's Review," unidentified clipping from the *Sunday Republican*, FSNMPL. Mann also described the review in a letter home, November 21, 1861, Mann Papers, Brown University. "Such a sight was never seen before," he wrote. See also John L. Parker, *Henry Wilson's Regiment: History of the Twenty-Second Massachusetts Infantry* (Boston, 1887), 55.

task they had set themselves. I remember Mr. Lincoln, and the appearance he made riding, almost as [if] it had all happened yesterday instead of 36 years ago. It was the first time I saw him, and I looked for all my eyes were worth. I saw the president many times after that day, but never when he interested me as then. He was called a homely man, and he was. His devoted admirer could hardly call him otherwise. With his long, angular form, seemingly largely made up of arms and legs, clad in an ill-fitting suit of black that appeared to touch his person only here and there, and on his head a tall silk hat, well tilted back as he bounded up and down in the saddle—he was certainly a unique figure.

I do not think at that time that he was very much used to the saddle. He seemed to have all he wanted to do to keep his seat and guide his horse, but he had other work that proved almost too much for him. Every regiment he passed "dipped the colors" to him, and the regimental band struck up "Hail to the Chief"; and he, poor man, bobbing insecurely up and down in the saddle, had to raise his hat in answer to the salute as on he dashed. Hardly would he get it fairly stuck on the back of his head, then another set of colors would dip . . . President Lincoln was a patient man and had endured many hardships and privations in his youth and early manhood, but I doubt if he ever was placed in a more trying situation, considering the suffering he must have endured physically and the anxiety he seemed to feel mentally for fear he might lose his balance in his frantic wrestling with that hat.

This grand review seemed to be the culminating act in the organization of the "Army of the Potomac," except the corps formation,[30] and from this time on all the political influence of the North was exerted, through Congress and the Executive department, to force it into action. The rank and file read the newspapers and discussed the "on to Richmond" question as freely as their fathers and brothers at home, though from a decidedly different standpoint, but the general consensus of opinion in the field was that McClellan knew his business, and when the time and conditions were ripe the army would move and win.

Resting in this faith [the army] settled quietly into winter quarters. Some regiments built log huts, using the regulation army tent for a roof, and constructed open fire-places within, though a small sheet-iron stove

---

30. Many men in the army retrospectively assessed the Bailey's Crossroads review as a decisive event in the army's development. Future cavalry general William Woods Averell recalled that the review "furnished needed tactical instruction and experience" and proved beyond a shadow of doubt that the national capital "was now permanently secured from the danger of capture." Edward K. Eckert and Nicholas J. Amato, eds., *Ten Years in the Saddle: The Memoir of William Woods Averell* (San Rafael, 1978), 347–48.

was often utilized instead of the fire-place for heating purposes. Other regiments, like the Eighteenth, continued all winter with only the army tent for shelter, pitched upon the bare ground. There seemed to be no higher authority for these different degrees of comfort enjoyed by the respective regiments than that of the colonel commanding, and why "Jimmy Barnes" wintered his troops in bare tents, with only the ground for a floor, on the crown of a bleak hill, remains a question to this day.

The colonel was a proud man, as well as a martinet—proud of the discipline of his regiment—and it was thought by some that the bleak winter quarters were a part of this discipline. No doubt the conspicuous French tents occupied by his command, pitched as they were in geometrical order, argued against their being struck for the irregular and unsightly log cabins of the less soldierly part of the army. These tents were circular in form, stood sixteen or eighteen feet high, and accommodated sixteen men each. They were made of heavy, strong, and coarse brown linen, but were not so good as the common cotton-duck tent for shedding water.

No provision was made by the commissary department for furnishing these tents, so the occupants provided in accordance with their tastes, or condition of their pocketbooks. Some purchased boards and made a floor—which was allowed if the tent was not raised out of line with its fellows—but many depended upon straw and pine needles to keep them from the ground. All were furnished with small, sheet-iron stoves, with the smoke-funnel passing through the top of the flap left for an entrance. More than one tent mess was burned out of even this "home and fireside" by the contents taking fire from the overheated stove; and being smoked out by a defective funnel, or because the wind blew from the wrong quarter, was a daily occurrence.

Regardless of the bleakness and bareness of this situation, the boys enjoyed themselves during the three winter months, and the health of this regiment compared favorably with that of any in the army. Baseball—or "round-ball" it was then called—clubs were formed and match games played between regiments, but the daily drill usually furnished all the exercise the men felt any necessity for, so cards, checkers, and chess were the favorite games. An important event in any one of these big French tents was the arrival of a box from the home of some one of the comrades. During the winter nearly all who had a home to hail from received a more or less elaborate box of good things therefrom. They were particularly numerous about Christmas time, though there was still enough Puritanism alive in old Massachusetts to select the "Thanksgiving" festival, instead of the other, during which to send substantial home-greetings in a box. It was all the same to the recipients, who immediately spread out the eatables for the whole tent-mess to share.

Discipline was strict, though hazing was indulged in accordance with the spirit or temper of the men for the time being. During the cold, drizzling, stormy weather that is characteristic of a Virginia winter, their spirits corresponded so that moroseness and sullen let-alonitiveness stuck out all over, but let a crisp, clear day show up and the temper of the army responded immediately.

"Penny-anti" was perhaps the most universally popular game when the soldier had pennies to anti with, though "high-low-jack-and-game," and "euchre" were close seconds. A few made a profession and business of the matter of "penny-anti," to the exclusion of all except the duties it were impossible to shirk. "I" company had two or three men who seemed to know or care for nothing else, and they would sit cross-legged through the long winter night, betting on the hundreds of different hands dealt from the worn pack of cards. Poker was meat, drink, sleep, exercise and religion to them. No matter how cold or wet the camp might be, from four to six congenial spirits of this sort could always be found in some quiet nest, closely shielded from the observation of officer or guard, intently shuffling the cards, and betting on the results as though the preservation of the country, or their individual eternal salvation, depended upon the nicety of the operation. The ingenuity displayed in covering the single tallow candle, which lighted the game, from the eyes of sentinel or officer, was equal to planning a battle. One, [Albert F.] Bates,[31] had the reputation of running up a big bank account through "penny-anti," but on the whole few either won or lost very much.

As March came round the peculiar soil of Virginia began to stir itself, and mud was the result. Why Virginia mud and the "Army of the Potomac" were so attractive to each other remains a mystery as profound as the love of some people for unadulterated cussedness. If the "sacred soil" of this proud state was about to turn to mud, then was the time the army must move and mix with it, lie down in it, and carry it from one country to another—help mix it, and 100,000 men can churn up some mud in a day when they feel just like it. So in March the army commenced to get ready to move—in accordance with orders from the politicians at Washington—and when the mud was puddling itself way down into the sub-soil of the state, in April, the army did move.

31. Private Albert F. Bates, a nineteen-year-old farmer from Bellingham. Wounded at Second Manassas, he would be discharged because of those wounds in January 1863.

THREE

Yorktown

"Chase them up some more!"

The army did more than just train that winter of 1861–1862. It also gained an identity. And that identity was to a remarkable degree wrapped up in the army's commander, Major General George Brinton McClellan. McClellan was younger than many men in the Eighteenth Massachusetts; he possessed youthful vigor and accomplishment. He had a magical touch with the troops, and by winter's end Mann and his fellow soldiers had embraced him heartily. For the Army of the Potomac, and for Mann especially, McClellan was something like a young man's first love: the feelings were intense, and the torch carried by each after the breakup (to come in November 1862) burned for a very long time. In late 1861, one man of the brigade wrote of McClellan, "In his hands I am willing to place my life and destiny, and blindly go where he may direct; for if the future of our country is not safe with him, then...."[1]

Many politicians and public outside the army had different views on McClellan. Politicians chafed at his reticence and secrecy. More importantly, they came to mistrust his motives. McClellan was arguably the most political army commander in American history, and he and his trusted subordinate, Fitz John Porter, hurled themselves into the debate over Union war aims. Their perspective on war—shared to the last syllable by Mann—was best described by Porter. "We will ... reconquer the country in a manner which will develop Union feeling and cause Virginia to rejoin us," he wrote to a newspaper editor in 1862. "The army goes as a disciplined body, not an armed mob, compelled to respect private rights and to win the respect of the people we will be with—and by a conservative course to

---

1. Letter of F. N. S. (Twenty-second Massachusetts), *Cambridge Chronicle*, November 2, 1861.

cause our enemies in the rear (the abolitionists) to be looked upon with contempt. How they are detested here."[2]

Many in Washington began to attribute McClellan's "slows" to his lukewarm support for a Union war policy that might include abolition— one that might bring the hard edge of war into Southern parlors. As January and February turned into March 1862 without movement from the army, the external criticism of McClellan intensified. In response, the army rallied around its commander. In letters home as well as in his memoirs, Thomas Mann would join the defense of McClellan. Indeed, it is a common theme throughout his writings.

Amid this climate of turmoil and intrigue, the Army of the Potomac embarked on its first major campaign. After a brief—and to much of the public, embarrassing—march against the empty Confederate defenses at Manassas Junction, McClellan and his army boarded transports bound down the Potomac and Chesapeake for Fortress Monroe, at the tip of the peninsula between the York and the James Rivers. McClellan eschewed the advice of so many others to take an overland route against Richmond and instead would lead his army up the Peninsula against Richmond from the southeast. For the next four months—April, May, June, and July— Thomas Mann and the Eighteenth Massachusetts would be part of the largest military endeavor in the nation's history prior to World War II.

Mann's first experience at "real war" came during the Siege of Yorktown, where the Confederates successfully blocked the Union advance up the Peninsula for a month. Mann's letters chronicle interminable shelling and unfathomable mud. He watched as McClellan and Porter worked the machinery of war into position for a climactic clash, only to watch (with a mixture of glee and disappointment) the Confederates evacuate on the eve of that supposed battle. Perhaps it was a fortunate indoctrination to war for Mann and the Eighteenth—a victory possessed of hardship but largely devoid of horror.

Criticism of army and corps movements, or of the plans of the commanding general, from 18, 19, and 20 year old privates, is worthless. But some of these boys, now 55 and 60 years of age, have lived to be men of affairs and accredited judgement in their respective communities, so may be par-

2. Fitz John Porter to Manton Marble (editor of the *New York World*), May 21, 1862, Marble Papers.

doned for occasionally emphasizing some of their earlier opinions with "I told you so." Sergeant Bill and Corporal Tom had opinions, and discussed army movements then, as they played chess, and some of their "I told you soes" are verified by history.

The army believed in McClellan and any blow aimed at him from Washington was spitefully resented by the 150,000 men that he commanded in March, 1862. The plans formulated by him for the defense of Washington and the capture of Richmond, though thwarted by the civil powers of the government, were forced [in 1864] upon General Grant by Grim War itself before the desired results could be obtained. One cannot blame McClellan altogether for failures when taking into consideration the constant depletion of his ranks, by repeatedly taking small armies of 10,000 and 15,000 men from them to allay the fears of the government, thus breaking up well considered plans of action. The men who would succeed under the restrictions thrown about McClellan are so few that a generation may pass into history before one is found. If he had been given the opportunity to climb by degrees, as was Grant, his star might have been the ascendent one.[3]

These deductions are from history, though an examination of the letters written to home-folks by our two heroes will explain some of their "I told you soes." While history was making things were not so transparently recognized.

Peremptory orders had been received for the army to make a forward movement on February 22d, the anniversary of the birth of Washington, but were not obeyed.[4] Others followed from the President until about the middle of March, when this vast army broke up its camps and made a feint

---

3. Mann's perspective on McClellan is entirely typical of the period. McClellan and most of his soldiers saw the detachment or withholding of troops to protect Washington as part of a political effort to foil the Army of the Potomac—to limit McClellan's political power by limiting his success in the field. For his part, McClellan and some of his subordinates cleverly used these perceptions to create something of a siege mentality in the Army of the Potomac and thereby intensify the army's identity with its commander. For vivid descriptions of the growing gap between the army and the government it served see Fitz John Porter to Manton Marble (editor of the *New York World*), May 21 and September 30, 1862; McClellan's "Harrison's Landing Letter," July 4, 1862, in Sears, ed., *McClellan Papers*, 336–38.

4. In late January, Lincoln issued orders for the armies of the nation to begin forward movement on February 22. Subsequently, McClellan talked Lincoln (though not the radicals) out of this idea, getting the deadline extended until March 18. See Sears, *The Young Napoleon* 149–51.

toward moving upon Manassas, where the Confederate army had made its winter quarters. The rebels had already left these quarters several days before, and retired behind the Rappahannock and Rapidan rivers, nearer their own capital.

As the Eighteenth reached the outlying fortifications left by the fleeing enemy, after a 20-mile march, those famous "Quaker guns" were all the arms that could be found, and they bore evidence of not having been manned for a week or ten days. . . . These Quaker guns were simply logs of wood mounted upon any old pair of wheels, to imitate mounted cannon looking through the embrasures of an earth-work fort, and were recognized by the army as boy's play. The Eighteenth, to a man, had gathered from some source that McClellan was about to change his base of operations to the York, Pamunkey, or James Rivers, and the reasons why this movement to Manassas was made by a part of the army were not understood at the time. McClellan, in his reminiscences, says that the army was moved out 15 or 20 miles to shake off the debris of winter quarters, and to put it upon its marching legs. The lesson was a good one, for this regiment left behind more than it carried. To some of the boys it was like burning the house and home and most of its treasures, but from this time on they knew how much of a load of "necessities" could be [discarded] without disadvantage on 20 mile marches.[5]

The route back was in the direction of Alexandria during the pouring rain that the army thoroughly mixes with the soil, to see how much mud could be made. Not all had yet learned to protect even a few necessary belongings from the soaking that a very wet rain expects to inflict, so that thousands went into camp that night without a dry thing about them. With few exceptions, which will be mentioned later, this watery, muddy march back from Manassas took more starch out of the rank and file than it was aware of possessing. As one old veteran has since remarked: "There is nothing that will cause courage and ambition to ooze so perceptibly

5. The army's march to the abandoned defenses of Manassas began on March 9, 1862. Porter's command and the Eighteenth Massachusetts departed early the following morning, passing through Falls Church, Fairfax Court House, and Centreville. McClellan viewed this march as the landward version of a shake-down cruise. The press and politicians generally scoffed, noting that McClellan only marched after he could be certain the enemy had evacuated northern Virginia. For other accounts of the march from men in Porter's command see Letter of A. G. C. (Thirteenth New York), *Rochester Democrat and American*, March 18, 1862; Letter of W. C. (Thirteenth New York), *Rochester Democrat and American*, March 19, 1862; Letter of H. M. G. (Forty-fourth New York), *Herkimer County Journal*, March 19, 1862.

from a private, loaded down with all his household belongings, as to let the water trickle down into the seat of his trousers." Imagine an army with the seats of its trousers wet, and plastered with red mud from foot to head, then its morale can be guessed at in a Yankee way.

It was seen the next morning that the troops were being embarked as rapidly as possible on all manner of transports that were moored in the Potomac about and below Alexandria; river and ocean steamers, and scows towed by steamer or tug-boat.[6] One small steamer accommodated the Eighteenth and all its camp equipage, baggage wagons, horses and mules. It began to be noticed by the ranks that "Jimmy Barnes" always managed to have the Eighteenth pretty well looked after. The sail down the Potomac, past Mt. Vernon, out into the Chesapeake, and around Old Point Comfort, to the landing at Fortress Monroe,[7] was thoroughly enjoyed by all except the few who were inclined to pay tribute to Neptune, as the ocean swell was felt at the mouth of the bay. Tom, while recalling to mind one of the standing inducements that was a part of every handbill, so freely thrown out to encourage enlistments in the regular army, allowed that the "chance to travel," in this instance, filled the bill very pleasantly—an improvement over paddling in the mud three days before. He had succeeded in drying the seat of his trousers.

After landing, the regiment marched to the ruins of the old, aristocratic city of Hampton, about two miles from the grim fortress, and made its camp in the midst of them. The only building left standing was the Episcopal church in which George Washington had worshiped. . . . Company "I" pitched its tents immediately about this ancient church and in the churchyard that was filled with the remains of historical personages of 100 years ago. The massive stone and crumbling brick tombs, singly, in pairs and family groups, were built on top of the ground, for digging two feet beneath reached to the water level. It was a novel and suggestive spectacle to see the small, shelter tents of the soldiers leaning against the walls of the church, thus utilizing them to enlarge their capacity. Others made use of the larger tombs for the same purpose, while many actually made their beds on the tops of the marble, slate, or soap-stone slabs that covered the remains of a Randolph, Tucker, Lee, or Curtis.

6. This was, by far, the largest amphibious operation in the nation's history to that time, involving 389 vessels. For additional background on this (and incidentally all other aspects of the Peninsula Campaign), see Stephen Sears's *To the Gates of Richmond: The Peninsula Campaign* (New York, 1992), 23–24.
7. Located at the tip of the peninsula formed by the York and the James Rivers.

Corporal Tom wrote: "The whole city was burned some time ago. Not a whole house was left. The houses were all brick and there were some splendid churches and other public buildings. They were built in the old English style, [with] paved streets and brick sidewalks. It must have been a splendid city and quite a large one. You know that next to Jamestown it is the oldest place in Va. Among the ruins I could see many indications of wealth. Numerous piano strings, marble fireplaces stairs and in one or two places marble floors."[8]

During the four days that the Eighteenth occupied this camp, no duties were exacted of the men except a small detail for guard, and many of them improved the opportunity to visit the shores of the Chesapeake Bay. . . . One fascinating object of interest to our two heroes was the largest cannon owned by the United States, up to this date. It lay dismantled and useless, between the fort and the beach, was 15 to 18 feet long, and with a bore large enough for an average sized man to crawl into. In a clear day the smoke arising from Norfolk, and its Portsmouth navy-yard, could be seen across the bay; even then it was rumored that the rebels were preparing some kind of floating battery to play the mischief with our massive, oaken men-of-war that were hovering about these waters.[9]

Thus far war was rather pleasant. The bay was the natural home of oysters by the bushel, and at low tide thousands of men waded out, fished for them with their toes, gathered, opened, and ate their fill without leaving the water. Others were more fastidious, preferring to boil them into tough little bits of leather before venturing to add James River bivalves to the regulation army ration. Fresh water was scarce, and shallow wells were dug in the sand to obtain it; still it was too brackish for drinking or making coffee. Whatever means the burned-out inhabitants of this city had provided to furnish themselves with water had perished by the fire that destroyed everything else.

Four days after landing at Old Point Comfort, knapsacks, blankets, and shelter tents were slung on shoulders, three day's rations taken in haver-

8. This section is inserted by the editor from a letter from Mann to friends at home, March 24, 1862, Mann Papers. Hampton had been destroyed by the Confederates during the fall of 1861, fearing a rumor that the Federals intended to turn it into a settlement for freed slaves. Sears, *Gates of Richmond,* 28.

9. "These waters" had been, three weeks before, the scene of the clash between the *Monitor* and CSS *Virginia (Merrimack).* Though the battle was indecisive, the presence of the *Monitor* neutralized the *Virginia* and thereby eliminated a much-feared threat to army shipping.

sacks, and a start was made to find the enemy. It was quite evident, to even the youngest drummer boy, that this march was not to end until formidable obstructions were encountered. The Eighteenth was not absolutely the head of the column that started up the Peninsular for Yorktown, but it took the van before the historic place was sighted.

The distance from Hampton [to Yorktown] is about 20 miles, and the first day's march though unobstructed was, for some unaccountable reason, very slow, not more than half the distance being covered. The second day it rained incessantly, and the artillery, baggage, and supply wagons were constantly mired, blocking all the roads so that the infantry took to the woods and fields. The country was low and in many places swampy. Route step was the order, so the men picked their way through the woods and across morasses covered with water, in accordance with the best judgement they could bring to bear upon the situation. In attempting to jump from one fallen log to another or from one firm hillock to another that looked as if it was equally firm, the unlucky soldier often plunged bodily into the water of the swamp, knapsack, rations, musket, and all. Very few crossed this swamp without a ducking from the water beneath, and all were soaked from the clouds above.

During the second day the baggage trains and artillery were left behind, stuck in the mud, while the infantry plodded on alone. Later it was learned that this particular swamp had been fixed by the rebel general, Magruder, to block the invading army. It was done by damming the mouth of Poquosian creek, which flowed into the York River, and the mouths of Warwick and Deep creeks, which flowed into the James, thus backing up the waters of these three creeks and flooding the swamps that extended nearly across this whole Peninsular. It succeeded in checking the artillery, with the down-pouring rain for an ally, for several days, and in delaying the infantry twenty-four hours. The supply trains were also left on the Fortress Monroe side of the flooded swamp, so most of Porter's division were without rations for 48 hours.[10]

10. While the march to Yorktown was indeed difficult, Mann exaggerates the effect of the Confederates' attempts to create impassable swampland. In fact, Confederate damming efforts were largely confined to enhancing preexisting mill dams on the Warwick River. The mud alluded to by Mann was not the product of the Confederates, but of the rains, which fell into the dusty soil copiously for many hours on April 5. See Sears, *Gates of Richmond*, 36–37. For an excellent account of this march by another member of Porter's division, see the unidentified letter from the Fourteenth New York, [Utica] *Oneida Weekly Herald*, April 29, 1862.

Just before dusk, during a lull of the rain, the Eighteenth deployed through the woods in the van of the army, and was proceeding cautiously to advance as a skirmish line, when the deep, sullen boom of a heavy gun was heard coming from the direction of its movement. It was the sun-set gun fired from the main earth fort in Yorktown—from the same fort, partly rebuilt, that Lord Cornwallis constructed in 1781, and now, as then, defended by the enemies of the country. In a few minutes the advancing line found its progress obstructed by a fence that divided the forest and swamp from the open fields beyond.[11]

There was no order to halt so the men commenced to scramble over [the fence]. Across the fields, a mile away, could be seen the fortifications of Yorktown. Outside, drawn up on dress-parade, a Confederate regiment was enjoying the music of its brass band, the faint strains of "Dixie" being distinctly heard by the occupants of the fence. It was the first sight the Eighteenth ever had of armed rebels, and was drunk in with the eagerness of men who had been waiting nearly a year for it. The general expression, for the instant, upon the faces of all was that of surprised curiosity, mingled with a look as if further investigation was eagerly invited. In another instant a shell came whizzing toward our men, and in bursting it scattered several panels of the fence in all directions. Curiosity was immediately changed to a panicky, nervous look, as if the explosion had killed nearly the whole crowd while the few left living were examples of a miracle; and the men fled back into the forest without standing upon the order of their going.

But "Jimmy Barnes" was at hand, probably the only officer of the regiment who had smelt that kind of powder and iron, and he soon had his command under perfect control, safely hidden in the depths of the woods. Several more shots were fired into the forest, as if searching for this devoted regiment, but that first one, and all that followed, did no particular damage.

This first screaming and hurtling shell from the enemy, which was probably a 64-pounder,[12] crashing into and bursting among the rails of that

---

11. The earthworks visible at Yorktown today are largely the product of Civil War, not Revolutionary, soldiers. Only a handful of the 1781 works were not improved by the combatants in 1862. For a complete summary of the Eighteenth's experience at Yorktown see Colonel Barnes's report in U.S. War Department, *Official Records of the War of the Rebellion* (Washington, 1880–1891), Vol. 11, Part 1, 293–94. Hereinafter referred to as O.R.

12. Civil War cannon were routinely identified by the weight of the projectile they fired. Both sides would bring heavy guns into play during the siege at Yorktown. Rarely thereafter would the Eighteenth see such iron behemoths. Mobile guns on the battlefield rarely fired

fence, even knocking them out from under several of the boys, did more in five minutes to teach every blessed mother's son of them the value of discipline than the whole previous year's training. True, the training had prepared them for the lesson, and "Jimmy Barnes" was, providentially, at hand to press it home, but, gee-whiz, it came so sudden! From this time the regiment believed implicitly in Colonel James Barnes.

This was the evening of the 5th of April, and the night was spent in the swamp as a picket guard. Tom says he could not find a spot to stand upon without covering his ankles with water, and that he spent most of the night hugging a partially fallen tree that rested at an angle of about 30 degrees. By crawling along up its trunk he managed to keep clear of the water, though incessant wakefulness was necessary to prevent losing his hold and rolling off. The night was a long, wet, and dismal one, during which this regiment protected a front about one-quarter of a mile long. Later it was learned that to the right and left other regiments were doing similar duty from the Warwick to the York rivers. Yorktown was thus completely invested except upon its river front.[13]

Morning found the haversacks of this part of the army empty; the soldier had not yet learned what three day's rations meant. Enough had been issued at Hampton but fully a third of it was left behind, and while each took what would have been sufficient if lying quietly in camp, this kind of work played havoc with the supply. These two days and nights of active campaigning used up rations that ordinarily would suffice for three, so the third day and night there was plenty of grumbling and growling but nothing to eat. Going without food is of little account if one can become accustomed to it, but the first test of that kind of endurance is almost as surprising as the initial smell of gun-powder from a sixty-pound shell. It was known that the supply trains were somewhere on the way, stuck in the mud, and Colonel Barnes, in this instance as in many another, knew just what to do. He sent back a picked lot of men with a competent officer to help one supply wagon out of the mud and drag it to regimental head-

---

projectiles exceeding twenty pounds (4.5 inches in diameter). Most fired ten- and twelve-pound rounds.

13. Though Yorktown was indeed fully invested in 1781, it was not—contrary to Mann's assertion—in 1862. The Confederate line ran nominally southward from Yorktown along the Warwick River for a distance of about six miles, blocking the Union advance up the Peninsula and preventing the "investment" of Yorktown claimed by Mann. The Eighteenth Massachusetts and the rest of Porter's command held the extreme right of the Union line, within sight of Yorktown.

quarters, with the alternative of bringing a supply of rations to the troops upon their own backs. The regiment had found dry ground and waited impatiently for something to eat.[14]

Tom, in writing home from Yorktown under date of April 14, says: "Our camp is in a peach orchard of 30 acres." In fact the whole of this Peninsula was noted for its peach orchards, and as the army gathered about the historical Yorktown during the first week in April, these orchards were in full blossom. The request to preserve the trees as much as possible, not to wantonly destroy them, came from headquarters and was very generally observed. Notwithstanding the fact that Tom wrote to his home folk, "It is the prevailing opinion here that as soon as Yorktown is taken the government will begin to discharge some of its troops," there were some who suggested that if the peach-trees were preserved the Eighteenth might have a chance at their fruit in its season. And it did. After the terrible seven days fighting in and about the Chickahominy, when General Porter's division marched to the support of Pope at Bull Run, this regiment again passed through the peach orchards of Yorktown while they were loaded down with luscious fruit: as the natives said: "One of the heaviest crops the trees were ever known to produce."

The camp was a very pleasant one, under the shade of the peach-trees, but war had commenced in grim earnest, and the shot and shell were being tossed back and forth between the two hostile armies as carelessly as snow-balls are thrown between rival cliques of school-boys. This was by the artillery and sharp-shooters, while the volunteer infantry were engaged night and day throwing up entrenchments with shovel and pick.

For one whole month the "Army of the Potomac" dug away until a perfect network of "defences" and "approaches" so completely protected itself that it was a rare occurrence for a man to be killed. These breast-works drew nearer and nearer, by parallels and angles, to the formidable earth-forts of the enemy that they confronted. In a night a line of defences would suddenly appear, 50 yards nearer the rebels than the night before. Invariably, new "parallels" or "approaches" were commenced in the night, under cover of the darkness, which required the labors of the Eighteenth three nights of each week. But after the new works were well under way

---

14. At this point in the memoir, Mann veered off into a lengthy treatise on army mules. For the sake of continuity, that section has been relocated to the rear of the memoir, as Appendix A.

they could be finished during the day, because the work of the night had been sufficient to afford protection for day-work. Reliefs were changed under cover of the night, so that it was necessary for a day-relief to remain in the trenches from between three or four in the morning to seven or eight in the evening; the night squads making shorter hours.[15]

Men, like animals, can accustom themselves to almost any condition. The farmer boys who made up a large percentage of the army, knowing the fright exhibited by a farm animal at the discharge of a single fire-arm, were astonished at the total unconcern with which army horses and mules received the smoke and crashing of a battle. So the men soon became accustomed to the howling and sputtering and bursting of the shell that the enemy were continuously throwing into the Union lines—due in part, no doubt, to a confidence that the protection of these simple earth-works quickly inspired.

Although this regiment was under the fire of the rebel batteries every day for a month, not one of its number was seriously injured by them. Early in the siege, and through the carelessness of some officer, a part of the 22d Mass. regiment that was at work near this one, exposed quite a large body of its men, and a single shell from the rebel fort burst in their midst and killed seven. Under date of April 22d, Tom writes to his father:

> Yesterday we were engaged in finishing up an earth-work which was within half a mile of those occupied by "Secesh." We had completed all that was required by one o'clock in the afternoon, so were laying off and taking all the comfort possible under the circumstances, for we could not leave the protection of this breast work to return to camp till after dark. Most of the men were playing cards, though many of them were taking a nap. I was stretched along up the side of the fort so that my head was about 18 inches below the top, half asleep, though watching a game of "high-low-jack" that was going on below where my feet rested. We heard the heavy boom of a gun but paid no attention until the next second when I was knocked heels over head, down into the midst of the card players, and all of us tumbled to the bottom of the trench, half buried under a cart-load of dirt.
>
> It took some time to find out what had happened and how much we were hurt, but when it was discovered that not one of us had a scratch we began to laugh with the rest of the company that had gathered around to see what all the fuss was about. A large rebel shell had struck into the top of our breast-work and, after burying itself pretty well, bursted, and the dirt it threw up tumbled down upon us.

15. For an excellent account from another member of Martindale's brigade, see unidentified letter from the Thirteenth New York, *Rochester Democrat and American*, May 12, 1862.

At no time during the war was the efficiency of sharp-shooters so apparent as during this siege. A regiment, known as Berdan's sharp-shooters was attached to Porter's division, and it was made up of men above the ordinary in abilities for this kind of life. Colonel Berdan was himself a noted rifle shot throughout the country, and in gathering his men into a regiment he subjected each recruit to a rigid test in the use of a rifle. That was the deciding test that was applied, consequently his command was made up of noted Indian fighters, scouts, and the crack shots of the country. These men were not subjected to the drill and discipline of other regiments but, to quite a large extent, did their fighting on their own hooks, each armed with his own favorite rifle.[16]

During the early part of the siege these men were scattered between the opposing lines, where each man usually dug a hole large enough to get into, using the dirt thrown out as a breastwork for himself against the fire of the enemy. Later, when the earth-works had been built closer, these men were stationed at intervals behind them and, from their positions, picked off the rebel gunners who attempted to load the heavy guns upon the parapets of the forts. They thus succeeded in keeping several of the sixty-four pounders quiet for days at a time, which afforded much protection to the thousands of men who were constantly engaged in strengthening and building the Union defences and approaches.

The Confederates also had their sharp-shooters who quite frequently let daylight through a Federal soldier, though they could not approach near

16. Colonel Hiram Berdan commanded the First United States Sharpshooters, one of the truly distinctive units of the Civil War. Bedizened in green uniforms with rubber buttons (manufactured by Goodyear Corporation) to reduce glare, the men of the regiment hailed from across the country, but had one thing in common: excellent marksmanship. They routinely served as skirmishers in the Fifth Corps, fanning out in front of attacking or defending formations to probe, deflect, or deceive. The regiment did not operate as haphazardly as Mann suggests here. Moreover, by 1862 the entire regiment carried breech-loading Sharps Rifles, and not the mish-mash of weapons that characterized the unit in the war's early months. See C. A. Stevens, *Berdan's United States Sharpshooters in the Army of the Potomac* (Reprint, Dayton, 1972). Though the First Sharpshooters earned a great reputation for effectiveness, Berdan himself—though an accomplished mechanical engineer and marksman—failed as a leader. He repeatedly vanished when battle seemed imminent and repeatedly found himself refuting charges of cowardice. For a scathing assessment of Berdan by one of his soldiers see an unsigned letter in the *Penn Yan Chronicle,* November 6, 1862. See also William Y. W. Ripley to Berdan, July 21, 1862, copy on file at Richmond National Battlefield Library, originals held by Roy Hodges of Annapolis, Md.; Frederick T. Locke to Fitz John Porter, May 26, 1886, Porter Papers, Reel 15 (container 36), frames 417–19, Porter Papers, Library of Congress; Ripley to Porter, June 12, 1886, Reel 15, frames 460–65.

enough to interfere much with the operation of the heavy siege guns. The reach of the 32 and 64 pound rifled guns, used by McClellan's army, was such that nothing was gained in posting them near enough to be within range of an ordinary rifle. The besiegers of Yorktown also had several 100 pound rifled cannon, and at least one 200 pounder,[17] and these were in a well sheltered position from two to three miles away, throwing their shell completely over the Union army and landing them within the defences of the doomed place.

Under date of April 14, Tom writes to one of his brothers:

> I saw one of these sharp-shooters, known as "California Joe," shoot three rebels this morning. He was stationed behind the earth-works we were throwing up, with his heavy, telescope rifle resting on the top of the loose dirt, watching some rebel pickets or rifle-men that were stationed behind the partially fallen brick walls of a house which had been recently burned. The rebels were nearer our lines than their own, and must have got out there the night before. One of our 32 pound rifled guns was battering down the remaining walls of this house, which made it too hot for the rebels, so they attempted, one at a time, to make a break for home. Then was the time the old California scout got in his work, causing the remaining four to throw down their guns and make a quick run for our lines to give themselves up. They informed us that there were nine men and a sergeant behind those brick walls, where they reckoned upon being all right till night if our 32 pound gun had not discovered their hiding place; and that the shell from that gun had badly injured the sergeant and two men which were probably already dead.[18]

In another letter to his brother, written eight days later, Tom speaks of this sharpshooter again, prefixing his description of the scout's accuracy with his rifle by describing the rifle he used. Both Tom and his brother at home were lovers of a rifle, and Tom writes: "I had an opportunity to examine

---

17. In fact, the Union army had two two-hundred-pound guns, each weighing eight tons. The "32-pounder" guns referred to by Mann were likely thirty-pounder Parrott rifles; the "64-pounders" were probably the many large-caliber rifled guns brought forth by McClellan. For a summary of Union armament during the siege, see Sears, *Gates of Richmond*, 57–58.

18. "California Joe" was one of the most famous enlisted men of the war. His name was Truman Head, and he was grizzled, hairy, and proficient. It is true, however (as the regimental historian of the First Sharpshooters notes), that "almost everything relating to the Sharpshooters in the way of extraordinary shooting was credited to 'California Joe.'" "California Joe's" accomplishments at Yorktown were particularly noted, and it is entirely possible that the soldier Mann observed was indeed Truman Head. See Stevens, *Berdan's Sharpshooters*, 49–50.

'California Joe's' rifle this morning, as he is behind the earth-work where I am now writing, laying for a chance to pick off a rebel gunner. The rifle weighs 32 pounds, and has a small telescope running the whole length of the barrel, which he uses to sight his target by. This telescope will make a man who is a mile away look as if he was only 200 or 300 yards off."

Here our hero breaks in upon his enthusiasm over the rifle by the exclamation, written with an excited and heavy hand, followed by some scrawling exclamation points: "There!!! The scout has just shot a secesh!! And he was a good half mile from where we are!!!"

He continues:

> It looked as if the rebels had been trying all the morning for a chance to load the 64 pounder which was pointing directly toward us, and a few minutes ago one of their officers jumped up to the top of the parapet and waved his sword, as if to encourage the men to come up and load the gun. It seemed for a minute or two that he was going to succeed, but the scout had his rifle sighted on the officer who was making such a fine target of himself, and when he fired down came the rebel, heels over head, outside his own fort toward us, evidently stone dead. It was a fine shot for the man must of been a full half mile away.

"You think it is a grand sight to be in full view of the siege of Yorktown," says Tom, in the same letter to his brother, "and to be in amongst the whizzing shot and shell?" And adds: "Well, it is. But it looks better on paper." In describing the appearance of the rebel shell, under date of April 29, he says:

> Something is going to happen pretty soon. The cannonading is getting to be almost incessant, day and night, and I have been doing picket duty in the outmost rifle-pits for the past 24 hours, right under the rebel forts. They are shelling us all the time, but we keep well behind the breast-works so that no one is hurt. A big piece of shell struck one of our stacks of muskets and scattered them in all directions, of course ruining most of them. But you ought to see these big shell in the dark night. They look like a red-hot ball coming at you; and when one bursts it shows a large sheet of fire, and each piece that flies from it looks as if it was red hot.

No more graphic description of the closing days at Yorktown, from the private's standpoint, can be had than Corporal Tom's boyish letters to his Massachusetts home, and under date of May 1st he writes:

> Last night about six o'clock we went out to work in the trenches, leveling the top off, which is the most dangerous part of the whole, and we came in

about midnight. The rebels threw 14 shells at us during the five hours of our stay. When we saw the flash of the gun that was throwing them we would jump down behind the works into the trench, and so dodge them. One of them just skimmed the top of the earth-work and bounced off over us, but it covered three or four of us pretty well with dirt. We have got a little used to the rebel shell so that we do not crouch and cringe quite so much when one comes hissing over. When one of them bursts, just before reaching us, the pieces that fly and scatter make the awfulest buzzing you ever heard.

The camp of the Eighteenth was in a ravine, and only a short distance from the York river, below the town. Porter's division occupied the right of the besieging army, and a mile farther down the river were located the batteries where the 200 pound gun was mounted. In his letter Tom tells about the opening of this gun upon Yorktown:

> About noon we got everything ready and chucked a shell into the 200 pound gun, and the first shot sent the shell a mile beyond the rebel fort, and the fort was three miles from the gun. We fired in all, this afternoon, about 15 shots, and all but the first one was plunked into or burst over the rebel fort. The secesh soon quit firing their 64 pounders, finding that they could not reach as far as this battery, and it was thought by some that they had left their fort.

As before stated, privates can know little, in fact absolutely nothing of the plans of a campaign or siege; but as the animal world possesses the instinct that foretells the on-coming of an unusual storm, so the rank and file of an army seem to scent an important move or battle. In Tom's next letter home, two days later and under date of May 3d, he says:

> Something is going to drop pretty soon. It is now half past two in the afternoon, and I have just come from work in the trenches. The rebels troubled us all they could, by throwing shell at the rate of eight per hour. They struck, skipped, and burst all around us; they chucked into the works we had thrown up, and bursting, scattered the sand all over us, though the only man I saw hurt belonged to another regiment. He was at work about two rods from myself when the piece of a bursting shell, weighing half a pound, struck him on the shoulder, knocking him down and his shoulder out of joint—nothing but what he will easily get over. It was a constant bang!! whang!! buzz!! buzz!!
>
> I have just learned that A. K., of Medfield, was shot through the body, yesterday, just above the thighs and lived about an hour, but I cannot get a

chance to see him.[19] The 200 pound gun, down below us, is tossing its shells into the centre of Yorktown at the rate of one every five minutes, and the 100 pound guns chime in. The rebels are replying to them with the best they have got, and their shells are buzzing in all directions.

On the last page of this letter, our hero adds this postscript: "Sunday morning.—THE REBELS HAVE EVACUATED YORKTOWN! THE STARS AND STRIPES ARE FLOATING OVER YORKTOWN! We have just been ordered to pack our knapsacks to march. They say the rebels have spiked all their guns. When are the cowards going to make a stand? Well, I suppose we have got to chase them up some more!"[20]

During the whole of this siege the army was deprived of its accustomed music. Not even a fife or drum was allowed to play, and the sudden bursting forth of all the brass bands, accompanied by the screaming fifes and rattling drums, made the army feel as though the resurrection morn had dawned. The excitement in the camps was beyond any ordinary expression, as the army crawled out from behind its entrenchments into the freedom of the open fields and woods.

19. Allen Alonzo Kingsbury, a member of the First Massachusetts Infantry. Kingsbury shared a hometown with many in the Eighteenth. He was one of the first volunteers from Medfield, and his correspondence home was frequently published in local newspapers. He died in a skirmish along the front of the Union Third Corps on April 26, 1862. His death stimulated an intense outpouring from his home town; his letters, diaries, and many postwar tributes were published in *The Hero of Medfield; Containing the Journals and Letters of Allen Alonzo Kingsbury* (Boston, 1862).

20. The Confederates evacuated their Yorktown/Warwick River line on May 4, 1862, after a month of siege. Much of the Union army responded in the same joyous literary fashion as did Mann, and source material on the fall of Yorktown abounds. For a summary, see Sears, *Gates of Richmond,* 59–62.

FOUR

Peninsula Campaign

"Next Door to Defeat"

From Yorktown the armies churned toward Richmond, until they lay glaring at each other only seven miles from the downtown spires. In this movement, the Eighteenth Massachusetts received the first of many strokes of good fortune it would receive on the Peninsula. Rather than fighting its way through choking dust that "filled every open receptacle . . . ones eyes, ears, nose, mouth, etc.," the Eighteenth Massachusetts and the rest of Morell's division traveled up the Peninsula by ship, disembarking at White House—the ancestral home of Martha Custis Washington.[1] From there the Bay Staters got their first real look at Rebeldom. Mann called it "a fine looking country here but very wild and neglected." He also recorded his first observations of freed slaves. As the army moved, "contrabands" flocked to it, "and we hire many of them to carry some of our baggage, &c. Each commissioned officer has now one or more of the black personages as an attendant to black boots, run for water, &c."[2]

Good fortune also shone on the Eighteenth when it came to the battles of the Peninsula Campaign. On May 27, Porter's corps fought a significant and successful battle near Hanover Court House. The Eighteenth Massachusetts, on picket near Mechanicsville, missed it. Four days later, major fighting flared at Fair Oaks and Seven Pines. The Fifth Corps was not called upon.

Instead, the corps remained north of the Chickahominy River, separated from most of the army, which lay south of the river in front of Richmond. The Confederate army's new leader, Robert E. Lee, found Porter's isolation north of the Chickahominy too tempting. On June 26, he at-

---

1. The quote is from John D. Wilkins to his wife, May 14, 1862, John Wilkins Papers, Clements Library, University of Michigan. Wilkins was in the Third U.S. Infantry of the Fifth Corps. See also Mann to his mother, May 14, 1862, Mann Papers.

2. Mann to his mother, July 7, 1862, Mann Papers.

tacked, initiating a bloody series of battles. Again, fortune would shine on the Eighteenth Massachusetts. While the Fifth Corps suffered horrendous casualties at the Battles of Beaver Dam Creek, Gaines Mill, and Malvern Hill, the Eighteenth was sent on an expedition to the north to try to delay, or at least discern, the approach of Stonewall Jackson's command from the Shenandoah Valley. The assignment led to an exhausting series of marches back to White House Landing, but no bloodletting. As the bulk of the Union army toiled in bloody retreat across the Peninsula, the Eighteenth helped break down the huge supply depot at White House Landing. Then—fortune smiling again—the men were ordered on ships and floated around to the new base of operations at Harrison's Landing on the James. There they rejoined an exhausted, discouraged, and depleted army.

There can be no doubt that the evacuation of Yorktown took the army completely by surprise. It was a way the rebels had that was characteristic of all their movements. They never did what the commanders of the Union armies anticipated, until during the last year of the war when the Confederacy became so exhausted in material and men that it had to. This is a compliment to the enemy, but the rebels earned it.[3]

The "skedaddle" from Yorktown and its defences [on May 4th] was known at headquarters by daylight, but not a single cavalry-man was started in pursuit, to say nothing of the infantry, till noon or after. To say that the army was angry and chagrined at the situation is drawing it mild. When it took into consideration the amount of work expended in digging the woodchuck out, and the ease with which the woodchuck left his hole and hied himself to pleasanter surroundings, it was simply stupefied. The new 100- and 200-pound rifled guns had only been tried for a day. Four hundred or 500 pieces of artillery had been posted to assist in the grand pyrotechnical display of burying Yorktown under a scrap heap of broken iron. A hundred thousand well-equipped soldiers were spoiling for a fight, and hardly a regiment had thus far been afforded the opportunity. The general feeling and sentiment of the rank and file of this army were not overdrawn in an emphatic expression of Sergeant Bill's, while discussing the situation with Corporal Tom, soon as the fact of the evacuation was substantiated.

> 3. In fact, the high command of the army was not entirely surprised by the Confederates' evacuation of the Yorktown line. Union intelligence produced a number of clues. None of these, of course, reached the men in the ranks. Sears, *Gates of Richmond*, 61.

"Well, Tom," said he, "our fourth-of-July is a pretty d——d flat one." In truth, that is a comprehensive sizing up of the expressions heard on all sides after the music from the brass-bands had tired itself out.[4]

There was intense indignation over the killing of two or three of the first troops that entered the rebel works. They were murdered by the explosion of some infernal machines that had been buried in such a manner as to explode upon the slightest touch. A hundred or more prisoners were gathered in . . . and these were immediately compelled to unearth all the buried bombs and infernal machines before any more troops were allowed to explore the camps of their vanished adversaries. This fact of burying bombs and baiting them in such a manner as to lead a body of men to examine, handle, and thus explode them, has been strenuously denied by the Confederates. Nevertheless it is a fact that they were so placed, that men were killed by them, and that two or three hundred captured Confederates were made to unearth more than a score of these infernal machines.[5]

In the pursuit of the retreating army, which was allowed to gain fully twelve hours on its pursuers, Porter's division was left behind for another purpose. Perhaps the fact that General Porter had immediate charge of the artillery trains and of superintending the general siege of the place [caused]

4. Mann's observations here bear the mark of hindsight. There was indeed frustration in the army, but only over the fact that the Confederates had abandoned Yorktown before the mighty weight of a month of Union preparations could be brought to bear on their certain-to-be-doomed lines. There is little evidence of contemporary frustration in the ranks over a slow Union pursuit. Mann's letters fail to mention it; other letters from the army are likewise absent the chagrin. Indeed, for the men in the ranks, May 4 and 5 were hectic as an entrenched Union army gathered its traps and prepared to pursue up the Peninsula toward Richmond. See Mann letter (no salutation), May 7, 1862, Mann Papers; Sears, *Gates of Richmond*, 65–66. For other accounts of the fall of Yorktown from members of Martindale's brigade, see letter of "Scorer" of the Thirteenth New York, *Rochester Union and Advertiser*, May 16, 1862; unidentified letters from the Thirteenth New York, *Rochester Democrat and American*, May 14 and May 17, 1862.

5. The men killed by the Confederate "torpedoes" belonged to the Eighteenth's sister regiment, the Twenty-second Massachusetts. These "infernal machines"—the Civil War equivalent to land mines—engendered outrage among Union troops, as nearly every contemporary letter from Yorktown attests. Some were "laid down carelessly in bags, hoping we would mistake them for food," remembered a man of the Twenty-second. The torpedoes were the idea of Confederate general Gabriel Rains. That even Confederates decried their use is confirmed by the fact that such deadly contraptions would rarely, if ever, see service again in Virginia. See John L. Parker, *History of the Twenty-Second Massachusetts* (Boston, 1887), 94–95; Sears, *Gates of Richmond*, 66; Letter of Scorer (Thirteenth New York), *Rochester Union and Advertiser,* May 16, 1862; Letter of C. M. H. (Twenty-second Massachusetts), *Chelsea Telegraph and Pioneer,* May 10, 1862.

his division to be left in charge of the evacuated place.[6] Tom writes, under date of seven o'clock in the evening of May 4th: "I have been out to General Porter's headquarters nearly all day, loading ammunition upon wagons. The ammunition we loaded was for ten and twelve pound rifled guns, and we loaded 15 wagons, which are drawn by four mules each."

The next morning, Monday, this division moved up to and camped outside the immediate defences of Yorktown, which gave the boys of the Eighteenth an opportunity to explore the whole place. It was found that a general attempt had been made by the departing enemy to destroy all valuable stores that could not be conveniently carried away, but this division found plenty of flour, bacon, and cooking utensils, so that a decided change could be made for a few days from the regulation United States diet. Griddle cakes, fried bacon, with a few eggs, were adopted instead.

On May 7th, Tom wrote a description of Yorktown and its defences, from the inside:

> Many of us got the tents that the rebels left in the fort, myself among the number, so that we [now have] quite a large house, and plenty of room. We also got plenty of flour, pots, kettles, spiders, &c. Soon as we had pitched our camp, I went to baking griddle cakes. I made a great pile of them for Dennis [Short] and myself out of the secesh flour and baked them in a secesh spider. Short and me got nearly a bushel of flour and lots of eggs. We lived high yesterday and shall today. . . .
>
> Yorktown is a very pleasant looking place or was before the place was spoiled by throwing up so many earthworks. The rebels had a breast-work all round the village. The trench was 15 feet deep and 25 wide, and they had cannon mounted all around. I saw that big gun of theirs that burst. It killed 10 of their men besides wounding many more. They had two other guns that were bursted. . . . When we arrived in the town and inside the breastworks, we found it the most squalid stinking place I ever saw. . . . We found some 300 graves of the rebels that had died and were killed. Any quantity of dead horses, pork & ham lying round. . . .[7]

---

6. Porter was indeed appointed "Director of the Siege" by McClellan. This likely resulted from Porter's intense involvement with the nascent Union balloon service, which gave him unequaled visual access to the situation around Yorktown. See Fitz John Porter, "Advance on Yorktown," MS in Porter Papers (reel 11, frames 437–42), Library of Congress.

7. Thomas Mann letter (no salutation), May 7, May 9, 1862, Mann Papers. The text of this letter does not appear in the original memoir, but is substituted for a rather muted summary of the missive offered by Mann. Corporal Mann also wrote of seeing "a brick house within the village, in which were imbedded, near the ridge, two cannon balls that had found lodgement there during the Revolution nearly 100 years before."

Late in the afternoon of the seventh, Porter's division went on board steamers and transports, on the York River, upon which had been loaded immense quantities of army stores, together with ammunition for the artillery, and on the morning of the 8th the whole squadron sailed up the river. The troops landed at different points, from 25 to 30 miles above—some at West Point, at the junction of the Pamunkey and Mattaponi Rivers (which unite to form the York), and others at the White House, several miles farther up on the Pamunkey. The Eighteenth left the steamer on the shore opposite West Point, and a part of the regiment was immediately asked to volunteer in burying the dead and assist in bringing the wounded from the battle-field of [Eltham's Landing]. Tom says that he assisted in burying about 50 of the dead, and in helping in 25 or 30 wounded men.[8]

This was all the Eighteenth, or Porter's division, saw of that battlefield, though all day on the 5th, before leaving Yorktown, the sound of fighting [at Williamsburg] was distinctly heard, and they knew that Hooker, Keyes, Hancock, and Heintzelman were hotly engaged with the retreating rebels.[9] The men were constantly expressing impatience at [the circumstances] that kept them away from the immediate field of battle, but were consoled by the colonels and brigadiers with the statement that they were performing an important part in McClellan's plans, and would take their turn in due season. A few months later the anxiety to engage in an open fight with the enemy was not so pronounced.

In writing from "Camp near West Point" on May 9th, Tom unconsciously sizes up the status of the negro, or slave question, at this stage of proceedings, as follows: " 'Colored Pussons' are flocking into our lines every day, by twos and threes and by the dozzen. *We don't meddle with them, only to keep them within the lines after they once get in.*" In this same letter he also tells his father, evidently in reply to an inquiry from him in regard to what the army is doing: "We have to read the New York or

---

8. In the original memoir, Mann misidentified the battle that produced the dead as Williamsburg. Rather, as indicated by the brackets in text, they were the product of a heavy skirmish between the Confederates and the first Union troops ashore at Eltham's Landing, near West Point (twenty miles from Williamsburg). In this fight, the Confederates lost 48 men, the Federals 186. Mann wrote in his May 7/9 letter, "They called for volunteers of our Regt. to help remove the dead & wounded. There was but very few volunteered. I went over and helped them. It was trying to ones nerves to do it, but I will not describe it to you. You can imagine it." See also Sears, *Gates of Richmond,* 85–86.

9. The Battle of Williamsburg, fought May 5, 1862, pitted the Union advance under Joseph Hooker against the Confederate rear guard under James Longstreet. Though eventually driven off, the Confederates managed to blunt the Union pursuit up the Peninsula.

Philadelphia papers to get the news ourselves. And as near as we were to Williamsburg at the time of the fight, our regiment could obtain no authentic information till the *Philadelphia Inquirer* arrived." Brigadier and Major-Generals were about as free in giving the rank and file the particulars of a fight then as railway managers now are in promulgating information to the public about a rail-road disaster.

On the morning of the 13th the "long roll" beat to arms at three o'clock, and by six the troops laying along the banks of the Pamunkey, including the Eighteenth, with three day's rations in haversacks, started forward again. For the first time in its marching history dust was encountered instead of mud, and much of the 14 miles covered that day was through clouds of it that found its way through clothing and into knapsacks and haversacks, irritating the skin and suffocating to the lungs and throat, with no escape for any. The kind of soil adapted for making mud is equally efficient for producing a fine, powdery dust when conditions change from wet to dry. And with the roads filled for miles by marching men, galloping cavalry, artillery and baggage trains, it was soon pounded into an ash-like dust that the thousands of tramping feet were constantly kicking into the hot, still air. Nor is anything gained by taking to the fields. A Virginia field is as bare as a newly plowed one in New England, and the dust will soon fly from it as readily as smoke from a fire.

At this stage of the war the opinions expressed by the men in the ranks, as written to friends at home, are extremely interesting as reminiscences—first, because the few that have been preserved fairly represent the general trend of them all and, second, because they largely reflected the opinions of the heads of regiments and brigades. In reply to one of Tom's letters his father seems to have discouraged the idea that the war was to be of short duration, or that the soldiers who had enlisted for "three years or during the war" would see the end much before the years had expired. Our hero, in replying, writes: "Very likely father is right in regard to our being discharged, but I don't see what these secesh are thinking of. I should think they would throw down their arms and give up. Still they may be foolish enough to think that they are going to whip us. I think that by next Sunday our troops will be in Richmond . . ." In less than six weeks Tom had occasion to revise his opinions.

By the 20th of May the army had settled down on both sides of the Chickahominy river and swamp, in the worst possible position that could be selected within a radius of 40 miles, either for offensive or defensive purposes. Fitz John Porter had been promoted to the rank of Major General, and was placed in command of a corps that ultimately became famous as the "5th Army Corps." His old division, now commanded by General Morell, became the 1st Division of the corps, and a division of regular troops of the United States army, under General Sykes, was added.[10] It soon became generally understood that Porter's corps was being held as a reserve force, and upon it devolved much of the duty of guarding ammunition and supply trains, railroad and stores, interspersed with frequent sorties to feel out the enemy, picket duty, besides doing its share of building corduroy roads and bridges through this treacherous swamp.[11]

Much of the time during the next month the camp of the Eighteenth was pitched on moderately high ground above the swamp, near Gaines's Mills, and by the side of a famous spring whose waters were both copious and cool. "Jimmy Barnes" could be trusted to find a good camp for his regiment, every time, if there was one to be had. Instead of picks and shovels it was now engaged with axes and saws, and in shouldering and carrying logs from the choppers to the road and bridge constructors.[12]

This was famous tobacco country, every plantation having its peculiar barns for storing and curing the weed, and although foraging was still strictly prohibited, no objections were raised to the boys helping themselves from these barns. The tobacco was of the finest quality, the barns

10. General George Sykes—"Tardy George," as he was sometimes known. An old regular, Sykes commanded the only body of Regular Army troops connected to the Army of the Potomac. He would command the entire Fifth Corps at Gettysburg. Today, a unit of the U.S. Army still bears the moniker "Sykes Regulars."

11. The term corduroying roads refers to the simple but important process of "paving" a road with logs by laying them crosswise on the road bed. Porter's corps had a more important assignment than just corduroying roads, protecting ammunition, supply trains, and a railroad. McClellan put the Fifth Corps north of the Chickahominy to also link with the expected advance of additional Union troops from the north, from Fredericksburg. Indeed, much of McClellan's strategic and tactical thinking throughout the Peninsula Campaign was constructed around the expectation that up to thirty thousand Union troops would be advancing southward to join in a general assault on Richmond.

12. Gaines Mill was associated with the expansive plantation of Dr. William Gaines. The mill sat astride Powhite Creek, a mile west of New Cold Harbor. Dr. Gaines's residence sat nearer the river, just west of Powhite Creek, along River Road. A man in Martindale's brigade called Gaines's place "a splendid residence." The soldier also asserted that Dr. Gaines had been arrested for declaring, "If any Union soldiers were buried on his place he would dig them up and burn them after the army moved away." Letter of Scorer, *Rochester Union and Advertiser*, June 23, 1862; Samuel S. Partridge (Thirteenth New York) to Ed, June 10, 1862, Samuel S. Partridge Papers, FSNMPL.

well filled with a finely cured crop of one, two, and three years before, and there were plenty of men in every regiment who were cigar-makers by trade. The sutlers who had been supplying the army, at a dollar a pound, soon commenced to buy instead of sell. The tobacco was brought in by the bushel, and the army rioted in "long nines" and "short sixes."

From being held as reserves, this corps was soon worked around to the right until it held a position on the extreme right of the army, with its picket lines, for days at a time, within seven or eight miles of the rebel capital. In taking this position, Porter's old division, now Morell's, was sent well to the right and toward Richmond, in the expectation of connecting with McDowell's army, which was marching from the direction of Washington to aid McClellan. On the night of the 26th of May, the Eighteenth was occupied in picket duty, thus escaping the fight that took place at Hanover Court House the next day.[13]

In a letter addressed to his brother, dated "In camp Eight miles from Richmond," May 31, Tom writes:

> For the past week we have been having pretty hard times, scurrying from one place to another; doing picket duty one night and marching to protect some exposed position during the day. We have discarded for good all unnecessary baggage, tents, and even our knapsacks. The only shelter now used by this regiment is what we carry on our backs. For tents every man carries a piece of cotton cloth, a little heavier and closer wove than ordinary sheeting, and about six feet square. Three sides of each piece are provided with buttons and button holes so that two pieces can be readily buttoned together, to make a roof, by spreading them over a pole or fence rail which makes a ridge-pole. The third piece is buttoned to the two others so as to close up one of the gable ends, leaving the other open. Of course it requires the material carried by three men to make one such tent, and as each man also carries both a woolen and rubber blanket, they are used to make the three who must occupy this little shelter tent as comfortable as possible. This answers very well in pleasant weather, but we have to huddle pretty close to keep warm in a frosty night, or to keep dry in wet weather; even then it is

---

13. The Battle of Hanover Court House (sometimes called "Slash Church") occurred on May 27, 1862. Much of the Fifth Corps participated in a move northward to dispense with a brigade of North Carolinians near Hanover Court House. All of Martindale's brigade, except the Eighteenth Massachusetts, was involved in the movement, which culminated in a clash that cost the Union 355 killed and wounded. The Twenty-fifth New York, one of Martindale's regiments, suffered nearly half of the Union casualties. See Robert E. L. Krick, "The Battle of Slash Church (Hanover Court House), May 27, 1862," in William Miller, ed., *The Peninsula Campaign of 1862* (Campbell, Ca., 1995), Vol. 1, 1–38.

hardly ever a success. Such a camp, however, can be pitched and occupied in about half an hour, and all gathered up, slung on our backs, and the men formed in line for a march in ten minutes.

Continuing, in the same letter, he says:

> We were relieved from picket, on the morning of the 27th, by Sykes' regulars in order that we might join our division, with the understanding that the whole command was moving out to clear the way for McDowell to unite with the right wing of McClellan's army. The movement started about four o'clock, during a heavy rain, but our colonel was ordered to give his regiment a few hours rest before following on, so we did not start till nearly 10. The roads were very bad but our regiment had them all to itself, consequently we could pick our way and get along quite rapidly. After marching about five miles we began to hear cannonading and volleys of musketry, and "Jimmy Barnes" began to fume and swear and hurry us up, but with all the speed possible the Eighteenth did not arrive on the battle-field where our division was engaged till it began to grow a little dark, and the fight was over.

It seems that our hero's courage is still in first-class condition for he ends up this letter by writing:

> The Eighteenth has not succeeded in getting into a good square battle yet, and I am becoming a little discouraged. We were in hopes of taking a hand in this fight to show the rebels what kind of metal we were made of. Our regiment, being the only fresh one on the field, were ordered to bury the dead of both armies and bring in the wounded, working till 10 o'clock. We found 60 of our own men, and about 100 rebel dead, and more than three times that number were wounded on both sides. We also captured 1200 prisoners, two or three wagon loads of muskets, equipments, etc. This morning I climbed to the top of a large oak tree, from the top of which I could see the spires of Richmond, which seemed to be from four to five miles away, and the heavily wooded Chickahominy swamp lying between.[14]

There was much sickness in the army during June. The Chickahominy swamp[15] was not conducive to good health, and Northern men were commencing their first summer's experience in the South under these adverse malarial surroundings. Probably the Eighteenth was as carefully looked

---

14. Mann exaggerates the Confederate prisoners taken at Hanover Court House. They lost a total of 345 men captured in the battle. Krick, "Slash Church," 33.

15. The Chickahominy River was a typical Virginia tidewater creek, with uncertain banks and a sluggish flow. As it flows through Hanover County, the main channel is only eighty to one hundred feet wide, but in places swamps extended up to a mile on either side of the river, creating a formidable and significant military barrier.

after, and its sanitary surroundings were as favorable as any regiment in the army, yet by the end of June out of the thousand men borne upon its rolls only about 600 were present for duty. There is every reason for estimating the loss to other regiments throughout McClellan's command full as high.

This rapid depletion of the fighting abilities of this army has never been properly taken into consideration in connection with the fearful Seven Day's fighting that was about to take place. Of the 600 out of every 1000 who did take some part in the prolonged struggle, many were weakened by the hydra-headed forms that the Chickahominy malaria took so as to incapacitate in degrees varying from slight indisposition to an almost helpless stage. Both our heroes, Bill and Tom, though always keeping their place in the ranks, without any hospital record whatever, were constantly complaining to their home folks of the debilitating effects of this climate and the swamp air.

Company "I" left three or four of its men behind when it broke camp at Hall's Hill. Before leaving Yorktown, five or six more gave out and disappeared into hospital wards, among them its orderly-sergeant, Preston Soule [who died on May 14]. But [on the peninsula] thirty . . . dropped out of the ranks during June alone, killed or incapacitated by the climate and malaria. The loss of Soule was severely felt by the company because he was one of the brightest and best, and his death, which occurred after a short sickness, produced a shock upon the sensibilities of the men that was not easily shaken off.

The Battle of Fair Oaks took place on May 31st, to the left and on the opposite side of the swamp from the position occupied by Porter's command. During the afternoon of that day the heavy cannonading was almost continuous, while the repeated volleys of musketry wafted to the ears of the right wing, telling of a heavy engagement. It was renewed again during the next day, Sunday, and only died away about four in the afternoon. All this time Porter's corps were under arms, ready to move at a moment's notice to the relief of their comrades, or to repel the attack that was hourly expected from the north of it. The battle of Saturday kept approaching nearer, which indicated that the Union forces were losing ground, but on Sunday the battle sound constantly moved farther and farther away, and the anxiously waiting 5th Corps knew that the rebels were giving way while its own comrades were winning.[16]

16. General Joseph Johnston's Confederates attacked the Federals at Fair Oaks on May 31, 1862. As Mann's narrative indicates, the Confederate attacks initially made significant gains against the Federals, but were reversed on the following day. The Federals lost 5,031

Tom writes at four o'clock in the afternoon of June 1st: "The firing has ceased; only a cannon shot once in a while. I know the rebels have been driven because the sound of musketry has receded further from here. Many of our men have fallen today, and it hardly seems right that we were not doing our share of the fighting; but some troops must remain this side of the river as a protection, and the lot fell to us."

This battle was known as that of Fair Oaks or Seven Pines, after which the opposing armies lay comparatively quiet for nearly the whole of June. It was a rainy month, which caused the Chickahominy to overflow and flood the swamp land on both sides, making it very difficult at times for the two wings of McClellan's army to communicate with each other. The inhabitants about Gaines's Mills said that the overflow of this sluggish stream, during the first two weeks of June, was greater and more prolonged than within the remembrance of any living. . . . The increase of malarial disorders corresponded with the humidity with which the troops were surrounded, so for days at a time full half the men were under the surgeons care.[17]

Many of the dead bodies of men and horses, only slightly buried after the battle, were uncovered by the floods of rain and filled the air with poisonous gasses. Every morning a scorching sun shone upon this wet soil, while during the succeeding evening thick, black clouds rolled up, accompanied by brilliant flashes of lightning, and all night long it rained as if another inundation was to cover the earth. The country all about was one vast swamp, and some of the heavy guns actually settled into the quicksands underneath so they could not be extricated. They are there yet.

June 9th, Porter's corps was reviewed by a number of noted Spanish officers, led by General Prim.[18] On the 11th, Tom writes: "We anticipate every other minute for the next. We are here in camp; nothing to do but

---

killed and wounded, the Confederates 6,134. Perhaps the most important outcome of the battle was the wounding of Johnston. He would be replaced in command of what would henceforth be known as the Army of Northern Virginia by Robert E. Lee.

17. The most common disorders were not malarial, but rather chronic dysentery.

18. Spanish General Juan Prim y Prats, accompanied by a substantial staff and trailed by a retinue of politicians from Washington, visited the army on June 8. In part due to his prewar travels in Europe, McClellan attracted a steady procession of European visitors and even a few European volunteers. Mann wrote of Prim in a June 11 letter, "His uniform was all covered with gold & silver laces on his breast, the insignia of Spain and of his office. His cap I should think was made of silver lace altogether. His is an ordinary sized man with very dark complexion, black hair, and head. Quite a smart looking man." Mann to friends at home, June 11, 1862, Mann Papers. See also Sears, ed., *McClellan Papers,* 293; Robert G. Carter, *Four Brothers in Blue* (Reprint, Austin, 1978), 63.

have an inspection at four o'clock; a real dog's life! Those that like it I hope will get their fill."

The 14th, he writes:

> Yesterday we marched out about three miles for picket duty. It was our orders not to shoot at the rebel pickets, and they were acting under similar orders, but we were expected to fire upon any officer who was seen approaching the picket lines. That was one of the times when the private discounted an officer. Of course there was an occasional officer scattered among the men, though he had to dress like a private and behave like one, or take the chances of having a hole bored through him. I saw whole regiments of rebels, about three miles away; they seemed to be marching to some designated point. Our cavalry and artillery were crossing the river all day, so I believe that only our division is left on this side. Things begin to look as if they were approaching a crisis.

But the "crisis" did not arrive for yet two weeks longer. Meantime McClellan made his daily trips into the air by means of a large balloon, under the charge of Prof. Lowe. Little Mac was undoubtedly the first general commanding an army to use the balloon for military purposes, and it first made its appearance while his army was being organized about the immediate defences of Washington. Its utility became very manifest during the siege of Yorktown, at least obliging the rebels to make all their important moves under cover of the night or of a dense forest. This balloon was moored to the ground by ropes, allowed to rise in the air above the reach of the enemy's firing, and there held while [the occupant viewed] the surrounding country, and something of the rebel operations. As at Yorktown, so at Gaines's Mills on the Chickahominy, McClellan or some corps commander, took daily observations from this balloon while the Confederates wasted several tons of iron in trying to reach it with their best rifled guns.[19]

19. Professor Thaddeus S. C. Lowe, a civilian aeronaut, supervised the Union army's balloon operation, which for most of the campaign consisted of two balloons. Mann is incorrect in asserting that McClellan ascended in Lowe's balloon's during June 1862. According to Porter, McClellan ascended in a balloon only once, in early 1862. Porter noted that such "sudden elevations not unfrequently unsettled one's nerves—but a rapid rise to an aerial sphere attended by the jerking of the rope holding one to earth, the twirling of the balloon causing dizziness, causes a nervous uncertainty of one's hold to life. . . . Whatever Genl McClellan learned of the value of the balloon, he certainly never gratified any desire to renew the trip." Porter, "Signal and Balloon Services," undated MS, Porter Papers, reel 25, frames 412–24. An excellent summary of the Union balloon service on the Peninsula appears in Tom D. Crouch, *The Eagle Aloft: Two Centuries of the Balloon in America* (Washington, 1983), 375–95. For some of the dispatches sent by Lowe during his June ascensions, see T. S. C. Lowe Papers, Library of Congress.

By the middle of June this air ship began to make three or four trips skyward each day, sometimes making one in a clear night. During one of these trips it broke from its moorings and sailed away over Richmond, but a fortunate change of wind brought it back to the Union lines in safety. Prof. Lowe said: "While hovering over the city of Richmond we shook the stars and stripes at the gazing thousands, from our car, and in some instances were answered by waving handkerchiefs from the ladies, while hundreds of rifle shots were aimed at us for a target."

During these long, hot June days, while the regiment had only from two to three day's duty to perform out of the seven, time hung heavily and our two non-commissioned officers wrote to the home folks extended descriptions of everything coming under their observation, including the minutest particulars. The country, soil, produce, manner of living among the natives, and the climate, were all new to New England men. In describing the architecture of Virginia Tom writes: "It is an invariable rule in Virginia to build the chimneys on the outside of the houses, generally one on each end. It looks as if a good spot was picked out for the chimneys, the chimney built, and finally the house constructed between the chimneys."[20]

June 23d, he writes: "A thunder shower has just given us a wetting. It lasted about fifteen minutes, while all the time the sun was shining and our own and the rebel guns were booming away, as if trying to drown the noise made by heaven's artillery." This was the last letter written by Tom until July 4th. Between those dates occurred McClellan's change of base to the James River, and the murderous seven days fighting that drove him there. The booming of the guns mentioned above, though unrecognized in that connection by the non-coms, was the preliminary to the grapple for the mastery of the army of Northern Virginia with the army of the Potomac.

Again the Eighteenth was in luck. [On June 26th and 27th] it escaped the onslaught made upon Porter's corps of 25,000 by a Confederate force of 60,000 men during which this devoted corps lost 7,000 of its numbers in killed, wounded, and prisoners, within a few hours.

The escape of the Eighteenth was due to its being one of the crack regiments of the 5th Corps, and the fact that a very delicate and important piece of work was to be performed that required intelligent colonels and men of proved discipline. The service required was not less than to swing loose from the army and its connections, engage and hinder, by every possible device, the union of the dreaded "Stonewall" Jackson's command with that of Lee's at Richmond. This task was to be performed regardless

---

20. This was a common criticism of Virginia architecture by New England soldiers—almost a cliché.

of the consequences, and to be undertaken by the Eighteenth Massachusetts, under Colonel Barnes, the Seventeenth [New York],[21] a light battery of artillery, and a squadron of cavalry, all under the command of General Stoneman.[22] Less than 2,000 men were pitted against Jackson's whole command, and held it away from Lee nearly 24 hours without losing a man except less than a score by capture. It was the principal device used to delay this intrepid fighter, and was the only successful ruse ever employed against his usual methods.[23]

In these reminiscences only the fortunes of the Eighteenth are being followed, so the tremendous grapple between the two armies, lasting seven days and resulting in a loss to McClellan of 15,249 killed, wounded, and missing; to Lee of 25,000, must be left to other historians, while the side movement of this regiment receives particular attention.[24]

Leaving all their baggage behind—taking nothing but a woolen and rubber blanket, haversack, canteen, cartridge-box with 40 rounds of ammunition, and musket—the men of this regiment marched 14 miles . . . toward Mechanicsville, where a line of battle was immediately formed.[25] This was on open, high ground, so this little handful of men would present to the enemy an imposing appearance. Just at dusk its line was shifted to another position half a mile away and camp fires built as if to remain for the night, but soon as darkness was complete and more than double the usual fires started, it stole away to still another position, [distant] about two miles and a half, where the night could be passed in safety—though without campfires or a voice above a whisper.

21. Mann misidentified the regiment as the Seventeenth Pennsylvania. See *O.R.*, 11, Pt. 2, 330–31.

22. George Stoneman, commander of the army's so-called "advance guard," a mixture of cavalry and infantry. An old regular and Mexican War veteran, Stoneman would be one of the army's more prominent commanders until his departure from the eastern theater after the Chancellorsville Campaign. Warner, *Generals in Blue*, 481.

23. Mann claims accomplishments for this detachment that no historian has discerned. His claims at delaying Jackson are completely unsupported by other accounts. That Jackson was indeed slow arriving on the field was attributable not to Mann and the rest of the Stoneman detachment, but to Jackson. See Sears, *Gates of Richmond*, 199–200. See also *O.R.*, 11, Pt. 2, 223, 298–99, 330–31.

24. Lee in fact lost 20,204, not 25,000. The Federals lost 15,855.

25. Mechanicsville would be the scene of major fighting on June 26—a battle sometimes called the Battle of Beaver Dam Creek. The village of Mechanicsville, through which the Eighteenth often passed during the campaign, was (recorded Sergeant Alderman) "one of those Virginia towns or places that requires one's being told of the fact when he gets there." Alderman, "Experience of the 18th Regiment during the Memorable Seven Days' Fight before Richmond," unidentified clipping from the *Sunday Republic*, FSNMPL.

Heavy firing was heard in the direction of Mechanicsville before sundown [on June 26], and early the next morning quite a number of stragglers found their way into the ranks of this little band, from McCall's division.[26] Several times, in the early morning, Bill and Tom who acted as videttes with Company "I" during the night, were on the point of shooting down these stragglers, mistaking them for the prowling enemy.

Early on the second morning [June 27] the sound of battle became very heavy, extending over the whole line from Mechanicsville to the camps that had been left at Gaines's Mills, and many more stragglers from McCall's division came in. Colonel Barnes had the chief command of these two regiments of infantry, and quite early in the morning of this second day he informed his command that the duty it had been sent out to perform had been accomplished, but that it was entirely surrounded by the enemy—that a large part of Lee's army was between them and their own, and a part of Stonewall Jackson's force was about to make a descent upon them from the other side. Continuing in this little speech, he stated that it was General Stoneman's intention to cut his way out at all hazards, giving no consideration to surrendering. Then he called upon the men to keep their ranks well closed up, obey orders promptly, promising under these conditions that the chances were in favor of safely reaching White House Landing, on the Pamunkey. On the other hand, he emphatically asserted that any man who loitered or straggled would be immediately gobbled by the rebels, who were hovering about like bees.

About noon the race commenced. The infantry marched on both sides of the road with the artillery between. One small squadron of cavalry was in advance, and another brought up the rear. Between noon and seven o'clock in the evening these troops marched twenty miles, to Tunstall's station where the 6th Pennsylvania [Reserves] regiment, belonging to McCall's division, was found, suffering a loss of less than twenty stragglers. These found their way back to the several regiments upon the first exchange of prisoners from Richmond.[27]

[The 18th] alongside this Pennsylvania regiment during the second

---

26. Brigadier General George McCall commanded the Pennsylvania Reserve division—part of Porter's corps. The Pennsylvania Reserves would bear the brunt of the fighting on June 26 at Beaver Dam Creek.

27. The Sixth Pennsylvania Reserves had been at White House since mid-June, guarding the massive supply depot there. Richard A. Sauers, "The Pennsylvania Reserves: General George McCall's Division on the Peninsula," in William Miller, ed., *The Peninsula Campaign of 1862* Vol. 1, 43.

night, only to have the race forced again by nine o'clock the next morning. At that time the pickets were driven in . . . Within ten minutes three regiments formed into line of battle for a fight. No attack was made, however, and about two in the afternoon a bee-line was struck for the White House, some three miles away. We reached that place in 30 minutes, thus affording this little band the protection of the gun-boats, where safety was assured.[28]

At this place . . . a large force had been busy for four days loading vast quantities of ammunition and army supplies onto the transports [on] Pamunkey river. The work was nearly completed when Stoneman's racers arrived, and the material that had not been loaded was rapidly and effectually destroyed. The locomotives used in conveying supplies to the army over this 20 mile line of railway were blown up and the rolling stock likewise . . . together with the bridge that the railway crossed [the river] a few hundred yards away. One unnecessary piece of vandalism was accomplished, no one knew how. The White House itself was burned to the ground. Although this was not the identical house once occupied by the Widow Custis who became the wife of Washington, it was built upon the same ground, commanding a fine view of her ancestral acres, now the property of General Robert E. Lee's [son].[29]

Strange as it may appear . . . greater efforts were put forth to preserve the property of the rebels who were in arms against the Union than to guard and protect the sutlers. Let an act of vandalism occur, or if a Virginian complained to the commanding officer that one of his pigs, the contents of his smoke-house, or hen roost, had been appropriated by a soldier, and extraordinary efforts were made to find the culprits.[30] A sutler's team

28. These were probably the advance elements of Stuart's cavalry, who would arrive at White House Landing only after the Federals had abandoned the place.

29. The property was owned by W. H. F. "Rooney" Lee, Robert E. Lee's son. Moreover, the house there in 1862 was indeed the home once occupied by the family of Martha Custis, later Washington's wife. The landing at White House—the primary supply depot for the Army of the Potomac—was, said one man, "a vast forest of masts, and for a half mile the shore was covered with the commissary stores and ammunition. . . . Some distance back from the river was a canvas town, consisting of several hundred hospital tents, arranged in regular streets with board floors and beds in them." Evan M. Woodward, *Our Campaigns* (Philadelphia, 1865), 104. For a marvelous description of White House Landing see Mary Acton Hammond, ed., " 'Dear Mollie': Letters of Edward A. Acton to His Wife, 1862," *Pennsylvania Magazine of History and Biography*, Vol. 89:1 (January 1965), 17.

30. McClellan insisted that the war "be conducted upon the highest principles known to Christian Civilization. . . . It should not be, at all, a war upon population. . . . Pillage and

might be rolled wrong side up, his whole stock in trade appropriated by a gang of soldiers on a lark, and it was a rare thing for him to obtain any sympathy from the commanders, to say nothing of redress. Perhaps the officers recognized that the average sutler was making such enormous profits from the knick-knacks supplied to soldiers that he might suffer a total loss of every third or fourth load and still come out ahead of the game.[31]

At the White House these sutlers had collected to the number of half a hundred, and all well stocked for the soldier's trade. The fighting about Richmond prevented their moving to the front with their loads, so they had gathered here for protection, while hoping the officer in command would allow them to take ship with the other supplies for more favorable surroundings. Hardly one of their loads was allowed to crowd the already overcrowded shipping, and there was weeping and wailing and pleading and plentiful offering of uncounted "greenbacks," by this horde of Levies, but all to no purpose. The horses were either driven overland by their owners, in company with the two cavalry squadrons, or confiscated to cavalry use. The wagons and their contents were burned, except what was appropriated by Stoneman's men to refill empty haversacks.

Three steamers were reserved for the troops, and Tom, in writing from the deck of one of them says:

> Our haversacks had completely caved in, and just before going on board we filled them from the sutler's stores that were already on fire. I caught up several pounds of loaf sugar, a peck basket full of sweet crackers, a whole cheese, some baker's pies, several bottles of pepper-sauce, pickles, jellies, and brandied peaches, all of which I succeeded in getting on deck. Some of the boys on this deck toted on a whole crate of sardines which we divide up. All are well supplied with one thing or another, and it is well that we are because the army supplies have been hastily loaded upon barges where we cannot well get at them, or were burned at the landing.[32]

Sergeant Bill adds:

> A large boat, the John Brooks, was to take us off, and as we were by this time nearly out of rations, the first thing in order was to take on board what-

---

waste should be treated as high crimes; trespass sternly prohibited; and offensive demeanor by the military toward citizens promptly rebuked." Sears, ed., *McClellan Papers*, 344.

31. Sutlers were merchants who traveled with the army, selling niceties to the soldiers—food, especially. Mann is correct in asserting that soldiers not infrequently attempted to sack sutlers' wagons, though not nearly so often as Mann suggests here. Mann's obvious resentment toward sutlers, who often charged (successfully) high prices, was typical.

32. This extract is from Mann's July 4, 1862, letter to friends at home, Mann Papers.

ever we wanted in the way of food. I shall never forget the sight that 2000 or more men made running back and forth from the river bank to the boats and carrying whatever their fancy selected on board. There were men with great cheeses on their heads, and men carrying in each hand a ham of generous proportions. Others were toting a tub of butter, while still others went in for tin and hardware, pots and pans, kettles and all manner of hollow ware, brooms and brushes, tobacco and cigars, baskets and boxes of various kinds of canned goods, with sugar and coffee galore. I actually saw one man with a "grindstone" that was at least two feet in diameter, tugging and working his best to carry it aboard. . . .

Meanwhile the match had been applied to everything combustible and fire and smoke added another feature to the wild and reckless scene. The immense stacks of provisions made fearfully hot fires and it seemed wicked to destroy it all, but it was burn it or leave it for the enemy. By dark the work of destruction was completed by blowing up the railroad bridge across the river just above the landing; and, all aboard, we steamed down the river with the good boat packed with men and things saved from the supplies.[33]

One of the Hudson River steamboats, the Vanderbilt [along with the John Brooks], conveyed the Eighteenth from the White House down the Pamunkey. This is a narrow, deep, and crooked stream—so narrow throughout its course to the York that the steamer could not have turned around without its prow impinging upon one bank while its stern rested against the other. It doubled upon itself several times, making the bee-line distance of 15 miles into 30 by the river's course. Two or three of its loops were so sharp that this steamer twice ran its nose well into the soft bank, while its stern was pulled from one side to the other by hawsers to enable it to make the turn. The men on deck gathered leaves and flowers, and cut canes and switches from the tree branches that were constantly brushing along its side. It was a strange sight to have so large a steamer as this navigating what seemed to be a brook in comparison. From the low-lying adjacent fields it looked as if it was traveling on land, and the whole spectacle was heightened by the string of craft that followed in its wake, made up as it was of every conceivable kind of floating thing, from the palatial three-deck steamer to a four-oared flat-bottomed scow.

33. Alderman, "Experience of the 18th Regiment during the Memorable Seven Days' Fight before Richmond," unidentified clipping from the *Sunday Republic,* FSNMPL. This passage has been added by the editor; it does not appear in the original manuscript. Like Mann, below, Alderman identifies only one of the ships that carried the Eighteenth away from White House Landing. The *John Brooks* and *Vanderbilt* each had five companies of the regiment on board. See O.R., 11, Pt. 2, 299.

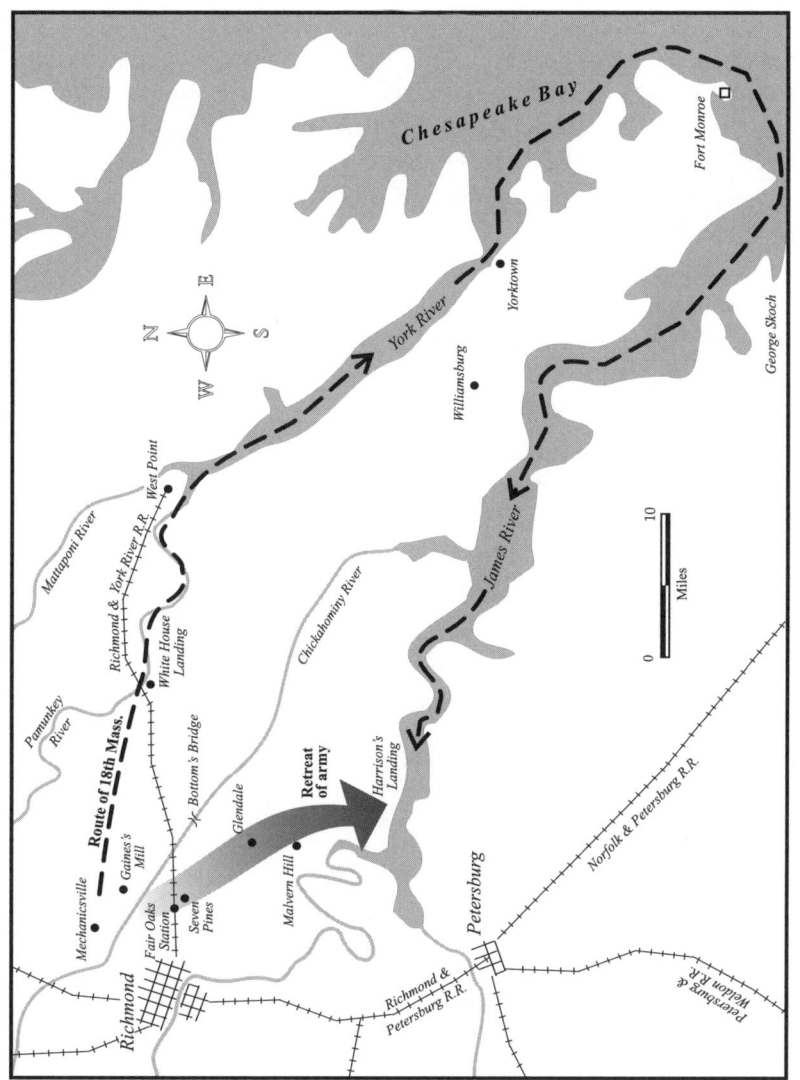

The Eighteenth's roundabout route to Harrison's Landing.

The York is quite wide and straight—a tide-water stream to the Chesapeake—and down this out into the historical bay and around Old Point Comfort sailed this regiment for the second time, and anchored in the waters of Hampton Roads for a day and night. Not being permitted to go ashore, most of the men who could swim enjoyed the luxury of a sea-bath by jumping into the water from the decks of the steamer and climbing back over ropes provided for the purpose. Although this proved an exceedingly pleasant trip for troops who had so recently used their legs to the extent of between 70 and 80 miles in three days, anxious thoughts and dark forebodings in regard to the fate of battle from which they were barred were uppermost in the minds of all. Any attempt at hilarity was quickly crushed out as if spontaneously, for the fate of comrades they were going to seek absorbed all thought and conversation.

Everything was heading up the James river, the Eighteenth with the rest, and a landing was made at Berkeley's[34] during the night of July 1st. . . . As the Vanderbilt rounded the [last] bend of the river . . . the sound of booming cannon and fitful musketry [from Malvern Hill] again wafted to the ears of this regiment.[35] It had listened to the first day's fighting, was not out of sound of the heavier guns on the second day, and was now sailing into the closing hours of that terrible conflict only to land after the last gun had been fired.

The distance from Berkeley to the battle-field was some [nine] miles, and scattered bodies of troops were arriving on the banks of the river all through the night, though the bulk of the army [did not arrive] from Malvern till the next day, so this regiment did not unite with its brigade and division until the evening of July 2d. Then it began to realize something of the results of the struggle that had taken place.[36] As a sample, Tom wrote

---

34. Berkeley Plantation, or Harrison's Landing. At the outset of the Seven Days battles, McClellan had designated this as the destination for, as he optimistically put it, his "change of base" from the York to the James. Berkeley Plantation is perhaps the oldest continually operated postcontact settlement in Virginia, receiving a patent in 1618. It later became home to a family—the Harrisons—that would produce two presidents of the United States: William Henry and Benjamin Harrison. For a complete history see Clifford Dowdey, *The Great Plantation: A Profile of Berkeley Hundred and Plantation* . . . (Charles City, Va., 1967).

35. The Battle of Malvern Hill—the last of the Seven Days battles—ended in repulse for Lee and the Confederates. Malvern Hill is located about nine miles northwest of Berkeley Plantation.

36. Mann's memory was flawed here. Martindale's brigade arrived at Harrison's Landing to reunite with the Eighteenth Massachusetts on the morning of July 2. *O.R.*, 11, Pt. 2, 299.

in his letter of the 4th: "The 22d Massachusetts regiment, which is always along side of us in Martindale's brigade, was in the midst of the battle at Gaines's Mills, and equally so during the closing hours at Malvern Hill. In the commencement it had fully 600 men; now only 250 can be found." Porter's corps alone suffered nearly one half the total loss to the whole army, though the losses in some regiments were in excess of others, the 22d Mass. being one of the heaviest sufferers. The Eighteenth began to feel crestfallen, as if in a sense disgraced by being able to muster nearly 600 men while its comrade regiment could only show 250.

Soon, however, as Generals Porter and Martindale learned that Colonel Barnes had arrived with his regiment, safe and sound, they rode in among the ranks, shaking hands with officer and private alike, expressing surprise that it had escaped capture or annihilation. Soon the men changed their bearing of shame-facedness to that of pride, the compliments bestowed by both generals for the valuable service the regiment had rendered, and its masterly escape, had a magical effect.[37]

. . . The fact that this brilliant move of Stoneman's force, in the face of Jackson's army, was due almost entirely to the generalship of Colonel Barnes resulted in the promotion of the Eighteenth's colonel to the rank of brigadier. This is no reflection upon General Stoneman, for he rose from a sick bed to lead the force, and during its four day's service he was obliged to rely very materially on Colonel Barnes. It was several months before Stoneman was able to return to his cavalry command, as the slight part he did take in the maneuver totally incapacitated him, and he was sufficiently a soldier to report Colonel Barnes' service at its full value.[38]

In a few days the army became settled about Harrison's Landing, occupying a vast level plain, and massed altogether too compactly for comfort or proper sanitary conveniences. It was like retiring within a circular fort two miles in diameter, with the bend of the James river forming nearly one-half the circle, and earth-works thrown up to complete the remainder of

37. During the night following Malvern Hill, Martindale had suffered a spasm of panic and proposed the surrender of the army to the Confederates. A month later, he would be relieved of command and subject to a court of inquiry. O.R., 11, Pt. 3, 352–53.

38. In fact, Stoneman would not return to cavalry command, but to infantry command—a change largely attributable to his poor health after the Peninsula Campaign (one man said he thereafter had "a somewhat sleepy appearance"). He would command the Third Corps of the Army of the Potomac at the Battle of Fredericksburg, in December 1863. In 1863, he would return to cavalry command, leading Hooker's cavalry during the Chancellorsville Campaign. Regis de Trobriand, *Four Years with the Army of the Potomac* (Reprint, Gaithersburg, 1988), 337. Warner, *Generals in Blue*, 481.

the defences. On this circular, flat plain the army of about 80,000 men, 8,000 or 10,000 cavalry horses, and 12,000 to 14,000 army mules, squat in the mud or ash-like dust for more than a month, with the thermometer ranging from 95 to 112 degrees in the shade.

This is a safe statement to make in regard to the range of the thermometer because there were no thermometers to measure with, and scant shade except what was afforded by the groves left about the celebrated "Westover Mansion"[39] and the Harrison estate, under which no rank below that of a colonel was allowed to loiter. It was mainly on this estate, where President William Henry Harrison was born, that McClellan's army settled, and the old mansion, built of brick brought from Europe, was still standing. Some of the more simple-minded privates did not understand why brick need be brought so far for building purposes when, to all appearances, enough of the finest kind of brick-clay must have been thrown out for the foundations of this house to make its walls. They forgot that the first settlers of Virginia were FFVs, not Yankees.[40]

The Eighteenth received no tents for 20 days, consequently obtained the full benefits of sun, rain, midnight dews, and flying dust, and took on about the color said to have been adopted first by the Malay race. The boys made themselves the best shelters possible by the use of their blankets alone.

Sometime . . . there appeared within the lines of the Army of the Potomac an imposing organization known as the "Lancers," who acted their part in this war drama.[41] Their presence was the most noticeable at Harrison's Landing and was made up of 12 companies of 100 men each, hailing from Pennsylvania. Sergeant Bill, who was the most sarcastic member of company "I" after Orderly-sergeant Soule's death, thus sizes them up:

> They were mounted, but in places of sabres they carried lances. A lance Webster defines as a species of spear with a long handle, etc., used by the ancients. I presume our lancers would have been "great stuff" with the ancients. They evidently didn't get on the stage of action within 2,000 or 3,000 years of the time they ought, and if they failed of the appreciation in the

39. Westover was the seat of the Byrd family of Virginia, and Berkeley's downstream neighbor by a half mile. The house still stands, though only its grounds are open to the public.

40. FFV is an abbreviation for "First Family of Virginia"—in Mann's eyes a term indicative of impracticality and opulence.

41. The Sixth Pennsylvania Cavalry or "Rush's Lancers," who would be armed with lances until the spring of 1863.

army that their projectors seemed to expect, it must have been the fault of the army and not their own. They made a circus-like appearance with their lances, at the head of which each had a small piece of red flannel cloth fastened, calculated, I suppose, to strike terror to the hearts of the Johnnies who might behold them. If that was not the reason, I don't know what was, unless it was to look pretty. Or perhaps the flannel might have been intended to work on the Johnnies the same as it does on a mad bull. If that was it, 'twas a mistake; the Johnnies didn't need anything of the kind. They were always ready to go for a Yank without the addition of the red flannel; besides, our lancers never got near enough to aggravate the rebels much.

The boys had a way of jeering at them . . . with such remarks and epithets as: "The great American toad-stickers," or "Father Abraham's sucker spearers," and other pleasing observations calculated to make the lancers feel that they were appreciated and their appearance noticed. Fellow-soldiers engaged in one pursuit, and occupied in accomplishing the same end, are bound together by the common ties of sympathy more firmly than men are united in the ordinary avocations of life, but let one, or many, fail of being or doing what is expected, or what is considered their part and the bond flies asunder with a snap, and is never rightly adjusted until things are evened up and all stand squarely on their proper footing.[42]

On the 7th of July, the steamer coming from Fortress Monroe landed a very unpretentious passenger. He was wholly unattended and unannounced, a man simple in his dress and manners who for a few moments excited only curiosity, for he wore a silk hat and . . . stood head and shoulders above all with whom he mingled. It was Abraham Lincoln, come to consult with the commander of the Army of the Potomac.[43]

Life on the James continued without incident worth passing into history until the night of July 31st. . . . At two o'clock on the morning of that date the Eighteenth was aroused, and ordered to be prepared in 30 minutes with rations for 24 hours, and its working tools, arms and ammunition. Before daylight it had marched six miles away from the camps and halted for a short rest, where the information was communicated by Major Hayes, now in command of this regiment, that the forces thus detached consisted of 800 cavalry, four pieces of light artillery, and the Eighteenth

42. This extract from Alderman, "Should 'Joe' Have a Pension? The Inglorious Career of the Pennsylvania Lancers," unidentified clipping from the *Sunday Republican*, FSNMPL. The Sixth Pennsylvania Cavalry would serve credibly with the Cavalry Corps of the Army of the Potomac until the end of the war.

43. Lincoln visited the army for only a day and during that time reviewed the troops and consulted inconclusively with McClellan. See Sears, *The Young Napoleon*, 226–29.

Massachusetts Infantry. The business at hand was to make a reconnaissance of the country in the direction of the Chickahominy.

[The 18th] continued the march until 8:30 in the morning, when the vicinity of the Chickahominy was reached, a distance of 18 miles. Finding nothing there to oppose, the infantry rested and foraged while the cavalry followed the bank of the river well down to its junction with the James. Returning about three in the afternoon, the whole force started back for camp by the way of Charles City Court House. By 5 o'clock the foggy, leadened clouds that had been hovering all day began to leak, and in another hour every man was thoroughly drenched, while the mud grew ankle deep in the road. To the tired legs of the infantry it seemed unusually slippery, like so much jellied soft-soap spread three or four inches deep over the whole surface.

Camp was reached at 9:30 in the evening after a march of 36 miles, said at the time to be the record-breaking march up to date. In his letter to friends at home, dated August 1st, Tom writes: "Our march was a pleasant one, through some fine looking country, and we passed one field containing over 100 acres that was heavily covered with growing corn. It was so rank that much of it reached a height of 12 or 14 feet, and the ears were in their prime for roasting, which circumstance we immediately took advantage of with avidity besides toting some back to camp. We also found plenty of pears and peaches, while the ripening blackberries fairly covered acres of ground."

The blackberries of Virginia, in their season, were a plentiful luxury and did more for the army than all the surgeons quinine, pills, and potions combined.

Sometime during the early evening of July 31st, under cover of the darkness, the rebels succeeded in planting a battery at Coggin's Point, on the opposite side of the river from McClellan's camps. . . . About 11 in the evening of this dark, stormy night, [the rebels] opened upon this circular pen of 80,000 soldiers with eight or ten pieces. The guns were worked as rapidly as possible, some giving their attention to the huddled shipping in the river, but more seeking the very centre and thicket of the Federal camps. It is not surprising that the respects of the first shot were paid to the Eighteenth for this regiment occupied about the centre, and the rebel gunners, being experts, calculated well upon the thickest location of men for their target.

Tom wrote, "I had just drank my coffee and fairly got to sleep when I was suddenly awakened, could hear nothing but a perfect thunder of artillery. I first thought it was a gun boat fight. . . . The rebels had collected a large force on the other side of the river and had planted a battery under cover of the woods."[44]

> Cannon to right of them,
> Cannon to left of them,
> Cannon in front of them
> Volley'd and thunder'd;

So quoted Sergeant Bill, after the melee quieted down enough to allow scurrying men and horses to decide whether they were still on earth, and where they "were at." Bill was great at quotations, and usually had an apt one ready to fit most occasions. This one fitted to a T the pandemonium that was launched over the Army of the Potomac for 30 or 40 minutes shortly after the return of the Eighteenth . . . The first shell burst within the regimental lines of this weary legged scouting party, as if in retribution for its raid through the country of the day before. . . .

Battles and desperate charges and hand to hand encounters by dragoons, grenadiers, and infantry have been described by prolific writers, often in a masterly manner. The onslaught of desperate thousands has been told in prose and verse, and recited by every English-speaking school boy. But none of it seems to fit the rattle and crash and confusion of one hour of that night. The bursting and splintering, whirring, whizzing and smashing of things generally; the blinding flash from the missiles as they flew apart and the wicked; the singing of the hundreds of sharp, jagged-pointed pieces of iron that were thrown in all directions with a force to kill; the darkness of the night, which was so black that a soldier could not be distinguished from a horse ten yards away. All this can be imagined as a pandemonium, but not as poetry. There was no poetry of motion about it. Men not half dressed, springing up from their earth-couches over almost every square yard of area, and all talking, ordering, swearing or praying at once; with 10,000 stampeded horses and mules running amuck, did not have a tendency toward smoothing "war's wrinkled front."

The men did little or no wandering away from their respective regimental belongings, except a few of those nearest the river bank sought shelter beneath it. There was no place where safety was any more promising than right where one happened to be, and before time was given for any concerted action, or before any was attempted, the whole affair was over.

44. Mann to friends at home, August 1, 1862, Mann Papers. The quotation from the letter has been added by the editor.

The damage done was very slight compared with the display and estimates: ten men killed, a few horses and baggage wagons destroyed, and two small barges sunk in the river. But the scare and excitement of that hour were prolific themes in the army for several days. In the morning several thousand men were sent across the river to take possession of Coggin's Point, which was accomplished without opposition. The rebel battery had only been out there for a night's lark.

The campaign done, Tom wrote gloomily of the war's prospects.

> You will see by the papers that McClellan is not defeated, but it was the next door to a defeat. . . . I have no hopes of seeing home until my three years are up. I think foreign nations will soon interfere in some way, and this war will end in a long and bloody way in which England if not France will be engaged. Just as sure as the Rebelion [sic] is not utterly put down by Sept., we shall have a foreign war on our hands. We shall in all probbability be able to meet it but it will take years to extricate ourselves from it. It would be much better to bring on the men if it takes a million and put the rebellion down in a hurry.[45]

45. This letter extract does not appear in the original memoir. See Mann to his brother, July 7, 1862, Mann Papers. Mann's fear of foreign intervention was shared by many in the North that summer. Conversely, the Confederates ardently hoped for it. Indeed, it was a major motivation for Lee's invasion of Maryland in September 1862. Mann's hope for more troops would be realized when Lincoln called for three hundred thousand more men in the wake of the Peninsula Campaign. To that, Mann proclaimed, "Long live Old Abe!" Mann to his brother, August 17, 1862.

FIVE

Second Manassas and Antietam

Mann and much of the army would spin McClellan's failed Peninsula Campaign into a masterful change of base. "McClellan's plans were deep," Mann explained emptily to those at home. He, like so many other soldiers, blamed officials in Washington for not supporting the army's beloved commander (McClellan loudly made the same contention on his own behalf).[1]

McClellan complained of a lack of support; Lincoln claimed he had no more support to offer. After a month of contentious stalemate, Lincoln and his new general-in-chief Henry Halleck ordered McClellan to evacuate the Peninsula. The objective: to unite the Army of the Potomac with a new Union army operating in northern Virginia under John Pope, then to resume the campaign against Lee. In mid-August Mann retraced his steps down the Peninsula, back onto the transports, and back up the Chesapeake and Potomac to Aquia Landing and Fredericksburg. From there, Porter's corps would march up the Rappahannock River to join Pope's army near Rappahannock Station.

A Yankee hallmark of 1862—shared by both McClellan and Pope—was the persistent expectation that the Confederates would do precisely what Union generals hoped they would do. Perhaps Joseph E. Johnston, the Confederate army's first commander, could be depended upon for such certitude. But Robert E. Lee could not. Lee chose not to await the massive junction of two Union armies in northern Virginia. Instead, he concluded to try to dispense with Pope before McClellan could fully join him. On August 18, Lee would embark on a campaign that would culminate on the plains of Manassas—on the same ground where the war's first major battle had been waged in July 1861.

Mann, the Eighteenth Massachusetts, and the Fifth Corps joined Pope's

---

1. Mann to friends at home, July 4, 1862, Mann Papers.

*army in the effort to foil Lee. As the Wrentham Company hauled its traps along a meandering course through central and northern Virginia, it did so as a veteran organization. Colonel Barnes had moved up the command ladder and would miss the campaign. Lieutenant Colonel Ingraham had left the service, taken ill on the peninsula. Command of the regiment fell to the new major, Stephen Thomas, an overweight foundry worker from Middleboro.*² *Months of toil on the peninsula had taken a heavy toll on the Eighteenth; the original 850 men had shrunk to about four hundred. But those who remained were fast becoming inured to the hardships of soldiering. The Peninsula had delivered to them the full range of soldier trials. All, that is, except one: battle. That, however, would change along an old unfinished railroad embankment on August 30, 1862.*

History, as a rule, only takes cognizance of the movements and plans of commanders—the battles they win or lose and their political results. The rank and file receive even less notice than is accorded to well running horses or the keen noses of a pack of hounds in a successful fox hunt. The late civil war, however, will be likely to go down into history somewhat modified in detail and narrative, differing from the stereotyped methods of the ancients by receiving the impress and certifications of thousands of the common soldiers who acted their part in it. As Sergeant Bill well says: "It happens sometimes, in narrating events, that the little incidents are quite as interesting to the reader or listener as are the recorded histories of great occurrences. Besides there are always great writers, and it is their peculiar province to write of great things, leaving the little things for the little fellows to tell."

So, leaving the military expediency of the next move of the Army of the Potomac to the . . . Major Generals, this [memoir] will concern itself with a few of the details in which the privates took a profound interest. The expectation of the men who fought seven days about the rebel capital, inflicting upon the enemy nearly double the loss of their own, would naturally be for reenforcements to enable them to give the Confederates another trial. And when the rank and file became fully cognizant of the

---

2. Stephen Thomas received his commission as major on August 25, just five days before the Second Battle of Manassas. The status of Lieutenant Colonel Ingraham can be found in the *Boston Herald*, June 14, 1862.

fact that McClellan's change of base had not taken the army, practically, any farther from Richmond, the order emanating from General Halleck to withdraw it was a surprise to say the least to the lowest "private in the rear rank."[3]

The Eighteenth started from Harrison's Landing, with its corps, at midnight of August 14th, and toward evening of the next day reached and crossed the Chickahominy near its junction with the James, where [the Eighteenth] was allowed to rest for one night. The distance marched was 30 miles, and the [Chickahominy] was crossed on a pontoon bridge three-fourths of a mile long.... Next day the march was continued to Williamsburg, and the battle-field of three months before became the camping ground during the night of the 16th, after a march of only 12 or 14 miles. On the 17th an early start was made, and Yorktown was again visited. Here the old camp of the regiment was repossessed and occupied for a night. The peaches in the old orchard were ripe and dropping to the ground, and the two army corps just arrived succeeded during that one night in taking care of them all.

From Williamsburg to Yorktown is 16 or 17 miles,[4] and from the latter place to Fortress Monroe, 25 miles—the distance marched during the day and evening of the 18th. The next day many of the troops, this regiment among them, moved up to Newport News, some seven or eight miles, where steamers were awaiting to transport them to Aquia Creek on the Potomac River.[5]

At Harrison's Landing the men had been supplied with new knapsacks, replacing those left on the battle-field and gobbled by the rebels at Gaines's Mills. These were now packed with extra underwear, overcoats ... and sent on board transports for conveyance, thus leaving the regiment under light marching conditions—with just muskets, haversacks, canteens, cartridge-boxes, and rubber and woolen blankets. These knapsacks did

---

3. General Henry Wager Halleck, the new general-in-chief of all United States armies. Though Halleck had the authority to act broadly and decisively, he shied from the task, instead acting more as advisor to Lincoln than the director of vast armies. Halleck issued the order for McClellan to withdraw from the Peninsula on August 3, 1862. See John Hennessy, *Return to Bull Run: The Campaign and Battle of Second Manassas* (New York, 1993), 10.

4. In fact, the distance is about nine miles.

5. About twelve miles north of Fredericksburg, Aquia Landing would be a major Union disembarkation point and supply depot in late 1862 and early 1863. From here, Union troops and supplies could move easily toward Fredericksburg on the Richmond, Fredericksburg, and Potomac Railroad.

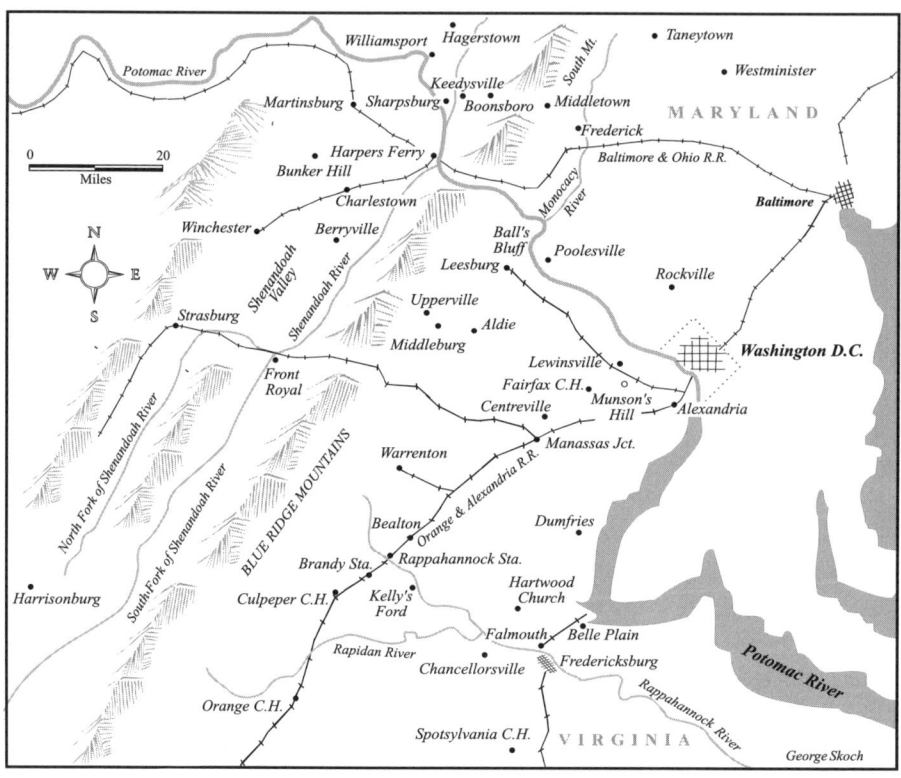

Northern Virginia and Maryland, scene of the Eighteenth's operations August–September 1862.

not find the regiment again until nearly the 1st of November, weeks after the battle of Antietam.

In Tom's first letter home, which he had no opportunity for writing until a month after the last one quoted from, he says: "During the whole of our marching from Harrison's Landing to Newport News, we had plenty of peaches, pears, melons, and blackberries; and being allowed to forage pretty much as we pleased, supplied ourselves very well with fresh pork and some chickens. Only hard-bread, coffee and sugar had been given us for rations, which soon played out, so the pork and fruit helped us out fairly well. All previous orders in regard to foraging now seem to be of no account."

The landing at Aquia Creek was made on the morning of [August] 21st, and a part of Porter's corps, probably the whole of Morell's division, which included the Eighteenth, was immediately transported to Fredericksburg by railroad, where a day's and a night's rest was allowed. From this time to August 30th, no reliable data of the movements of Morell's division can be found except what is given in letters to home friends, written after the battle of Bull Run which was now close at hand.[6] Tom writes:

> About dusk of the second night after reaching Fredericksburg, we were again on the move, marching the greater part of the night, only resting two hours just before daylight and pushing on the next day, thus putting about 25 miles between us and Fredericksburg; but we found ourselves in a dangerous locality. For the next four or five days we posted pickets every night, sometimes advancing and sometimes countermarching though making from 10 to 20 miles every day, and always in [view of] the Blue Ridge mountains. One night we camped on the banks of the [Rappahannock].[7]
>
> At last we struck the railroad within a few miles of Warrenton Junction. . . . Then our marching commenced in earnest, for when we did march our movements were often in double-quick time. When close upon Manassas our artillery had a brush with the rebel guns, and the division was quickly thrown into line of battle behind it, but did not go into action. We could see

---

6. By the time Porter reached Fredericksburg, Pope had withdrawn behind the Rappahannock, about thirty miles northwest of Porter. Porter's assignment was to join Pope by marching along the north (left) bank of the Rappahannock, finding him, presumably, somewhere near Rappahannock Station. The first of Porter's troops would make contact with Pope on August 22, with most arriving late on August 23. Hennessy, *Return to Bull Run*, 81.

7. In the original letter, Mann misidentified the river as the Rapidan. The Fifth Corps never approached the Rapidan during this period.

the long lines of dust raised by the marching rebel troops as they came through a gap in the mountains.[8]

This last movement that Tom describes was on Friday, August 29, and the succeeding moves of this regiment and division are easily followed. The marching abilities of the Eighteenth had now been pretty well tested, having traversed 200 miles on foot, besides nearly as many more by steamer and railroad. Since leaving Fredericksburg the weather had been very dry and hot and water, on the lines of march, very scarce. In one instance, after camping down for the night, the men spent full half the time in searching for it, then finding only muddy puddles in a creek that had ceased to flow. During that particular night, which was not very dark, Tom started out with several of his comrades about nine o'clock, and declares that he traveled over four miles of territory, following the dried–up creek a mile before a puddle could be found that was deep enough to fill a canteen. On his return, loaded down with ten or twelve [canteens] filled with muddy water, he had a gruesome story to tell.

After leaving the dry creek on the return trip, which was probably a mile and a half from the camps, a peculiar bunch of something moving between two closely growing trees attracted the attention of these water carriers. A nearer inspection showed that the fluttering was from the remnants of a grey, Confederate uniform, still partially covering the skeleton that had put it on while flesh and life were there. The cartridge-box still hung by its leather strap from the shoulder, but the canteen and haversack had dropped to the ground, while the musket, weather beaten and rusty, was by its side. Only the skeleton of the soldier remained; the flesh had been stripped as clean as only the ever present turkey-buzzards of Virginia knew how, and to reach the last shred of flesh the strong home-spun cloth of the uniform had been torn away by beak and claw.

These remains were lodged between two large chestnut trees that grew

8. Mann's brief passage on August 29 obscures the events that grew from the activities of Porter and his corps that day. The Fifth Corps operated on the extreme left of the Union army, just northwest of Manassas Junction, and faced the extreme right of Lee's army about three miles south of the main Bull Run battlefield. Though Porter did not receive direct orders to attack from his position until nearly dark, Pope would claim that those orders were sent to Porter and that Porter disobeyed them. Porter, a strong devotee of McClellan—and an ardent opponent of Pope—would be court-martialed and (wrongly) dismissed from the army for his inaction on August 29. The Porter case was one of the celebrated cases of the nineteenth century and produced volumes of testimony and debate. For a summary, see Hennessy, *Return to Bull Run*, 464–65.

from a common root, making the conditions favorable for a wounded soldier to wedge himself into while leaning against the crotched trees to rest. The appearances were that he was a retreating participant of the battle of Bull Run of the year previous.

On the morning of August 30th, the Eighteenth reached the brow of quite a ridge [Henry Hill], which overlooked much of the old Bull Run battlefield of the year before, and from which glimpses were caught of nearly the whole of Pope's army. Even then, in the eyes of the 20 year-old soldier boys, it presented a jumbled, confused appearance as if without a head, or with too many heads and no concentration or purpose. This regiment immediately moved down into the midst of it all and was ordered to "stack arms" and cook its coffee—the first opportunity afforded to cook lunch for 24 hours. . . .[9]

The battle was raging furiously, in spurts, while this regiment coolly broke its fast with hot coffee, hard-bread and fried salt-pork, and Tom writes: "They were bringing in the wounded by hundreds and surgeons were at work sawing off legs and arms not 20 yards from where I was swallowing my rations, too hungry to allow the business to disturb me much."

A few minutes before noon, the position of the regiment was changed about half a mile to the right, bringing it to the front and into line of battle [on Dogan Ridge]. Skirmishers were immediately sent out to find the exact position of the enemy. At least two brigades of Morell's division were thus placed in front of the artillery and ordered to lie down while the batteries, firing over the long line of prostrate infantry, engaged those of the rebels.[10]

It was not many minutes before the skirmishers were heard cracking away, and soon an occasional shell whizzed over, "plunked" into the ground a few yards short, or burst directly over the lines of men who lay hugging the ground.

Tom wrote in a letter home: ". . . a shell from a rebel cannon came whizzing toward us striking the ground some 50 ft. from where I lay, but it did not burst. Our cannon then opened upon them and they had a regular ar-

9. The regiment's position at this time was on Henry Hill, scene of much of the fighting during the 1861 First Battle of Manassas, and on August 30 a busy place just behind the main Union lines.

10. This all occurred on Dogan Ridge, the virtual center of the Union army's position. Though largely ignored by visitors today, on August 30, 1862, Union artillery crowned Dogan Ridge and dense formations of Union troops formed behind the ridge. Jackson's line along the unfinished railroad lay just under a mile away.

tillery fight over our heads as we lay in front of our cannon. Of course the rebel shells being aimed for our battery burst over & all round us, for we were close by our cannon. We lay there and [watched] the ball go on for about an hour, when our battery changed its position to give us a chance to advance."[11]

Being called to "attention," the order was: "Forward,—guide right and left, keep the touch toward the colors,—March!"

This movement was continued through half a mile of forest [Groveton Woods] that was so open that the men experienced little difficulty in keeping a respectable line. The movement continued to the edge of the open fields, where the order ran along the line: "Halt,—lie down!" From this position the work [at] hand began to loom up and cast its shadow before us. Either the Union troops would soon charge across, or the rebels would make a like move in the opposite direction.

The skirmishers were busy between the hostile forces, partly hidden by the tall grass, slight ridges in the ground or behind low bunches of brush that grew in these open fields, which were 800 to 1000 yards across. The land sloped from both sides toward a depression about midway between the opposing forces, to where the dried up bed of a small creek seemed to act as the dividing line to separate the battle now growing more imminent every moment.[12] On the opposite side from that occupied by the Federals the land was higher, and along its ridge a constant, dropping fire of musketry was covering the field, though not yet reaching to the position of the Eighteenth. In a few moments, however, the rebel gunners trained their artillery upon the crouching Union infantry and this regiment received its full share of bursting shell.

Tom writes:

> We lay on our faces on the edge of the woods. Across this field we could see the rebels every once in a while pop their heads above a fence or from a little bank and fire at us and drop down again. Our sharpshooters kept their heads down a little as when they fired they were pretty sure to fetch their man.... The rebels soon discovered us lying in the woods. Then the shell flew at us in earnest. You may depend it was no pleasant duty to lay on the

11. In the original manuscript, Mann simply paraphrased the very vivid account in his letter to friends at home, September 7, 1862, Mann Papers. The editor has replaced the summation with the words of the letter.

12. Known today as Schoolhouse Branch, this wet-weather stream bed sits about three hundred yards in front of the Eighteenth's position in Groveton Woods.

ground with a rebel battery playing at us but little more than a half mile distant.

The shell bursting all about us, Mr. Skinner[13] was hit in the shoulder as he lay on the ground but no harm done. Then a minie ball from a rebel sharpshooter struck and went through a blanket rolled up on the back of one our men and then struck Mackavoy[14] on the heel, disabling him for further duty—and he limped to the rear. That was all that happened to our Co. as we lay there.[15]

Then the startling order: "Attention, 30th,—forward! Double-quick! Charge!!"—rang out to the New York regiment on the right, and it started across the field.[16]

The Eighteenth rose to its elbows, watching the rush, expecting to move the next instant. The rebels got up in masses from their position behind the ridge and poured volley after volley into the New York regiment, which left nearly half its numbers strewing the ground along the way. But the remnant kept right on till reaching the ridge occupied by the enemy, then it stopped and held its ground.

We heard the thrilling words, words that fixed determination in the countenance of nearly every one of us: "Attention, Eighteenth! Forward." We sprang to our feet, and marched some 8 rods [50 yards] out into the open field in a perfect line as though we were going through a drill. Then came the word "Charge Double quick" and we started on a run across the field for the top of the hill. The rebels pouring into us from the right of the regt—in the hill, and also from the left. What there was left of the regt. soon reached the brow of the hill where we commenced to fire upon the rebels as fast as possible. We could not see much of the rebels[,] only their heads & shoulders at any time. They were behind a fence & in a pit that had been dug out for a railroad. . . . We were in a bad pickle as we had advanced into a half circle

---

13. Private Zenas Skinner, at forty-six the oldest man in the company (hence the "Mr. Skinner" identification no doubt). He was a factory hand from Wrentham.

14. Frederick McAvoy, a nineteen-year-old upholsterer from Fall River. McAvoy would return to service, but would be discharged for disability in December 1863.

15. The letter text (Mann to friends at home, September 7, 1862) has been added by the editor. A brief, redundant deletion follows this paragraph.

16. Mann's letter indicates, correctly, that the Thirtieth New York of Hatch's division lay to its right, the Twelfth New York of Butterfield's brigade to its left. While in the woods, Mann's brigade was aligned in columns of regiments—that is, each regiment in line of battle, one behind the other. The Eighteenth Massachusetts was the lead regiment, followed by the Thirteenth New York and First Michigan. As the brigade moved out of the woods and across the field, the two regiments behind the Eighteenth Massachusetts (the Thirteenth New York and First Michigan) moved abreast of the Bay Staters. See John Hennessy, *Second Manassas Battlefield Map Study* (Lynchburg, n.d.), map 11, p. 294.

of the rebels. Soon the 12th N.Y. came up on our left,[17] but not far enough to our left, so . . . they crowded our Co. and we stood 3 and 4 ranks deep. The men were falling thick and fast around us. My comrades. I fired 27 times and each time with my piece sighted on a rebel head or shoulders. My comrades falling round me seemed to make me calm with a fixed determination to do my duty. I was not excited. Let me tell you the reason. *I expected to die.* After the battle I was much excited, that is when I found myself in a safe place. We started across the field with 44 men in our Co. In 1¼ hours we returned with 13 men. . . . I was struck on the left hip with a piece of shell weighing I should think more than a pound. It made me stagger some and drew blood, but no harm done altho it made me a little lame for two or three days.[18]

This regiment, in common with others, had run up against "Stonewall" Jackson's troops, strongly entrenched in the cut of an unfinished railroad, which afforded the rebels the protection of an improvised earth–work, and this brave and persistent charge of Morell's division made no perceptible impression. A movement was being made by the rebels to capture the remnant of this division and a quick change to the rear became necessary, but the officers experienced some difficulty in making it understood amid the stifling smoke and deafening noise of the crashing musketry. Finally the colors were started back, word passed from man to man to "follow the colors," and the retreat across the death-strewn field was inaugurated—which added still others to the harvest of death.

17. Other sources confirm that the Thirteenth New York, not the Twelfth New York of Butterfield's brigade, linked with the left of the Eighteenth Massachusetts at about the site of the present-day "Groveton Monument," less than twenty yards from the unfinished railroad. (Indeed, adjutant Fisher Baker, who returned to the ground the following week, claimed that dead from the Eighteenth lay within twenty feet of the excavation.) The First Michigan, to the right of the Eighteenth, lagged slightly behind, closing only to within fifty yards of the Confederates. Letter of B. F. Messervey (Eighteenth Massachusetts), *Norfolk County Journal,* September 20, 1862; Letter of T. S. (Eighteenth Massachusetts), *Taunton Daily Gazette,* September 5, 1862; Testimony of Fisher Baker in U.S. Congress, *Senate Executive Document 37; Proceedings and Report of the Board of Army Officers in the Case of Fitz John Porter* (Washington, 1879), Part 2, 246–48; undated report from Major Thomas of the Eighteenth Massachusetts, T. C. H. Smith Papers, Ohio Historical Society; George C. Hopper, *The Battle of Groveton* (Detroit, 1913), 8–10 (First Michigan); E. W. Everson, Diary (Eighteenth Massachusetts), excerpts in the Fitz John Porter Papers, Library of Congress.

18. This long letter excerpt is inserted in lieu of the less vivid, distant, less-accurate account included in the original memoir. The editor surmises that Mann, for some reason, did not have access to his September 7, 1862, letter to friends at home, in which he provides a detailed, emotional account of his first experience in battle. Indeed, it is one of the most compelling letters Mann wrote during the entire war.

The charge across the field, the emptying of cartridge-boxes on the ridge, and the return to the edge of the woods from whence the movement commenced, occupied from 45 to 60 minutes, during which the Eighteenth lost 67 men killed, 212 wounded, and a few prisoners or missing. Company "I's" quota of the loss was four killed, 21 wounded, and three missing, out of the 44 men who were supposed to be engaged in this charge.[19]

Few campaigns of the war would stimulate more bitter recriminations than Second Manassas. Pope—a darling of the radicals on Capitol Hill—would be reassigned to the Northwest to fight Indians, but before leaving he would level charges of disobedience against Fitz John Porter. History would prove the charges largely baseless, but in 1862 the politically charged atmosphere blurred most everyone's vision, and Porter would ultimately (in early 1863) be dismissed from the army—"ruined," said Lincoln's secretary John Hay, "by his devotion to McClellan."[20] For Mann and other men in the Fifth Corps, this would only steel them in their devotion to McClellan and antipathy toward the emerging policies of the government they served.

Confederate victory at Second Manassas sent the Union army into a brief, but intense, bout of depression. Two things quickly rectified this psychological swale. First, as Mann describes, McClellan returned to the army. But perhaps even more important than that—and unmentioned by Mann—was what Robert E. Lee did next: he crossed the Potomac into Maryland. If anything was bound to revitalize a dispirited Union army, it was the Confederacy's first incursion onto Northern soil. Within a week after the end of the Second Manassas Campaign, the army—with its beloved McClellan at its head—was moving into Maryland after Lee. Mann, as will be seen, would struggle to keep up.

The Fifth Corps would play a tangential role in the Antietam Campaign

---

19. Mann overstates the loss of the regiment at Second Manassas. Official records indicate the regiment lost 34 killed, 106 wounded, and 29 missing—by far the regiment's bloodiest day of the war. Only four Union regiments at Second Manassas would suffer a higher death toll. Examination of the rolls indicates that Company I suffered 3 killed, 18 wounded, and 5 missing.

20. Hennessy, *Return to Bull Run,* 465. The best modern study of the Porter case is found in Henry Gabler's "The Fitz John Porter Case: Politics and Military Justice," a Ph.D. dissertation, City University of New York, 1979. See also Otto Eisenschiml, *The Celebrated Case of Fitz John Porter* (New York, 1950).

until its closing drama. On September 20, 1862, after Lee's army had retreated to Virginia, Barnes's brigade would lead a cross-river attempt to swipe at Lee's rear guard. The effort would go awry, and the Eighteenth Massachusetts would be witness to one of the greatest disasters to ever befall a regiment of the Army of the Potomac.

Meanwhile, the war's great issues would come into full debate on the public stage. The military calm following Antietam belied the unrest and controversy surrounding the issues of slavery and emancipation. Mann, a devoted proponent of the "conservative patriot's" mode of war espoused by McClellan and Porter, would join in the debate with his abolitionist family at home. His writings reflect those of thousands in the army.

. . . From the battle-field of Bull Run the Second, the regiment . . . marched with the remnant that still rallied about its colors, some 300 men, to Centreville, and camped during the remainder of the night around the little church in this straggling village[.][21] The next day [we listened] to the battle of Chantilly, where the brave General Kearny was killed and Pope's campaign ended.[22] During the night of September 1st, the march toward Washington was resumed by way of Fairfax, in halts and hitches, now blocked and then on for a few hundred yards, for the roads were filled with artillery and baggage trains.

Sometime between 10 and 11 o'clock of September 2d, a horseman, with one or two companions, was seen approaching, picking his way in and out amid the artillery and scattered troops. It was noticeable that he hailed every squad that was met, and soon it was remarked that while he spoke the men swung their caps and greeted him with cheer after cheer. Before he reached the little squad of men to which the Eighteenth had been reduced, they knew that it was "Little Mac" by the reception accorded, and which the "Army of the Potomac" never gave any other man. Soon he

21. The "old stone church" in Centreville still stands, now surrounded by intense development along Braddock Road.

22. General Philip Kearny, commander of a division in the Third Corps. Kearny was perhaps the best division commander in the army and certainly one of its more vivid personalities. He had lost his arm in Mexico, fought overseas for European armies, and carried on a notable personal life that stimulated much comment. His death at Chantilly marked the loss of the first prominent officer in the history of the Army of the Potomac. See William B. Styple, *Letters from the Peninsula: The Civil War Letters of General Philip Kearny* (Kearny, N.J., 1988).

approached within hailing distance, and big, fat, Major Thomas, who was moping along with the rest of the boys, called out: "Here comes McClellan, give him three cheers!" Up went every cap, and the whole squad hurrahed itself hoarse.

"What regiment is this?" McClellan asked, while trotting alongside. "Eighteenth Massachusetts!" yelled back a hundred voices. "Go back to your old camp on Hall's Hill!" he replied, and rode on.

In an hour the spirit of everything was changed, for during that time nearly the whole of this discouraged, bedraggled, forlorn army discovered that its beloved commander was restored to it again. The march was continued to Hall's Hill, in a go-as-you-please manner, but the morning of September 4th found 400 of this regiment crawling out from its old company quarters, on this old camp-ground, to answer the roll-call. It was remarkable, the influence this single horseman exerted upon this straggling, defeated army, as attested by the answering of 60,000 men to the roll-call on their old camp grounds this same morning. But what a change. The Eighteenth left these camps five months before with 900 men, and not half of them were now present to answer to their name.

The stay about these old familiar camps was of short duration, for Colonel, now General, Barnes was ordered to take his brigade back to Fort Corcoran, and here the famous 118th Pennsylvania regiment was added. That body of men was always known as "The Corn Exchange" because it was recruited and armed by the stock brokers, the Corn Exchange, of Philadelphia . . . At the same time the 20th Maine was added to the 3d brigade of Morell's division, and this regiment was as fine body of men as New England ever sent to the front. . . .[23]

All sorts of rumors were afloat in regard to the victorious army of General Lee. [Some said] that he was about to grapple with McClellan again by turning the tables and laying siege to Washington. But the most plausible explanation of the cessation of battle, and the alarums of war, held that

---

23. Deleted here is a brief passage claiming that the Twentieth Maine suffered an outbreak of smallpox upon its arrival in Virginia. Mann was incorrect. The Twentieth Maine suffered its smallpox outbreak nine months later, on the eve of the Chancellorsville Campaign. The regiment would later gain fame for its exploits on Little Round Top. See Alice Rains Trulock, *In the Hands of Providence: Joshua L. Chamberlain and the American Civil War* (Chapel Hill, 1992), 110. For more on the 118th Pennsylvania, see the newly published, excellent letters in J. Gregory Acken, ed., *Inside the Army of the Potomac: The Civil War Experience of Captain Francis Adams Donaldson* (Harrisburg, 1998). In a deleted sentence of the memoir, Mann erroneously asserted that the 118th Pennsylvania had twelve companies.

the rebel host was so badly used up for lack of rations, ammunition, etc., that Lee found it necessary to fall back to recruit. In a few days, however, the boys had settled upon the fact that the rebel army was headed North, for Baltimore or Philadelphia, because the usual work of this regiment, marching, was resumed in that direction.[24]

Across the Aqueduct Bridge to Georgetown, then directly through Rockville in the direction of Frederick City, Md., moved Morell's division in the rear of all the other army corps. So far as the marching of this division is concerned, until it reached the battlefield of Antietam it was unimportant—though the men were in a destitute condition in respect to clothing or tents for shelter, and in anything but prime condition physically. The worst feature was the wearing out of shoes, for which no provision had been made, and hundreds of the men of this division marched to Antietam barefooted. Naturally, considerable straggling resulted.

Straggling in Virginia was dangerous. In Maryland it was anything but that for the boys in blue (though Lee, with his boys in grey, did not receive the hearty welcome with open arms that he was led to expect, as the sequel proved).

The corporal and his chum, Dennis [Short], fell out of the ranks while the regiment was passing through Rockville, which is 25 or 30 miles north of Washington, and meandered along at their own sweet will for four days. Usually one can travel more miles and do it easier when having the whole way or line of march to himself than while moving in the ranks. The path can be picked for the feet in bad places, while moving in the crowded ranks over an uneven, muddy or difficult place no such opportunity is afforded. In a moving column the individual must keep his place, slumping into a muddy hole one moment and climbing over a fallen log or large boulder the next. The [mounted] field officers guide a marching column, ordering the onward march and halt at pleasure, no doubt correctly gauging the average needs of the men for rest or motion, but taking little cognizance of the individual.

So it often happens that men who were half sick or considerably indisposed could, by falling out of the ranks and moving or resting as their own judgement dictated, keep within easy reach of their [regiment's] place though straggling a mile or two away. Men who could be relied upon readily obtained permits to leave the ranks when making long marches—though not in the immediate vicinity of the enemy—with the caution not to lose track of their respective organizations.

24. Lee started crossing the Potomac near Leesburg on September 4. The Union army began its move to confront him days later.

But there were stragglers and stragglers. A straggler with a written pass from his captain was quite a different kind of soldier than the one without a pass. And straggling on the long marches, where no enemy was near to make the possibilities of a fight a constant expectation, was considered in a different light than the kind that was more or less prevalent when the "skulker's" comrades were swinging into line of battle.

A good illustration of the straggling in Maryland is given in the corporal's letter to his father, written after the battle of Antietam. He says:

> Before leaving Fort Corcoran I began to feel dull and stupid, but managed to keep along with the regiment until it reached Rockville; my skin and the whites of my eyes were as yellow as gold, and the surgeon said I was jaundiced—whatever that may be—anyhow, I felt like sleeping all the time, and know that I marched several miles in the ranks while sound asleep. The next morning the captain gave me a pass to fall out of the ranks, and the first thing I did was to lie down in the corner of a fence, on a bunch of fodder that had been placed there for some cattle, and immediately fall asleep.
>
> Sometime during the morning Dennis found and awakened me. He left the ranks the night before, though for what reason we never fully explained, but I was glad of his company so we started on a pace together. Both of us were bare-footed, for our shoes had become so worn as to be of no use, but that did not worry me much for I rather liked to go "bare-foot" so long as I could keep out of the ranks and choose my own walking. The worst deprivation of all was the lack of a shirt; the only one I have had since leaving Harrison's Landing had become so filthy that I threw it away. We had been promised that others would be issued in a day or two while at Fort Corcoran, but we had to come off without them.
>
> Dennis was all the time hungry but I had no appetite, and it worried me, for the people that we met at the different houses along the road gave us all kinds of "home-cooked" eatables, which Dennis enjoyed and I could not. Sometimes the people would take money for a pie or cake, though generally they refused it, acting very different from anything I have met in Virginia. It seemed to be a question whether the Maryland people were secesh or not, particularly since the experience of the 6th regiment in Baltimore, but I can assure you that the country people of the state are Union all the way through.[25]

25. The Sixth Massachusetts had been attacked by a mob during its passage through Baltimore during the first days of the war. Four soldiers and twelve citizens died in the mayhem, which defined most Northerners' view of Marylanders. The Federals' experience during the Maryland Campaign, sixteen months later, demonstrated vividly that central and western Maryland were vastly different from the more pro-Southern eastern reaches of the state. Lee's army received a chilly welcome as it moved through Frederick and Washington Counties,

The next day after leaving Rockville I had a very pleasant talk with a farmer's wife, where we stopped to rest under the shade of the trees that made a grove about her house. She said I had "jaunders," and needed some saffron tea; that if I could wait a few minutes she would make me some, which I was glad to do, and I drank about a pint. Probably it did me some good, though all the time I wanted something sour, and toward night, just before going into Frederick, we found some plum trees on which the fruit was beginning to ripen. Those plums were the first thing I found for three or four days that tasted good; they were very sour and I ate quite a lot. Afterwards I began to feel better. Maybe the saffron tea had began to work but I think it was the plums that waked me up.

We reached Frederick in the evening, and the next morning I wrote you a line or two to keep you posted where I was. Nearly all the churches of the city were being used as hospitals, and in the one from which I wrote the letter I managed to stay only the one night and day, but without seeing a doctor during the whole time. The ladies of the city were in and out all the time, bringing every variety of delicacies for the sick soldiers. Before night I learned that Morell's division passed through the day before, while the fight was taking place along up the side of South Mountain, and I began to be homesick so tried to coax Dennis to start on with me for the regiment. But he would not budge, so I left him just before sundown and starting with two others, who I found were as anxious as I to be with our division, pushed on in the trail of the army over the mountain.[26]

We did not go more than three miles that night because it was difficult to find the way, so bunked down by the side of a board fence where there was plenty of hay for a bed. Early in the morning we climbed to the top of the first ridge of mountains from which a magnificent view was spread out before us, looking over Frederick on one side, and the Middletown Valley, which lay between this ridge and the South Mountain on the other. I think the Middletown Valley is the finest looking country I ever saw, and as we walked down through it large, fine looking farms were passed on each side of the road until beginning to climb the South mountain.

The fight [of September 14] along up the side of [South] Mountain was over the roughest kind of ground, rocks piled upon rocks, and the troops must have pulled themselves up in many places by clinging to the bushes or

---

while the reception accorded Mann and Short during their trek through the same region was typical of that given Union troops.

26. The Battle of South Mountain, September 14, 1862. South Mountain (more properly a ridge extending north and south for more than twenty miles) lay about twelve miles west of Frederick and constituted a considerable barrier to an advancing army—if defended. The Confederates attempted to block the gaps on South Mountain, but ultimately failed. The Federals would pass through on September 15, advancing toward Sharpsburg.

taking hold of each others hands. Toward night we found ourselves among the scattered dead that were left just as they were killed. There were hundreds of them still unburied, among the rocks and wedged into clumps of bushes, and all much swollen, turned black, and stinking horribly.

A little further on and we began to hear the boom of cannon and see the smoke from the battle ahead, in the valley on the other side. By dark we reached the foot of the mountain, and were looking for a good place to camp down for the night when one of the fellows found the carcass of a hog that had been killed sometime during the day and a part of it taken away, so we had plenty of pork steak for supper, and a good bed by the side of a straw stack.

In the morning we hurried on again as fast as possible. Either the battle was over or had moved further away; at the time we did not know which, but I found the regiment about four o'clock after crossing one battle-field that was covered with dead men and horses as far as I could see. You may believe that I felt a good deal relieved when I found that it had not been in a fight, and that the battle was finished.

Porter's corps was held in reserve during the whole of the Antietam fighting, and much adverse criticism was immediately set flying in regard to holding this corps of 11,000 men inactive during these battles where the army lost over 15,000 in killed and wounded. It emanated from men high in the political councils of the government, with perhaps General Halleck as their sole military authority. Military critics universally commended McClellan's wisdom. Of that, however, the rank and file were not proper judges, but the men who made up Porter's corps, particularly Morell's division of it, had not forgotten that they left one-third of their number on the battle-field of Gaines's Mill only two months before, and nearly one-half its remaining number on the field of Bull Run but 15 days before, and felt that a slight respite was due them, even if Halleck and the Administration thought otherwise. Evidently Porter was already marked for decapitation.[27]

Morell's division arrived at Antietam on the evening of September 16th, and was held in reserve near the center of the lines; it was also charged with the protection of the ammunition and supply trains of the whole

27. Mann's mistrust of Halleck and the administration was typical of soldiers of the Army of the Potomac. In this instance, Mann grossly overstates the influence of Washington in the handling of troops on the battlefield at Antietam. The decision not to put the Fifth Corps into the battle was entirely McClellan's. As for Porter, Mann here foreshadows his eventual relief from command as a result of supposed "misconduct" at Second Manassas.

army. The battles along Antietam Creek and about Sharpsburg commenced near four o'clock in the afternoon of the 16th and ended during the evening of the 17th.[28] Toward noon of the last day's fighting a part of this division, including the Eighteenth, was sent some distance to the right to act as a support to General Sumner's corps, but was not called into action, though under a severe fire of shot and shell from the rebel batteries for more than an hour.

During the whole of the following day the armies remained quiet as if afraid of each other. Both Generals Lee and McClellan seemed to require all that time to make up their respective minds what to do next. Lee, as usual, formed his conclusions several hours earlier than his opponent and retreated across the Potomac during the night of the 18th, while McClellan concluded to attack him on the morning of the 19th. Then it was discovered that the Johnnies had become so disgusted with Maryland that they [decided] that Virginia was a more congenial side of the Potomac for themselves.

The honors of Antietam were practically even, a drawn battle. If McClellan was defeated and Lee the victor in front of Richmond, three months before, then Lee was defeated and McClellan was the victor at Antietam. The losses in killed and wounded were about the same in both armies, though Lee lost considerable material and more prisoners, leaving his dead for McClellan to bury and his wounded to the tender mercies of the Union surgeons. Despite the continual hue and cry of the Southern press against the "mud-sill Yanks," as blood-thirsty, cruel monsters, whose mission was to devastate and murder, invariably the commanders of the Confederate armies preferred the Union surgeons to their own, and the comforts and tender care of Union hospitals over anything within their own lines.

On the morning of the 19th the 5th Corps took the initiative, and Morell's division was soon posted along the east bank of the Potomac, its artillery commanding the heights on the Virginia side, with its skirmishers or pickets covering the fords across which Lee had moved a few hours before. Apparently the Confederates were guarding, with equal vigilance, their own side of the river, for shot and shell were exchanged at intervals between the batteries on either side, while sharpshooters and pickets kept up a continual popping at each other all day.

28. In fact, the fighting on September 16 could not be characterized as more than heavy skirmishing, stimulated by the Union army moving into position. Antietam is uniformly recognized as a one-day battle—indeed the bloodiest single day of the entire Civil War.

As night approached volunteers were called for from the 18th and 22d Massachusetts, 4th Michigan, and 118th Pennsylvania regiments, and they crossed the river at Blackford's Ford in charge of General Griffin to investigate.[29] Only the rebel pickets were encountered. They immediately took to the woods and allowed this small scouting party to capture five guns of a battery that had been commanding the ford all day. One of these guns, which they drew across the river on their return, had been captured from battery "D" of the 5th U S artillery at the first Bull Run, more than a year before.[30]

Early the next morning a larger force was sent across at the same ford, including the whole of Barnes's brigade. . . . The river where this brigade crossed is 300 or 400 yards wide and the ford, which was found with difficulty by men unaccustomed to it, was made passable at low water by a kind of bar thrown up by the action of the swift running water after flowing over a dam that was a hundred yards above. . . . With the utmost care in picking one's way the water was found to be waist deep, while very few succeeded in crossing without wading to the armpits, and many were swept from their feet by the strong current. . . .

As the troops left the river they moved by a narrow cart–path that followed one of those ravines that cut through the cliffs on the Virginia shore, and bearing to the right by an easy ascent it led into the village of Shepherdstown. Some of the buildings of this place almost overhung the river from the top of the cliff, which was from 100 to 150 feet and almost perpendicular in height. The path that Barnes's brigade followed was used to reach a large stone mill, built down near the water's edge, which was grinding what is known as Portland cement from the rock of which the cliff was largely composed.[31]

[The brigade] formed into line of battle on the cliffs above, pushed a skirmish line to the front, and commenced to move cautiously forward. It was soon stopped, however, by the appearance of an overwhelming force

---

29. Shepherdstown, Blackford's, or Boteler's (pronounced Butler's) Ford was about a mile below the present-day highway bridge linking Maryland to Shepherdstown, West Virginia. Dennis E. Frye and John W. Schildt, *Antietam Remembered* (Sharpsburg, 1987), 15–16.

30. Two guns of Griffin's Battery were captured on Henry Hill; the others were seized at the bridge over Cub Run during the retreat from the First Manassas battlefield.

31. Mann's account of the fight at Shepherdstown Ford is uncharacteristically disjointed (literarily speaking). The editor has reordered some of the text to allow for a more chronological narrative, and a brief deletion of a needless description of the topography on the Maryland side of the river has been made. Mann's words remain largely unaltered.

of rebels who had not retreated so far as was supposed. A few rounds were exchanged, but it was plainly seen that unless the river was regained in double-quick time this brigade would be scooped in. "About, face! Double-quick,—march!" was the order rolled out by "Jimmy Barnes," and back the whole force went in a hurry.[32]

The results of this little affair of Shepherdstown were amusing, disastrous, and thrilling, all in one—amusing as an interesting episode of history, thrilling to every participant, and terribly disastrous, particularly to the 118th Pennsylvania. . . .

As this brigade was driven back, the 18th and 22d Massachusetts, 13th and 25th New York, 1st Michigan, and 2d Maine, about 1,200 men in all, upon reaching the top of the ravine marched by the left flank and filed into it, thus practically dropping out of reach of the rebel fire for a time. But the 118th Pennsylvania, hardly three weeks in the service, with nearly as many men as the other six regiments combined, were driven to the brow of the cliff where no means of escape seemed available except down its precipitous face to the river, and to the dam that was abreast of the cliff.

Naturally they huddled a few moments, like sheep, on the brink. There they presented the best possible targets for the pursuers and were also in the range of the Union artillery on the opposite cliffs, which was being effectively used to check the hooting, yelling, rebel brigades. To all appearances, it was every man for himself with this unfortunate regiment, and soon they began to drop over the cliff by the score. Some crawled down along safe crevasses to the dam; others found the ford. The whole brigade afforded targets for a scattering fire from the Johnnies as it recrossed the river, though soon as the "Corn Exchange" regiment left the cliff the Union guns re-opened and kept back the main body of pursuers. Many of this unfortunate regiment tried to cross on the slippery dam, which barely afforded a foot-hold for a single person, and many deaths from drowning was the result.[33]

32. The small foray of the night before had alerted Lee to the vulnerability of his rear, and he had ordered A. P. Hill's division to hustle back toward the ford the following morning. It was Hill's men that the Federals so unexpectedly and disastrously found on the morning of September 20. For Colonel Barnes's report of this affair, See *O.R.*, Vol. 19, Pt. 1, 345–47. See also Joseph Hayes's MS Journal Extracts, Joshua Chamberlain Papers, Library of Congress; James V. Murfin, *The Gleam of Bayonets* (New York, 1965), 305.

33. A vivid, extensive, and accurate account of the 118th Pennsylvania's travails at Shepherdstown Ford can be found in Acken, ed., *Inside the Army of the Potomac*, 129–37. The bloody rebuff at the ford ensured that McClellan would not resume his effort to pursue Lee and inflict a final, devastating blow. See Cecil D. Eby, ed., *A Virginia Yankee in the Civil War: The Diaries of David Hunter Strother* (Chapel Hill, 1961), 115.

The whole loss to the brigade was 361 killed and wounded, but of this number the 118th lost 269. The Eighteenth lost but three, only one killed.

In connection with this affair of Shepherdstown, in which only 1,750 men were engaged, the spread-eagleism of Confederate reports of battles was illustrated. In Gen. A. P. Hill's official account of it to the Administration at Richmond he says:

"Then commenced the most terrible slaughter that the war has yet witnessed. The broad surface of the Potomac was blue with the floating bodies of our foe. But few escaped to tell the tale. By their own account, they lost 3,000 men killed and drowned from one brigade alone."

When it is noted that these figures represent just 990 more men than were killed in the Union army during the whole of the Antietam fighting, this sample of rebel reporting stands out more unique than any of Sergeant Bill's indictments against "our special correspondent."

During the next six weeks the army lay comparatively quiet, the causes of this inaction being still a matter of controversy.[34] McClellan made repeated requisitions upon the quartermaster's department for supplies, particularly for clothing and horses. The nights were becoming frosty, and whatever may have been the condition of supplies in the army at large, Morell's division was without shirts, overcoats, shoes and stockings, tents, or knapsacks, until the last week in October. During the warm weather there was no suffering, but it must be allowed that this division was in no condition for a late fall campaign in hostile and barren Virginia.[35]

Morell continued to guard the banks of the Potomac, and the position of the Eighteenth was in the immediate vicinity of Blackford's Ford, watching the bluffs of the Virginia side where the rebel pickets were posted to pay the same attention to the Maryland side. After the first few days

---

34. Mann mused in a letter home on September 29, "I cannot think what McClellan is about. It has been remarkably still. . . . There don't seem to be anything going on." For a discussion of the Union nonadvance after Antietam, see Stephen Sears, *Landscape Turned Red* (New York, 1983), 288–303, 313–14.

35. Mann's testimony on the condition of the Eighteenth is consistent with many other sources that speak to the deteriorating condition of the army in the fall of 1862. This trend flies in the face of the traditional interpretation of McClellan as master organizer and manager. Much evidence—including Mann—supports the thesis that the army's poor condition during the early winter of 1862–1863 was not solely the product of Ambrose Burnside, but in fact had its genesis under McClellan. This neglected subject is worthy of further study and interpretation. See also letter of "C" in the *Kingston Argus,* November 26, 1862; unknown letter from the Sixteenth Maine, Lewistown, Maine, *Daily Evening Journal,* October 28, 1862; Letter of George Breck, *Rochester Union and Advertiser,* October 24, 1862.

following the Shepherdstown affair, during which the pickets were constantly passing and receiving compliments from the muzzles of their respective rifles, by mutual consent all out–post firing ceased, and the corporal and several of his comrades did considerable successful fishing below the dam at the ford while exchanging gossip instead of rifle-shots with the Johnnies on the other side.

President Lincoln again visited the army, on October 1st, remaining three days, during which he rode over the battle fields, visited the wounded in the farm houses and barns, and reviewed the army. The corporal writes home, under date of October 7: "As the President rode along our thinned ranks his face looked careworn and sorrowful, which was plainly noticed as he rode in front of our regiment, while we dipped the shattered colors in the customary salute. He must have observed the marks of rebel bullets and shell which they bore, though they were received at Bull Run instead of Antietam. The state and national colors together, which the regiment always carries, had 28 bullet holes through their folds, and one of them was badly torn by a bursting shell."

In another letter, dated October 20th, he says:

> I have been detailed with six men of the regiment to guard the property of Mr. Blackford who lives down below the cliffs, and right abreast of the dam across the Potomac. Mr. Blackford seems to be quite a wealthy farmer, this year raising over 1,000 bushels of wheat and nearly that amount of corn, but the rebels took it all from him or destroyed what they could not use or carry off. He has given us a room in the house with table and chairs, and it seems very odd to sit at a table to eat and write, something I have not had the opportunity of enjoying for over a year. We turn in our regular rations of hard-bread, salt beef or pork, sugar and coffee, and his two negro cooks give us all the "soft bread" and home cooking that we can ask for. About 100 yards from the house a large spring gushes out from under the cliffs, a stream large enough to run a saw-mill, and the water is clear and cold. Mr. Blackford says that no matter what the weather or the season may be this spring keeps an even temperature and throws out exactly the same amount of water every day.[36]

36. Mann and six other men acted as provost guard for Blackford's house, taking a room in the house for lodging. Mann wrote that Blackford "has five slaves and a hired white man. Two are women and do the work in the house. They are now very busy every day baking bread for the soldiers, which they sell from 25 to 40 cts a loaf. About three times the price of bakers bread in Mass. but it is worth double." Mann to his mother, October 14, 1862, Mann Papers.

The corporal remained in these pleasant quarters six weeks, writing long letters to the home folks, in which the slavery question, the expected emancipation proclamation, and the adverse criticisms upon McClellan, were discussed. The regiment received a few recruits from Massachusetts, and a few of the absent sick ones returned, still its numbers were less than 600 men.

In October Tom writes to his mother:

> I [don't see] the necessity of the President's [Emancipation] Proclamation at the present time. And you cannot imagine the misery that will be brought upon the inhabitants of the slave states if slavery should be immediately abolished. Half of this generation of the slaves would starve to death before they will learn to provide for themselves, and I am sure that would not be benefiting the slaves. The only humane and correct way to free this country from the curse of slavery is a very gradual emancipation and to confine slavery within its current limits. But it seems the government has arrived at that state where the President's Proclamation is absolutely necessary for the salvation of the country. . . . One thing in regard to the President's Proclamation: If he was not a Christian it would never have been issued.[37]

37. This letter text is not in the original memoir. Letter of Mann to his mother, October 14, 1862, Mann Papers.

SIX

Fredericksburg

"Wicked and Murderous"

After six pleasant weeks in Maryland recovering from the intense summer campaign, the Eighteenth Massachusetts and the army—spurred again by an impatient president, public, and press—took to the field. Their march south would be, like all those directed by McClellan, deliberate. But it would also be picturesque, and it would offer Mann much to remember. This march came at a time when the war was changing. No longer would it be a purely military exercise. President Lincoln had issued the Emancipation Proclamation on September 22. Many in Washington wanted the South at large—including civilians—to suffer for their defiance. While Mann did not subscribe to those motivations, he gained an increasing awareness of just how devastating the war was for the civilians unfortunate enough to be in this one-hundred-thousand-man army's path.

The conflict between those (like Mann) who simply wanted a restored Union—eschewing a broader, harsher war—and those who wanted to use the war to transform Southern society came to a head in the months following Antietam. This debate's most vivid public expression came on November 7, 1862, when the administration relieved George B. McClellan from command of the Army of the Potomac. Shortly thereafter, corps commander Fitz John Porter was also relieved, and soon division commander George Morell left the army too. The government had elected to end the army's participation in the debate to shape Union war aims by removing the debaters from the army. Mann and thousands more wailed in protest. Many officers threatened to resign. A few even whispered about taking the army and marching on Washington.

But as always with this army, the grumbling proved to be just grumbling, and soon the army took to the road again. Ambrose Everett Burnside rode at the helm now, a man largely unknown to Mann in November—a man who would display few qualities that would endear him to anyone in the next three months. Burnside's immediate objective: Fredericksburg. It would be the army's last journey of 1862, and for a time it bore the markings of wild success.

When the darkness of the night of October 30th had become complete, Morell's division was relieved of its picket duties and moved a mile or two back from the cliffs, out of sight and hearing of the watchful enemy who still their vigils kept along the Virginia heights. At the same time General Morell was detached from this command and left in charge of another body of troops . . . and General Griffin superseded him. Griffin was a regular army captain, winning his spurs while in command of the efficient battery that bore his name, and the rank and file were rather pleased with the change, though entertaining no reflections against Morell.[1]

Without mentioning his name, the captain of company "I" concluded to resign his commission and retire to private life before another campaign was undertaken in Virginia.[2] Uncomplimentary remarks had been freely indulged in regard to his absence from Bull Run battlefield, and it was also noticed that he could not be found during the "little affair" at Shepherdstown. At this stage of the war the right to resign commissions and retire from the conflict, even by the lowest lieutenants, was accorded. A few months later, however, such resignations were denied.

This company allowed its captain to take leave of his command without saying "good-bye" or showing marked regrets. About the same time, one of its most efficient commissioned officers, 1st Lieut. [Samuel] Bugbee, was

---

1. Brigadier General Charles Griffin was viewed as the prototypical old regular, though only thirty-seven years old. As aforementioned, Griffin commanded a battery at First Manassas and then rose steadily under the command of Porter. He would become a mainstay of the Army of the Potomac—one of only a few officers who served in every campaign from First Manassas to Appomattox. A staff officer described him as a "tall, slim man with that air of decision, stalking walk, drooping moustache and sunken cheeks. . . ." Another called him "king of the wardogs," and still another tagged him as "one of the most devoted ladies' men I ever saw. He is constantly after the girls." Griffin married the sister of a fellow officer in 1862 and presumably calmed thereafter. See Morris Schaff, *The Battle of the Wilderness* (Reprint, Gaithersburg, 1986), 88; Letter of Cicero (Thirteenth New York) in the *Rochester Democrat and American,* December 22, 1862; Alexander S. Webb to his sister, February 26, 1862, Webb to his wife, March 12, 1863, Alexander S. Webb Papers, Yale University Library.

2. Captain Frederick D. Forrest, twenty-four, a shoemaker from Wrentham. Mann was remarkably restrained in not commenting about Forrest's shortcomings in his letters. Forrest is recorded to have been discharged for disability (not resigned) on October 23, 1862.

obliged to resign on account of broken health and injuries received at Bull Run, and Lieut. Edson from company "D" was placed in command.[3]

Early the next morning the line of march was taken up in the direction of Harpers Ferry, and the movements of the Eighteenth, its brigade and division, for the following 20 days, are described and commented upon by the corporal in a communication to the home lyceum. The corporal had resigned the secretaryship of this debating society, which was the institution of the little country village [Wrentham] from which he hailed at the time of enlisting, and he was in the habit of entertaining it from time to time, not only with thorough descriptions of marches, places, and battles, but also with spirited defences of McClellan—until his town's people charged him with being a "copperhead," then he refused any further communication with it. The article referred to is dated "Camp near Falmouth, Va., November 28, 1862," and is here given nearly verbatim:

> We have entered upon another campaign on the "sacred soil" of the Old Dominion. Thursday night, October 30, we struck our tents and shouldered them, together with other equipments, and moved off in the darkness behind the hills, about a mile, soon as our pickets could be relieved by the 2d Massachusetts, which came up from Harpers Ferry for that purpose. By daylight the march was resumed and we were soon among the mountains that I love so much.
>
> At times we climbed steep ascents, then filed round almost to the mountain's top where the road was hewn from the solid rock into the face of the cliff that hung over our heads above, and fell shear away from us a hundred or more feet below. Then our course descended by a winding road, barely wide enough for six men to walk abreast, to the valley below. We passed large quarries from which a bluish stone, with a grain like lime-stone, was being blasted out, while in other places large slabs of soap-stone were being hoisted to the surface and sawed.
>
> Harpers Ferry was reached soon after noon, and it came suddenly and unexpectedly into view as we filed down from the heights through an archway of overhanging ledges, like entering a barrel through the bung hole, and when once within the basin-like place it looked as if there was no way out. The bridge across the Potomac having been burned, we crossed by a pontoon bridge to the place made famous by John Brown, marched past the remains

---

3. The records do not show that Bugbee was wounded at Manassas. Lieutenant Charles F. Edson, mentioned here, was just twenty-two and a tinsmith from Middleboro. He would be commissioned Captain of Company I on November 1, 1862, and would retain the rank and position until mustered out on July 26, 1864.

of the old arsenal, and almost immediately crossed the Shenandoah by another pontoon bridge.[4]

I would like to have remained about this place for a few days, long enough to explore its curious ledges and caverns and cliffs, but the opportunity was not given. The march was continued about a mile down by the side of the Potomac then, turning suddenly to the right, we left this basin amid the cliffs and rocks as mysteriously as we entered. The whole place, which occupies the pointed tongue of land between the Potomac and Shenandoah rivers, appeared like a vision, and in an hour and half it disappeared as completely as if no such place existed on the map.

The march was extended for seven or eight miles, until we had passed completely through the Blue Ridge and around the spur of Loudoun heights, when we camped for the night, and also remained a day and another night. This camp was a very pleasant one, affording a fine view of Maryland Heights on that side of the Potomac. To the south it overlooked some of the best appearing country in the state. Here we received a complete supply of clothing, so that the dilapidated appearance of the Eighteenth underwent a change for the better, and its spirits were correspondingly improved. In fact, all the troops we met seemed to take on more of the old, enthusiastic elasticity of a year ago.[5]

Sunday morning, November 2d, we again moved forward, passing through a thrifty looking farming country and, keeping along the southeastern edge of the Blue Ridge, arrived at the little cross-road village of Snickersville about dark, making a march of something like 20 miles. This place occupies the entrance to the gap of that name that cuts through the mountains to the Shenandoah Valley, and the country, for miles around, looks as if this was the first time it had been visited by either army. The fences were all up, chickens, pigs, and sheep were quite plenty about the farmhouses, and an effort was made by General Barnes to prevent the de-

---

4. In 1859, abolitionist extremist John Brown led a raid on Harpers Ferry, with the intent of seizing arms from the arsenal, distributing them to slaves in Virginia, and inciting an armed insurrection. Though Brown succeeded in capturing the government buildings in Harpers Ferry, he never made it out of town. A contingent of U.S. Marines led by Colonel Robert E. Lee surrounded Brown and his party in a small "engine house," or firehouse, and killed or captured them all. Brown was hung two months later. The engine house used by Brown was dismantled for display elsewhere in the late 1800s, but now sits about fifty yards from its original location. The site was, when Mann passed it in 1862, perhaps the most famous place associated with the decades-old sectional struggle in America. Today, the core of the old town is preserved and operated as a National Historical Park.

5. A report on the Eighteenth Massachusetts published in the *Boston Herald*, November 19, 1862, confirms the good condition of the regiment. The paper noted that the regiment could count 468 men in its ranks, and only 6 of the 468 were sick.

struction of property. During the three days we remained at this place, however, pretty much all the live stock disappeared and not a soldier seemed to know what had become of it.

Among the other orders a peremptory one was issued to let the fences alone, which caused much growling among the men for a day, as no means of obtaining wood for cooking purposes or pitching of tents are so convenient as from the common Virginia fence. On the second day, therefore, a delegation waited upon General Barnes with a request to be allowed to use the rails because other fire-wood was hard to obtain. His consent was finally granted to take only the top rail, which completely solved the difficulty. These Virginia fences are generally built eight rails high, run in a zig-zag manner so that the ends of one panel ride the ends of another, thus doing away with posts and post holes that are used in building fences in eastern Massachusetts.

Of course soon as all the fences thereabout were relieved of the eighth rail the seventh rail become the top one, which was also appropriated, and so on until all the rails disappeared while literally not infringing upon the orders of the general. He made a move to stop the mischief and caused several of the culprits to be sent to his headquarters, each with a rail across his shoulders, and among them was [John] McGinnis of my company, who acted as spokesman for the whole crowd.

"What does this mean," questioned General Barnes, in pretty severe tones, "did you not understand the orders to only take the top rail?"

"May it plase yer honor, gineral," replied McGinnis, "there were nary a bit of rail on top o' this when I tuk it."

General Barnes saw the point without further explanations, and sent them to their quarters and the rails were allowed to go too. That was the last we heard of the rail business, except to tell as a good joke on our old colonel, and he seemed to enjoy it as well as any one.

One of the brigades of this division had a little skirmishing with the rebels, up through the gap, the day that ours arrived, and the next day our regiment scoured the mountain on one side of the gap, sending skirmishers in all directions but found no signs of rebels. We left Snickers Gap on the 6th, marching 15 or 20 miles each day until the 9th when we camped near Warrenton . . . in the midst of a heavy snow storm. This white mantle covered the ground to the depth of three inches before morning, but the sun melted the last vestige of it during the following day. Our march to this place brought the regiment through Middleburg, which is one of the best looking places I have seen in the state, and also within 10 miles of the battle-field of Bull Run. There seems to be some fatality about Bull Run that causes the Army of the Potomac to look it up about three or four times a year, to see if it is yet on the map, or to make certain there are no rebels loafing near the place.

It may sound strange to you good people in the country towns of old Massachusetts, but the severest blow ever dealt the Army of the Potomac, or that ever can be aimed at it, has just fallen with crushing effect upon us: McClellan was superseded on November 10th by Burnside! I am fully aware of the sentiment about home in regard to "Little Mac," but if you could witness the feeling, and hear the talk in this army, as displayed and out-spoken during the past 15 days, it would frighten you. This protest extends from the higher officers in the saddle to the lowest private in the ranks, and among whom two sentiments are prominently expressed; first, that the game of politics will continue at Washington regardless of the consequences; and second, that the civil authorities who are in control are totally ignorant in this instance of the step they have taken.

Yes, this army has been deprived of its leader, and he took leave of us all, by riding the whole length of the ranks with uncovered head, while cheer after cheer followed his course, the men raising their caps from the ends of their bayonets, as high as they could swing them. It was the greatest ovation I ever knew any man to receive, or ever expect to see again. When Adjutant Baker undertook to read his farewell address to our regiment he broke down, and tears rolled down his cheeks upon the paper from that he was trying to read. I think every man in the ranks shed tears—the men who are in the habit of standing up to their duty, I mean, not the other kind.

Do you imagine that this disposal of McClellan, for which you non-combatants of the North are responsible, will hasten the time when the rebellion will be put down? You people about our homes, who have been clamoring so persistently against him, have now succeeded, but the mistake that has just been committed will surely result in some more "Popes." Wait and see!

The day following McClellan's farewell, we were notified that General Porter, our corps commander, was deprived of his command and ordered to Washington to answer to charges preferred by Pope. A petty man, Pope is, to prefer charges against Porter! Why, Porter has forgot more and learned more during the past year than Pope will ever know. The safest thing for the country to do next is to discharge this entire army, from the commanding general to the last drummer boy: send us home to take your places and let you come out and try this business awhile. There is considerable talk all through the camps that most of the higher officers are likely to resign their commissions.[6]

6. William Alderman's reaction to McClellan's removal was similar: "My courage is all gone and I don't care a little who gets whipped. The only man that ever done anything is circumscribed and not allowed to do a thing." William Alderman to his parents, November 10, 1862, William Alderman Papers, in private hands but a photocopy in FSNMPL. For a typical officer's reaction that confirms Mann's description of dissatisfaction among officers

We remained in and about Warrenton a week, then moved forward to this place, which is about two miles from Falmouth and on the opposite side of the Rappahannock from Fredericksburg. It has rained every day for the past week, and during that time I have not had a dry thread of clothing about me; however, it is not very cold so we pay but little attention to the wetting, though you would hardly know this was the same army which moved down the side of the Blue Ridge 20 days ago.

General Hooker is now in command of our corps, and is a general favorite with the army. If we could have had our choice after Porter we should have selected Hooker, so cannot find any fault with the commander of the 5th Corps. He has been christened "Fighting Joe," and I think he got it at Williamsburg.[7] I sincerely hope that in my next communication to your debating club I shall be able to speak a good word for our new commander, General Burnside, but since his management at Antietam we fear he is not the man for the place.[8]

Little need be added to the above except to note that the army was thoroughly organized, in good condition, 125,000 strong, and on December 1st lay along the northern bank of the Rappahannock, while receiving its supplies by the way of Aquia Creek—and undecided whether to construct winter quarters or attempt another move against Lee. The Confederate army occupied the heights on the south side of the river, evidently waiting to see what Burnside was there for.[9]

---

see John Gibbon to his wife, November 12, 1862, John Gibbon Papers, Historical Society of Pennsylvania.

7. Hooker would command the Fifth Corps for a short time only. He would rise to command of a Grand Division, and then, on January 26, 1863, to army command. During the Fredericksburg campaign, Major General Daniel Butterfield—a longtime presence in the First Division of the Fifth Corps (the Eighteenth's)—commanded the corps.

8. Alderman—"Sergeant Bill"—agreed entirely with Mann's assessment. See Alderman to his parents, November 27, 1862, Alderman Papers, FSNMPL.

9. In fact, Burnside had taken the army to Fredericksburg in an effort to cross the river quickly and move on Richmond. That the Confederates Mann saw had been given a chance to contest the Union crossing was due to one of the most spectacular logistical misunderstandings of the war, when the pontoons that were to have carried the Union army across the river were two weeks late. Lee and the Confederates—initially outmaneuvered by the Federals—used the grace period to establish a strong position on the south bank of the Rappahannock. Burnside was not deterred and would decide to force the matter anyway. The best treatment of Burnside before Fredericksburg in November 1862 is from James Ogden in "Prelude to Battle: Burnside and Fredericksburg, November 1862," in *Morningside Notes, An Occasional Publication of Morningside Bookshop*, Catalogue 23 (Dayton, n.d.), 3–12.

Burnside's move to Fredericksburg had been, in fact, wildly successful, leaving Lee and his army flatfooted and outmaneuvered. What Lee lost by Union maneuver, however, he gained back by Union mismanagement. The pontoon bridges that were to have carried the Army of the Potomac across the Rappahannock at Fredericksburg were late in arriving, and by the time they did arrive, Lee had recovered and placed his army squarely on the heights behind and south of Fredericksburg, awaiting the Union approach. To the astonishment of many, Burnside obliged Lee. (For Union commanders it was always a mistake to expect Lee to do what the Union commanders expected him to do; mistake turned to disaster when those Union army commanders did exactly what Lee hoped they would do. Such was the case at Fredericksburg.)

On December 11, the bloody crossing of the Rappahannock began. The city of Fredericksburg found itself devastated by this war as Union cannon tried to subdue Confederate harassment of the bridge builders by bombarding the place. Eventually, the Confederates yielded, the city smouldered, and preparations for the climactic battle progressed. The Eighteenth Massachusetts and the rest of what was now Barnes's brigade would be among the last of the Union troops to join the battle. Their late entry did not, however, spare them horror and suffering.

The last days of November and the first few in December were extremely cold for Virginia, and the Eighteenth, speaking for one regiment, suffered accordingly. Its camp was on a bleak elevation, with only the small, portable shelter tents for protection, and the raw winds swept the smoke of the camp-fires close to the ground so that it penetrated everything and everywhere. The rail fences had been quickly disposed of, which sent the soldiers to the woods for green timber, and that only increased the smoke nuisance four-fold. In three days the men were as black as the average "contraband," and their eyes were becoming red and inflamed from the acridity of the smoke thrown off from the multitude of great fires that were built in the efforts to keep warm. It was plain that a change of camp and conditions were crying necessities.

Undoubtedly the delay in building winter quarters was owing to the expectation of Burnside that he would be required to fight a battle before allowing the army to hibernate for the winter. However, General Barnes did not seem inclined to have the bleak experience of the year before repeated, so during the first week in December his brigade was moved down into quite a heavily timbered valley where the men were told to make themselves comfortable as possible, and here the Eighteenth built themselves log huts. These were fashioned to accommodate three, four, or more men, as messes could agree. Very few of them required more than two days to finish with open fire-places, bunks, wooden chimneys plastered with mud, and using the shelter tents that were stretched for roofs. Through these cloth roofs the only light of the several domiciles were obtained, except . . . from the sputtering blaze of green wood in the small fire-place, or a candle.[10]

Probably two reasons operated to produce haste and incompleteness in this first attempt of the regiment toward imitating the house-building of primitive man—a feeling that their inhabitation was uncertain and the "tender-foot" experience of most of the boys. They were made comfortable, however, by continual patching after having been deserted and reoccupied twice during this memorable winter, each time being materially improved over the original. But this camp will be referred to again. Meantime there are more stirring things brewing and, first, General Barnes and his brigade must do a little independent work of its own, a kind for which he was supposed to be peculiarly adapted else he would not have been so frequently selected.

Some eight miles from Falmouth an out-post of cavalry had been stationed, under the command of one [Captain] Johnson, at a place known as Yellow Chapel, and on the 28th of November the rebel Wade Hampton, with 200 of his cavalry, swooped down upon them and gobbled the whole crowd of men and horses, about a hundred of each. Undoubtedly Captain Johnson was wholly to blame as his duty called for special vigilance while, on the contrary, he was taken completely off his guard. Immediate dismissal from the army, and rightly, resulted in the case of this careless captain, but the affair called General Barnes to the scene post haste with his whole command.[11]

---

10. The winter camps of the Fifth Corps were located around Stoneman's Switch on the Richmond, Fredericksburg, and Potomac Railroad in Stafford County—astride modern Leeland Road. Many of the campsites from that winter still survive, though they are being lost to bulldozers weekly.

11. Captain George Johnson commanded a troop of the Third Pennsylvania Cavalry. His position at "Yellow Chapel"—better known as Hartwood Church—was on the western perimeter of the Union army; his job was to prevent precisely the sort of disaster that befell him on November 28. Johnson was promptly dismissed from the army on December 2, 1862. For perhaps the best account of this affair see William H. Powell, *The Fifth Corps* (Reprint, Dayton, 1984), 364–65. Hartwood Church still stands, about three hundred yards north of Route 17 (Warrenton Road), six miles west of Route 17's junction with Interstate 95. For

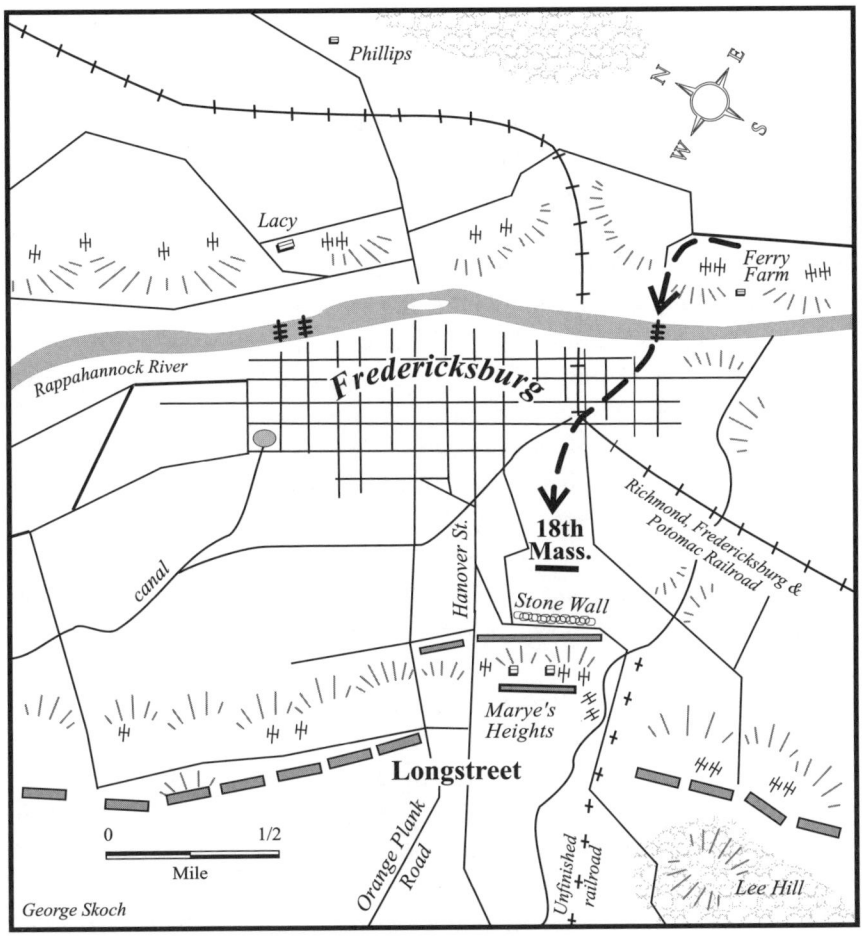

The Eighteenth Massachusetts at Fredericksburg.

With two day's rations, the brigade started out on what was known as a "secret mission" on December 1st, proceeding immediately to the spot where Hampton captured the Union cavalry. There it remained over night without catching a Johnny or seeing one, though "Jimmy Barnes" put up quite a job to entrap some of them. This was one of the times when the private soldier was taken just enough into the confidence of the officers to spoil the whole business, while there is little question that if the soldiers could have been told the ruse, the undertaking might have had a better showing of success—that is, if there had been any rebels thereabouts to act their part, which is doubtful.

In short, Barnes endeavored to set a trap for some rebels and bag a lot of them. To do this the seven regiments were put under cover of the woods, on three sides of an open field, where they were supposed to be completely sheltered from observation. At the same time a small show of force was made in one edge of this field as a bait to the Johnnies to make another swoop. The rank and file had an inkling of what was up though not enough to carry out their part well, as within an hour hundreds of fires were started for the purposes of warmth and boiling coffee, and these must have disclosed the presence of the whole brigade to any enemy who might be within miles of such a transparent trap. The next day the brigade returned to camp by the way it moved out while enjoying, all through the ranks, good-naturedly pointed jokes at the expense of "Jimmy Barnes" over his "rebel trap."

Before attempting to describe the part that the Eighteenth took in the wicked, uncalled-for, and murderous battle that was about to take place, it will be well to examine a little into the lay of the land, for in this instance it was spread out before the naked eyes of the privates almost as completely as through the commanding general's field-glass. As before stated, the Federal army was stretched along the north-eastern bank of the Rappahannock river, on the opposite side from the city, while the Confederates occupied the south-western and Fredericksburg side. On the Federal side the banks were 50 or 60 feet above the river, and rose as bluffs almost directly from the water's edge. Fredericksburg, in its best estate holding a population of 4,500, occupied a plain only a few feet above the water level of the river, and lay along the river's edge where there were a few primitive

---

more on the history of the church see Homer D. Musselman, *Stafford County in the Civil War* (Lynchburg, 1995), 91–92.

wharves for the landing of small sloops and schooners, for which the Rappahannock was navigable to this place.[12]

On the Fredericksburg side, the land did not rise into the heights occupied by the rebels until it had receded about a mile back from the city. This condition left a moderately rising plain, some nine miles long by one mile wide between the river and the fortified position of the enemy. . . . The position of Fredericksburg was so low that the Union army could look freely over it to the heights beyond. With this comprehensive view of the rebel position and—without the aid of field-glasses—the reception the Johnnies were preparing for the Yanks was nearly as well comprehended by the sergeants, corporals, and privates, as by those who rode horses and wore stars on their shoulders. When the rank and file were drawn up on the banks of the river during the 11th, 12th, and 13th of December, the general results were theoretically as certain to them as the practical demonstration proved.

The morning of December 13th was passed by the Eighteenth behind the artillery of the army [on the heights opposite Fredericksburg], from which it had been, [two days before], engaged in riddling the devoted city with shot and shell. Nearly 200 pieces were thus used [on the 11th] to drive 300 or 400 Johnnies out of the streets and houses from which they were pegging away at the Union engineers who were trying to bridge the river with pontoons. No doubt such a proceeding was good tactics, but before any impression was made upon the persistent enemy the 7th Michigan and 19th Massachusetts regiments had to be ferried across in pontoon boats and clear them out at the point of the bayonet.[13]

About one o'clock in the afternoon of the 13th Barnes's brigade crossed by the pontoon bridge leading over to the city, and lay along in its streets nearly two hours awaiting the orders to move out, which were received about three o'clock. Every man of the regiment knew the business that was at hand, and the chronic skulkers managed to lose themselves about the

12. Sitting just below the fall line of the Rappahannock, Fredericksburg had long had aspirations to be a major inland port. It succeeded in a measure—becoming a significant outlet for crops and goods from the Virginia Piedmont—but was vastly overshadowed by Richmond to the south and Alexandria to the north. For an excellent summary of pre- and wartime Fredericksburg, see the introduction to Noel G. Harrison, *Fredericksburg Civil War Sites*, Vol. 1 (Lynchburg, 1995).

13. In the original memoir, Mann placed this forced crossing on December 13, not December 11. On the morning of December 13, Barnes's brigade lay at "Ferry Farm," the childhood home of George Washington—just opposite the so-called "middle crossing." Carter, *Four Brothers in Blue*, 193.

houses and cellars of the place while the men who represented the Eighteenth unslung knapsacks, left them in the streets, and moved out to the rear of the city. In crossing the railroad immediately on the outskirts the shell from a rebel battery, which was posted on the heights nearly to the extreme left of their lines, plowed the ranks of the regiment twice. The movement across was so quickly executed, however, that but two shots were received before a cover from that battery was reached, though they made two bad gaps that were as quickly closed up.

The brigade marched partly through and across this railroad by the right flank, so when it was faced to the front it stood in line of battle facing the frowning, fortified rebel lines known as "Marye's Heights," which were from one-third to one-half mile away. The rising, sloping ground [in front of the heights] was already thickly strewn with the dead and dying, the debris of previous and unsuccessful charges against the gloating, insatiate enemy.

The lines were straightened up by the edge of the sluice-way or deep ditch, then ordered forward across it.[14] The scramble for the other side was a difficult one for its sides were so muddy and steep that the men had to help each other by pushing and lifting and pulling. Then the lines were straightened for the second time, while officers and men were gathering themselves for the charge that they well knew was to be immediately attempted.

The narrator, who was himself a participant in these scenes, and who is putting forth his best efforts to tell the simple, unvarnished truth, hesitates for the moment before marching himself and his comrades into the storm of death, overcome by his own memories of the terrible destruction that resulted. While the men of this brigade were sliding, and slipping and pulling each other across this ditch, they were sheltered from the enemy's fire by the slightly rising ground in their immediate front. But soon as the brigade was across and its lines corrected, the commanding voice of General Barnes was distinctly heard from one end of it to the other: "Attention, First Brigade! Trail,—arms! Forward,—march!" And soon as the first step

---

14. This millrace powered several factories in Fredericksburg. The three bridges spanning the race had been destroyed by the Confederates, leaving Union soldiers to either cross on the remaining stringers or ford the obstacle. Few features on any battlefield received more consistent mention in Union accounts than did this one. Harrison, *Fredericksburg Civil War Sites*, Vol. 2, 161–62.

or two forward was taken his voice again rang out: "Double-quick, First Brigade!—Charge!!!"¹⁵

With the full, round, vocal "hurrah" characteristic of Northern troops, the wild run was commenced for the stone wall that crowned the heights, and behind which the enemy was safely intrenched while delivering that murderous fire of musketry that swept these open fields with a hail-storm of lead. Four or five hundred yards from the starting point, one wing of the regiment encountered a high board fence that acted as an obstruction for a moment or two, and it also offered a target for the enemy whenever the heavy clouds of smoke opened a rift sufficient to uncover it. This fence was riddled with bullets like a sieve, and behind it was found a heavy windrow of dead, but onward was the word, and the section struck by the Eighteenth was soon knocked into kindling wood by the butts of its muskets, and the onward charge continued.¹⁶

Without disparaging any other regiment of the brigade, the whole seven doing well their duty, it is true that the Eighteenth—that is the few who were left of it—penetrated 50 yards nearer that formidable stone wall than any other troops that were hurled against it. No doubt General Barnes, who rode in the immediate rear of his old regiment, stimulated somewhat the determination of the men, but flesh and blood could not face the decimating fire and leave a live man to tell the story, and the line grew thinner and thinner until it practically melted away altogether.

The corporal says he went so near the stone wall, from behind which a constant flash of flame was leaping through the smoke, that unburned powder was blown into his face from the rebel muskets, and for a moment he stood alone enveloped in the stifling smoke without a comrade to be seen. Then he coolly turned about, deliberately retraced his steps for a few yards to where a number of his comrades were, and joined them in hugging the ground behind a slight hummock that afforded a little shelter from the leaden hail.

---

15. Barnes's brigade was ordered to relieve part of the Ninth Corps—Sturgis's division. *O.R.*, Vol. 21, 408–09.

16. The Eighteenth Massachusetts advanced virtually alone, having become separated from the rest of the brigade (to the Eighteenth's left) by as much as two hundred yards. Joseph Hayes, MS Journal Extracts, Joshua Chamberlain Papers, Library of Congress; Erastus W. Everson, "Forward Against Marye's Heights: The Last Onslaught at Fredericksburg—A Line of Dead Heroes," *Philadelphia Weekly Times*, March 4, 1882; *O.R.*, Vol. 21, 408–09.

Tom writes in a letter home:

> The first time we charged I fired once just as we turned to come back. Myself and Wm. Laird went further than any other man in the regiment. I think we went to within five rods [80 feet] of the stone wall, behind which the rebels were posted. I was hit five or six times by spent balls[;] two bullets smashed my rifle, one of them blowing the lock completely off. . . . Another bullet went completely through my tin dipper and haversack, going through a chunk of salt-pork and six thicknesses of woolen bag in which the pork was wrapped, and finally penetrated my overcoat. Amid such a perfect shower of bullets it was my luck to come off with my life.[17]

In a few minutes the remnant of the regiment was recalled in such a manner that the men scattered back to near the place where the board fence had been encountered. There the lines were partially reformed, the men turned about, and another attempt made to possess the stone-wall entrenchment of the enemy. In this second charge every member of the color-guard was shot down, and for a moment the regimental colors lay in the mud, but there were yet men left to bear them aloft and still others to follow and keep in touch with them.

Again the newly compacted lines of this brigade, which now presented more the appearance of a small regiment, were pushed back, decimated and torn by the deadly, leaden storm. The third time, the almost superhuman efforts of General Barnes succeeded in reforming his lines near the ditch at the foot of the slope, but the whole brigade presented the appearance of seven color-guards protecting the standards of the 18th and 22d Massachusetts, 2d Maine, 1st Michigan, 13th and 25th New York, and 118th Pennsylvania regiments.

"Forward, First Brigade!"—the general commanded for the third time, and it moved up again to the farthest point reached by the first charge. Only a few, however, penetrated that distance, and they scattered doggedly back to where quite a heavy line, made up of the remains of many regiments, lay behind a slight rise in the ground that was screening them from the withering fire. Behind this slight hummock-like ridge, a very respectable battle-line had voluntarily formed, beyond which it was practically

---

17. Mann to friends at home, December 17, 1862, Mann Papers. Mann's claim to have reached to within eighty feet of the stone wall is likely exaggerated. It is unlikely any Union soldiers approached so closely—though hundreds, like Mann, claimed to have done so. Still, the Eighteenth got as close as anyone did. The Eighteenth's attack took them past the Stratton House, whose pocked walls still stand on Littlepage Street in Fredericksburg. See George M. Barnard to his father, December 16, 1862, George Barnard Papers, Massachusetts Historical Society.

impossible to exist. It was on its belly, and digging and squirming itself into the muddy earth for protection, but with its face to the foe and loading and firing as rapidly as such a position would admit. To raise a head two feet from the ground was practical suicide.[18]

This line, which lay only 100 to 150 yards from the heavy and well protected rebel lines that were behind the stone wall, was held by this brigade for 46 hours, and the sixty rounds of ammunition that each man carried were discharged at the foe during this first evening and the next day. . . . Toward midnight of that day Humphrey's division silently stole out to this exposed position. . . . An hour or two later Humphrey's division was also withdrawn, and this battle was ready to be handed down into history.

Company "I" moved to this battle–field with 28 men, three of these were killed and 14 wounded, not counting the slight injuries that were only exhibited as marks of the storm.[19] The corporal showed six of them, not one of which was disabling—hence he was not counted in the returns of wounded. Probably no one of the company escaped without the marks of bullet or shell about his person or equipments, and this statement is representative of the casualties in the brigade.

Amid all this suffering, carnage, and death, the soldiers who hugged this muddy plain for 46 hours were quick to see fatalities that exhibited the shadow of a comical side and, strange as it may appear, such incidents stick to memory the longest. When, therefore, the participants in that bloody mistake of Burnside's are asked to recall the scenes, the serio-comic ones are first to spring forth.

While making the first charge toward the heights, during the moment's check caused by the board fence, the corporal was struck in such a manner as to suddenly force the breath from his body and double him into a heap on the ground. As he expressed it: "It felt as if a ball big as my fist went

18. Though the ground the Eighteenth crossed is now covered with houses, the "hummock" spoken of by Mann—as well as dozens of other men who owed their survival to it—is still visible on the streets of Fredericksburg, especially Mercer Street, just to the north (right) of the Eighteenth's position. The most vivid account of the postbattle ordeal on the battlefield is in Joshua Chamberlain, "My Story of Fredericksburg," *Cosmopolitan*, 1912, 148–59. For another excellent description of these assaults by a member of the Eighteenth see Barnard to his father, December 16, 1862, George Barnard Papers, Massachusetts Historical Society. Barnard recorded, "Col. Hayes threw his arms about me and almost cried at this wicked murder and it is no satisfaction to me that I led brave men to death. I wish no more responsibility."

19. Examination of the roster indicates that only one man was killed, fourteen wounded, and one missing.

through my body." It was but a minute before he regained his wind, examined damages, and found that a heavy bullet had passed through the tin dipper hanging to his haversack, penetrated through the contents of the haversack and flattened itself against the heavy brass fastening of his belt. The haversack had worked its way from the side where it belonged, to the front, and thus received the whole impact of the lead.

As he gathered himself to move forward, two bullets struck his musket so nearly together that he could not tell which came first. One hit the stock opposite the lock and carried the latter entirely away. The other bent and opened a rent near the muzzle of the barrel and clinched the bayonet to it in such a manner that they could not be wrenched apart. Plenty of good muskets were scattered about, and the corporal quickly appropriated one that was freely used a few minutes later. All this occurred within the space of three minutes, while a part of the line was pounding the boards from the fence with the butts of their muskets, and he was ready to move forward with his comrades. In firing his 50 rounds the next day, several different muskets were used, discarding one soon as it became so foul as to refuse duty, and seizing another that had been rendered useless by the death of its owner. In attempting to load one piece it proved so foul that the iron ram-rod could not be withdrawn, and rather than lose that round of ammunition ram-rod and all was discharged with good aim at the sheet of fire appearing along the top of the stone wall.

The sergeant [Alderman] acted as file-closer, whose duty it was to see that the men kept their places and did not get rattled. In the performance of this duty his special attention was given to one man who thus far had managed to shirk every fight, or appearance of a fight, and during the first charge his man was kept in place practically at the point of a bayonet. But, with the sergeant, he did some pretty tall sprinting when the regiment made its first partial break for the rear. For a minute or two they ran side by side, then suddenly the sergeant's protégé threw down his musket, leaped into the air and fell to the ground, limp and apparently lifeless. On rejoining the regiment where it was again reforming, the sergeant reported his man as dead as a herring, and expressed some compunctions over the part he played in the poor fellow's taking off. Two days later, while the non-com was in the act of telling the story of the incident, in walked his man without a scratch, but the general expressions of "disgusted delight" with which he was received were not calculated to raise him in his own estimation.

Company "I" had one little German soldier, not over five feet four inches in height, who was true grit clear through and who was not one of the reported wounded men. He could be depended upon to be in his place every time, and was holding up his end when that board fence was reached. Like the rest of the boys, he had to gasp for breath at times in the thick powder smoke, and during one of them a ball struck him a glancing blow in the mouth, breaking two of his teeth and spinning him round on the ground like a chicken with its head cut off. It dazed him for the moment, but quickly regaining both his senses and feet, and discovering that the only damage was the loss of two teeth, he shook his clenched hand at the enemy and, while spitting the blood and teeth from his mouth, sputtered:—"Py tam, I fights mit you now! I likes not ze doctors vat pulls me out doze teeth!"

While campaigning, old soldiers take good care that their canteens are kept full of water. While on the march every opportunity is improved to refill them, or empty and replenish with a fresher supply, well knowing that no combination of conditions will produce such a consuming thirst as the excitement of battle mixed with the suffocating smoke of burning powder. During the night and day and part of the second night that Barnes's brigade lay hugging the ground in front of Marye's Heights, the suffering from thirst was past understanding by any one who has not had a similar experience. By dark of the first night every canteen was empty. A few venturesome ones crawled back, under cover of the darkness, dragging a dozen canteens in their track, to find water at the foot of the hill, and they returned in the same manner, but this supply barely sufficed through the night.

The keenest suffering for water culminated during the afternoon and evening of the following day [December 14], when no movement could be made without attracting a hail-storm of lead from behind the stone wall. To the right, and only a few feet in the rear of that part of the prostrate line occupied by the Eighteenth, was a well, already choked by dead men, and one dead horse lay partly across it. Its water, which was found at a depth of 10 or 12 feet from the surface, was reddened with blood, and men revolted when its use was suggested. But it was the only supply within reach for more than 16 hours. It could be reached by crawling like a snake upon the ground without exposing enough of the person to present a target, and thirsty throats were producing a species of delirium. Toward the close of the day this thirst overcame all sense of smell, taste, or squirmishness, so the water was raised by stringing one canteen to another, and then drank.

Hugging the ground under ordinary circumstances, when it is dry and warm, is not hardship. The soldiers of '61 and '65 lived on the ground, slept on the ground, and at times ate and drank from the ground without growling. But the kind of ground the 1st brigade hugged in front of Marye's Heights was mattressed with about three inches of cold, slimy, sticky mud. The ground had been frozen to the depth of two or more inches; considerable snow had fallen [several days before], and during the two days this battle-field was occupied a cold fog pervaded everything, thawing the snow and frost into the characteristic Virginia mud, and it was working deeper and deeper every hour.

The Confederate forces were massed behind a heavy stone wall that was more than a mile in length, supplemented by fresh earth breast-works, from which the sloping fields in their front were swept by the muzzles of their rifles, and only under cover of night, or during the moments when the dense battle-smoke hid everything, could a movement be made. To illustrate: A few yards to the rear of Barnes's brigade, a horse had been lying all the morning apparently dead; finally it showed symptoms of life and made an effort to regain its feet, the next instant it was riddled with half a hundred bullets.

Off a mile or two to the right, near where the heights occupied by the rebels changed their direction toward the east, thus forming the northeastern angle of this battle-ground, they had posted a battery or two so that its use could make a clean sweep of a mile or more of the ground-hugging Union lines. Why those batteries were not more freely used could only be conjectured at the time, and Sergeant Bill declared: "Lee wants the fun of another set-to with this army, which he will miss if he annihilates it now." They did send a few shots with a fearfully raking effect on some of the lines, and about three in the afternoon a bursting shell from that direction carried the top half of a comrade's head clear away while spattering the corporal with his brains. Death was instantaneous, but our hero was obliged to keep the ghastly company of the slain within the reach of his hand for several hours.

Incidents of this character might be told to fill a volume, but enough have been repeated to convey some idea of the conditions thrown about one part of this battle that has been passed into history as "Burnside's Slaughter Pen."[20]

20. For a summary of the condition of the Eighteenth after Fredericksburg, including a complete list of casualties, see the *Boston Herald*, January 7, 1863.

SEVEN

Mud and Renewal

The horrors of Fredericksburg were but prelude to more struggles. Ambrose Burnside sought redemption and recovery for the army, not in rest, but in a new campaign. In mid-January the army hauled itself out of its camps again for a new campaign. This time nature intervened. Days of rain turned Virginia's roads to quagmires. The Union army slogged to a halt, knee-deep in the mud that Mann so loved to describe but so hated to experience. Most soldiers would have agreed that the spectacle of one hundred thousand Union troops wallowing for days would have been humorous had it not been so serious and miserable (though certainly the Confederates found great joy in the debacle!). The failed "Mud March" marked Burnside's end and in many respects constituted the nadir of the Army of the Potomac's experience. That winter had all the appearance of being, as one man put it, "the Valley Forge of the War." Lamented another, "Oh my country, how my heart bleeds for your welfare."[1]

Before the men's boots were dry after the Mud March, the army received a new commander—"Fighting Joe" Hooker. Despite his moniker, Hooker's greatest contribution to the Army of the Potomac would come not on the battlefield, but in the army's winter camps during the early months of 1863. Hooker tended mostly to simple things long overlooked. Regiments were paid (many after seven months without pay); fresh bread appeared in camp; furloughs became available; sanitation improved (Hooker went so far as to order the entire army to bathe in early April). He also instituted a popular system of corps badges and staged prominent reviews. By April, he had taken a grumbling army on the edge of functional collapse and turned it back into a splendid fighting machine. As it

---

1. Daniel Woodward, ed., "The Civil War of a Pennsylvania Trooper," *Pennsylvania Magazine of History and Biography*, 87 (1963): 51.

would prove, however, Hooker—like McClellan—would be better at creating the machine than using it.

Though Mann and the men of the Eighteenth clearly appreciated Hooker's organizational efforts, they did not embrace their new commander—or for that matter any commander—with the same fervor they had McClellan. Pining for McClellan was a popular pastime in the army that dreary winter, and Mann shared in it wholeheartedly. He also engaged those at home in some lively debates about slavery, politics, Copperheads, and the course of the war. Mann's musings on these subjects are a useful summation of the momentous gulf that rent Northern society in early 1863.

More important to the army's health than any of Hooker's reforms was the mere chance for extended rest. Until the end of the Mud March, the army had been campaigning almost constantly since early March of 1862. Its longest respite had come after Antietam, and that respite lasted weeks rather than the requisite months. Rest was a balm that corrected many ills—physical and mental—and by the time the leaves burst to green in late April, the Army of the Potomac was, as one man recorded, ready to "make Richmond howl."[2]

During the latter half of the night of December 14, and until near noon of the 15th, the few soldiers of the Eighteenth who had kept in touch with their regimental colors slept in the open streets of Fredericksburg. Perhaps there were a hundred of them, maybe not more than eighty, but they slept the sleep of men who felt that their duty had been performed to the last requirement of human endurance and patriotism. The nerve tension of the past 48 hours was relaxed, but the exhaustion produced by it had drawn deep lines in the faces of even the 20-year old boys. They were thankful for the freedom afforded from the strife, though their beds were made on the hard, stone pavements of this old aristocratic city.

In the afternoon Barnes's brigade returned to its camps on the peaceful side of the river. Before morning of the 16th the rest of the army did likewise and pulled its pontoon bridges up after itself. The thrashing it had received did not endear the commanding general's [Burnside's] personality

---

2. Numa Barned (Seventy-third Pennsylvania) to his sister Emma, March 27, 1863, Numa Barned Papers, Clements Library, University of Michigan. For a complete summary of the army during the winter and spring of 1863 see John Hennessy, "We Shall Make Richmond Howl: The Army of the Potomac on the Eve of Chancellorsville," in Gary Gallagher, ed., *The Chancellorsville Campaign* (Chapel Hill, 1996), 9–14.

to brigade, regimental, company, or individual memories, and the Eighteenth did its share of criticizing his tactics. The sergeant, with an emphasis that verged on the profane, allowed that, though honest enough, he did not know enough to lead a drove of steers from one Berkshire hill to another without losing half of them. The sergeants have the first rights of opinion in the rank and file, but the corporals come in a close second and the sergeant's right hand corporal [Mann] thought it about time Burnside superseded Halleck, as that general-in-chief knew more things that weren't so than any man with stars on his shoulders, and he needed a rest. Besides, Burnside was a very imposing looking man on horseback.

But the Army of the Potomac had this "imposing" looking man with it still, and a more strategic move than the "slaughter-pen" variety was to be attempted before his final leave-taking.

For a month, however, the army settled into the winter quarters it had constructed, sadly missing the comrades left on the other side of the river but hoping and praying that the majesty of the government, to whom these sacrifices were being made, would find a leader who could at least move pawns, castles, knights, and bishops with sufficient skill to prevent being check-mated for a few months—even if he could not administer one to General Lee. Meantime, General Barnes and his brigade must have their little outing again, all by themselves.

It was only a scouting expedition, this time, to the opposite side of the Rappahannock—perhaps undertaken as much to give the men a little exercise and change as for any definite purpose.[3] [The expedition] required a march of 12 or 15 miles up the river on the 30th of December. We forded where the water was waist-deep and so cold that the ice must be broken except where the current was running swift enough to carry men off their feet. Then came a cold, cheerless camp where the night was used up in thawing and drying the effects of the wintry river. Considerable moving about from one place to another [on the rebel side of the river] was the program of the next day . . . The next night we re-forded the same river to the safer side, and another thawing and drying; then a return to camp on

---

3. The expedition was in fact part of a grand scheme by Burnside to renew the offensive against Lee. Barnes's division and William W. Averell's brigade of cavalry would provide an upstream diversion while the main force crossed about six miles below Fredericksburg. The offensive would be aborted by Lincoln himself—and so it seemed to the men of the Eighteenth that their chilly march had no purpose. A. Wilson Greene, "Morale, Maneuver, and Mud: The Army of the Potomac, December 16, 1862–January 26, 1863," in Gary Gallagher, ed., *The Fredericksburg Campaign* (Chapel Hill, 1995), 180–81.

New Year's day, 1863. It has been disputed that men can sleep while carrying muskets and other equipments of soldiers and keep their places in the ranks of a moving column, but men did sleep during the march back to Falmouth on the first morning of that new year.[4]

January 8th, the 5th Corps was reviewed by General Burnside, a premonitory symptom of another campaign, and the boys began to speculate as to where next, but without a shadow of enthusiasm. Dissatisfaction, homesickness, and discouragement had settled over all like the chilling fog clouds so prevalent during a Virginia winter. At this review it was discovered that General Meade had been placed in command of the corps—a man little known by the rank and file, so they had no criticisms to offer at the time.[5]

The next day a lot of packages and boxes, which had been accumulating in Washington, were brought out to the regiment and eight or ten of them fell into the lap of company "I." They had been packed by loving hands at home, and many were six weeks overdue, but the most pathetic feature centered about one box received by this company that was directed to one of its members whose dead body was left in front of Marye's Heights a month before. Its contents were divided among his messmates, except the little keepsakes, which were returned to the tender hands that sent the box on its mission.

On the 16th [of January], orders were issued to strike the camps and be ready to move the following day, but by the time the comfortable quarters were well demolished the order was changed to the 18th, and again changed to the 20th, thus keeping the army in a state of hesitating expectancy for three days. This early breaking up of camps, and the restless

---

4. The camp of the Eighteenth Massachusetts was in fact located about three miles northeast of Falmouth, though Falmouth constituted the heading for most of Mann's letters during the winter of 1862–1863. Mann visited the village of Falmouth rarely, calling it a "a sunken, dirty hole." Mann to friends at home, January 16, 1863, Mann Papers.

5. George Gordon Meade replaced Daniel Butterfield as Fifth Corps commander in late December—the fourth commander the Fifth Corps had had since November 1 (Porter, Hooker, Butterfield, and now Meade). A Philadelphian and a career officer in the Topographical Engineers, Meade had offered steady but unspectacular service to this point in the war. A member of Lincoln's cabinet observed him to be "a tall, thin man, rather dyspeptic, I should suppose from the fits of irritation to which he was subject. He was totally lacking in cordiality toward those with whom he had business. . . . He was an intellectual man, and agreeable to talk with when his mind was free, but silent and indifferent to everybody when he was occupied with that which interested him." George Meade, *The Life and Letters of George Gordon Meade* (Reprint, Baltimore, 1994), Vol. 2, 341–42; Charles A. Dana, *Recollections of the Civil War* (Reprint, New York, 1963), 171–72.

moving about of the different regiments, in itself would have given ample notice to the enemy that a move was about to take place. But there were also plenty of apparently half-witted country people within Burnside's lines to whisk accurate information across to their friends every few hours, so if the hero of Fredericksburg dreamed for a moment that any move he could make would surprise the enemy, he knew even less than the soldiers he commanded gave him credit.

He did, nevertheless, take the enemy by surprise, but the character of it was so ludicrous that instead of giving him battle the Johnnies put their fingers to their noses and wiggled them at his army.

Both the sergeant and the corporal have expressed themselves freely in their different descriptions of this short campaign; the one was in a mood to give the comical side while the other gave a gloomy one to friends at home. They practically slept under the same blanket, drank from the same canteen, went out on the campaign together and returned from its arduous duties side by side. It was only their temperaments and moods at the time of writing that differed, for both wrote the literal truth, and both descriptions are necessary to make the picture of "Burnside stuck in the mud" complete.

The sergeant prefaces his narrative with a short prelude on the peculiar mud of Virginia. This mud subject has already been touched upon several times as playing an important part in the movements and comforts of the army, for it rarely moved without being vexed by its depths and adhesiveness. But the changes cannot be too frequently rung on that important factor if one wishes to comprehend a soldier's life between November and May in Virginia. The sergeant says:

> The winter season in Virginia is very properly called the "rainy season." The snow-fall here in New England is the rain-fall there; and the frost of winter that penetrates and freezes the ground here frequently one, two and even three feet deep, there seldom gets as many inches. Besides, the "sacred soil" is a very peculiar soil. It isn't like any other soil, at least any Massachusetts soil. The clay of Virginia is the most adhesive, the most tenaciously sticky that ever was, and will get pasty like dough with very little wetting. When in this condition anything coming in contact with it becomes more entirely besmeared than would be believed by one who had never experienced its peculiar property of stickiness.
>
> A shoe or boot once sunk in its soft depth, requires a surprising amount of muscle to extract it, and when extracted it is a sight that is calculated to inspire remarks that are forcible, if not elegant. All these peculiarities were well known to the men who composed the Army of the Potomac. They had

had many a wrestle with it, and knew, or thought they knew, all about it. Alas, how easy a thing it is to be deceived! There were degrees to the compound that had not been tested, and depths they had never sounded—as the near future was soon to teach them.

In the afternoon of what had been a very bright and pleasant January morning [January 17], the bugle sounded the assemble, and we got the order to prepare for marching at once with several day's rations and an unheard-of number of rounds in our cartridge boxes. Tents came down in a hurry that had cost us a good deal of hard labor to prepare, for we had expected that we were in camp for the winter and had "fixed up" accordingly with quite elaborate log-houses with chimneys and fire-places "built in" of sticks laid "cob-house" fashion, and thickly cemented with mud, of which we always had enough; and over all canvas was stretched for roofing. But all that went for nothing. The order was to strike tents, and down they came, with many remarks as an accompaniment that sounded like "More blamed fool business!" "New pastures for Father Abraham's pet lambs," etc.—for the boys were given to making remarks on occasions that didn't meet their unqualified approval.

It was near the middle of the afternoon, three days later, before we started on our January campaign. The road was full of men, artillery, baggage and ammunition trains and all that pertains to a moving army, so much so that we made very little progress, most of the afternoon being passed in waiting for what was in front of us to get out of the way and give us the road. So that night found us only 2½ miles from the old camp. Meanwhile, the clerk of the weather had been getting in his fine work, and by the time we filed out of the road and went into camp close by, the ominous, dismal-looking clouds began to dribble. We pitched our little A tents as best we could, lighted fires and cooked our coffee and ate our primitive meal, filled our pipes and smoked in solemn silence over the situation. Before our evening smoke round the campfire was fairly concluded the dribble became a deluge and we crawled under our little shelters, made everything as snug as possible, and composed our eyes and limbs to sleep.

There is something fascinating in such a bivouac notwithstanding its discomforts. The weird blackness of night, now and again lit up by the fitful flickering of the camp-fires, the wind sighing in solemn cadence through the tree-tops, the pattering of the rain upon the frail canvas under which we lie, and withal the sense of weakness and littleness as the dense pall of darkness over and around all draws its impenetrable curtain and gloomy night reigns over the sleeping thousands.

Oh, yes, there is a side to "grim war" that is not all stern reality. There are times when imagination runs rampant, and the poor, tired body forgets its weariness, its aches and pains, while the mind contemplates the mysterious and hidden by which we are surrounded, and loses itself in the vast unknown. And so the night passed with the "Storm King" abroad, and the morning showed that the pattering rain of the beginning had developed into the pelting, pitiless downpour that defied our best efforts at keeping dry.

It looked discouraging—everything did. It was depressing, as all limp and sodden we tried to coax the damp and dying embers of our camp-fires into life and warmth again, and many a "blankity-blank" should occur in a faithful portrayal of the remarks and conversation indulged in while the boys, with very indifferent success, attempted the boiling of coffee and frying of pork.

If I remember rightly, it was Sergeant Bly[6] who was wrestling with the problem of making his coffee boil and whose mind was evidently harking back to times when he had helped to sing in the "revival meetings" at home, broke out with: "Oh, that this dry and barren ground in springs of water might abound, and fruitful soil beco . . ." He was promptly suppressed right there and given to understand that anything more in that line wouldn't be tolerated.

And now troops began to move along the road and take up the line of march again. And what a crowd they were! A soldier's skin is supposed to be water-proof and shed rain like a duck's back, but this beat everything and penetrated everything. Of course, we got our marching orders, too, and joined the procession. By this time the road was a sight to behold. With every added footstep, either of man or beast, the mud took on a somewhat different consistency—got just a little thinner, and penetrated down a little further, while the artillery and wagon-trains sunk deeper and deeper. The teamsters shouted and applied their whips with many an expletive; the marching column of infantry as it floundered on shouted out taunts and jibes at the stranded wagoners and artillery drivers, glad to see those whom they considered as generally having a "soft snap" in such a predicament, while the wheels of all of them sank down clean to the hubs, and no amount of shouting profanity would induce them to make another revolution. I actually saw mule teams so utterly discouraged that after being unhitched from the wagons they refused to budge, and either stood knee-deep in the mud or lay down in it. And still it rained! It came down in sheets, and it came down in continuous streams. There wasn't any "let up"—it just kept right at it and improved every moment . . .[7]

The progress made the second day was about the same as the first. It being quite impossible to get on, we were ordered into camp, having made

---

6. Sergeant Ezra K. Bly, a twenty-one-year-old "tinman" from New Bedford had been wounded at Fredericksburg the previous month. He would serve out his entire term of service.

7. The original included another paragraph following this—an expostulation of an old Methodist yarn that, while amusing, simply breaks the narrative. It has been deleted here.

but little more than two miles, perhaps five miles from the old camp. And still it rained just as hard as ever. The road by this time had become a raging sea of mud—quite thin and liquid on top, but growing thicker the further one sank in it. Night came on and still no signs of a let-up. We were near the Rappahannock and the Johnnies were on the other bank. Their pickets on the opposite side caught on to the situation, and they painted on a board in large letters, "Burnside stuck in the mud." This they set up conspicuously where the "Yanks" could see it, and thus the famous campaign of General Burnside was named by the rebels themselves. It proved to be a name that "stuck," and was always referred to by that title.

Another morning came, and still it poured. Things began to look serious. The question of subsistence began to demand attention, for rations had run low, and there was no way of getting more. Something had to be done at once, and so the whole army was set to work corduroying the road back to camp. A corduroy road is built by cutting small trees, say six to eight inches thick, into lengths of 10 feet perhaps, and laying these sticks or small logs side by side [across the road] close to and touching each other. This makes a continuous "log road" which gives a surface over which trains and artillery can be moved, even if the mud is hub deep. And that is just what the army was set to doing, the idea being to corduroy the whole five miles back to camp. Still it rained; but when one is just as wet as one can be, it goes without saying he can't be any wetter. So we worked with a will to get a way back to camp and subsistence. This we accomplished after being away just four days, and as we once more began to set the old camp in order the clouds rolled away and the "glad and glorious sun" once more showed his face.

The corporal says:

As we were drawn up in line ready to move, about one o'clock on Tuesday (which was January 20th) an order was read from General Burnside informing us "that we were about to meet the enemy again, face to face; that their army on the Rappahannock had been weakened by our recent successes in North Carolina and the Southwest, and now is the time to strike the deathblow of the rebellion in Virginia."

This order was received in perfect silence; not a cheer, not a response except the suppressed, undertone mutterings such as: "Another political move!—more blundering!—the army won't fight!" How different was the reception of an order, any order, read at the head of the Eighteenth from McClellan's hand!

We were soon on the move in the direction of Hartwood Church while every man was growling and snarling, or else glum and "stuffy." No matter what or where the movement was headed for, any disinterested party could have gathered from the demeanor of the men that nothing but defeat would result. The thinking volunteers wondered at the hardihood of a man who dared undertake to lead such a disgruntled force.

Before we had marched two miles it commenced to rain, and it was apparent to a number two private in the rear rank that we should get stuck in the mud. Did not get three miles from camp before it was night and we went into camp in a pine forest where every blessed mother's son of the Eighteenth found wood ticks sticking all over them in the morning. Boiling coffee with green wood during a drenching rain, is not fun, and trying to find rest during a long winter's night with every thread of clothing wringing wet is discouraging, and waking from a fitful sleep to find one's body one-third submerged in a puddle of water is a forceful reminder of rheumatism, but such is a soldier's lot.

Next morning we packed up in the rain, and after wringing all the water possible from blankets and clothing, the moisture that would not wring added many pounds to the shoulder-pack. We tried to move forward, but did not get a foot until afternoon because the roads were already blocked with artillery and supply-trains. Then we managed by jerks and stops and starts to hitch along a couple of miles when, the second night overtaking us, we camped in the woods again.

On the morning of the 22d, it was found that the army was stationary, with its artillery strung all through the country, to the hubs in the mud, and settling deeper every hour. The supply trains were also immovable, and the pontoon train, which was near the river, was under the command of General Lee instead of Burnside, as the former had covered it with his guns.

The Eighteenth had succeeded in marching five miles during two days, and it had been two as hard day's marching as we ever put in. Standing in the marching column, loaded with from 60 to 80 pounds of baggage and equipments, everything wet as water can make it, is more exasperating and fatiguing than a good swinging march. The uncertainty whether the halt of the column will be for one minute or forty keeps the soldier on his feet, shifting his load from one shoulder to the other. If we conclude to unsling knapsacks to rest aching shoulders and stretch ourselves upon the ground to relieve aching legs, there may be only time to draw one sigh when: "Attention,—company,—forward,—march!"—brings the column to its feet, and on we go for a few hundred yards, to have the same tactics repeated again and again.

In the course of the day we were informed that the troops would be allowed to find their way back to camp in the best possible way but the artillery and supply trains must go first. So the roads were corduroyed; the men took the places of horses and mules, pried and pulled guns, caissons, cracker and ammunition wagons upon the log roads. The pontoons were left behind, and it is reported that General Lee sent his compliments to General Burnside, accompanied by the tender of 20,000 picked men to help us out of the mud.[8]

It is currently reported that our corps has lost 3,000 men by desertion during the past two weeks, 300 having taken that kind of leave from one regiment. The Eighteenth has lost less than a dozen by desertion . . . but hundreds of horses and mules have gone under. I crawled into the log hut left in camp near Falmouth on the 20th toward night on the 25th, pretty well discouraged with the whole blamed business.[9]

Nature beneficently interposed to prevent a serious blunder on the part of the commander of the army in his second attempt to demonstrate how a thing should not be done, and before his army was extricated from the mud he wrote an order, subject to the approval of the President of the United States, dismissing from the service every important officer under his command.[10] Of course the President disapproved it and, in its stead, immediately accepted the resignation of this disappointed commander. This sweeping order that was never issued was quite comprehensive but not comprehensive enough to suit the rank and file. It stopped at the rank of brigadier general. To have included all of the army that took no stock in his abilities it should have been extended down through and included the colonels, majors, captains, sergeants, corporals, and high privates. If such commanders were the best that the government could furnish, the army was ready to go home.

But the President had discovered this state of feeling in the army and probably gave it the best man who was then within its lines to reorganize and re-establish its morale, General Joe Hooker—the very man who headed the list in Burnside's sweeping order. He assumed the command January 26. Next to McClellan, Hooker organized and enthused the army

---

8. Not literally true, but no doubt offered by one of the Confederate wags watching from the south side of the river.

9. By far the best modern discussion of the Mud March can be found in Greene's "Morale, Maneuver, and Mud," in Gallagher, ed., *The Fredericksburg Campaign*, 171–217.

10. General Orders Number 8, composed on January 23 but never issued, called for the dismissal from the army of generals Hooker, W. T. H. Brooks, John Newton, and John Cochrane—all intriguers of the first order. Burnside also sought to reassign Generals William B. Franklin and William F. Smith, both of the Sixth Corps, and Samuel Sturgis and Edward Ferrero of the Ninth Corps. Burnside presented the order in person for Lincoln's approval, indicating that if the president found the order objectionable, then he (Burnside) would be compelled to resign. Lincoln elected not to approve the order and reassigned Burnside to duty elsewhere. O.R., Vol. 21, 998–99. For a complete discussion of this unprecedented episode see Greene, "Morale, Maneuver, and Mud," in Gallagher, ed., *Fredericksburg Campaign*, 209–11.

better than any other in its history, and it was only a few days before his hand was apparent in showing a regard for the comfort and welfare of the men by ordering better rations, inspections of the camps to see that the men were comfortably housed, and by instituting a system of furloughing the men, in their turn, for ten or twelve days that they might have an opportunity of visiting their homes.[11]

By March 30th, reorganization was complete, and well tried men [were] in command of the different corps except, perhaps, that of the 11th. Generals Butterfield and Warren were included in the formation of Hooker's personal staff, with the first named as chief, and in these two he had able advisers. Butterfield was well known throughout the 1st division of the 5th Corps from the beginning as commander of the third brigade, which contained two or three crack regiments that were more persistently drilled even than "Jimmy Barnes' " prize regiment of the 1st brigade.[12]

A system of corps badges was devised by Butterfield that designated the organization to which every soldier belonged. It was ordered to be worn in the centre of the top of the cap, and proved a most excellent mark in aiding stragglers to find their place. [The badges] also assisted the provost marshal and his aids in placing a class of men who displayed no special anxiety in regard to where they belonged, and this devise also acted as a check upon line officers who were lax in regard to straggling. The 5th Corps badge was a Maltese cross; 1st, a circle; 2d, a clover leaf or ace of clubs; 3d, a diamond; 6th, a square cross; 11th, a crescent; 12th, a star; these constituted the army of the Potomac. The first division of each corps was red; 2d, white, and 3d, blue. All the corps throughout the Union armies soon adopted a distinctive badge, in imitation of the Army of the Potomac, for other commanders were quick to perceive the advantages thus afforded.

Heretofore the cavalry arm of the service had been the laughing-stock,

11. The reforms instituted by Hooker—and their dramatic positive effect on the army—are most completely documented in John Bigelow, *Chancellorsville* (Reprint, New York, 1995), 39–51. See also Hennessy, "We Shall Make Richmond Howl," in Gallagher, ed., *The Chancellorsville Campaign*, 9–14.

12. Many of those who worked closest with Butterfield had a far less charitable opinion of him. Fifth Corps artillery officer Charles Wainwright said of him, "Butterfield has not made so good a chief of staff as I expected. Much to my surprise he does not seem to have practical common sense in all points, the very trait of character it was supposed he would excel. He is most thoroughly hated by all the officers at headquarters as a meddling, overconceited fellow." Butterfield was, in 1862, the fastest-rising citizen soldier in the army, moving from regimental to corps command in a year. Allan Nevins, ed., *A Diary of Battle: The Personal Journals of Colonel Charles S. Wainwright, 1861–1865* (New York, 1962), 215.

like Sergeant Bill's Lancers over which he grew so sarcastic, and a dead cavalry-man was so rare that neither the sergeant or corporal had yet seen one. The cavalry's use seemed to be wholly monopolized in adding eclat to the several staffs of the brigadier and major-generals, while the general commanding utilized full half of the available sabre-jinglers to keep him from getting lonesome. Hooker changed all this while organizing the cavalry into a corps under the command of General Stoneman, so that eventually it became a match for the Confederate horsemen under Stuart.[13]

Another noticeable improvement instituted was the effectual check put upon the spy system, which thus far had been able to report to the authorities at Richmond every order issued or move contemplated in ample season to give the Johnnies all the information they could possibly desire. It was not wholly stopped, for the enemy had a well organized bureau of information at Washington, and the War Department was not yet conducted on military principles—politics still having precedence. The dashing rebel cavalry leaders, by their frequent raids about the army, also kept General Lee well informed, but General Hooker imitated him in his organization of the Federal cavalry, so that very soon some dashing leaders began to develop to match the enemy.[14]

Heavy details were made every day to corduroy the roads for miles in all directions leading out from the camps, and quite a system of earthworks was thrown about the positions occupied by the several corps. At least two corps were detached and sent to other parts of the country.[15] Some recruits were received by the various regiments, the Eighteenth obtaining about 100 from among their immediate acquaintances in Massa-

13. In fact, the organization of the cavalry had been evolving steadily since 1861. Hooker's move to establish a corps of cavalry culminated that process, which had seen the cavalry go from operating in detachments of a regiment or two, to organization as brigades under Pope, to the establishment of divisions. The "dashing" leaders under development would not reach the top of the command structure until late 1863 and 1864. For the moment, the army's cavalry would be commanded by Brigadier General George Stoneman.

14. Hooker's redoubled efforts at intelligence gathering and security are emphasized strongly throughout Stephen Sears's excellent new study, *Chancellorsville* (New York, 1996). Hooker appointed Colonel George H. Sharpe of the 120th New York as the director of the new "Bureau of Military Information." Sharpe performed his job admirably. Ibid., 68–70, 100–02, 130–31, 391–92. The "imitations" Mann refers to were two cavalry raids undertaken by Hooker. The first culminated in the Battle of Kelly's Ford, March 19, 1863. The second was "Stoneman's Raid," an attempted raid deep behind Lee's lines as the army moved into action at Chancellorsville. The raid failed to achieve its lofty goals. See A. Wilson Greene, "Stoneman's Raid" in Gallagher, ed., *Chancellorsville Campaign*, 68–98.

15. Only one corps was detached—the Ninth. It would return to the Army of the Potomac in 1864.

chusetts. And squad, company, and battalion drills were taken up in an efficient manner, though not with that absorbing interest, perhaps, by the old soldiers as during the previous year.

Picket duty was performed along the banks of the Rappahannock with an earnestness and calmness quite different from the feverish, nervous manner of the first year of soldiering. The Johnnies had discovered that the Yanks could and would fight, and the latter began to acknowledge in their letters to friends at home that it took all of one Yank to whip a Johnnie, or anyhow, that one at a time was enough to tackle with any promise of success. In fact the two armies that stood facing each other, with only the Rappahannock flowing between, were beginning to entertain a decided respect for each other. Only the pickets ventured to the water's edge on either side, and in several places the river narrowed so that the lines were separated by less than 200 yards. This gave an opportunity among the privates to swap gossip with the enemy at various times and in favorable places where, by common consent, firing at each other was omitted for weeks at a time.

The alertness and watchfulness of either picket force was not abated one iota while the Blue and the Grey found these opportunities to exchange coffee for tobacco. To facilitate these exchanges, [one or the other] tossed a stone with a twine attached across the river, thus establishing a rope ferry—very efficient for towing small packages from shore to shore. As on the Potomac several months before, so now on the Rappahannock, officers must keep out of sight or become targets for rifle-shooting.

Foggy weather along the river banks was the rule, and a conversation was easiest carried on when the fog shut down so thick as to hide one bank from the other. Then it became a good conductor of sound, and transmitted it across the water more readily than in any other direction. On the Fredericksburg side one of the piers of the burned rail-road bridge was usually occupied by a small squad of Johnnies, while directly opposite on the Falmouth side a picket post of Yanks was comfortably installed under the bluffs. At this place badinage and repartee were freely swapped and, though never taking on a very serious character or showing any temper except with a sarcastic cast, at times "twitted" pretty closely upon the actual condition of things as, for instance:

"Uncle Robert is kinder inquirin when you alls are going to get ready to give we'uns another try."

"Oh, well neow, don't yer go ter borrowin no sort of trouble on that pint. If yer wants to take a turn come right over hier any day."

"Seems you'uns kinder pettered out, tired like, I recon, trying to flank Uncle Robert."

"Tired nothin,—tired of flanking yer d——d mud!"

"When you alls gwin to look roun Bull Run some more?"

"Well, Johnnie, 'bout the time yer Uncle Bob wants ter take 'nother look at Baltimore."

"You alls Yanks talks too much; you'uns no fighters, nohow."

"I say, Greyback, why don't yer drive us out'en yer front yard and give a feller a chance to get shook of yer sacred soil?"

"Maybe Uncle Robert knows the lay of these plantashuns a heap sight better than you alls."

"How did yer Uncle Bob like Maryland?"

"We'uns calculated to be a heap hungry and called round that thar country for raciness."

"Well, Johnnie, yer got yer 'raciness.' Ye going ter git hungry agin soon?"

The Johnnies did get hungry again sooner than was expected—but this kind of picket duty was decidedly different from firing by platoons on negro huts a year before.

April 22d, Tom wrote to his mother: "I little incident occurred here a few days ago that has attracted considerable interest throughout our corps—a corporal of the 118th Pennsylvania regiment gave birth to a bouncing baby. Both are doing well though still confined to the hospital. The story is that she followed her lover by enlisting in the same regiment, unbeknown to him; was soon promoted to the rank of corporal and about to be commissioned when this unusual thing took place. She must have been a plucky woman, and I think she has earned a commission."[16]

Under the same date, replying to a recommendation from his father to study the "Report of the Committee on the Conduct of the War," he writes: "I have read enough of the committee's report to become completely disgusted with it. It shows profound ignorance of military affairs in general, and of McClellan's case in particular, and there are statements made in that report that I know to be false of my own personal knowledge. That report only proves the bitter-differences existing between the Republican and Democratic parties; that the politicians at Washington have taken the pains to distinguish between a republican and a democratic general, and set them to pulling each other's hair."[17]

16. This blessed event is confirmed by other sources. See Samuel S. Partridge to his brother, April 10, 1863, Samuel S. Partridge Letters, FSNMPL.

17. The Joint Committee on the Conduct of the War was created in late 1861 to oversee the Union war effort and to expunge from it the incompetent or questionable. As the war progressed, it became a highly partisan organization—dominated by radical Republicans—

During the three months that the army lay comparatively inactive about Falmouth under the command of Hooker, both the sergeant and corporal discussed the situation of things pretty freely, besides keeping their friends at home well informed—at least of their individual opinions. These were, of course, shaded and influenced to a great extent by the consensus of the general discussions among their comrades, and by snatches of conversations that were overheard from time to time at brigade and corps headquarters; both our heroes were in the receptive ages of their lives when knowledge was rapidly absorbed. Evidently they had not been asleep during the 18 months just passed, for their voluminous correspondence shows rapidly maturing habits of comprehending things.

Wrote Tom to his mother in March:

> You spoke about my Semi Secession views. Mother, little do you know the state of mind the army has been in here since *McClellan* was removed.... Every man and woman and child might swear against McClellan and uphold your abolition principles but the army would have a mind of its own, and you may believe there is prescious little abolition sentiment in the army that McClellan once commanded. Never fear but the army will be loyal to Lincoln, in actions if not in feeling, *but* if the war continues beyond Lincoln's administration rest assured McClellan will be "commander in chief" of U.S. forces and president. If for no other reason the army will require it or disband....
>
> At our Brigade head Qrs. orders have been received to take from the ranks of the old regiments men to commission in the Negro Regiments and the adjutant has not succeeded in getting one yet who will take the offer of a commissioned officer in a Negro regiment.[18]

On the issue of the Emancipation Proclamation and slavery, Tom writes:

> You ask "what has abolition of the north to do [with the war]?" It keeps them [the Southerners] irritated, makes them more bitter toward the north.

---

and it reserved special attention for the strongly democratic high command of the Army of the Potomac. After most Union defeats, the committee convened an inquiry into the reasons for the defeat. The committee undertook a very visible inquiry into the loss at Fredericksburg in the weeks following the battle. See U.S. Congress, *Report of the Joint Committee on the Conduct of the War, Senate Reports,* No. 8, No. 108, 2 vols. (Washington, D.C., 1863).

18. Mann to his mother, March 4, 1863, Mann Papers. This excerpt does not appear in the original memoir. In a letter written to his mother on March 31, 1863, Mann declared, "I shall vote for him—if alive and where I can" in the 1864 presidential election. The sentiments about African American troops expressed here by Mann were seconded by thousands. A Pennsylvania surgeon declared that his regiment "would charge and drive [an African American regiment] with more delight than they would the rebels.... You have no idea how greatly

It is slavery alone that embitters the south so against the Abolitionists of the North. The constant meddling and harping. . . . If we are going to reform a drunkard it would be poor policy to continually make fun and criticize him at every turn. . . .

I would not have you entertain the thought that I uphold slavery, and believe it right; far from it. But I do *not* believe in desolating the country for the sake of freeing the slaves. When the war broke out, men enlisted to fight for the Union and our old flag, and of course we hail with joy any measure the President may take to hasten the vindication of that flag. But we cannot think that by declaring to the south, "Your slaves shall be free" will hasten the close of the war, but quite the contrary. Slavery is an institution that they are bound up in, and they will fight to the last to preserve it, let alone everything else. The President's Proc[lamation] will have *no* effect except in conquered territory. . . . [and] will prolong the war.[19]

Before and during the war, one of our heroes was nominally a democrat and the other a republican, by previous education and environment, and often these two disputants found it necessary to agree to disagree while taking their soup from the same dish. These bickerings are now uninteresting since time has decided them to their mutual satisfaction; but both were fond of figures and when they were appealed to, a common level was readily reached, and it was not long after the "mud march" before they began to reckon on the cost of the war. In this they showed, in common with all, the lack of ability to comprehend magnitudes, but their summing up of the amount of lead and iron it takes to kill or wound a man in battle, will excite a little curiosity if it does not add materially to the advancement of the arts and sciences.

Their application of the science of mathematics proved that in the battle of Fredericksburg it required 257 pounds of lead and $96\frac{1}{2}$ pound of iron to kill a rebel, and $33\frac{1}{3}$ pounds of lead and $12\frac{1}{2}$ pounds of iron to wound one. Stating it in another way; $4,111\frac{1}{2}$ musket rounds were required to kill a rebel, in addition to eight rounds of 12-pound shell. This computation was arrived at by taking the known facts of the rebel losses in that battle, which were 608 killed and 4116 wounded; and assuming that 50,000 men fired 50 rounds of ammunition each, and that 200 pieces of artillery fired 25 rounds each of 12-pound shell.

---

the common soldiers are prejudiced against the Negro." Paul Fatout, ed., *Letters of a Civil War Surgeon* (West Lafayette, Ind., 1961), 53.

19. Like the one above it, this excerpt is added by the editor to illustrate Mann's wartime thoughts on the huge social issues facing the nation that winter. This letter was actually written to his father on November 15, 1862, but is inserted here because it meshes better with Mann's postwar narrative.

The rebel execution upon the Federals was three times as great, per pound and round, assuming that the average weight of lead per round was one ounce, and that the weight of the average shell was 12 pounds. At Antietam the rebels did the greatest execution with equal weights of lead and iron, while during the "Seven Day's fight" in front of Richmond, McClellan's army did as much damage with two pounds as Lee's accomplished with three. McClellan made one pound of lead do as much execution in front of Richmond as Burnside got out of five pounds at Fredericksburg. Or, to make the comparison more complete, McClellan's reception of Lee in front of Richmond cost less lead per man killed and wounded than Lee's reception of Burnside at Fredericksburg.[20]

The average brigade that charged on Marye's Heights did not contain 2,000 muskets, so according to these computations each brigade must have fired two complete volleys to kill one rebel, and in firing one volley only four of the enemy were even touched by it.

Early in April President Lincoln again visited the army, accompanied by his wife and little son. He rode in and out among the different camps, the Eighteenth being called into line upon its own parade ground to receive him; "presented arms," "shouldered arms," dipped its colors, and gave him three rousing cheers. Two days later the army was reviewed, and in this review, according to the testimony of the rank and file, the ceremonies were "expeditiously and pleasantly" performed. A day or two later the First brigade was reviewed by a Swiss general, an old acquaintance of General Barnes, and under date of April 22d, Tom writes to home folks: "There is every indication around tonight that we are about to make another move."[21]

---

20. What these figures demonstrate—though admittedly by imprecise science—is the indisputable advantage Civil War armies had when on the defense.

21. Lincoln's visit to the army's encampment in April 1863 would be his longest visit to the front until the last weeks of the war. The reviews were immense spectacles that received intense press coverage and commentary from the rank and file. See Hennessy, "We Shall Make Richmond Howl," in Gallagher, ed., *Chancellorsville Campaign*, 11–12. The Swiss officer was Major General Follarde. He was not an acquaintance of Barnes, but rather of General Hooker, who assigned him to corps commander Meade for the visit because Meade spoke French. Mann wrote of him, "He appeared a smart looking man, and wore spectacles." Recorded Meade, "He seems like all foreign officers of rank, intelligent and educated. He expressed himself delighted and wonder-struck with all he saw, and says our troops will compare favorably with the best troops in Europe, and he has seen them all." Mann to his Mother, April 22, 1863, Mann Papers; Meade, *Life and Letters*, Vol. 1, 365; Samuel Partridge to Ed, April 12, 1863, Partridge Papers, FSNMPL.

Thomas H. Mann appears dressed in the Zouave-style uniform worn by the Eighteenth Massachusetts early in their service. The togs proved impractical and the regiment discarded them after a few months. Mann, who joined the Union army in the summer of 1861, is likely only eighteen years old in this tintype.

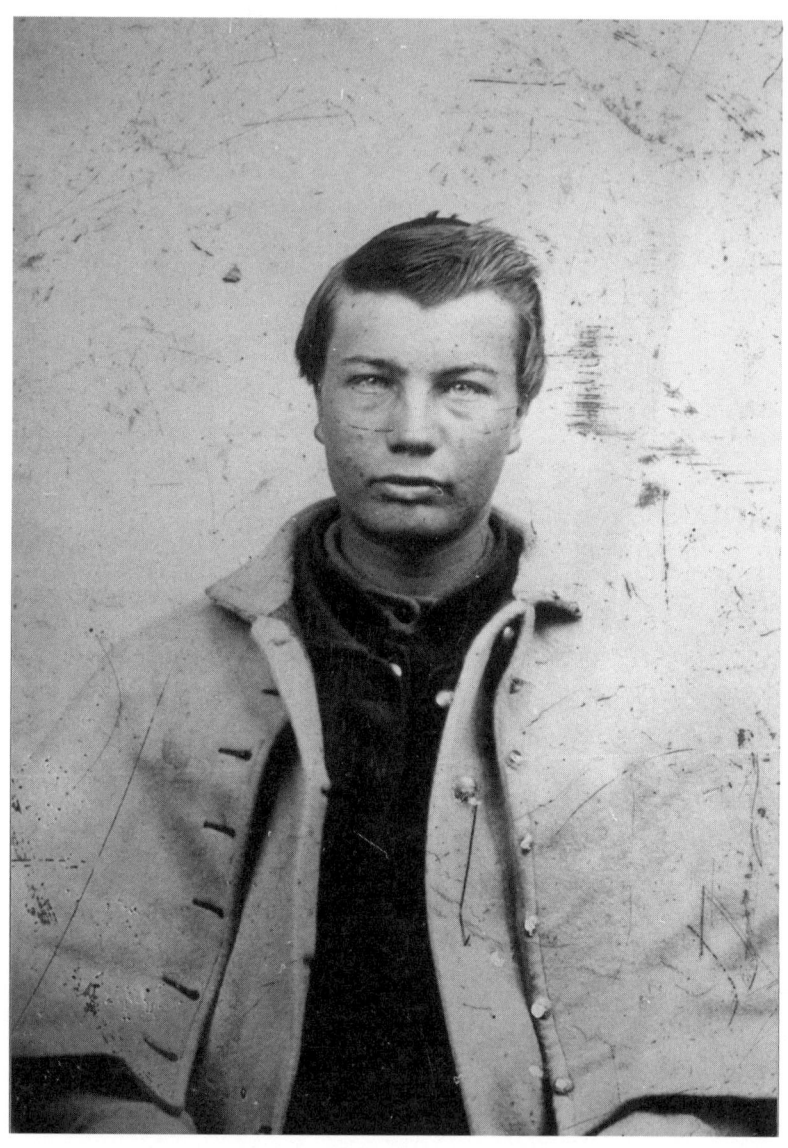

Tintype portrait of Thomas H. Mann in a more usual uniform of a Union soldier.

After recovering from fighting in the Civil War and from a debilitating experience as a prisoner of the Confederacy, Thomas Mann studied medicine and became a physician in Rhode Island. This tintype of the young veteran and doctor was probably taken in the early 1870s.

A view of the Mann family homestead in North Wrentham, now Norfolk, Massachusetts. From here, Mann departed as an eager volunteer in 1861 to return a worn veteran and ex-prisoner of war in 1865.

Thomas H. Mann retired from his Rhode Island medical practice in the mid-1880s and returned to Massachusetts, where he became a newspaper editor and publisher. In 1890, his prison memoir was published in *Century Magazine*.

EIGHT

Chancellorsville

"The Most Desponding Hours of My Life"

After four months of rehabilitation, the time for Joseph Hooker to test his renewed army in the field arrived. Hooker concluded not to repeat the mistakes of Burnside. Instead of plowing across the Rappahannock under Lee's guns at Fredericksburg, Hooker decided to move upstream, cross above Lee, and descend on his left flank. On April 27, 1863, the army shook loose their winterized legs and took to the field.

Mann, the Eighteenth Massachusetts, and the Fifth Corps would be part of the main flanking force—three corps designated to cross first the Rappahannock (at Kelly's Ford), then descend on the Rapidan Crossings and, beyond, Lee's left. Few Yankee campaigns of the war unfolded so precisely as planned. On April 30, the Fifth, Eleventh, and Twelfth Corps converged at the Chancellorsville intersection and stood squarely above Lee. Hooker declared virtual victory. But rather than keep the initiative, he yielded it to Lee (invariably a fatal mistake). He dared Lee to attack him at Chancellorsville, and Lee obliged in spectacular fashion. Mann and the Fifth Corps would mostly watch as Lee forged what many have called his greatest victory.

The depression that followed Chancellorsville is almost palpable in Mann's writings. Mann reverted—as he always would in times of defeat—to pining for McClellan. He, like most of the army, sought to place blame for the failures at Chancellorsville beyond the men in the ranks (in this case, he clearly blamed Hooker). The process of loss followed by scapegoating followed by recovery followed by renewed effort was becoming indigenous to the army—a rhythmic and resilient annual ritual. Fundamental to that resiliency was an unshakable optimism. Even the clear-thinking Mann could not escape it. Amidst the depression, he still saw hope. As he explained to his family, ". . . It is Hooker's first try. He may do better next time."[1]

1. Mann to his mother, May 17, 1863, Mann Papers.

Rumors that the army was about to move had been rife for several days, but the 5th Corps did not break camp until nearly noon of April 27. A day or two before that the unusual order was received to take eight day's rations in haversacks and knapsacks, indicating that the depot of supplies was to be abandoned, or that the army was about to put in some energetic work. Heretofore five day's rations were supposed to be the limit of the carrying capacity of marching soldiers, and is the utmost caliber of the regulation haversack. Ten days before marching, orders had been issued to pack all surplus clothing, such as could be dispensed with in a summer campaign, for storage, and the general explanation was promulgated that the army must present a light marching condition.[2]

To a certain extent these orders were complied with, though not radically enough, for during the first day's march toward Hartwood Church the roads were strewn with overcoats, blankets, and underwear that were discarded to lighten the aching shoulders that felt the strain intensified by the sun's heat.

Enough clothing was thrown away during the initial move for Chancellorsville to supply every inhabitant of that Virginia county [Stafford] with wearing apparel for a year. And the following autumn, when the army again returned to the banks of the Rappahannock from Gettysburg, it was noticeable that the darkies and "white trash" hereabouts had been plentifully clothed at the expense of the War Department. The blacks seemed to consider the heavy blue coats, flannel shirts, and woolen blankets, so generously scattered over the lines of march as a mark of special favor to themselves from Uncle "Lincum."

When the Eighteenth went into camp near Hartwood Church on the evening of the same day, after a march of about nine miles, the following order was read before breaking ranks: "Until further orders, in order to conceal the movements of the troops from the enemy, the usual duty calls will be omitted. Division commanders will see that their men build only small fires, and those for cooking purposes only."

2. Hooker's plan called for the Eleventh, Twelfth, and Fifth Corps to march upstream twenty-five miles to Kelly's Ford on the Rappahannock, then turn south and southeast by two routes. The Eleventh and Twelfth would cross the Rapidan River at Germanna Ford and move toward Chancellorsville from the west. The Fifth Corps—Mann's—would cross the Rapidan at Ely's Ford and move on Chancellorsville from the northwest. Darius Couch's Second Corps would cross the Rappahannock below its confluence with the Rapidan, at United States Ford. Other Union troops would cross the river in front of Fredericksburg, in order to keep Lee's attention distracted from his upstream flank. See Sears, *Chancellorsville*, 138–41.

This order was signed by General Meade, commander of the 5th Corps, and brought vividly to mind "Jimmy Barnes's rebel trap" of a few months previous, while the knowing ones allowed that the officers were beginning to profit a little by experience, and grew hopeful. It was also noticeable that the troops were being moved in a different manner than under Burnside. They did not obstruct each other; one corps or division was well out of the way before another was called into line for the march; the artillery kept from under the feet of the infantry; and all crept around behind the hills, as if to avoid notice, instead of crowding every eminence to attract attention.

Like the battles of Yorktown, Williamsburg, Seven Days, Bull Run, Antietam, Shepherdstown, Fredericksburg, and the Mud March, so with that of Chancellorsville . . . the stratagem and maneuvers that led up to it were supposed to be outside the ken of the rank and file. But, as already remarked, the high privates were learning full as fast as the major generals, and there were thousands of them making this strategic march for the Chancellorsville house on the 27th, 28th, and 29th days of April who have since taken higher rank in their respective communities than some of the generals who commanded. In other words, while a few generals, even a major-general or two, has dropped below the average standing of a citizen of the United States since this "little unpleasantness" between the North and South, hundreds of the privates they commanded have become members of Congress, of their respective State legislatures, judges of the higher courts, governors, and millionaires. When, therefore, the character of this class of men who carried muskets 35 years ago is taken into consideration, it must be allowed that, though only 20 and 25-year-old boys, their mental caliber was equal to a partial comprehension of military tactics.

In noting the preliminaries of the battle of Fredericksburg it was mentioned that the rank and file knew, before the attempt was made, that Marye's Heights were impregnable by any ordinary assault, and the affair was put down in their calendars either as an imaginary political necessity or [the product of] a grossly incompetent commander. So at this time, soon as Hooker had succeeded in getting three corps across the Rappahannock and Rapidan Rivers without a battle, the army he commanded knew that the Johnnies were, or ought to be, in a bad fix. In other words, Hooker had Lee at his mercy, if the former was half competent, and private soldiers were begging to be allowed to go in and spoil the "Army of Northern Virginia" right now.

Even the average private knew that the Federal forces were much superior in numbers, certainly three to two of the Confederates,[3] and every moment of delay, after crossing the rivers, was irritating the men who had eight day's rations on their backs. The character of this irritation was the opposite of that which kept them churning mud under Burnside. The exact causes of failure at Chancellorsville, the neglect to wipe Lee's army out of existence, lay with one man, and with that statement the matter is left to Sergeant Bill's "great writers" to discuss while the fortunes of the Eighteenth are being followed for the next seven days. To do this, recourse is had to the corporal's diary that was minutely kept and sent to his father a day or two afterwards.

The 5th Corps resumed its march from about Hartwood Church at noon of the 28th, after the 11th and 12th corps were well out of the way, and during a smart rain storm that continued seven or eight hours, passing the United States Ford, and camped at 10 o'clock, for the night, near Kelly's Ford. While passing the former ford, a squadron of cavalry crossed the Rappahannock, captured a rebel out-look post of 30 men, and returned with them to the marching column before the rear brigade of the corps had passed. On the morning of the 29th, the march resumed at seven o'clock, crossing the Rappahannock on a pontoon bridge half a mile below the fording place, then moving directly for Ely's Ford of the Rapidan, which was reached a few minutes before six in the afternoon.

The river at this ford was found to be about 250 yards wide, with a swift current, but no pontoons.[4] As at Kelly's Ford, so at this one, the cavalry preceded the infantry and crossed an hour or two before any large body of the latter arrived (though the 11th and 12th corps had moved farther up the river, to Germanna ford, and were within striking distance in case of trouble). Here the cavalry captured the outposts of the enemy and made it certain that infantry could be safely crossed, so two divisions, Griffin's and Sykes's, of the 5th Corps, forded the stream and were all in camp before midnight. The Eighteenth, being one of the first regiments to cross, bivouacked before dark on the right [south] bank.

To ford the Rapidan, under garments were removed, made into a bundle with the knapsack, haversack, and equipments, and strapped about the neck upon the shoulders and heads of the soldiers, thus producing a top-

---

3. The odds were more lopsided than that. The Federals had about 130,000 men available for the campaign, the Confederates about 61,000.

4. Only in its tidal sections is the Rappahannock 250 yards across. The width of the river at Ely's Ford was about 400 feet.

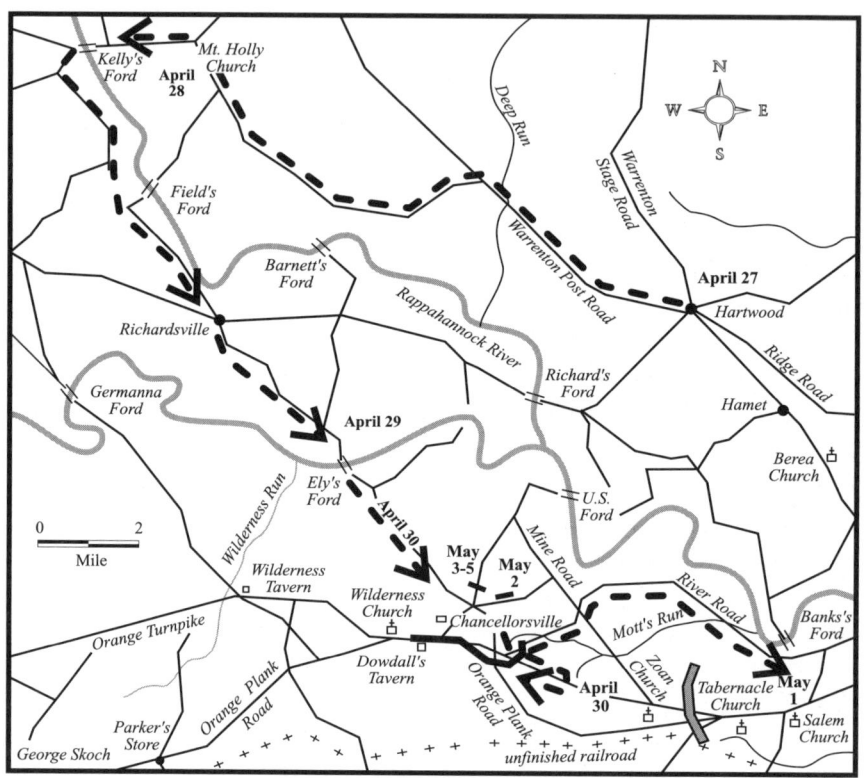

The Eighteenth Massachusetts's route to Chancellorsville.

heavy condition not calculated to insure one's equilibrium in a swift-running, three-foot deep current. In this instance, however, the rebels were not making targets of the men who were attempting to keep their footing, as was the case in the Potomac [at Shepherdstown Ford]. The men generally escaped a ducking, though an occasional one had to be fished out by the cavalry who were scattered across to meet emergencies of that kind.[5]

After cooking his coffee and partaking of one-third of one of his eight-day rations, Tom wrote in his diary [for April 29]: "The cavalry are bringing scattering rebel prisoners about every hour. The Rapidan was not fortified here, and very slightly defended. Think we must have taken the Secesh completely by surprise, as a small force might have held an army in check at this place."

April showers seemed to prevail in Virginia as in New England at this season, and the thousands who were congratulating themselves upon their escape from a ducking in the river were thoroughly soaked during the night by a heavy rain storm. But such little things were of no consequence now for the whole army was ablaze with enthusiasm over the fact that the enemy were being flanked out of Fredericksburg—from behind its murderous Marye's Heights.

On the morning of the 30th, Sykes's division moved directly down the river for the United States Ford,[6] and the division of Griffin followed about seven o'clock. After crossing quite a stream, known as Hunting Creek, it halted until noon, then moved . . . for a short distance toward Chancellorsville.[7] Before three o'clock, Barnes's brigade moved out alone on the [Orange] Turnpike . . . leading directly toward Fredericksburg. In this advance the Eighteenth Massachusetts and 25th New York regiments were deployed as skirmishers and kept up a running fire upon a like force of rebels

---

5. Speaking of the crossing at Ely's, an officer of the Eighteenth recorded, "The men took off their clothes and held them on their heads and it was a regular sight to see the army marching down to the ford with nothing on but shirts and coats." George M. Bernard to his father, May 4, 1863, G. M. Bernard Papers, reel 17, Massachusetts Historical Society (MHS). Bernard was assigned to General Griffin's staff.

6. This movement by Sykes came in response to a report that a Confederate brigade was blocking United States Ford. Sykes's job was to uncover it to clear the way for the crossing of Couch's Second Corps. By the time Sykes approached United States Ford, whatever Confederates had been there had vanished. Sears, *Chancellorsville,* 176–77.

7. A country crossroads where the Orange Turnpike, Orange Plank Road, and Ely's Ford Road come together, about five miles south of the Rappahannock River. The "ville" at Chancellorsville consisted of just a single house, the home of the Chancellor family. See Noel G. Harrison, *Chancellorsville Battlefield Sites* (Lynchburg, 1990), 16–20.

who were steadily pushed back for nearly two miles, until a large body of the enemy was encountered advantageously posted on a ridge.

While making preparations to attack, General Barnes received orders to simply hold his ground until dark without bringing on an engagement, then to retire under cover of the woods in the direction from whence he had moved out. As directed, the skirmishers were silently called in, and the whole brigade as silently stole back and bivouacked in the woods for the remainder of the night.[8]

During the morning of May 1st, congratulatory orders from General Hooker were read at the head of the regiment, in which he said: "The army has thus far met with complete success, and the enemy must come out of their fortified position and fight us on ground of our own choosing or ingloriously retreat." This was cheering and encouraging.[9]

Near 11 o'clock the whole division, Griffin's, moved toward Banks's Ford some five miles, to within two miles of it, then countermarched to nearly the place it left [six hours before]. There a line of battle was immediately formed with a heavy force of skirmishers thrown out.[10] These kept up a brisk firing well into the night, but no general attack was made in front of this division. It was learned, however, that Sykes was heavily engaged during the afternoon, and an appearance of the enemy was momentarily expected by Griffin. It was already pretty generally understood that the Union forces were not to be the attacking party, but were being placed in advantageous positions to receive any demonstrations that the enemy might be disposed to make. The results of this understanding were becoming plainly evident in the rapidly rising spirit of determination among the rank and file to hold any ground that was required and at all hazards.

8. Barnes's men encountered parts of Richard H. Anderson's division on high ground east of Lick Run, not far from Zoan Church. While Barnes's regiments advanced along the Orange Turnpike, corps commander Meade was back at the Chancellorsville intersection, bristling under Hooker's new orders not to push forward from the intersection and to wait for the rest of the army to come up. Ibid., 180–81.

9. The order, issued on April 30, read, "It is with heartfelt satisfaction the commanding general announces to the army that the operations of the last three days have determined that our enemy must either ingloriously fly, or come out from behind his defenses and give us battle on our own ground, where certain destruction awaits him." *O.R.*, Vol. 25, Pt. 1, 171.

10. The abortive march toward Banks's Ford—though glossed over by Mann—reflects a major turning point in the campaign. Meade had intended to reach the ford and clear it so that other Union troops could cross. But before Meade reached the ford, Hooker's main advance along the Orange Turnpike and Orange Plank Road encountered Lee's advance guard. Hooker immediately decided to fight a defensive battle and issued orders for the entire army to pull back to the Chancellorsville intersection. Sears, *Chancellorsville*, 201–14.

The position of the Eighteenth at this time, evening of May 1st, was in a heavy forest a mile or less from the Chancellorsville house, and about sundown this place became a pandemonium on earth where the bursting shell and shrapnel shot from the rebel batteries tore through the trees as if to make kindling wood of the whole. The effect of 15 or 20 guns throwing that kind of ammunition into a heavy forest is very much like a storm of hail upon a field of growing grain, only the hail-stones in this instance were jagged pieces of iron hurtling through the air, shot to kill, and cutting and slashing the heavy timber as if it was standing grain. The crashing of shot and bursting shell among the trees multiplies the racket of noise and seeming danger four-fold, yet but one man of company "I," Simmons, was seriously injured during the two hours that the company was exposed to its iron missiles and flying splinters.[11]

After midnight Barnes's brigade moved a mile or more to a new position where for three hours it was not under fire, though muskets were stacked in line, ready to be immediately snatched, while the men essayed to obtain a little sleep by the side of them. Three hours later, or about three o'clock on the morning of May 2d, Company "I," of the Eighteenth, went to the front as skirmishers and remained thus deployed until after six in the evening, while the whole of Griffin's division lay stretched upon the ground, massed within easy supporting distance, though little firing was done in the immediate front of this position. Some distance to the right, however, heavy skirmishing, repeated volleys of musketry, and the quick booming of cannon, as if firing by whole batteries, kept reminding these troops to be on the alert [all day on May 2].[12]

11. The wounded man was Isaac R. Simmons, thirty-five, a "seaman" and a later recruit who had joined the regiment in August 1862. Simmons's wound would be serious enough to lead to his discharge from the Eighteenth. Simmons was wounded while Barnes's brigade held position in woods north of the Orange Turnpike, about eight hundred yards east of Chancellorsville. The division came under fire from Confederate guns on the ridge that is now occupied by McLaws Drive—part of Fredericksburg and Spotsylvania National Military Park. Frank O'Reilly, *Chancellorsville Troop Movement Maps* (1998) FSNMPL. All references to the position of the Eighteenth at Chancellorsville are taken from this excellent set of maps.

12. At this time, the Fifth Corps' main position was along the Mineral Springs Road, facing southeast, about a mile north of the Chancellorsville intersection. One man described the building of the works here: ". . . all hands were set to work entrenching and making abattis and breastworks[.] [T]his continued all the next day and by night we had a most splendid line of fortifications." Those works remain today, though most of them fall outside the boundary of Fredericksburg and Spotsylvania NMP. George Bernard to his father, May 4, 1863, Bernard Papers, MHS.

This incident of heavy firing just before dusk [on May 2], noted in the corporal's diary, must have been the time when the rebel General Jackson struck the right flank of the 11th Corps, doubled it up, stampeded it, and changed it into a flying, crazy mob. The position of the Eighteenth at this time, however, was such that but little of that stupid disaster was comprehended by its men.

A little before dark, company "I" was relieved from the skirmish line and withdrew a few hundred yards, rejoining the regiment and brigade where all lay in line, ready to spring into action at a moment's warning. This line was shifted several times during the night, so sleep was only caught in snatches.

At sunrise of May 3d, Barnes's brigade moved about a mile and occupied, with the corps, a place near the center of the army, within a few yards of General Hooker's headquarters and near the Chancellorsville house, to add support to the line at that place. Repeated charges were made by the enemy to drive the 5th Corps from this position, commencing at sunrise and continuing at uncertain intervals until noon, but without making the slightest impression. Then a lull was enjoyed for a few hours. It was evident, however, that the enemy were concentrating for a heavy massed attack.

It was during this interval of fighting that the story of "Stonewall" Jackson's being carried from the field, mortally wounded, was told from regiment to regiment, and, though rejoicing in his elimination from the conflict, his ability, energy, and nobleness of character were recognized by all.[13]

The place occupied by the Eighteenth on this day was only a few yards—most of the time less than 100 yards—from the fighting line, unable to fire a shot yet exposed to the enemy's compliments of musketry and shell. . . . Too many troops were unnecessarily massed at this point, only inviting death when it was uncalled for, and during the three hours the regiment was thus exposed one of the most promising captains of the Eighteenth, Hewins of company "B," was torn in two by a shell, and eight of its men were wounded. The same shell that killed Captain Hewins tore away the arm of another man, and the leg of still another.[14]

13. In a postbattle letter, Mann commented, "Jackson was a smart man—one of the truest and best they have—and a Christian. I admire him as a man. If we had a few such men, affairs would have a far different appearance." Mann to his mother, May 17, 1863, Mann Papers.

14. Captain William G. Hewins, a twenty-five-year-old auctioneer from Boston. George Bernard said of this incident, "Capt Hewins of my regt was killed by a shell; he carried my

General Meade was soon convinced that the rebels could be handled here without exposing so heavy a line, and Barnes's brigade moved 500 or 600 yards to one side just as the expected charge came, thus taking it from under the immediate fire of shell.[15] It was received almost entirely by the 5th Corps artillery, which was posted as thickly as the guns could be advantageously worked, and they poured into the charging, yelling masses volley after volley of canister, which cut swaths like a reaper's cradle in a field of grain.

In this almost hand-to-hand encounter, which occurred a little before sundown, the 3d Massachusetts battery lost every horse and more than 20 of its men, while the guns became so hot as to blister the hand that touched them. Through it all the infantry lay partially protected in the rear, ready if the guns failed, but the artillery did the business.[16]

From the position occupied by the Eighteenth . . . the location of the rebel guns could be seen, and it was observed that the accurate firing from a few of the Union Parrott guns[17] blew up several of the enemy's caissons. This called out very audible grunts of satisfaction, suppressed cheers in fact, as it was not worth while to invite attention and a rebel shelling by a full Yankee hurrah.

After dark this regiment moved back to its place, then advanced into the open field over which the battle had raged all day and immediately threw up earthworks. All were suffering for want of sleep, and during the night many a soldier was doubled up by sleep, with a shovel in one hand and his musket in the other, but by snatching five minutes sleep and ten minutes work enough earth was thrown into a line of breast-works to give all the protection needed.[18]

---

watch home for me to you last summer, and had only got back from another short visit to Boston a few days before." Bernard to his father, May 4, 1863, Bernard Papers, MHS.

15. This new line of Griffin's division (and Barnes's brigade within it) tracked along Ely's Ford Road, its left resting near the Bullock Farm. The line faced southwest and was just out of the zone of major fighting on May 3—fighting that would be as severe as any in the war. See Bigelow, *Chancellorsville*, 343.

16. While Mann is correct in asserting that the artillery of the Fifth Corps saw service at Chancellorsville, he is incorrect in his reference to the losses of the Third Massachusetts Battery. The battery lost no horses and men at Chancellorsville. See O.R., Vol. 15, Pt. 1, 522–23.

17. Parrott Rifles—a type of rifled cannon named after its inventor, Robert P. Parrott. Most Parrott rifles used in the field fired ten-pound projectiles, though a few twenty-pounder guns also saw service.

18. Another man of the Eighteenth noted something that Mann chose not to include in his recollection: "With the wood still full of dying and wounded men, they were set on fire and the poor wretches burned to death. Fancy their position, crippled and unable to move,

These trenches were occupied by Barnes's brigade until the morning of May 6. Matters were very quiet along the front during the morning and a part of the afternoon of the 4th, the reasons for which were not understood by those who were grimly holding their muskets in one hand, momentarily expecting an attack from the enemy, while fishing from the rapidly depleting haversacks a bite of "hard-tack," raw salt-pork, and scattered grains of coffee with the other. All were suffering from lack of sleep, and even while munching something to appease the stomach, many obtained their "forty winks" as they stood, sat, or partially reclined in the trenches, though never relaxing a soldier's grip upon the loaded musket....[19]

During [the afternoon of May 4], the cheering news was passed from rank to rank that Sedgwick and his corps had captured and were now occupying the heights of Fredericksburg. Cheer after cheer broke loose and resounded so as to be heard above the firing as the news passed from one regiment to another. But within an hour men in the ranks were earnestly discussing the reasons for this inaction about Chancellorsville. Sergeant Bill became so thoroughly aroused that his words were hot and inflammatory enough against every general on the field, and the general commanding in particular, to have indicted him for high treason if he had worn shoulder-straps. He swore roundly at the "devilish cowardice and rank incompetency of the infernal set of imbeciles who had the army dangling at their heels; a set of ignorant Negro-lovers who didn't care a rap about ending the rebellion so long as they could have their brandy and champagne, ride fine horses, and order an army about. These d——d quack officers are giving Lee all the opportunities he wants to play his usual tricks of thrashing the Army of the Potomac in detail, and he's going to do it, or you may take me for a jackass."

The sergeant's temperament was a little choleric, while the corporal's was more sanguine and hopeful. "Wait awhile, Sarge," pleaded the latter, "it's possible the commander of the Army knows more about the situation than we poor devils in the ranks. Maybe Sedgwick has men enough to hold his position, and the Graybacks will be rolled back upon us by morning."

---

seeing the flames approach and all within short musket range of us." George Bernard to his father, May 4, 1863, Bernard Papers, MHS.

19. The reason for the quiet on the Fifth Corps front lay miles to the east, where part of the Union army under John Sedgwick had crossed at Fredericksburg. This forced Lee to break off fighting at Chancellorsville to confront this dire threat to his rear. Speaking editorially, the paragraph following this one in the text has been deleted. It included a speculative and erroneous discription of an assault on the Fifth Corps front that did not occur.

Thus the men took sides in the trenches over the unusual quiet of the evening of May 4th and all the next day, dividing about even over the two sides of the question as expressed by the sergeant and corporal. All were becoming impatient of the apparent delay. "Now is the time to give them h——l," said one, which was none too forcibly expressed to represent the rank and file. Belts were tightened, blankets re-rolled, and muskets and cartridge-boxes were carefully examined in momentary expectation of hearing the word "forward!" from all along the line.

It never came, but instead, a few days later, while Tom and his comrades were plodding their weary way back across the fords of the Rappahannock, wearing the chagrined, downcast look of whipped dogs with tails between their legs, they had to acknowledge that Sergeant Bill's display of temper had been a prophecy.

Heavy cannonading wafted to these impatient men during the late afternoon and well into the night of May 4th from the direction of Fredericksburg, and they did not need to be told that Lee's army had turned upon Sedgwick. Corporal Tom, in his diary already mentioned, wrote on the morning of May 5: "Heavy cannonading near or at Fredericksburg last night. Fear the rebels have massed their forces upon Sedgwick and will crush him." At noon of the same date this entry is found: "It is rumored that Sedgwick has been driven across the river by Jackson."[20]

Though only a rumor with the Eighteenth, the fact was a crushing, disastrous reality, while for nearly 24 hours, from noon of May 3d, Joseph Hooker, commander of the army of the Potomac, lay in his tent, incapacitated by the shock of a rebel shell, or drunk. There are two sides to that story that will not be discussed here. The statement that for 24 hours the army was without a commander, and at the very time that Lee withdrew large forces from the front of Chancellorsville to strike Sedgwick at Fredericksburg, however, will not be disputed.[21]

On that night of May 5, a cold, northeast, foggy rain-storm covered the whole, hanging like a pall of blasted hopes to add misery upon mortification to the discomforted mind—a verification of the old adage that "misfortunes never come singly"—bringing acute suffering to the body as well

---

20. Sedgwick's move toward Lee's rear was met by the Confederates at Salem Church. In a brisk battle, the Union advance was stopped on May 3, then reversed on May 4. Sedgwick would tumble back across the river at Banks's Ford on the evening of May 4.

21. Hooker had been knocked unconscious by a shell early on May 3 and remained in a stupor for the remainder of the battle. Some, like Mann, wrongly attributed his stupor to alcohol. See Sears, *Chancellorsville*, 505–06.

as the soul. The Eighteenth found it all for its duty was on picket, in the open fields that spread out in front of the works from which the rebels had been several times repulsed, during this long, minute-counted, forsaken night, until four o'clock the following morning, while the army was hastening back to the fords it so enthusiastically and buoyantly crossed seven days before.[22]

No one can ever know the amount of physical suffering the body is capable of enduring without putting the matter to an absolute test. This regiment made one of those tests on the night in question. In the wet and cold several hundred men shivered and shook for ten hours without the privilege of movement for exercise or fires for warmth, as though attacked with the spasm of intermittent fever that shrivel and pucker the skin into folds while driving the blood from the surface, to produce a raging fever about the heart, brain, and nerve centers.

The sergeant says it was a night that eternity will not be long enough to make him forget. And the corporal wrote in this diary: "The worst and most desponding twelve hours of my life," while Chancellorsville was passing down into history.

Barnes's brigade were the last troops to leave the battlefield of Chancellorsville, and the Eighteenth did not steal away from its advanced posts in the open fields until the last organized body of troops were well underway to the fords. Then the men were called in singly and silently, taking their places in the line of march with the brigade.... The march to the Rappahannock was made after four o'clock in the morning of May 6th, taking the most direct route for the United States Ford, four or five miles distant. We used all the haste it was possible to obtain from the worn-out, thoroughly chilled men who were wet, hungry, and actually dropping by the wayside to sleep. Most of the march was made during the cold, grey dawning of the morning, and was somewhat hindered by the efforts of the more robust to aid weaker or exhausted comrades so they might not be left behind.

When the ridges that command a view of the river were reached [a mile from the river] the brigade formed a battle line, cut the trees in its front to

22. The Fifth Corps, like most of the army, crossed at United States Ford during its return march to the Falmouth camps. For a thorough description of United States Ford see Harrison, *Chancellorsville Battlefield Sites*, 7–9. For a brief synopsis of the role of the Eighteenth Massachusetts see Joseph Hayes, MS Journal Extracts, Joshua Chamberlain Papers, Library of Congress.

obstruct the road, and threw up slight earth-works with the expectation of soon meeting the van guard of Johnnies. But they seemed well enough satisfied with their manner of handling the Yankees during the past four or five days; anyhow, they made no attempt to scare Hooker any further during this campaign.

For three or four hours on this morning the 5th Corps were the only troops left on the right [south] bank of the Rappahannock. The stream was considerably swollen by the constant down-pour of rain, and the 11th corps was slowly filing across upon one pontoon bridge that threatened every moment to be swept away. It was evident, by the actions of the different brigade officers, that they felt the extreme danger . . . if Lee should make a break for it. Providentially he did not, and about eight o'clock Barnes's brigade tramped across the loosened, swaying bridge to the peaceful side of the river once more.

During all the remainder of the day this brigade was detailed to assist in taking up pontoons, after which the tired, disgusted Eighteenth had nothing to do but wend its way back to the old camping grounds beyond Falmouth. A few of them, Bill and Tom among the number, plodded back that night, a distance of ten miles, but neither remember the hour of arrival. In his first letter after to home folks, the corporal wrote: "I am pretty well used up, as we have just arrived back in camp after marching out to the United States Ford, yesterday, to finish up our job with the pontoons that it seems we left half done, two days ago, owing to the drunkenness of our officers."[23]

A long rest was now before the Army of the Potomac, or that portion of it still left along the banks of the Rappahannock, for the Chancellorsville loss was 17,287 killed, wounded, and missing. . . . The forces about Falmouth were still further depleted by the expiration of the terms of service, two years, of many regiments, so it was plain that no aggressive movement would be attempted in this direction until the condition of things was materially changed—or the rebels forced it.[24]

23. This is a paraphrasal of the content of Mann's May 9, 1863, letter to friends at home. It may be that Mann is quoting from another letter he wrote at the time, which has not survived.

24. Mann erroneously asserted in a deleted passage here that the army suffered the detachment of an army corps after Chancellorsville. He is correct that the army lost many thousands of men when the enlistments of the so-called "two-year" regiments expired. Indeed, controversy over the date of the expiration of these enlistments—before or after the Chancellorsville Campaign—stimulated more than one uprising among the two-year regiments. Mann's corps commander, Meade, noted that the Fifth Corps stood to lose nearly eight thou-

As the days lengthened out away from Chancellorsville, and its mistakes were more fully comprehended by the common soldiers, General Hooker rapidly lost caste under . . . the discussions that were freely indulged around every company's quarters, particularly after the universal army pipes of the evening were lighted. The testimony given by Hooker before the "Congressional Committee on the Conduct of the War," in relation to McClellan, breathed so general an atmosphere of condemnation of everybody but himself, and showed his own ambition in such unmistakable characters, that the ridicule of the rank and file predominated over all previous admiration for his fighting qualities.[25]

To a great extent, Hooker redeemed himself soon as his abilities were properly sized up by the Administration, and after his command was reduced to correspond with his mental powers. But his testimony before that Committee so stirred up the army that every newspaper that published it was strictly excluded from his own army-lines, and even a personal search was made by the provost-marshal's department, through company quarters, to confiscate the few copies that had been smuggled through the mails. In a letter to his father, written by the corporal on May 17, he says: "Hooker showed his egotism in his testimony on McClellan, and I was surprised to read such an array of falsehoods from so high a source. It was so ridiculous in its deliberate perversion of the truth as to be apparent to every reading and thinking private in the army, and it did not take us by surprise when it became known that he was taking every possible precaution to keep it out of our reach."

In replying to his soldier-son's radical language and statement in relation to the suppression of the testimony, the corporal's father suggested that perhaps General Hooker did not believe it best for private soldiers, whose duty it was to obey, to know too much. That only added fuel to the flame, for the corporal replied: "When a man lies, and knows that he is

---

sand men due to expiring enlistments. Meade, *Meade Letters,* Vol. 1, 367. The unrest surrounding the date of expired enlistments seems to have been focused most in the First Corps, though the Second Maine of Barnes's Brigade would undergo an uprising just prior to Gettysburg. See John Gibbon, *Personal Recollections of the Civil War* (New York, 1928), 112–13; Proceedings of the court of inquiry for General Alfred Sully, *Herkimer County Journal,* August 30, 1863 (deals with a mutiny in the Thirty-fourth New York).

25. Hooker testified before the committee on December 20, 1862, and March 11, 1863, declaring (among other things) that the failure of the Peninsula Campaign "is to be attributed to the want of generalship on the part of our commander." U.S. Congress, *Report of the Joint Committee on the Conduct of the War, In Three Parts* (Washington, D.C., 1863), Pt. 1, 575–82, 665–73.

lying, naturally the printed evidences of that kind of testimony would be kept from those who knew better, and from this army in particular who he must have known would hold such falsifying in contempt; perhaps Hooker is afraid his army knows too much already."

For several weeks the different regiments, particularly the New England and New Yorkers, indulged in considerable base-ball playing, which was encouraged by the colonels and brigadiers. On May 17th a match game was played between the picked elevens of the Eighteenth and Twenty-second Massachusetts, which attracted considerable attention throughout the corps. It was played for a prize of $25, a purse made up among the field officers, and bets upon the result were freely made, the Eighteenth being the favorite. The game, which was hotly contested and only finished when it became too dark to continue longer, was decided in favor of the Eighteenth, 50 to 47. Naturally the 22d was not satisfied with so close a game so a return contest was held the next week which resulted in a tally still worse for the 22d, consequently the winning regiment became the champion. Company "I" fathered all of the Eighteenth's eleven but one.

The camps about Falmouth were becoming very filthy from the debris of dead animals, fragments of refuse from the cooking operations of thousands of messes, worn-out and cast-off clothing, and other leavings of an army of 100,000 men, in addition to that of thousands of animals, all of which had occupied these camps for six months. From the beginning no guarantee had been given that this ground would be occupied from month to month, so no elaborate or proper sanitary regulations prevailed. Square miles of territory had been denuded of every tree and shrub and green thing, leaving every inch of it as bare as a traveled road, except for the short, scattering stumps of the forests, which only added to the desolation. Every shower converted it all into a sea of filthy, stinking mud. Naturally the army was glad to move out and away to pastures new.

NINE

Gettysburg

"One Continuous Roar"

The steady diet of adversity suffered by the Army of the Potomac had an ironic effect: the army hardened and developed a resilient self-identity that few military organizations in history would match. It no longer bonded with its leaders, but instead bonded with itself. One of Mann's cohorts in the Fifth Corps stated it most eloquently: "True, yes, too true, we have not been victorious. But the fault is not in the troops, for never have men been known to fight as this army has fought, even when we knew we were outgeneraled and defeated. Any man will fight when flushed with former victories, but it is only this army that will face the enemy though defeat be certain."[1]

The army would need every bit of this resiliency in June and July of 1863. In the North, unrest rampaged because of the draft. The Democratic party evermore embraced a conservative, peace-at-any-price philosophy. The soldiers read all this as a lack of support for their efforts, and though many of them (including Mann) embraced the individual political philosophies that characterized Northern conservatives, their brotherhood with the Democrats ended—abruptly—on the issue of peace at any price. For the soldiers, the costs had already been immense. Their sacrifices could only be, and must be, justified by ultimate victory. Mann and his fellow soldiers railed against the "Copperheads" as intensely as they fought Lee's army on the battlefield.

Robert E. Lee, of course, avidly read Union newspapers and was acutely aware of the divisions that threatened the Union war effort. Indeed, this military man largely constructed his strategy with an eye toward

---

1. James R. Woodworth (Forty-fourth New York) to his wife, Phoebe, July 21, 1863, James R. Woodworth Papers, James Schoff Civil War Collection, Clements Library, University of Michigan.

Northern politics. "It seems to me," he wrote, "that the most effective mode of accomplishing [our] object . . . is to give all the encouragement we can, consistently with truth, to the rising peace party in the North."[2] *His chosen means to do that was to bludgeon the major Union instrument for winning the war and, thereby, demoralize the home-folk who supported the army. He saw no better way of doing that in the wake of Chancellorsville than by raiding northward, into Maryland and Pennsylvania. There, Lee hoped to win a convincing victory that would inflict a fatal wound on the Union will to fight.*

In mid-June 1863, Lee's army started north. Hooker shadowed him, trying constantly to pierce a veil of cavalry that shielded Lee's movements. By this point in the war, as Mann repeatedly notes in his memoir, the Union cavalry had achieved equal footing with the Confederates. As the armies moved, the cavalry clashed. Mann and the Eighteenth would be shuttled forward to support these efforts. Many infantry units in the Fifth Corps would be directly engaged. The Eighteenth, for its part, would just watch and march to exhaustion—Centreville, Aldie, Middleburg, and a dozen villages in Maryland would be added to its travelogue. Finally, on July 1, the boom of distant cannon told that the armies had clashed. For Mann and the Eighteenth, the status as bystander would abruptly and bloodily end.

Barnes's brigade bid adieu to [the camps near Falmouth] at 8:30 on the morning of May 29th, marching toward Hartwood Church, passing that place about noon and soon after bivouacking for the night. The next day it marched as far as Morrisville and went into camp about five in the afternoon. At four o'clock in the afternoon of May 31st, the brigade moved about three miles and camped in the vicinity of Grove Church, where there was a quartz mill that had been in active operation extracting gold before the war.[3] At this place the brigade camps were strung out over a mile and half, and the Eighteenth was fortunate in securing a clover-field for its

---

2. Clifford Dowdey, ed., *The Wartime Papers of R. E. Lee* (Boston, 1961), 508.

3. Gold mines were common along a line running from southern Fauquier County (around Morrisville) southward across the Rapidan and Rappahannock into Spotsylvania and Orange County—part of the Southern Appalachian gold district. Though never a threat to California gold mines, the mines in central Virginia produced profitably for many decades. The last were abandoned in the 1930s. See Erik F. Nelson, *Historic Resources along the Rappahannock and Rapidan Rivers* (Fredericksburg, 1997), 45–47.

camp. The clover was in full blossom, and the boys reveled in it for 13 days like a herd of worn-out stable horses. The second brigade was at Kelly's Ford, about four miles distant, and the third at Ellis Ford, still farther up the river.[4]

The whole division was simply guarding the fords of the Rappahannock, and on the 9th of June a part of it witnessed a hand-to-hand encounter between Stoneman's cavalry[5] on the Union side and Stuart's Confederates. It took place across the river near Kelly's Ford, to which place Barnes's brigade was called in haste about 11 o'clock in the morning, reaching the high banks of the river that overlooked this play of Yankee and rebel sabres in season to see the Johnnies cleared from the field. Evidently the Union cavalry had been trained already to other service than gallivanting about the headquarters of the various generals, and from this time the infantry began to respect and fraternize with the "sabre-jinglers."[6]

. . . Some idea may be obtained from the corporal's diary in regard to the depletion going on in the ranks, the result of two years of campaigning in Virginia, for in it was noted under the date of June 12: "The Eighteenth only numbers 350 muskets at the present time, yet we have a full compli-

    4. Grove Church was located about halfway between Hartwood Church and Morrisville—just west of Deep Run in Fauquier County—on the road linking Falmouth and Warrenton. In a June 5 letter to home, Mann termed the move to Grove Church from Falmouth "like moving out into the country from a crowded city." Mann was incorrect in saying that Ellis's Ford was upstream from Kelly's Ford. In fact, it was almost directly south of Morrisville, about four miles *downstream* from Kelly's Ford. For an excellent summary of the Rappahannock and Rapidan fords, see Nelson, *Historic Resources Along the Rappahannock and Rapidan Rivers,* 93–135.

    5. Stoneman had been relieved in the wake of Chancellorsville, and the Union cavalry was now commanded by Alfred Pleasonton.

    6. Mann refers to the Battle of Brandy Station. Little of the battle was likely visible to Mann and his fellow Fifth Corps soldiers north of the Rappahannock, and indeed he makes no mention of actually seeing the battle in his letter to his mother on June 12, 1863. A handful of infantry regiments crossed the river to join the fight, but arrived too late to play a part. Reflecting in his letter on the fight, Mann wrote, "Our cavalry are beginning to be of some service now, and they have proved themself equal to the best of the rebels. The prisoners taken say Gen. Lee was gathering his cavalry for a move upon Maryland and Pa." Though the Confederates ultimately repulsed the Union horsemen at Brandy Station, the battle did indeed mark the ascendancy of the Union cavalry to a level competitive with Stuart's horsemen. Within a year, the Union cavalry would outstrip the Confederates in equipment, horses, numbers, and effectiveness. A comprehensive modern study of Brandy Station is much needed. Until (if ever) that study arrives, see Gary Gallagher, "Brandy Station: The Civil War's Bloodiest Arena of Mounted Combat," *Blue and Gray Magazine,* October 1990, 9–22, 44–53.

ment of commissioned officers, both field and line, so that the pay of these amounts to more than that of the whole rank and file. Our whole division of three brigades only numbers about 4,500 men, less than one brigade ought to have, with four brigadiers under pay. The regiments ought to be filled to their full number of 1,000. It is quite plain that somebody does not understand war, and that its cost is of no earthly consequences."

During the 12th and 13th of June the 1st and 3d Corps moved past the lines occupied by Barnes, going in the direction of Bull Run. . . .[7] The Army of the Potomac [had] started upon [Lee's] trail or along his flank [as he moved north], and the Eighteenth left its camp in the clover–fields about Grove Church on [June] 13th, moving by way of Catlett's, Manassas Station, and Centreville to Gum Springs. It camped so as to present a line of battle . . . with the rest of the division facing Thoroughfare Gap in the Bull Run Mountains.[8] As in the march from Fredericksburg to Manassas of the year before, so in this the weather was very dry, dust flying in clouds from the finely pulverized roads, and long detours were made to find water. Even then it was only to be had from puddles left in the deeper holes of dried-up creeks, and was invariably thick and red with mud. While at Gum Springs, on the evening of the 18th, a heavy thunder shower gave the country a good soaking down, which was the first rain in sufficient quantities to lay the dust for seven weeks.[9]

On the 19th the whole division moved hurriedly to Aldie's Gap [in the Bull Run Mountains], distant four miles, and camped to the right of the road leading through it in such a manner as to be in battle line whenever called to "attention." It was found that the Second Division of the Corps [the Regulars, commanded by Sykes] was occupying the left of the road in the same manner, as if expecting the enemy would make another attempt to crawl through this gap like the year before when Pope was at Bull Run.[10] The 1st Rhode Island and Massachusetts Cavalry had had a sharp,

---

7. This move marked the beginning of the Gettysburg Campaign. With the Confederates moving northward through the Shenandoah Valley and, eventually, across the Potomac, Hooker and his army shadowed him to the south and east, moving northward toward Manassas, Fairfax, and the Potomac.

8. Gum Springs was located along the Little River Turnpike (modern Route 50), about ten miles north of the Manassas Battlefield. Thoroughfare Gap was, and is, the best of the passages through the Bull Run Mountains, a tall ridge that runs from New Baltimore northward to Aldie, Virginia.

9. Since the torrential rains that followed the Battle of Chancellorsville.

10. Aldie Gap lies at the northern end of the Bull Run Mountains. The second division referred to by Mann was that composed of the army's regular army troops, commanded during the Gettysburg Campaign by Romeyn B. Ayres.

running skirmish with the rebel cavalry the day before, in which the former received pretty rough handling and lost the bulk of their men as prisoners.[11] It required a force of infantry that preceded Barnes's brigade to clear the gap, and at two o'clock in the morning of the 21st the whole of Griffin's division moved through in quick time to Middleburg, reaching that place an hour after sunrise. During this march the cavalry were constantly skirmishing, but kept the roads clear well in advance of the movement of the infantry.

A short check was received at Middleburg, but as soon as the infantry deployed to go in, the rebel cavalry took to their heels, and again the division moved on toward Ashby's Gap of the Blue Ridge,[12] going into camp near this place about sundown. During the cavalry skirmishing across the Middleburg valley 60 prisoners were secured, but it was found that a strong rebel force held the gap, so this division was turned back at three o'clock on the morning of the 22d, and reached its camps at Aldie an hour before sundown.[13]

As soon as the enemy's force was discovered in Ashby's Gap, it was so well known as to become the common remark of the rank and file that Lee's army was off for another invasion of Maryland or Pennsylvania. It was only a question of a few hours before the Eighteenth would be moving across the Potomac to do its part toward driving that audacious commander back to his own "sacred soil." In a letter to his father, written June 18th, the corporal wrote: "If Lee has ventured this way again with his army, I think he will get hustled around pretty lively and sent back much worse off than he came. At least, I hope he will. I see, by the papers, that you people of the north have been pretty well roused up by Lee's threatened invasion. Well, it will do you some good."[14]

Before the troops with which the Eighteenth was intimately connected crossed the Potomac, they tacitly understood that the settled policy of Hooker in regard to the coming campaign, gathered from a circular order that was read at the head of the brigades, was to favor the movement of

11. For more on this bloody clash, see Wilbur S. Nye, *Here Come the Rebels* (Reprint, Dayton, 1984), 173–77.

12. Where modern Route 50 crosses the Blue Ridge.

13. For a complete summary of the division's movements on June 21 and 22 see *O.R.*, Vol. 27, Pt. 1, 598–99.

14. This was a common sentiment among Union soldiers—the idea that a Confederate invasion would stimulate the Northern populace to action. See also letter of George Breck in the *Rochester Union and Advertiser*, May 15, 1863.

Lee's army well into Pennsylvania while following closely in his wake. All possible efforts were to be put forth to prevent his returning, but none to obstruct the heads of his columns in their northward march.

Two reasons were current, and discussed about the campfires at night among the officers as well as men, which made that kind of tactics very popular. . . . These reasons were:

First, that by such a movement Lee might absolutely be prevented from taking even a squadron of cavalry or a single gun back to Virginia if he could be coaxed far enough into Pennsylvania. A serious invasion of the North of that character would release thousands of troops that were loafing about the fortifications at Washington to assist in watching and guarding every avenue that might be open for a return escape. Second, with Lee's army in Pennsylvania, rioting among its rich farmers and thriving manufacturing towns, a general awakening of the whole North would result in overwhelming the weakening Confederacy in a short time.

The Army of the Potomac was never handled better than on this race after its old opponent toward that state.[15] But Hooker had gained the contempt of his Corps commanders by his marked failures to take advantage of the successes gained during the first days of Chancellorsville. The Administration dared not risk him with another battle, so he was superseded by General Meade on the morning of June 28th, and General Sykes took command of the 5th Corps.[16]

Of these arrangements the rank and file of the army knew nothing about until after the Battle of Gettysburg had been fought. On the contrary, during the evening of June 30th Colonel Hayes of the Eighteenth called the regiment to attention and informed it that General Halleck had been superseded by McClellan and the latter was now commander-in-chief. The cheering that followed this announcement was tremendous, prolonged, and given with the old spirit that he always called out. This pe-

---

15. Most in the army did not share Mann's charitable view of Hooker on the eve of Gettysburg. See, for example, Acken, ed., *Inside the Army of the Potomac*, 289–90.

16. Sykes has been mentioned before. A forty-year-old career army officer, he had served in all the campaigns of the Army of the Potomac. Plain, simple, and tenacious, he stimulated relatively little comment from the rank and file. Sherman said of him in 1861, "Sykes has in him some dashing qualities," but these qualities certainly paled compared to some of his compatriots. Sykes would command the Fifth Corps for ten months. Warner, *Generals in Blue*, 492–93; Rachel Sherman Thorndike, ed., *The Sherman Letters: Correspondence between General Sherman and Senator Sherman from 1837 to 1891* (New York, 1969), 123. See also Timothy J. Resse, *Sykes' Regular Army Infantry Division, 1861–1864* (Jefferson, N.C., 1990), 293–94.

culiar information was given to the whole division, and perhaps to the whole corps, at about the same time, and the wild cheers that broke from the men as the news communicated from regiment to regiment resounded along the various roads on which the army was moving well into the night. It put new life and renewed spirit into the tired veterans who had been making forced marches for the past three days and aided much in moving thousands forward who, otherwise, would have fallen by the roadside. This incident will be referred to again after Gettysburg.[17]

The Eighteenth left Aldie at eight o'clock on the morning of June 26, marching through Leesburg to Edward's Ferry. It crossed the Potomac into Maryland by a pontoon bridge about four o'clock and continued until nine in the evening—making a march of 20 miles during this wet, drizzly day over slippery, muddy roads. By seven o'clock on the next morning [June 27] this regiment and corps were in motion, and during the morning Barnes's brigade made a detour that took it four miles away from the line intended.... At noon the Monocacy River was forded within sight of its junction with the Potomac. The water was waist deep, with the added danger of a strong current that took quite a number of the men off their feet, even threatening to sweep some to the Potomac.

The march continued during the afternoon [of the 27th] for some miles along the right [west] bank of the Monocacy, then leaving the river the brigade moved through Buckeystown and went into camp two miles from Frederick about seven in the evening, after a march of 24 miles. In a letter to "friends at home," dated June 28, the corporal wrote: "Our march yesterday was through wheat fields. On both sides of the road as far as the eye could reach nothing but wheat was in sight, with an occasional cornfield, but no wood or grass land. Reaping machines were clattering in all directions, as the grain is just ripe for cutting. The army pays no attention to the wheat but marches right through it, and we made a wide swarth through more than ten miles of it yesterday, choosing to tramp through it rather than in the muddy roads."

Before closing this letter he further notes: "I am sorry for the farmers in

17. For confirmation of this incident see Hayes, MS Journal Extracts, Chamberlain Papers, Library of Congress; John L. Smith, *History of the 118th Pennsylvania Volunteers, Corn Exchange Regiment* (Minneapolis, 1905), 237. While some members of the army fought the Battle of Gettysburg under the misimpression that McClellan had resumed command, the vast majority did not. Most letters written between June 28 and the beginning of the battle on July 1 accurately reflect the change in command from Hooker to Meade. See Sears, *The Young Napoleon*, 353–54.

this splendid country through which we are passing, for the army is worse than a plague or pestilence."

After a rest of 36 hours, the march again resumed at seven on the morning of the 29th, moving through Frederick and out on the turnpike road toward Westminster—camping two miles beyond Libertytown. On the 30th, moved by daylight . . . and bivouacked at Union Mills for the night, within ten miles of the Pennsylvania line, making a march of 24 miles.[18] This bivouacking was only in name, however, for Barnes's brigade was almost immediately scattered to the front for picket duty, and it was midnight before . . . some of the men caught a few hours sleep.

[The regiment] was called in from picket about eight o'clock in the morning of July 1st, and at 10 again resumed the northward march, crossing the Pennsylvania line soon after noon. It reached Hanover at five o'clock, where a rest was allowed for two hours and a half. Before eight in the evening all were again hurried forward, but the forced marching was beginning to cause men to drop out from sheer exhaustion. At 11 o'clock that night the corporal [and his friend McGinnis] dropped into a fence corner by the roadside, rolled himself in his blankets, and was soon oblivious to the tramp, tramp of the army, and the steady rumble of the artillery that kept moving by all night.[19]

Old soldiers remember that the reception of the Union army by Maryland was generally very cordial. The Marylanders displayed a genuine hospitality that is characteristic of the South when kindly disposed toward her visitors. Perhaps a share of this reception was due to the fact that the rebels were hungrier than the Yankee. It was different in portions of Pennsylvania, and this change was noticeable soon after crossing the line and all the way to Gettysburg. The Dutch farmers seemed to be very closefisted, never giving but always selling, and making careful note upon the spot of every penny's worth of damage, real or fancied, that their property received from

---

18. Mann also recorded that he marched through Middleburg this day, but that's an impossibility—Middleburg was well west of the Fifth Corps' route of march.

19. Sykes was responding to a summons from army commander Meade. The Fifth Corps had halted in Hanover at about 4 P.M. when Sykes received a courier from Meade. Meade's message informed Sykes of the events of July 1, then ordered him to march with the Fifth Corps to Gettysburg with all haste. "Scarcely had arms been stacked," when the Corps took to the road again. It reached Gettysburg after midnight, bivouacking about two miles southeast of the town. The army would complete its march three hours later, arriving at the front at 7 A.M. on July 2. *O.R.*, Vol. 27, Pt. 1, 600; Harry W. Pfanz, *Gettysburg: The Second Day* (Chapel Hill, 1987), 49–51.

Yankee or rebel, to present later for payment to the treasury of the United States.

One of these thrifty Dutch farmers, whose fine, lordly acres must have spread out to almost touch "Mason and Dixon's" line, was caught selling water by the glass to the tired, thirsty, marching column of soldiers that was hastening after the invader. His trade only lasted until a Pennsylvania regiment that was marching in this column reached the spot. Then he was so roughly handled that he soon had the appearance of having been passed through a threshing machine. This case is not an exaggeration, it was characteristic of a large class of the farmers mentioned. But happily, the matrons and maidens counteracted to a great extent transactions of that kind by dealing out with a liberal hand . . . bucket-full after bucket-full of lemonade, iced water, coffee, and in some instances rather hard cider.

The booming of cannon to the northward told us that Lee's army was halted and that another grapple was about to take place, which stirred my Irish comrade's Irish blood to the boiling point. We both felt as he expressed it: "Thim divils have got as far North as is hilthy for thim!" and that we were out of place. The inhabitants about us were becoming badly scared and were leaving in all directions, in all manner of teams, away from the sound of the cannonading. Among them was a mule harnessed to a two-wheeled hayrick, driven by a frightened negro. We halted the driver to make inquiries but found him too demoralized to give us intelligent answers. Then McGinnis offered him a dollar to turn about and carry us on a piece, but it made no impression. Comrade McGinnis is an educated man and there were occasions when he dropped his Irish brogue; this was one of them, and his next speech was a command given in terse English:

"You black rascal, turn that mule's head in the other direction and give us a lift!"

"Deed, Massa, dis nigger mit killed, sur!"

"Kilt, is it? Sure, its an honor to yees to be kilt these days! B'gorra, a black Corpse wont stink worse nor a white! Turn round I say!"

"O massa, massa, de air am full of iron pots dat am bustin and he make big hole tru de cabin!"

"Ye black fool, it's not the loikes of ye they do be after! Turn that mule's head tother and forenist!"

And McGinnis, to emphasize his remarks, gently prodded the darkey with his bayonet. Our negotiations were very short for, already, while he was managing the colored gentleman I had got the mule by the head and was turning it about. Then we jumped aboard and took command of the whole outfit, keeping the mule in the direction we wished to go regardless of the negro's importunities. The reins were still in his hands but the bayonets were ours and with them we kept prodding the mule and threatening the darkey, thus riding for several miles until an occasional shell from the rebel guns reached over and dropped in our immediate vicinity. The negro had dropped into the bottom of the cart, ash-colored from fright, and the mule was becoming unmanageable in our hands.

"Sure, it's quoite time we ixecuted a flank movement!" said McGinnis, so we dismounted from the cart, and the next instant were convulsed with laughter to see that darkey and the mule get to the rear. The mule really showed speed....

About one o'clock in the afternoon we found our regiment and were congratulated by the captain, to whom we reported, upon being all right in spite of our straggling, as the regiment had not yet been engaged!

A curious commentary upon this incident was given by [the corporal's] father, in reply to the corporal's account of this straggling, characteristic of the "abolition" feeling at the North at the time. He wrote: "Do you think you was using the poor colored man just right in forcing him in the manner you relate?"

The 5th Corps reached Gettysburg at five o'clock on the morning of July 2d, after a march of 60 miles since the morning of June 29th, and was held as a reserve in support of the batteries until three in the afternoon. By that time all the stragglers who cared to be at the front had come up, and they made up full half of the Eighteenth—which was, no doubt, in about the same exhausted condition as other veteran regiments of the Corps. About two o'clock in the afternoon the 6th Corps came straggling up in very much the same condition in which the 5th Corps did in the early morning, taking the place of the latter as a reserve while the 5th was sent to the front to have its little experience in the edge of the "Devil's Den."

Mann and the Fifth Corps arrived at Gettysburg in the midst of quiet, but on the cusp of some of the war's most intense and dramatic fighting. Throughout the night of July 1 and the morning of July 2, General Meade had arranged his lines in that famous "fish hook," extending from Culp's Hill on the right to Cemetery Hill, then southward toward (but not quite to) Little Round Top. Just after midday, Third Corps commander Daniel Sickles took it upon himself to adjust Meade's line, moving his troops westward to the Emmittsburg Road and the Peach Orchard, bending his left back toward Devil's Den. Though possessed of strong ground, this line reeled under heavy Confederate attacks that afternoon. As Sickles's line withered, calls went out for reinforcements. The Fifth Corps responded first. Some units went to Little Round Top. Others, including Barnes's division, headed toward the soon-to-be-famous Wheatfield. On the stony hill just beyond that field, the Eighteenth Massachusetts would play out its part in the Battle of Gettysburg.

At three o'clock in the afternoon of July 2d, the 5th Corps went to the front to retrieve the ground lost by Sickles's 3d Corps. General Barnes was in command of the division, Colonel Tilton, of the 22d Massachusetts, commanded the 1st brigade and Lieut. Col. White led the Eighteenth.[20] The 3d brigade was sent to Little Round Top where it would make itself famous under the leadership of Colonel Chamberlain of the 20th Maine, as the commander it started with, Colonel Vincent, was almost immediately killed.[21] The 1st and 2d brigades undertook to fill the gap between the right of the 5th Corps and left of the 3d Corps, which brought them a little to the right of the foot of Little Round Top and to the edge of the "Devil's Den."

The battles around Gettysburg have been so vividly written from the standpoint of men who were in a position to comprehend the vast and complicated movements as a whole, both from the Federal and Confederate sides, that nothing of the kind will be attempted while sketching the little part acted by the Eighteenth and its immediate connections, and what it saw of this, one of the great historical battles of the world.

In moving to the front Tilton's and Sweitzer's brigades, the 1st and 2d, passed to the left of a stone house and across a lane leading to it that was heavily fenced by rolling large boulders together to form a wall.[22] Then

20. Major William B. White, former commander of Company G, was a twenty-five-year-old shoe manufacturer from East Abington. He would eventually rise to lieutenant colonel of the regiment. The brigade's commander at Gettysburg was Colonel William S. Tilton, the former colonel of the Twenty-second Massachusetts.

21. Mann refers to Colonel Joshua L. Chamberlain of the Twentieth Maine, who won a Medal of Honor for his efforts on Little Round Top. Contrary to Mann's assertion, Chamberlain did not command the Third Brigade after Vincent's death. Rather, command devolved upon Colonel James Clay Rice of the Forty-fourth New York.

22. The house referred to belonged to J. Weikert; it still stands. The road was the so-called "Wheatfield Road," which today is part of the National Park Service road system at Gettysburg.

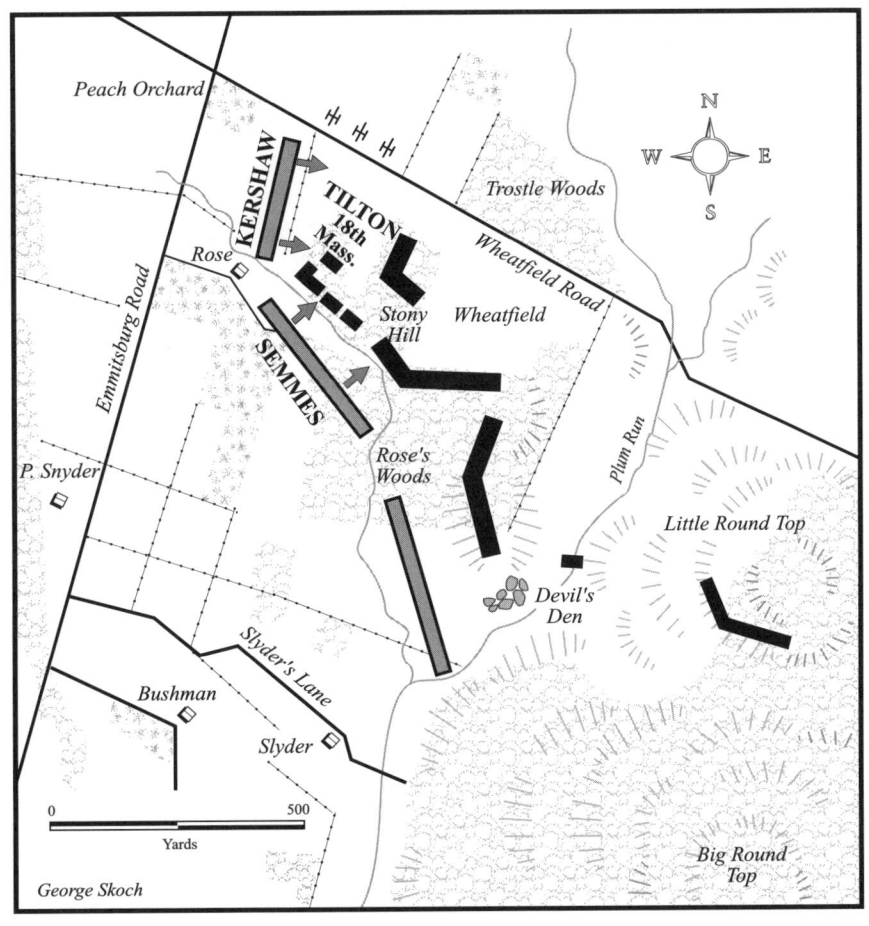

The Eighteenth Massachusetts on the Stony Hill, Gettysburg, July 2, 1863.

they entered a piece of woods where a small brigade was passed over that it was understood belonged to the 3d Corps; it was lying down upon the ground. The line of Barnes's division was formed in the edge of this piece of woods, the ground to the front being open and sloping away to another piece of woods that was 200 yards or more away. It was hardly straightened in position to the satisfaction of General Barnes before an unusual movement was observed in the edge of the woods beyond, and in another moment a rebel line of battle emerged with that peculiar Indian yell that was very familiar to these veteran brigades. The line was a heavy one, struck the 1st brigade, on the extreme right of which was the Eighteenth, at an angle of 23 degrees, and lapped a long distance past where any troops were at hand to face it.[23]

A quick, sharp order was passed along the line: "Reserve your fire till the order is given!" As the Greybacks scattered out of the woods, an instant's halt was observed while they straightened their lines, then the [Confederate] order to fire was distinctly heard by the right half of Barnes's line, and it was quickly executed. Its effect was astonishing though not unusual. The volley was delivered at a distance of 200 yards, and from a line that was 40 or 50 feet below the elevation of the Union line, so instead of doing the fearful execution that was expected, nearly the whole shower of bullets passed harmlessly 10 or 20 feet over these Yankee heads. As the rebel order—"fire!"—was heard, the counter order—"down!"—was given by General Barnes, but too late to be effective even if it had been necessary to preserve lives.

Then the enemy sprang forward, and as they emerged from the smoke of their own volley, half way up the slope, the order for which the Union line was impatiently waiting—"aim, fire!"—sent a raking swarth of bullets into the yelling ranks that made many gaps and caused a decided check. Barnes's men aimed for the rebels' feet, having been taught in an instant not to fire over their heads, while the lack of casualties from the heavy rebel delivery had decidedly steadied their aim.

23. The Eighteenth Massachusetts and the rest of the brigade—which numbered only 654 men in four regiments—took position on what is today known as the "Stony Hill," just west of the Wheatfield. Mann's precision in measuring the angle of the Confederate approach reflects the intense interest Union veterans took in events of Gettysburg after the war. While other battles faded to muddled flashes of horror; the veterans measured and remembered (or at least attempted to) Gettysburg with unprecedented exactness. The troops advancing on Mann's regiment and brigade were South Carolinians commanded by Joseph B. Kershaw. See Pfanz, *The Second Day*, 243, 256–57; O.R., Vol. 27 , Pt. 1, 600–02.

But half that charging line had no such fire to meet and was rapidly wrapping itself around Barnes's right. The 1st Brigade must immediately change its line by facing about and making almost a half wheel to the rear. This was done, and the movement required the longest race on the part of the Eighteenth because it was on the extreme right, while Sweitzer's brigade to the left was disturbed but very little.

In making this change the swing back took the regiment again across the lane and heavy stone walls that fenced it, and as the men jumped them advantage was taken of each to give the rebels a volley or two and to reload under their protection. The brigade thus swung back some 500 or 600 yards to where it was able to hold its ground without any further flanking on the part of the enemy. But by this time—nearly dark—its ammunition was exhausted, and a brigade of Pennsylvanians from the 5th Corps came to its relief.[24]

Although not a man of the Eighteenth was injured by that first, full volley from the rebel line, the formation of a new line in the face of the charging, flanking enemy, cost this regiment 32 men out of a total of only 108, nearly all of whom were only slightly wounded or taken prisoners. Corporal Tom was a prisoner a half hour or more, but a bloody incident secured his release as well as his capture—one of a hundred exciting and interesting episodes of the "Devil's Den," not all, however, with so happy an ending.

The corporal had disposed of half his 40 rounds of ammunition, had just discharged his musket in the face of the advancing line of rebel flankers—which was less than 50 yards away—and was crouching behind the last wall of the lane when one of his comrades undertook to climb over it and was shot dead. The body fell across Tom in such a manner as to pin him and his musket, which he was in the act of reloading, to the ground. Not dreaming that the comrade was dead, Tom berated the prostrate form as a careless "lunkhead" until the copious stream of warm blood, which was thoroughly saturating him, led him to comprehend the state of things and to untangle himself from the corpse. But the incident had so absorbed Tom's attention that he did not observe his live comrades moving still farther to the rear, and by the time he was ready to move the Johnnies were

---

24. The Eighteenth would continue to be tangentially involved in the battle, helping to support Bigelow's Ninth Massachusetts Battery near the Trostle House. As will be seen, Mann would not be witness to this action. The Pennsylvanians Mann refers to were the Pennsylvania Reserves, commanded this day by Brigadier General Samuel Wylie Crawford. In the original, Mann misidentified the Reserves as being part of the Sixth Corps. Ibid., 316–17.

leveling their muskets across the wall, over his head, and into the ranks of the 1st Brigade.

Tom had no alternative but to lie quietly while the Greybacks took their turn in firing several volleys after his vanished comrades. Then they jumped the wall and moved a few yards farther toward the Union lines, which made the corporal a prisoner of war. To make a picture of the situation complete it must be understood that a dense pall of smoke, from the heavy fire of musketry, hung so close to the ground at this stage of the action that nothing could be seen 15 yards away.

As Barnes's lines were brought fairly to face the charging foe they remained firm, and the further onward movement of the rebels was checked. A lull in the battle occurred that lasted 15 or 20 minutes, though quite a scattering fire was always dropping its hissing and zipping bullets against the walls and boulders that covered these fields, making the corporal's position a hot one from the fire of his own comrades.

A little later several members of the rebel hospital department made their appearance while attending to their duty of helping the wounded, and one of them, noticing the live corporal all saturated with blood by the side of the dead man, asked how badly he was hurt. At the same time, in a matter of fact manner, he reached for Tom's musket, which he immediately clubbed across the wall in such a manner as to ruin it. Like a flash the condition he presented prompted Tom to reply in a faint voice:— "Don't know, but think I am used up!"

"Well, you all do the best yo' knows and we'uns'l tote yo' back d'rectly." And away they moved, leaving the corporal to his own devices.

Our hero immediately crawled between a big boulder and the wall where he was not only pretty well protected from stray bullets, but well hid, though he was hardly settled into a comfortable position when the Pennsylvania Reserves, of the 5th Corps, charged down, cleared the field and lane, and gave the corporal a chance to crawl out, pick up a serviceable musket, and report to his regiment. He was received back by company "I" just at dusk as one raised from the dead, for Hemenway[25] was about to send in the company reports for the day, in which Corporal Tom appeared as "left on the field mortally wounded."

The difference between the number of men reported as present for duty and the number that actually take part in a battle was very marked in this

25. Lieutenant William W. Hemenway—wounded at both Second Manassas and Fredericksburg.

Gettysburg campaign, as has been casually noted in others that preceded it. And in showing the discrepency [*sic*] in the Eighteenth, it may be taken as an average, covering all the veteran regiments of the Army of the Potomac, for this was not a peculiar or an exceptional one.

For two years either Sergeant Bill or Corporal Tom had kept the company accounts, made out its pay-rolls, and knew exactly how every man was accounted for; whether at the hospital sick, absent without leave, prisoner of war, or present for duty. At this time Sergeant Bill had also much to do with the regimental rolls, so was well posted in regard to its standing as a whole.

Considering the reduced numbers of the Eighteenth, therefore, which were *reported* present for duty—only 314—in contrast to the 108 that were found at the front during the afternoon of this July 2d, the real fighting strength of the army must always have been far below the numbers represented in reports and upon paper. Some of these absentees were necessarily disabled in the forced marches to the front; others were detailed to guard wagon trains and camp equipage, but the fact remains that it is a rare thing for much more than half of the supposed strength of a regiment to be found in the line when a charge is made upon or received from the enemy.

By daylight on the morning of July 3d, the 5th Corps was in the position it was expected to hold at all hazards during the day. This was the two Round Tops, with the ravine between, and constituted the left wing of the Union army. The Eighteenth, with its own brigade, occupied the slopes of Little Round Top, from which the line of battle ran almost directly north to Gettysburg, two miles away, and spread out like a map to the gaze of the occupants of this hill the whole live-long day. To say that the little handful of men that composed the 1st Brigade enjoyed war for that day would be drawing it mild; they just gloried and reveled in it, watched it, cheered it on, elevated caps or articles of clothing upon the points of their bayonets, and flagged the giant hosts which, in their clash, marked an epoch in the world's history this 3d day of July, 1863.

Little Round Top was a mass of rocks and boulders, sloping quite abruptly into the valley that lay between these troops and the lower ridges that were occupied by some brigades of the rebel Longstreet's corps.[26] The men of the Eighteenth formed no distinct line of battle but distributed

---

26. Mann speaks of what is known today as the "Valley of Death," between Little Round Top and Devil's Den.

themselves in knots of threes and fours behind a convenient boulder, or temporized a protection for themselves by rolling smaller rocks into a breastwork. The corporal, [James] Snow, Higly, and McGinnis, were posted behind two quite large boulders, only a few yards below the crown of the hill. In a few minutes they had the open space between these boulders well filled with stones to present a pretty solid fort, in a small way, yet before night all four were well sprinkled with fragments of lead that spattered through the chinks, the result of volleys received from across the valley.

The rebel right was equally well protected, and both foes were in deadly earnest from early morning until Pickett's famous charge . . . was rolled back into a mass of ruins. Every moving thing across the valley, which was from 500 to 1000 yards between the lines, became a target for the heavy Springfield rifles whose minnie balls were dangerous at a mile distant.[27] From behind this miniature fort, sticks were dressed with cap and overcoat and raised into view, to be instantly pierced with rebel bullets, while rifles were cocked and leveled to catch the puffs of smoke from where the bullets came, hoping to get a minnie in before the rifleman had time to find cover. Every cap had its bullet-hole trophies to exhibit as a memento of Round Top.

Lieut. Hemenway dodged down to this post about noon, bringing a fresh supply of ammunition and, although not exposed 20 seconds, a dozen rebel bullets were planted uncomfortably close, one of them striking the iron scabbard of his sword so as to render it useless. He did not venture back until the fun was over for the day and, with his field glass, was quite an acquisition to this post, from which 100 Springfield-rifle minnies were sent with as deadly an aim as possible during the day.

Several 10-pound rifled Parrotts were planted a few yards above this post, near the crown of Little Round Top, which added their thundering compliments every few minutes to the efforts of the brigade.[28] Unfortunately, one of them burst about one o'clock and killed several of the men in its vicinity. It was supposed that the explosion was caused by the shell with which it was charged slipping away from the cartridge of powder before it was fired, owing to the sharp angle of depression.

At one o'clock heavy bodies of troops and considerable artillery were

27. This is an exaggeration. Common rifle-muskets of the period had an effective range of about 350 yards, and could kill up to a half mile away (850 yards).

28. This was Benjamin Rittenhouse's Battery D, Fifth U. S. Artillery—a battery formerly commanded by division commander Charles Griffin.

seen moving along in the immediate rear of the enemy's position, and all the guns on the Round Top opened upon them, which caused the Johnnies to drop out of sight. But this fire also called out a perfect storm of bursting shell from some concealed rebel batteries, and for a time the iron rattled and crashed among the rocks and men in a very loose manner to say the least. It soon ceased, however, having done but little damage.

It was about the middle of the afternoon that the rebel General Pickett made his famous charge upon Hancock's lines along Cemetery Ridge.[29] During the whole morning and the early afternoon the very absence of orders and information and the ominous silence that pervaded everything for an hour at a time indicated to the veriest novice that the gathering of the forces for the grapple and crash of a desperate engagement was in progress. At times the silence was so profound that the scattered posts on Round Top forgot their sharpshooting, and waited in breathless expectation for something to happen.

The signal gun that launched the fight, and gave notice to two armies that the time had arrived for Union and rebellion to meet again, was fired from one of Lee's batteries soon after one o'clock. In an instant the storm burst from the throats of 150 rebel guns, and the belching flame and bursting shell were directed at that part of the line held by the 2d Corps. They were leisurely replied to by about 80 pieces of Union artillery for a time, though the latter almost entirely ceased for a whole hour, while Lee's kept pounding away for more than two hours.[30]

Then the Confederates ceased firing, and the lull that followed for 20 minutes was more painful than the combined cannonading of two armies. The men occupying Round Top forgot their exposed position and jumped to the tops of the rocks and boulders, taking every advantage of elevation to catch a view of what was coming next. Instantly the whole hill seemed alive with Boys in Blue as if born out of the very rocks. The rebel gunners again trained a few of their pieces upon this covey of men, and the broken, hurtling iron flying among the stone made such wicked, shrieking, death-dealing noises that they quickly hunted their shelters, as a woodchuck hunts its hole.

Soon the rebel yell was heard, breaking the stillness, and sounding as if it broke from the foot of the mountain and ran their whole line on to, and

29. Winfield Scott Hancock commanded the Union Second Corps, in the center of the Union line on Cemetery Ridge. His command would receive and repulse Pickett's Charge.

30. Though largely anecdotal, the most commonly cited work on Pickett's Charge is George R. Stewart, *Pickett's Charge* (Reprint, Morningside, 1980).

beyond, the steeples of Gettysburg. It brought the guardians of the hill to their feet, and to the tops of their defences, to see Pickett's long, heavy line sweep out from the cover of the woods and on across the fields for Hancock.

For the next hour the Eighteenth witnessed one of the grandest, bloodiest and nerve-thrilling sights that has yet been produced on this continent. On came the grey, yelling host, across the fields, a line two miles long. The Union guns had ceased firing, but it was only to prepare to give the charge an appropriate reception.

The magnificent charge almost reached the woods that covered the Union artillery from the view of Round Top. Every man held his breath in suspense. What reception was that line to receive? Suddenly General Hunt's guns,[31] with one continuous, terrific roar, opened upon it and in three minutes it seemed to have melted away from off the face of the earth.

This appearance of vanishing into nothing that was given to that charging line was due, in a measure, to the rolling masses of powder smoke that hid it. But it was decidedly checked, and ringing cheers upon cheer resounded from Round Top, which brought another storm of shell among its rocks and sent its enthusiastic shouters to cover again.

Again the rebel yell pierced the heavy clouds of smoke, and rose above the boom of the guns. The smoke lifted so that a reforming of the mass for another charge became plainly visible; and on it came more determined than before. It met with the same reception, but penetrated nearer the guns that were dealing such fearful destruction. It was persisting. The penetrating wedge was given momentum by added numbers from other parts of the line. It penetrated the woods, to the guns, and for a few moments, which seemed hours, a few of the guns were silenced.

But new guns, that had not yet spoken, began to pour . . . canister into the flanks of this wedge-shaped mass, and it was almost annihilated. For the next few minutes comparative quiet reigned, and the smoke rose to disclose the feeble, third attempt of Lee's determined fighters to break the Union lines, but it was easily checked.

Half an hour before sunset, the round, full, Yankee hurrah was heard above the lessening, sullen discharges from the artillery, and a long, steady line of Blue moved out into view from the woods that had seemed to cover them. It swept across that portion of the field where Pickett's brave divi-

---

31. Henry Jackson Hunt commanded the Union artillery at Gettysburg.

sion had met it s fate, meeting with practically no opposition, but gathering in thousands of prisoners. The men on the Round Tops added their cheers to those of the victorious troops of Hancock and Hunt, and this time the return compliment of rebel shell was omitted.

Gettysburg was won.

TEN

Respite, Recruits, and Politics

The months after Gettysburg brought a period of quiet—some of it welcome, some of it not. The unwelcome inaction came in the days immediately following the battle as Lee's army managed to cross back into Virginia without bother from the Union army. Lee's escape stimulated cries of protest from Washington and from within the army itself. The soldiers wanted nothing more than to see Lee's army destroyed—even at the risk of their own lives—and to the ranks it appeared that no better opportunity had presented itself. Mann's tentmate Sergeant Alderman moaned to his parents at home, "Oh, what folly! What a precious chance to crush this rebellion, thrown away!"[1]

With Lee vanished into Virginia, the Army of the Potomac meandered southward, eventually returning to the ground made familiar during the Second Manassas Campaign along the Rappahannock River. For two months, the army would remain there, with time for reflection and even a few comic adventures (as Mann relates).

During August and September 1863, it became apparent to everyone in the army that the war had changed. No longer a purely military exercise, it had evolved into a conflict aimed at the South's armies, its economy, its institutions, and even its spirit. The army would come to embrace most of this change—recognizing, for example, that the abolition of slavery entailed real damage to the Southern ability to wage war—but Mann would accept the change more grudgingly than most. The virtues of the conservative McClellan would be, again, one of his recurring themes.

Nor was the war to be fought anymore only by men whose innate patriotism, enthusiasm, or sense of adventure had carried them to the front. While along the Rappahannock that August and September, the army—

---

1. William Alderman to his parents, July 30, 1863, Alderman Papers, FSNMPL.

and the Eighteenth Massachusetts—received its first infusion of draftees, bountymen, and substitutes. These soldiers-by-compulsion suffered much antipathy from the volunteer veterans, and the army used a heavier hand when managing them than had been necessary with the recruits of 1861 and 1862. The mass execution described by Mann in this chapter is vivid evidence of that.

Bearing witness to this execution constituted hardship of a new kind for Mann and thousands of others (as letters of the period attest). For the common soldier, the war had transformed into cycles of hardship without relief—battle, march, tedium, mud, sickness. Even periods of quiet entailed some measure of struggle and horror. All illusions of grandeur had vanished from the war. War had become, as one soldier had written, "a most hateful thing. I can imagine not one *redeeming feature about it anywhere. Even* Hell *cannot be more hateful than the murderous effects of war as we are seeing it now. . . . The horrors we behold are sickening enough to drive humanity to madness."*[2]

"The ghost of McClellan has won the battle of Gettysburg! I am all right," was the message the corporal sent to the home folks on July 5, 1863. Whatever may have been the knowledge of the officers within the 1st Division or the 5th Corps, the rank and file did not learn that Meade was the real commander until late in the evening of the 3d. When McClellan commanded the Army of the Potomac there were very few days in which he was not seen by every soldier who was able to crawl out of his bunk, so his absence during these three days of fighting had prepared his admirers to receive, in a kind of expectant way, the knowledge of the imposition that had been perpetrated.[3]

Two days later [July 6], the brigade was formed into a square to listen to congratulatory orders from General Meade. Adjutant Baker read them

2. Letter of George W. Barr (Sixty-fourth New York), June 10, 1862, Schoff Civil War Collection, Clements Library, University of Michigan.

3. McClellan too would subscribe to the theory espoused by Mann, i.e., that his "ghost" had helped win the Battle of Gettysburg. Indeed, in a draft of his memoirs McClellan used the term "McClellan's Ghost" in claiming some credit for the victory—a twist that brings into question Mann's claim to have used the same term in a letter on July 5. No letter from Mann on July 5, 1863, survives to verify the quote given at the outset of this paragraph. Evidence shows that both Mann's and McClellan's claims to McClellan's Ghost at Gettysburg are vastly overstated. Sears, *The Young Napoleon*, 354.

while standing by the side of Colonel Hayes, who was on horseback. As he finished the colonel swung his hat and called for three cheers for General Meade, but a deathlike silence was his only answer. The men felt a fraud had been imposed upon them and were not yet quite ready to take another hero to their bosoms. The chagrin of the colonel was very marked, for the whole corps was within sound of his voice, and in several near-by brigades some jeering was indulged at his expense. As the colonel replaced his hat and wheeled his horse his chagrin was very happily turned by remarking, "It is not necessary for the veterans who have seen the service that you have to cheer."[4]

When the same congratulatory orders were read at the head of other brigades, the several commanders profited by Colonel Hayes's discomfiture and called for "three cheers and a tiger for the Army of the Potomac!" which, of course, were given with a will. A year later the army learned to respect General Meade, and if he could have prevented Lee's recrossing the Potomac—if he could have sailed in again between the 5th and 12th,—he might have superseded McClellan in spirit as well as in truth. Then a call of cheers for Meade need not have been asked.

Gettysburg resulted in a loss of 23,049 to the army of the Potomac, and of 20,451 to that of Northern Virginia. But to return to the Eighteenth, which was left on the sides of Little Roundup during the evening of July 3.

Early in the morning of the anniversary of the natal day of the Republic, the 1st Brigade and a part of the 2d were sent to the front to reconnoiter. Deploying as skirmishers, they moved cautiously forward, down the rocky sides of the hill, across the valley and over the position occupied by the Confederates the day before, and on about a mile where the enemy was developed in force and strongly intrenched; evidently inviting attack. By 10 o'clock these [Union] troops were relieved by another and a larger force, and moved to the rear so to be given an opportunity to rest. But about noon a thunder shower broke with such fury that the flashes of lightning and crashing and rolling of the thunder seemed to echo the work of the day before. And the rain came in torrents, as if the fountains of the deep were broken up and the bloody fields were to be washed of all traces.

It continued all the afternoon and following night. Nothing could be

---

4. An officer in the 118th Pennsylvania described an identical reaction to a request to cheer the army commander. Acken, *Inside the Army of the Potomac*, 313.

kept dry, and if a battle had occurred only bayonets could be used. The muskets of the whole army were foul from use, and early during the 4th had been thoroughly washed out, but the continued heavy downpour of rain for 18 hours prevented drying, so it was doubtful if one musket in ten could have been discharged. No doubt the Johnnies were in the same defenseless condition and, though the Yankees presented a bedraggled, drowned-rat appearance, [the Confederates] had defeat added to their sum of miseries. Under any condition, a soaking on and about a battle-field is extremely depressing.

The 5th Corps did not start in pursuit of the retreating enemy until five o'clock in the afternoon of July 5, and although the Eighteenth was kept in motion until midnight, not over eight miles was made in the direction of Emmittsburg. It moved only a mile on the 6th, but on the 7th made a long march to the vicinity of Frederick, and on the 8th crossed the mountains to Middletown. On the 9th, [we] crossed over South Mountain, and the battlefield of the year before, to Boonsboro. On the morning of the 10th, it was seen that the Army of the Potomac was forming its lines parallel with Antietam Creek, on very much the same ground as the year before.[5]

It was pretty generally understood by the rank and file at this time that the Confederate losses had been severe, and prisoners by the score and hundreds were being brought in by the cavalry every day. The heavy rains had made the fords of the Potomac impassable, and the enemy were short of rations and ammunition. It was natural, therefore, that the hopes of the army should be raised to the highest pitch. To all appearances Lee's army was in a bad fix, while the Union Corps were enthusiastic, well closed up, and ready to sail in.

Upon advancing beyond the Antietam, the army moved in battle-array, each Corps in line, each brigade in columns of regimental front, and as the ground marched over consisted of open cultivated fields, the whole line could be seen, with its colors proudly floating in the breeze and the bayonets by the tens of thousands gleaming in the sunlight. For three days the artillery moved along two parallel roads, in the center of the mass, all ready for action, while hundreds of pioneers from each division moved to the front and swept away obstructions—fences, stone-walls, out-houses—everything but dwelling houses and large barns. The fields were covered with the heavy, bowed heads of the yellow ripened

---

5. Actually, about seven miles north of the 1862 battlefield.

grain, and when this army had passed everything bore the appearance of having a tornado pass over it. Hardly a stalk of wheat was left standing in the fields.

This battle line was several miles in length, and this magnificent exhibition so acted upon the morale of the men in the ranks, and upon the field officers who led, that if it had been precipitated upon Lee's army nothing could have stood before it. All day of the 13th the Union troops lay with closely drawn lines, investing the rebel position. Slight earth-works were hastily thrown up but never used. When [on] the morning of the 14th we discovered the fact that the Army of the Potomac had no opponent to face north of the river, the least that can be said for the men is that they were disappointed. Chagrin was added as this magnificent battle line swept into Williamsport to capture only one of Lee's small brigades. The Confederate army had built themselves a bridge and crossed it during the night of the 13th.[6]

Evidently the Administration at Washington was not pleased with Lee's escape, so the army was started on the chase without a moment's rest. The Eighteenth moved at daylight on the morning of the 15th, went through Keedysville, over South Mountain again, and into camp for the night, near Burkittsville, after a march of 24 miles. The next day it moved through Petersville to Berlin on the Potomac, and on the 17th crossed into Virginia. The campaign in Maryland and Pennsylvania had lasted 21 days and, if the army had not accomplished all that was hoped and expected, no one questioned the proposition that the Johnnies would not be likely to trouble loyal soil again for another year, at least.

From Lovettsville, where the division bivouacked during the night of the 17th, it moved a few miles early the next morning toward Snickersville, camping about nine o'clock by the side of a 25-acre lot of blackberries. For the next three months the army experienced little difficulty in finding all the berries it cared to gather and eat. The desertion of the plantations throughout eastern Virginia during the past two years caused the fields to

---

6. Part of the army crossed over the bridge mentioned by Mann, but the river had dropped enough to allow Ewell's Corps to cross at the ford at Williamsport. Meade's army did not capture a "small Confederate brigade," as Mann asserts, but it did capture as many as one thousand prisoners. By far the most intensive looks at Meade's efforts against Lee in front of Williamsport are found in A. Wilson Greene, "Meade's Pursuit of Lee: From Gettysburg to Falling Waters," in Gary Gallagher, ed., *The Third Day at Gettysburg and Beyond* (Chapel Hill, 1994), 161–201, and in Edwin Coddington, *The Gettysburg Campaign* (Reprint, Morningside, 1979), 535–74.

be overrun with the creeping, low-bushed blackberries, and by the middle of July they commenced to ripen. This kept the soldiers supplied until September, when the high-bushed variety followed in ripening. More or less of these berries had been gathered both years before, but never in such quantities as to afford [anything more than] a taste to the thousands who scoured the country in the vicinity of the camps. This year was a remarkable one for that very wholesome and welcome fruit, enough being passed over to supply three such armies.

During the next five days the division moved by easy stages along the south-eastern foot of the Blue Ridge, and on the 23d entered Manassas Gap.[7] At this place another very imposing display was made by the Third, Second, and Fifth Corps, all three entering the gap very closely massed. The Third was in advance, followed by the Fifth, and the third line was made up of the Second. It was known that the Confederates were moving up the valley of the Shenandoah on their homeward tramp for Richmond, while the Federals could prevent their coming through the gaps in the Blue Ridge or by dashing through possibly catch a glimpse of, and have a skirmish with, Lee's rear guards.

At Manassas Gap, however, the enemy appeared in some force, hence the display made during July 23d and 24th. In moving into the gap the 5th Corps marched by brigades in full regimental fronts, and this method of advance threw the Corps out of the road upon the steep mountain slopes. For several miles this line of battle had the appearance of the letter V, the bottom angle of the letter representing the road that wound through the gap, with either arm extending up the slopes of the mountains on both sides, thus making a huge V with an angle of about 45 degrees. This tactical display on a large scale was a beautiful one to witness, but to the men who had to pull themselves up by catching hold of the underbrush and tough sassafras shrubs or, in some places, by over-jetting rocks, the fun was not so apparent. The officers who rode along the turnpike that passes through this gap to Front Royal said that the spectacle was a magnificent one.

Just at dark a part of the 1st Division of the 5th Corps was sent to the extreme front to assist the Third Corps, which had met with quite a determined resistance,—though no difficulty was experienced in keeping the

---

7. Manassas Gap was the best of the many Blue Ridge Gaps. In addition to a major road (modern Route 55), the Manassas Gap Railroad traversed the defile—which offered an easy east-west passage. Just west of the gap, in the Shenandoah Valley, is Front Royal.

rebels on the move toward the valley. When too dark to proceed farther all bivouacked for the night.⁸ Early the next morning a general advance was made, but it was found that the Confederates had disappeared, having held the position long enough to permit Lee's trains to pass up the valley beyond. During the 25th, 26th, and 27th, the 5th Corps advanced by easy stages to Warrenton, about which the whole army seemed to be collected, and where it remained for several days.

In keeping up this thread of the movements of the Eighteenth, several matters of considerable interest to this regiment, as well as the rest of the army, have been passed by, which will now receive a little notice.

In the corporal's diary, under date of July 22, 1863, is this note: "Colonel Hayes, with six sergeants from this regiment, among them being Sergeant Thompson⁹ of this company, started for Massachusetts after 400 or 500 conscripts with which to fill up the ranks." And hereby hangs a tale, in which this army of volunteers was deeply interested.

Up to this period no conscripts, or drafted men, had made an appearance within its lines. But the draft riots of New York City had stirred up the temper of the Army of the Potomac from its profoundest depths, and the devilish results were the topic of conversation, bitter denunciation, and bluer streaks of profanity than had been called out by Burnside's Fredericksburg or his "Mud March." These riots took place during the 13th, 14th, and 15th of July, immediately after the army had whipped Lee out of Pennsylvania, and while it was in hot chase of his army along the Blue Ridge. Many a regimental commander begged the privilege of the general in command to take his troops to New York and teach the rioters a lesson, and the rank and file showed extreme anxiety to be allowed the opportunity of showing the Bowery toughs a little real war from the muzzles of their Springfield rifles.¹⁰

---

8. Mann speaks of the Battle of Wappings Heights—an aborted and botched attempt by the Union Third Corps to push into the valley and disrupt Lee's march southward. For an excellent description of this July 23 battle, see de Trobriand, *Four Years in the Army of the Potomac*, 529–31. Another member of Tilton's brigade, which supported the Third Corps during the fight, wrote, "3rd Corps battle plainly in view, with their skirmishers deployed and in action. Twas like a picture. The country very hill & near the enemy much wooded, their artillery plainly in view. Could see them fire and observe effect of shot." Acken, ed., *Inside the Army of the Potomac*, 320.

9. Sergeant George W. Thompson, twenty, a bootmaker from Franklin.

10. An artilleryman in the army eloquently expressed much of the army's view on resistance to the draft at home: "If violent resistance be made to the enforcement of the draft, we can easily spare a couple of veteran regiments who would enjoy nothing more than to drag

These men who were fighting, and had been fighting the battles of the country for two years at the front, were well aware that, in spite of the cost in blood and treasure, the great North was growing rich and populous. The times were being taken advantage of by hordes of speculators and contractors, and even farmers were piling money into the savings banks or investing in the government's bonds. All these conditions were receiving thorough and earnest discussion by the soldier boys, or soldier men, while moving again into Virginia for the third year's campaign, and sullen dissatisfaction with the failure of the country to reinforce their ranks was becoming marked.[11]

Finally two brigades of regular troops, under General Ayres, were detached from the 2d division of the 5th Corps and sent to New York. This did much toward smoothing the ruffled temper of the army, and from the day these troops left for the seat of war in New York the men breathed easier and slept better.[12]

The very presence of these veterans from the front immediately quieted the riots without the necessity of firing a gun or using a bayonet. They simply camped down in a few of the public squares of the city and the reign of terror was overthrown. It pleased the men at the front immensely to learn of the effect upon the great, maddened mobs of New York, when three or four thousand soldiers modestly camped within that great metropolis, and so the excitement in the army was abated.

At about this time, Corporal Tom explained in tart terms to those at

---

out concealed rebels and stay-at-homes, and make them bear their share of the burden. In fact, I should have no objections myself to be sent to New York with my section; there is a fine position for artillery on Broadway below Canal street, commanding the street as high as Eleventh, and the balls would ricochet splendidly on the hard pavement."

11. Hostility toward the Copperheads at home (those who sought peace through negotiation) became rampant in the army during 1863 and 1864. Though much of the army shared the conservative politics of the Copperheads, their commonality ended when the Copperheads began to suggest that the army was a tool in an unjust cause—thereby undermining (in the soldiers' view) popular support for the war effort in the North. Northern newspapers and mailboxes were filled with soldiers' diatribes against Copperheads. For some excellent examples see Alan A. Siegel, *For the Glory of the Union: Myth, Reality, and Media in Civil War New Jersey* (Rutherford, Teaneck, Madison, 1984), 148; Rufus Dawes, *Service with the Sixth Wisconsin Volunteers* (Marietta, Ohio, 1890), 127–28; Emil and Ruth Rosenblatt, eds., *Hard Marching Every Day: The Civil War Letters of Private Wilbur Fisk* (Lawrence, Kansas, 1993), 68–69.

12. The New York draft riots represent the bloodiest example of domestic unrest in American history. More than one thousand were killed or wounded.

home the difference between a "Copperhead"—those viewed as the instigators of the riots—and the conservatives in the army.

> James' letter of the 21st inst was received day before yesterday, and I improve this, my first opportunity to answer. I cannot exactly say I do not like James' letter, but if it had been from any other person, outside of the Home Circle, I should certainly give him or her a piece of my mind, and plain enough so there would be no mistaking what I thought of *any* person who accuses me or other volunteers of the "old army" of being *copperheads*. . . . I think it is very much out of place for those persons who are too much of the coward, or who love their ease better than their country, who are all the time barking upon politics, with not a thought of raising an army for the vindication of the "Stars and Stripes" to call us Copperheads—for such persons our remedy is "Silent Contempt."
>
> We own no Copperheads, Abolitionists or Democrats here in the Army. Our politics are Union to the soles of our feet and we are defending those politics with our best blood, and the best years of our life. McClellan a Copperhead!? I shall take the liberty of disbelieving *you* or *anyone else* that makes the assertion. Before McClellan was relieved from command of the army, but few of us knew what his politics were except that he was making every exertion in his power to suppress the Rebellion by *Force of Arms*. But supposing he was a Copperhead—He has received indignities enough from some of the people and the government to awaken bitter feelings toward the government.
>
> Perhaps you have read in the papers of the *Testimonial* preparing for McClellan in the "Army of the Potomac." Each private gives 10 cts., non comms .25, Lieut. 1.00, Capts. 1.50, Col. 5.00, Brig. Gen. 10.00, and Maj. Gen. 20.00. This is done throughout the whole army. *Not a man* have I heard of yet who is not glad to thus contribute. A committee is appointed of one staff officer from each Corps—to receive this money and decide upon the character of the testimonial. It will amount to upwards of $50,000. This will perhaps give you something of an idea of our, the "Army of the Potomac's" opinion of McClellan (without the necessity of my writing or saying another word).
>
> Another thing I would have to give you my opinion upon, and an honest unprejudiced one too. When a complete history of the rebellion and its subjugation is written, the Army of the Potomac will hold a high place, and present as fair a record as any of our armies. Mind you, I do not include all its leaders in this assertion.[13]

13. Mann to friends at home, September 25, 1863, Mann Papers. This letter does not appear in the original memoir. It constitutes such an excellent summary of the prevailing political view in the army, its views on its past deeds and founding leader, and its emerging sense

Later, when it emerged that the Democratic party would seek "peace at any price" and that McClellan was the likely Democratic candidate for president, Mann's—and the army's—view of McClellan changed dramatically:

> The army here are beginning to feel as tho' Pres. Lincoln would be elected by a vast majority for the next term and all I have heard express their mind, asserting that he is the only one they shall vote for. Even the hitherto strong Democrats, to a man, declare that to change the policy of the war at the present date would be to go over the whole of its past history again—that altho they would have had a far different policy pursued from the commencement, *now* they would not change. At the present. McClellan is dead with us. He has cut his own throat by dabbling in politics. It is not the place for a military member of the army to meddle with politics in the least. He should know no Politician but the Commander in Chief, and altho' we cannot but help admiring the *military genius* of the man, his *politics* and *meddling* we detest.
>
> We are satisfied beyond a doubt that a general's faith must coincide with their commanders in order to successfully prosecute the war. You are aware how bitter we have felt about the removal of McClellan. That feeling has in part abated, and he is now a dead letter. It is truly encouraging to us to read of the overwhelming majorities the Union and Republican candidates have every where received.[14]

---

of identity and history that it has been added here. The "testimonial" to McClellan referred to an effort by "friends of McClellan" to, as General John Sedgwick put it, "present him some little testimonial as a pledge of their esteem." By this time, McClellan was the clear front-runner for the Democratic nomination for president in 1864. One can only imagine Lincoln's reaction when he learned that the officers of the nation's most prominent army were arranging to make what amounted to a huge campaign contribution to his likely opponent in the next election. Once authorities in Washington learned of the "testimonial," it died a quick-but-quiet death. Nonetheless, it remains a vivid indication of the nature of the Army of the Potomac and its relationship with the civil authorities that controlled it. See John Sedgwick, *Correspondence of John Sedgwick, Major General* (New York, 1903), 155; David Sparks, ed., *Inside Lincoln's Army: The Diary of General Marsena Rudolph Patrick* (New York, 1964), 291. Patrick wrote in the aftermath of the testimonial controversy, "The idea seems to be that this Army will be broken up, that it is so thoroughly McClellan as to be dangerous."

14. This newly inserted passage is from Mann to his father, November 18, 1863, Mann Papers. It should be noted that though McClellan was removed from the army, he still retained his commission as major general throughout the upcoming campaign. This mixing of professions clearly irked Mann. McClellan would come to repudiate the Democratic party's peace platform, and Mann's views would change; by the spring of 1864, he was again ready

The use of Virginia fence-rails for camp-fires has already been alluded to, but at this stage of the war all restrictions in regard to their use had become obsolete, and during this summer and fall campaign about Warrenton, Culpeper, and the fords of the Rappahannock, every rail in two counties was appropriated and burned. The country through which the army moved during the last 10 days of July and the months of August, September, and October, was comparatively level. The seven Corps were closely massed, and were constantly changing camps and positions, the country being of such a nature that on many days these Corps were in plain view of each other. This maneuvering and marching and bivouacking made imposing pageants that were rather pleasing to the soldier's pride, and produced many graphic pictures for the artist's pencil.

After a march of a few hours, or a day, as troops bivouac for a short time or the night, sometimes each regiment forms a line as if for dress-parade, or line of battle (which is practically the same), stacks muskets, and then receives the order: "Break ranks!" At other times, governed somewhat by the nature of the ground, the regiment may be massed by company front, leaving plenty of room between each company for camping purposes. In either case one of the most picturesque and amusing sights immediately occurs and, if the lay of the country happens to be such that the different divisions and Corps are in close proximity and sight and the fence-rails are limited, some scrambling, wrangling, and even fighting is apt to result, to say nothing of swearing.

The haste and impatience of the men, as regiment after regiment swings into position, to be the first to get loose after the rails; the scattering of thousands upon thousands at a breakneck speed, and in all directions across the fields, to obtain possession of them; the disappearance of 25 miles of fences within 20 minutes, which changes the whole face of the country like a dissolving picture; to see those fences lifted bodily, and nearly every soldier of 50,000 bearing them in all directions, on their shoulders, toward their respective camps, made kaleidoscopic pictures that old soldiers will not soon forget.

There was one plantation in Culpeper County that has quite a history in regard to its fences. It was supposed to be one of the finest in the county, containing 1,000 or 1,200 acres, and belonged to John Minor Botts. This Botts was quite a noted politician before the war, took sides with the

---

to support McClellan for president—though Mann was in the decided minority on this issue. See Mann to friends at home, April 10, 1864, Mann Papers.

Union instead of the rebellion, and as a consequence was imprisoned a year or more by the Confederate authorities at Richmond. Later he was known as the author of "The Secret History of the Rebellion." He was noted among several decades of politicians at Washington as a very hospitable entertainer. Naturally, therefore, the rails of the fences on his plantation were to be let alone. But they were not. Whether they were burned by fresh troops that had never heard of this Union man or, on the contrary, were destroyed by the rebels out of revenge, does not appear. Anyhow, his plantation was stripped as thoroughly as any in the state. It was during this maneuvering of the army about Warrenton and Culpeper, in August and September, that the 3d Corps turned out, cut the chestnut trees from his forests, split the rails and relaid every fence over the whole plantation in four days—probably not less than 20 miles of it.[15]

Until September 16th, the army lay comparatively quiet, spread out to command the fords of the Rappahannock, changing camp often and for short distances, but making no important move or receiving none from the enemy. The 5th Corps covered Beverly Ford,[16] and both Meade and Lee seemed to be simply watching each other and waiting for the other to move first. The country had been swept so bare of everything that the boys had given up foraging, even for a "hoe-cake," though during one of the regimental excursions to the front for picket duty in September, the corporal and four of his immediate comrades stirred up a little excitement with a hive of bees.

15. Botts's Union sympathies stimulated his arrest by Confederate authorities early in the war. See *O.R.*, Series 2, Vol. 2, 1545–547. Though sympathetic to the North, Botts was found by Union soldiers to be mercurial, intolerant, and aloof. He lived in a home called "Auburn" (which still stands, just north of Route 29 in Culpeper County) with his wife and three daughters. Though the Union troops took great care of Mr. Botts's fences, one of them was less careful with one of his daughters. Rumor held that one of them got pregnant by a Massachusetts soldier. See Clark B. Hall's excellent summary of Union activities in Culpeper County, "Season of Change: The Winter Encampment of the Army of the Potomac, December 1, 1863–May 4, 1864" in *Blue and Gray Magazine*, April 1991, 8–22, 48–62. For specifics on Botts, see p. 50. For a wonderful treatment of the civilian experience in Culpeper County during the war see Daniel E. Sutherland, *Seasons of War: The Ordeal of a Confederate Community, 1861–1865* (New York, 1995). See also James I. Robertson, ed., *The Civil War Letters of General Robert McAllister* (New Brunswick, N.J., 1965), 356; de Trobriand, *Four Years with the Army of the Potomac*, 551–53.

16. About three miles above Rappahannock Station (today, Remington), Beverly's Ford had been a major crossing during the Battle of Brandy Station in June 1863.

There were several hives belonging to a plantation near the river, which bore the marks of having been disturbed by some one but not robbed. Perhaps the disturbers found the bees too hot and active and were not experts in handling them. The deserted brick mansion belonging to the plantation and its surroundings had been ransacked until not even an ear of corn could be found. The bees were holding the fort alone. The corporal had been somewhat accustomed to handling these active little insects on the home farm, and suggested that a way might be found to extract some honey from one of those hives with comparative safety during a cold, early morning before it was light, provided the crowd would leave the bees alone for a time.

The hives were the old-fashioned ones of braided and woven straw, and had the appearance of being well loaded with honey. The first night out on this picket line was too warm and light, and the bees had been too recently disturbed to suit the corporal's purpose. But the third night was cold enough to benumb the bees somewhat and make handling a safe possibility. The reserve was camped some 400 or 500 yards away from the aviary, by the side of a small pond of water that was fed by a fine spring that flowed out of a small brick house—evidently used by the owners of the plantation as a cold storage, while the pond, judging by the green scum and filth with which it was filled, had been utilized for geese and ducks.

Before daylight on the almost-frosty morning in question, the corporal roused his accomplices and together they proceeded to appropriate the heaviest hive. Two rails were carefully selected. The hive was gently placed upon them and borne to the camp between two of the boys, as the farmer frequently "poles" hay out of a wet meadow—all without the slightest difficulty. But on arrival in camp trouble commenced. It had been planned to smother the bees in the hive by burning wet powder under it, but in attempting to do so the powder was prepared with so much water that it could not be made to burn.

Meantime the nest, still resting on the rails, had been lowered to the ground not far from a large camp-fire, and if the bees were not warming up from the ground on which the hive rested, they certainly warmed from the fire and . . . were rapidly showing signs of angry life, as indicated by furious buzzing and the peculiar odor given off at such times. It was already daylight, and 90 to 100 of the boys had gathered around with watering mouths and a babel of advice. The bees were crawling out by the hundreds, over the ground and along the rails upon which the hive still rested, though not yet warmed quite enough to fly.

The corporal suggested that the whole nest be immediately taken away from the fire and burned in the ground, to smother the bees before time was given them to warm up any more, but a couple of the sergeant's "smart Alecs" caught up the rails and held the hive over the blazing campfire, expecting to smother the insects in that manner. Both ends of the rails were alive with bees, crawling away from the hive, and as they began to reach the bare hands of these "smart Alecs" total demoralization resulted, and this emblem of industry toppled over so and landed upon its side two or three feet away from the fire.

There is another variety of insects that will inflict severer punishment, and in quicker time than honey-bees—they are hornets—but as this full hive of bees began to warm up to their work, for all practical purposes they did about as well. They went for everything that was in motion, and it was only a question of seconds before the whole reserve camp was in motion, every blessed mother's son of them but the corporal. Edging away from the crowd . . . and, knowing well the nature of these domestic insects, he stood motionless while the tormented scattered for cover, rolled in the dirt, thrashed the air, and went for the goose-pond. A rebel shell bursting in the midst of these hundred men would not have produced such utter demoralization. Full a score of them plunged into the pond, and for several minutes it was the scene of more grotesque antics, splashing and profanity, than would be thought possible for such small insects to raise.

"Stung?" Yes, nearly every man had marks and wales to show for several days, except the corporal. He positively denied a sting, and a close inspection corroborated his assertion, but it was several weeks before he was approached on cordial terms by 20 or more of his comrades who had suffered the most—particularly those who sought the dirty goose-pond for relief.

"Was the honey made available?" Yes, the fire and other concomitants were too much for the bees and they finally deserted the camp. If the 25 or 30 pounds of honey had not been secured, the corporal's life, according to McGinnis, "wid be, not worth a cint."

During the last of August, and all the month of September, the army received heavy bodies of recruits. The Pennsylvania men came first, followed closely by those from the different New England states, and last from New York. On the 9th of September the Eighteenth received 200 men, 18 of which[17] were allotted to company "I." The majority were as good as the regiment ever had—these were the drafted ones, but as a rule the substitutes that were among them did not pan out so well. There is no means of knowing the proportion of conscripts to substitutes among these recruits, for the latter were hired to take the place of the former in the several towns that had a specified quota to fill, and in many instances these men kept their own counsel in regard to their status. These recruits outnumbered the old veterans present for duty.

It should not be taken for granted that all substitutes who had been purchased to take the place of the drafted were bad men, for such was not the case. The Eighteenth was honored with several of them who did their duty and became part and parcel of its history. But, on the other hand, a large proportion of the men who responded to the draft in person did so from a sense of duty, believing that when volunteers in sufficient numbers failed, a draft was right and patriots should respond. This draft, however, developed a "shady" class of people who were always existing on the "ragged edge" of things, and ever ready to act as if the government was lawful plunder. When the draft took place these unscrupulous men sprang up at once, ready and eager to profit by the opportunities that were immediately presented.

The sergeant handled these men—bounty-jumpers and agents—without gloves, yet truthfully, and his manner of sizing them up cannot be improved. He says:

> Thousands of men had been drafted who were bidding for substitutes, anywhere from $300 to $1000, and self-constituted agents to furnish material to fill the demand were immediately at hand. They raked the gutters of the cities for everything in human shape that there was any possibility of getting through the examining offices, and scoured the country districts for the rag-shag and fag-end of citizenship. Of course they got the lion's share of the substitute money; often the drafted man who paid never seeing or knowing who his substitute was, or caring, while the sub was an easy tool, or a fraudulent accomplice of the agent.

17. The draft law of 1863 allowed a potential draftee to hire a substitute to go in his place. These substitutes were often accorded like status with so-called bounty jumpers: both occasionally took their money, deserted, and then tried to reenlist under a different name. There is no record that Company I had any substitutes, though in 1863 it did receive fourteen draftees, as well as seven men who had enlisted voluntarily.

It was soon discovered that a profitable business was possible by securing the substitute money from a drafted man in one town or state, and at the first opportunity deserting; then find new pastures, under a different name, accept the like price of patriotism from another man, then make another jump for citizenship and still another chance. By keeping the thing going, and working the plan for all there was in it, these "bounty-jumpers" succeeded in selling themselves for a good deal more than even a good soldier would bring in the palmiest days of re-enlisting that followed a few months later.

It was a fine plan and, in the beginning, not over difficult to execute, but the military authorities soon "caught on" to their little game and became so vigilant that what at first was dead easy in another month was a mighty risky business. A military execution for desertion had not been pushed to the extreme and, though many convictions for that crime had been found by different court-martials, and sentence of death pronounced, the Executive power of the nation had always intervened. But the time had arrived when even the notoriously lenient President realized that Mercy needed the handmaid of Justice to remedy these high-handed evils.

The first examples of a public execution to come under the observation of the 5th Corps occurred on Saturday, August 29, and the culprits were five deserters, "bounty-jumpers," and criminals with a reputation gained before trying to fool with the patriotism of the country. Nominally they were recruits for the 118th Pennsylvania, already mentioned as the "Corn Exchange" regiment, but had never been fully enrolled with it. These men, whose names were George Kuhn, John Folaney, Emil Lae, John Rainese, and Charles Walter, had been court-martialed, found guilty under aggravating circumstances of enlisting with the intention of deserting; of having absolutely deserted more than once. They were promptly sentenced to be shot to death on August 26, but for some reason the date was changed to the 29th.[18]

The place selected for the execution was an immense meadow, in the shape of a large amphitheater, through which ran a small stream of water. Across this stream the pioneers of the 1st division had thrown a bridge, and on the other side of the stream, to the right of the bridge, five graves had been dug.

18. The executions were postponed at General Barnes's request in order to "obtain [a] Catholic priest and a Jewish Rabbi" for the doomed. Acken, *Inside the Army of the Potomac*, 332. See also J. L. Smith, *History of the 118th Pennsylvania Volunteers . . .* , 296–97.

From Sergeant Bill:[19]

> Military executions are conducted in a manner calculated to impress those who witness them with the magnitude of the crime committed and the awful reality of the death penalty. There is nothing omitted that will help to fill the mind with the dread and terrible solemnity of the occasion. Every detail is arranged with startling distinctness and carried out in a way that fixes it all in the mind with vivid clearness. The tap of the muffled drum has a fearful significance. It gives one a "creepy" sensation, a nameless dread, a shrinking, sickening foresight of the impending tragedy. We were used to scenes that were pathetic, harrowing, horridly repulsive. Death in its remorseless course had been with us in all it hideousness. We had grown familiar with it and callous by familiarity, but here we could see a purpose of showing death in a new and still more repellant form. . . .

About mid-day [on August 29] the 5th Corps was drawn up and massed in close column, one regiment back of another, in such a manner that an unobstructed view could be had by all. A chosen detail of 16 files, 32 men, under the command of Captain Orne of the Eighteenth, were drawn up ten paces in front of the open graves, condemned men, and empty, rough board coffins. Every fifth musket contained only a blank cartridge, but none knew who held it, while the other four-fifths were loaded to kill.

When all was ready, the signal was given, and the sound of muffled drums, mingled with the minor notes of the dead march from the band, was heard approaching from the direction of the guard tents. Soon the procession came within the enclosure formed by the Corps. Each prisoner was supported by two armed soldiers and walked behind his own coffin, then followed the band and the surgeons. On arriving at the open graves the coffins were set in their respective places and the culprits upon them, facing their executioners. Two were Catholics, two Protestants, and one a Jew, and were attended by a priest, a rabbi, and the chaplain of the 118th, who were given ten minutes in which to offer the last religious consolation.

A death-like silence pervaded everything. Their eyes were bandaged. The officer stepped quickly to one side and gave the command in crisp, sharp tones: "Ready, aim, fire!" and like one piece the 32 muskets belched forth their flaming tongues, and five men fell dead across their coffins. Then the bugle sounded the recall.

19. In the original memoir, Mann did not identify this passage as Alderman's, but it is lifted virtually verbatim from Alderman's "Fare of Three Bounty Jumpers," an unidentified clipping from the *Sunday Republican*, FSNMPL.

But what a change comes over the living thousands that have just witnessed the tragedy. How briskly ring out the commands as with quick step we march away to the lively strains of "Yankee Doodle," played by every regimental band in the Corps. And so we left behind all that remained of the five "bounty-jumpers," to sleep the sleep that knows no waking beside the river that had witnessed many pathetic events, and hushed its murmurs while sanguinary conflicts were being waged along its shores.[20]

20. In a letter to his friends at home on September 2, Mann added details not included in the memoir: "An alley was formed through the centre of our Corps, as it stood, through which the prisoners were conducted, supported by two guards each. All the prisoners but one walked with a firm step, though very pale. They were dressed with a white linen shirt and blue pants, each culprit walking behind his rough board coffin. On arriving at the graves the coffins were set in their respective places and each man—upon his coffin—facing his executioners, which were 50 in no., and drawn up 10 paces from the doomed." After the men had been shot down, "The old soldiers who had been in many a bloody fight without flinching . . . now turned pale and shed a tear, though but few would be found to raise their voice in against their execution, for we all felt that they justly deserved it. A deathlike stillness pervaded through the whole proceeding." For more on these executions, see Robert I. Alotta, *Civil War Justice: Union Army Executions under Lincoln* (Shippensburg, 1989), 77–80; Acken, *Inside the Army of the Potomac*, 334–36, 473–74n; Robert G. Carter, *Four Brothers in Blue* (Reprint, Austin, 1978), 346–48. August and September 1863 saw a slew of similar executions in the army. An artilleryman in the First Corps wrote, "The punishment meted to those guilty men has certainly had a salutary effect." Letter of George Breck in the *Rochester Union and Advertiser*, September 18, 1863. See also an account of an execution in the Fifth Maine of the Sixth Corps in the Lewiston, Maine, *Daily Evening Journal*, August 31, 1863.

ELEVEN

FALL 1863

SWIFT VICTORY AND NUMBING STALEMATE

To many historians, the fall of 1863 is a lost epoch largely overlooked. No legendary battles occurred; neither side gained advantage over the other. For the men, however, the period was anything but uneventful. Beginning in mid-October, the armies were in constant readiness or movement for seven weeks. Lee and Meade moved with their armies as if boxers, each looking to land a jab or better. Lee made a dash for the Union rear in October, only to be cut off and blunted (bloodily) at the Battle of Bristoe Station. Three weeks later, Meade dashed at Lee, this time catching the legendary commander unprepared at Rappahannock Station. There, Thomas Mann and the Eighteenth Massachusetts would play a supporting role in one of Army of the Potomac's most lopsided (on a small scale) victories of the war.

Though a balm to morale, the victory at Rappahannock Station brought Meade insubstantial fruits.[1] Pressured for action (as always) by Washington, Meade concluded on another campaign that he hoped would bring the year 1863 to a decisive end. On November 26, the army hauled itself out of its Culpeper County camps and headed, again, for the fords of the Rapidan, this time intent on passing downstream of Lee, forcing him into an open-field battle. The crossing succeeded, but instead of finding Lee in the open, Meade found him behind heavy earthworks along Mine Run. For four days, the armies glared across that stream, each determined to strike the other. But numbing cold, daunting topography, and forbidding earthworks dissuaded each. Despite the lack of bloodletting, Mann would call

---

1. The impact of the Battle of Rappahannock Station on the army's morale was noted by Emory Upton. The victory, he said, "had a most electrifying effect throughout the army, and I am sure, should he be manoeuvred with skill, the enemy will meet with a crushing defeat." Peter S. Michie, *The Life and Letters of Emory Upton* (New York, 1885), 86–87.

his experience along Mine Run "the hardest fought battle I ever experienced."

Just how difficult the forgotten campaigns of late 1863 were for Mann and his fellow soldiers becomes plainly clear in the memoir. He made no attempt to embellish the dozens of marches—now historically insignificant—into something they were not. Instead, in many places he uses tedium as a literary device, adopting a rhythm and style that conjures the blurred confusion of endless, directionless marching. There can be little doubt that the style is intentional; Mann was too clever and thoughtful a writer to have slipped into it unconsciously. Here Thomas Mann demands of the reader some of the stamina and determination that he and his cohorts in the Eighteenth had to muster to survive the final ordeals of 1863.

From the middle of September until winter finally closed in, the country about the Rappahannock and along the line of the Orange and Alexandria railroad became a chess-board, on which Generals Meade and Lee played a great game. The rank and file little understood it all at the time, except that the marching, counter-marching, breaking camps at all hours of the day or night, fording rivers and laying bridges, tearing up railroad tracks and re-laying them, feeling for the enemy with the skirmish-line, and in return being felt for, was the part they had to perform . . . It was rumored that Longstreet's division of the rebels had been sent West, but it was known that the 11th and 12th corps were detached from Meade, so this game of chess seemed reduced to a science between players who were nearly matched in their number of fighting men.[2]

Before daylight on the morning of September 16th, every corps was on the move to the front. The Eighteenth broke its camp at 2:30 but did not march until daylight. Crossing the Rappahannock, it moved out on the Culpeper road and camped at 1:30 near that village. The next morning this position was changed by moving out two miles beyond Culpeper, when a detail consisting of the 18th Mass. and 1st Michigan regiments, was ordered back to the village to act as provost-guards.[3] With marked satisfaction to the men these regiments immediately returned and established a

---

2. Longstreet's Corps of Lee's army had indeed been detached to join Braxton Bragg's army in Georgia and Tennessee. Longstreet's Corps was prominent in the Battle of Chickamauga. From the Union Army of the Potomac, both the Eleventh and Twelfth Corps—stepchildren of the army—were detached to the western theater in Tennessee.

3. Provost guards were the Civil War equivalent to the modern Military Police.

camp on the brow of a hill that commanded a magnificent view of the surrounding country, the village, and the Blue Ridge.

Here they remained 24 days, while the whole army lay comparatively quiet, though making an occasional reconnaissance, or engaging in a cavalry skirmish, but without any engagement of sufficient importance to give it a name. On the 24th of September a North Carolina regiment was captured by the cavalry and brought into Culpeper, and it was said that the organization was voluntarily surrendered because the state from which it hailed was tired of the war. It was true that the governor of North Carolina was having a bitter quarrel with the President of the Confederacy at the time, and the knowledge of the fact made this story of voluntary surrender quite plausible.[4]

The immortal Fates, or a fascination for the twice desolated place, decreed that this army must now make another visit to Manassas and Bull Run, and it proved to be a race between Meade and Lee for position. The Eighteenth stood in line for an hour waiting for the arrival of its brigade, on the morning of October 11th; fell into the line of march at 10 o'clock, marched to Beverly Ford and there formed line of battle at 5 o'clock in the afternoon. Not being disturbed at that place, the whole division crossed the river after dark and reached its old Beverly Ford camp at nine in the evening. Without being given the opportunity of cooking its coffee, the regiment was detailed for picket duty along the river bank, though it was not a very irksome one, and at nine the next morning the division was thrown into line of battle along the position occupied by these pickets of the night. The two other divisions of the 5th Corps had recrossed the river early in the morning and, shortly before noon, this division was relieved by a part of the 3d Corps, and also recrossed.

This corps was now in line of battle, moving [forward] toward Culpeper, through woods and marshes, across gullies and over hills, but without meeting the enemy, and at dusk it bivouacked on a ridge of hills near Brandy Station. There was some cavalry skirmishing at the front but it kept a mile or more away from the moving infantry. At one o'clock the next morning, October 13th, all the troops were moved quickly back to the ford, crossed the river for the 3d time in as many days and, about daylight, the Eighteenth was given the opportunity of cooking coffee in its old

4. This was pure rumor only. It likely grew from the capture of Confederate cavalrymen, some of them no doubt North Carolinians, during a bloody reconnaissance against Lee's left by Union General John Buford's cavalry on September 22–23. For more on this operation see William D. Henderson, *The Road to Bristoe Station* (Lynchburg, 1987), 53–60.

camp. By sunrise the march resumed toward Warrenton, two columns of troops moving together on either side of the road, while the artillery and supply-trains moved between them. Catlett's station was reached about sundown, at which place the corps bivouacked for the night.[5]

To the ordinary reader, a simple detail of the marching and counter-marching of an army, or a regiment, must be about as dry as the description of a working gang of common laborers. The story of one day's work might be told in an interesting manner, but the attempt to produce another story from the labors of the same gang, on the next day, would be likely to try the patience, and to reiterate the movements of that gang, every day for a month, would exasperate. But in telling the story of a regiment's experience of war in all its phases, extending over a period of three years, it must be remembered that this marching and counter-marching, hunting for the enemy and being hunted by the enemy, constitutes the real work and tests the endurance, patriotism, and devotion of the rank and file, and to them it is intensely real.

They feel that it must be told for, although the general reader would have every march or two spiced and sandwiched with a lively battle, these man were forced to their utmost endurance, night and day, rain or shine, through heat and cold, to checkmate the enemy, and only to offer battle on advantageous terms. So these dry details of the Eighteenth are a necessary part of the great game that was being played between Meade and Lee or, in other words, between the North and South for the vantage ground in this campaign. . . .

While at Catlett's station, about which at least three corps were camped on the night of the 13th, rations of fresh beef were issued at nine in the evening, being the first taste of meat the 5th Corps had been granted for three days. During the morning of the 14th some heavy firing was heard in the direction of Bull Run Mountains, and the appearances indicated another struggle for mastery between "Yank" and "Reb" on this historical field.[6] At 10 o'clock the 5th Corps was on the move, crossing Broad Run

---

5. By now, Meade was aware of Lee's dash around his right flank, and the entire army was in motion back toward Manassas and Centreville, over much the same ground covered by Pope during his 1862 retrograde. Catlett Station, mentioned here, was about twelve miles southwest of Manassas, on the Orange and Alexandria. In 1862, it had been the scene of a night raid by Stuart's cavalry that wreaked havoc among John Pope's headquarters impedimenta.

6. The firing described by Mann occurred not at Thoroughfare Gap (fifteen miles to the north), but at Auburn (four miles north of Catlett Station). There, just after dawn, some of Stuart's Confederate cavalry swiped at the Union army's rear guard—part of Gouverneur Warren's Second Corps. See Henderson, *Road to Bristoe Station*, 155–60.

near Bristow Station where a halt was made for the trains to cross and find protection in the rear. At one o'clock the 1st Division received quite a shelling from some rebel batteries, which lasted nearly an hour, killing and wounding 20 or more of the 1st brigade, but the Eighteenth escaped without losing a man.

This division was then hastened to Manassas Junction, where it arrived an hour before sundown. Late in the afternoon quite a heavy engagement had been brought on at Bristow's between the 2d corps and Hill's rebel division. The Eighteenth and a part of the rest of the division were hastened back to that place, which was reached soon after dark—after the battle had ceased in favor of the 2d Corps.[7] There was a little gratification, however, in seeing the 450 prisoners and five captured pieces of artillery marched to the rear. After an hour's rest our troops retraced their steps, crossed the stream near Centreville, and bivouacked from two o'clock in the morning until nine. Then they marched out in the direction of Fairfax and rested there, in line of battle, from four in the afternoon until sundown of the next day, the 16th.

The 1st and 2d Corps had been left at Centreville, from the direction of which quite heavy cannonading was heard by the 5th Corps for two hours after five o'clock. It rained heavily during the afternoon and night of the 15th, wetting everything very thoroughly and, no doubt, preventing some fighting that otherwise might have ensued. As has already been intimated, but little rain was required on this Bull Run soil to make all the mud that was necessary for blocking artillery and supply-trains, and things were looking a little uncomfortably that way. The men of the Eighteenth, in common with all, were becoming exhausted from the forced marches, short rations, and lack of sleep, and this rain was adding much to the sum total. But there was no rest yet; the game must be played out.

Again the division moved back to Centreville, and made a march between eight o'clock and midnight of the 16th during one of the heaviest thunder showers of the season, through mud and water that were knee deep and, except from the vivid flashes of lightening, in profound darkness. The 17th was spent in drying clothing and equipments, and early on the 18th the troops took the turnpike [eastward] for Fairfax where they arrived at eight in the morning. Tents were immediately pitched as if to

---

7. The Battle of Bristoe Station, where Warren's Second Corps drubbed the advanced-guard of Lee's army. The Battle at Bristoe effectively ended Lee's chance to cut off and destroy all or part of the Army of the Potomac.

make a stop of several days, but in less than an hour the bugle called to "strike tents" and this corps was moved out on the Vienna road [to the north of Fairfax], the 3d Corps marching in parallel column with it, while the 1st and 2d were left behind the earthworks of Centreville. Both corps bivouacked during the afternoon and night mid-way between Vienna and Fairfax, where plenty of chestnuts were found scattered on the ground from the well opened burrs, and no enemy to molest.

It was already apparent that if Lee intended to force another battle at Bull Run, all the advantages were with Meade, and that the former was fairly checkmated. Although the 5th Corps had been everlastingly hustled, it was becoming evident that the army was being handled by a master hand, and Meade's stock was rising in the estimation of these men who were being scooted from point to point like a pack of hounds after a herd of deer. Some of the camp-fire disputants intimated that the Confederates would make another break for Maryland, but the more knowing ones "reckoned" that Meade's outwitting them at Bull Run also prevented their venturing any farther from their own firesides for the present. In fact it was known on the morning of the 18th that Lee was retiring his army back to the Rappahannock.

On the morning of the 19th, the corps broke camp and moved over the Centreville road, crossing Bull Run, and went into camp about four o'clock on the old Bull Run battle ground of the year before. The Eighteenth's camp was only half a mile away from the scene of its charge upon "Stonewall's" division in the railroad cut, and soon as muskets were stacked many of the men started for the place to examine the ground and conditions that proved so disastrous. When the unfinished cut was reached, the ease with which the Confederates could keep at bay the charging divisions of the 5th Corps was noted and understood. It was found that but little attempt had been made to bury the dead after the battle, a trick the rebels always played, and the bare, bleaching skeletons of both armies were found scattered over the whole scene. Several of these whitened, fleshless remains of the Eighteenth were recognized by the comrades who had stood beside them where they fell, and in the evening a detail was made to properly inter them all, and to properly mark the graves of those that could be identified. Other regiments took like action, and all paid the same respect to the bare, unburied skeletons of the enemy.[8]

8. Because the armies quickly left the Second Manassas field after the August 1862 battle, the job of burying the dead was delayed by a week. The gruesome job of interring the dead fell initially to the brand-new 139th Pennsylvania. Others followed, and by September

The march resumed at daylight of the 20th, crossing the Manassas Gap Railroad [at Gainesville], then moving on the Warrenton turnpike and bivouacking in the Bull Run Mountains [at New Baltimore]. Here the regiment remained three days, obtaining a good breathing spell, and gathering plenty of chestnuts and blackberries. While in this gap two of company "I's" men, Ray and McCallum,[9] were returned from the "parole camp," having been captured during the night following the battle of Chancellorsville and recently exchanged. During the evening of the 24th the camp moved to Bristow Station, and the next day to Auburn plains. Here the whole corps stretched out in line, each regiment being in column by company, well spread out to make an imposing showing and a beautiful spectacle on this level plain, and here it established its camps for five days.

The Orange and Alexandria Railroad, which had been the only artery of supplies for the Army of the Potomac in its operations about the Rappahannock and beyond, was totally destroyed by Lee's army from Bristow to the point of its crossing the river. Bridges and culverts were blown up, and the iron rails either carried to Richmond or twisted into every conceivable shape by heating them upon the piles of burning sleepers that were fired for that purpose. It took the engineer and pioneer corps of the army until November 2d to repair and put the road in running order, and before that time Meade could not advance much farther in the direction of the Rappahannock.[10]

The corps moved from these camps on October 30th, some seven miles in the direction of Warrenton, and camped in the heavy forest of timber where it remained until the morning of November 7th. Corporal Claflin was received back into the company at this place, from the hospital to

---

23 the job of burying the dead was declared finished. While no doubt some bodies lay unburied—or had become uncovered—when the Union army returned to the field in 1863, in fact most of the dead had been interred. See Robert Guyton to his father, September 10, 1862, Robert Guyton and James B. Heaslett Papers, Duke University Library.

9. George A. Ray was a nineteen-year-old jeweler from Wrentham. Records show that he was "missing" after Second Manassas (not Chancellorsville). He would be captured again at the Wilderness and would spend the rest of the war in a prisoner of war camp. Gilbert McCallum, twenty-three, a bootmaker from Medway, would be captured in the Wilderness, would survive his imprisonment until his parole in March 1865, but would die in Wilmington, North Carolina, before he could reach home. He is not, as Mann asserts, listed as having been captured at Chancellorsville.

10. The destruction of the railroad—though comprehensive—did not inhibit Meade's movements for the rest of October. See Henderson, *Road to Bristoe Station*, 208.

which he had been sent, badly wounded, after the Bull Run fight of the year before.[11]

Reveille sounded at four o'clock on the morning of November 7th, and the whole corps was on the move at daylight. It passed Bealeton Station, then followed the railroad to within two miles of Rappahannock Station where a battle line was formed in the woods, muskets stacked, and the men remained at ease for nearly three hours. At three in the afternoon the sharp call to "attention" jumped along the line from one regiment to another and from brigade to brigade. The clattering of muskets as they were [grabbed] from the long lines of stacks produced a kind of music to which these veterans had become accustomed, but at this time the sound seemed to impress everyone that something was in the wind. Officers were riding along the lines and conferring with each other in a mysterious kind of way that betokened anticipated obstacles ahead.

The next order was, "prepare to load,—load!" and thousands of iron rammers sprang into the air in the act of sending the cartridges to their seat. Even while this military movement was being executed a regiment was seen to leave the line and rapidly deploy out to the front as skirmishers. Then the right and left regiments of the brigade, the 22d Mass. and 118th Penn., moved to the front and deployed into a single line of battle, while the 18th Mass. and the 1st Michigan . . . followed closely behind in column of division.[12] Thus moving through the woods for 20 minutes, the whole body of troops debouched into open fields and received a well aimed salute from several rebel guns that were defending the Rappahannock, a mile away.

Two strong rebel earthworks had been encountered, one on either side of the river . . . both now in plain sight of this brigade and playing into its ranks with shot and shell, protesting against a further advance. But the order was, "forward!" and on the troops swept ahead, keeping their alignments as if on dress-parade. The skirmishers in front began to engage with the like out-posts of the enemy, and steadily pushed them back toward the higher land that was occupied by frowning earth-works.

The first few shots sent from the rebel guns plowed some bad gaps in

---

11. George H. Claflin, a painter from Foxboro. He would be wounded again at the Wilderness, but would survive and serve out the war.

12. Columns of division refers to a formation where a regiment was aligned in a column of five lines of battle—each of two companies side by side. A line of battle, it should be noted, was composed of two ranks of men.

the lines, but there was no wavering or a moment's halt. The comrades simply closed them up, "touched the elbow" where it had been lost, and moved straight on. Soon the skirmishers approached near enough to the rebel gunners to bother their accuracy of aim, and the advancing line was too near for effective shell work, but not near enough for canister. It was a superb exhibition of the discipline and steadiness of veteran troops, though it made a few of the late recruits so deathly sick that they dropped from the ranks in a dead faint, and as white as real corpses. All the courage of a "Frederick the Great" will not make a man face the music whose nerves serve him such a trick.

Many of the shots aimed at this marching column fell short, rebounded, and passed 20 feet over the heads of the men, and it was a comical sight when 20 or 30 yards of heads were ducked as if expecting to dodge it. For the moment that part of the line appeared as if crawling on all fours, yet neither the step nor the alignment were lost. One shell struck the ground 30 feet in front of the line occupied by the corporal and skipped well over the heads of all, but in gouging the ground it threw a wheel-barrow load of dirt with such force as to send him, with comrades McGinnis and McCallum, sprawling to the ground before time was given to make even a motion to dodge. Not much injury was inflicted, and McGinnis remarked, while brushing the dirt from his face: "Faith, and be jabbers, the dum rebs are thrying to bury us before we are kilt!"

Company "I" occupied the van of the regiment, and the shot that floored the corporal and his two comrades burst immediately in its rear, killing Sergeant Brown and Private Barry of Company "E," besides severely wounding several others of the regiment. Through some mysterious manner, perhaps an instinct, this brigade became aware that it was only being used as a decoy—that other troops were edging closer to the fort on either side of these open fields, under cover of the woods and behind the railroad embankment, to storm the place. Although this brigade kept its lines steady and unwavering for two-thirds the way in the face of the whole fire, it was expecting every moment to see a rush from the cover to finish the work.

This parade had kept a magnificent front to within 500 yards of the rebel fortifications, when the two right regiments, the 18th Mass. and 118th Penn., received the order, "right-face! double-quick—march!" and they were soon under the cover of the railroad embankment [of the Orange and Alexandria]. Simultaneously the two left regiments were ordered to face to the left and file into the woods, and that part of the drama that had been assigned to this brigade was taken from the stage. The loss to the Eighteenth during the half hour it was exposed to this target practice of the rebel gunners was two killed and ten wounded. Among the wounded was Lieut. Weston of company "I," from the effects of which he soon after died.[13]

Just as the shades of evening began to lower, Russell's division of the 6th Corps[14] sprang from their cover, a little to the right and in advance of the position occupied by the Eighteenth, and charged the fort. They carried it handsomely in ten minutes and captured two brigades of rebel troops with four pieces of artillery. These [Confederate] troops belonged to the command of the rebel General Hayes, while the former major of the Eighteenth, now General Joseph Hayes commanding the 1st brigade, led the parade as described through the open fields.[15] The loss to Russell was less in numbers than were sacrificed by those who made the movement across the open fields during the afternoon. As the cheers of the charging column broke forth, Hayes's Union brigade sprang to its feet and to the top of the embankment and witnessed the whole affair, while adding its own voice of encouragement to the brilliant dash of Russell's men.

The veteran of many battles is usually a modest fellow; the soldier who isn't there is the one who is plum full of hair-breadth escapes, and one corps, division, brigade, or regiment, rarely shows a jealous side toward another. Particularly was this the case between the old 1st, 2d, 3d, 5th, and 6th corps. There was next to none in this case, though the 5th did entertain just a slight tinge of feeling because it was not allowed to close in upon that Rappahannock fort, instead of giving the glory to the 6th. But all that was as quickly forgotten until, several days later, when the New York papers were received which gave a minute description of the "brilliant" work

---

13. George F. Weston, twenty-five, died on January 5, 1865, in Boston.

14. Brigadier General David A. Russell would emerge as one of the best division commanders in the army in 1864—propelled onward by his excellent performance at Rappahannock Station. A New Yorker, he would be killed at the Third Battle of Winchester in September 1864. Warner, *Generals in Blue*, 417.

15. The Confederate general was Louisianan Harry Thompson Hays—no "e." The general was not captured along with the more than 1,600 Confederates lost at Rappahannock Station. The Federals lost just 419. For a good summary of the Battle at Rappahannock Station see Martin F. Graham and George F. Skoch, *Mine Run: A Campaign of Lost Opportunities* (Lynchburg, 1987), 18–29.

of the 6th Corps, and in which not even a mention of the 5th, or of the 1st brigade of the 1st division, was made. Then the boys were mad.[16]

But General Russell and a few of his brave men who climbed the parapet of that fort, in a hand to hand encounter, also had their little grievance. Although foreign to these particular reminiscences, it shows up the cold comfort and total lack of appreciation that these men at the front received from the head of the War Department, and will bear mentioning.

A sergeant of the 6th Maine was the first man inside the rebel works, but finding himself surrounded he called out that he surrendered. The next instant, however, seeing men of his command tumbling over the parapet, he yelled, "I take it back," and made a dash for the rebel colors, which he secured, and in General Sedgwick's orders of the next day this sergeant, Otis C. Roberts, was named and complimented.

General Meade ordered Russell to Washington, accompanied by this sergeant and the eight captured stand[s] of colors to present them formally to the government. In the armies of other nations such a mission when entrusted to an officer bearing the trophies of a victory won by his courage—particularly when suffering from a painful wound received in the action where the trophies were won, as was the case with Russell—results, as a matter of military etiquette, in promotion, or some complimentary recognition at least. His experience, however, was interesting though unsatisfactory. Upon arriving in Washington he addressed the Secretary of War, informing him of his mission and asking at what time it would be agreeable to him to receive the flags. After waiting the entire day and receiving no answer he called in person at the War Department, sent in his name, and was promptly informed that the Secretary was busy and could not see him. He thereupon sent the flags to the Department, and rejoined his command by the next train. Then some of the 6th Corps were mad.[17]

There were men in the army who didn't like the smell of gun-powder. They were all well enough in drills and evolutions. They could do camp and guard duty to the satisfaction of all concerned, and march as long and

16. History, incidentally, has not rectified this perceived injustice. The Union success at Rappahannock Station is universally and exclusively connected with the Sixth Corps. For Mann's contemporary account of Rappahannock Station (which he drew on heavily for his memoir), see Mann to friends at home, November 9, 1863, Mann Papers.

17. This episode is yet another reflection of the perceived animosity between the army and the government it served. For another view of this episode see David W. Blight, *When This Cruel War Is Over: The Civil War Letters of Charles Harvey Brewster* (Amherst, 1992), 266.

far as any—always provided they didn't scent saltpeter ahead. There were no predictions of a "move" or a "fight," no matter how wild and improbable, but what caught their ear and secured their close attention. They drank in the horrible details and hair-raising situations with as much avidity as ever-thirsty mortal drank clear, cool water from the bubbling spring.

All this was so noticeable that they at once became conspicuous, and were soon sized up for just what they were by everybody. They were experts in dodging and, like the war horse of "sacred story," they scented the battle afar off, but unlike that poetic steed they were not making any lively demonstrations of impatience to get there themselves. The Sergeant [Alderman] had an experience with one of company "I's" substitutes in this little affair at Rappahannock, which he thus describes:

> These substitutes were mostly a poor lot as far as I observed them, and the government was the party to suffer. One of them who was allotted to my company, and who went under the name of "Sherman,"[18] was a healthy, robust young man to look at, and physically all right, but he absolutely would not fight. He would turn up after a fight with plausible reasons explaining his absence every time. He could invent a story with wonderful facility, and he got to be considered a very able liar by everybody.
>
> It was finally determined to force him into the very next fight, and we were ordered to use any kind of force to keep him in the ranks, and to shoot him if we caught him running away. These orders were not simply for his benefit to operate as a scare; they were in earnest and meant to be obeyed just as much as any order, and the non-coms intended to obey them, too. Sherman understood this very well. He knew there was not a single officer or man to take any milder view of the situation, or look with any degree of leniency upon further shirking of a fight.
>
> As we advanced in line of battle toward the earth-works at Rappahannock Station, an occasional shell from the fort came over to us, and before long they got pretty thick—though in the beginning we were partly hid by a belt of timber. We all had our eyes on Sherman, and were just dead sure we would get him in this time. While marching in battle line through this timber belt, we came to an old log cabin that had evidently been at some time occupied by the negro slaves, but which was now abandoned. In order to pass this obstacle it was necessary to "break files to the rear," a movement that created some confusion for the moment and also took our attention away

---

18. The only "Sherman" in the regiment was Private Gilbert Sherman, twenty-six, a carpenter and resident of Medford. He would not die, but rather would serve out his term with the Eighteenth Massachusetts. The "Sherman" of Alderman's story is not known.

from Sherman. When we got straightened out again we had advanced a little beyond the cabin, and Sherman was gone.

If the earth had opened and swallowed him he couldn't have been any more out of sight. We all felt beat. We felt more than beat—we felt mad. There was no help for it, and we were obliged to go on without him. It was something more than a month afterward that Sherman showed up again. He had "bummed" about the army here, there, or anywhere that he could get a meal. He had succeeded in dodging the provost guard, whose business it was to pick up the shirks, sneaks, and skedaddlers of the whole army; but he evidently hadn't been having a very good time. He was about starved and had a played-out look clean through. Of course he was court-martialed, pay forfeited, and otherwise punished, but he never went into a fight.

During the night of the 5th of May following, after the first day's struggle between Grant and Lee, in the Wilderness, this Sherman was picked up by the rebel cavalry, several miles in the rear of where he belonged. He was taken to Andersonville, and finally to the Florence prison, where he died.

The sergeant winds up his picture of this typical skedaddler and constitutional coward with an expression of the predominating sentiment that actuated the men who faced the music and were always found where duty called, and all such heartily subscribe to the following: "What makes men face the enemy under deadly fire, do you ask, and are they not afraid? They are all very much afraid, I believe, good soldiers especially. It is pride that makes men stand. Not many, thank God, of our Massachusetts boys but would rather have left their bones on the 'sacred soil' than have had their names come back to the 'dear old home' branded as coward. No! No! Hunger they could endure, hardships and privations they could put up with, wounds, mutilations, sickness and death if must be, but dishonor—never!"[19]

The night following the Rappahannock affair, the Eighteenth camped in the woods about where the melee left it, and at daylight the next morning moved out to Kelly's Ford,[20] crossed on pontoons and went in to camp two miles beyond. All the appearances indicated that Lee's army had expected to winter along the right bank of the Rappahannock, with the right of it resting on Fredericksburg, for every sheltered ravine, through which

19. This section is largely taken from Alderman's "The Constitutional Coward: Instances of Soldiers Who Would Not Face the Enemy's Fire," unidentified clipping from the *Sunday Republican*, FSNMPL.
20. About five miles downstream from Rappahannock Station.

Meade's army was now distributed, had been utilized by the Johnnies for building elaborate log barracks. . . . Hundreds of finished and unfinished log-cabins were overhauled, demolished, and burned; [the Rebel camps] showed the marks of having been hastily abandoned. No doubt the unexpected capture of the protective earthworks and rifle-pits at Rappahannock, which thus uncovered some of Meade's movements, decidedly broke up Confederate plans.

This was corroborated by a half-finished letter, picked up by the corporal in one of those cabins. After quite a minute description of the complete wreck of the Orange and Alexandria Railroad as far as the Rappahannock, which was expected to act as a check to the further advance of the "Yanks" for the winter, the rebel writer went on to describe his own comfortable winter quarters, winding up with an urgent invitation to his home folks to "send me something good to eat."

With the exception of three slight changes in camps of a mile to a mile and half each the 1st Division's duty did not take it from the vicinity of Kelly's ford until the morning of November 26th, then was commenced the final dash at the rebels for this year. The initial move was attempted on the 24th, when the reveille and "strike tents" were sounded simultaneously, at four in the morning, but it had rained heavily all night, which puddled the surface of the ground so thoroughly that the moving troops did not average over two miles from their camps before all were blocked by the mud—very similar to the previous attempt of Burnside, though not so radical and disastrous. This resulted in a return to the quarters just left, and in adding another of those useless, exasperating, muddy and wet marches that were so outrageously discouraging to intelligent men who were necessarily kept uninformed of its intent.[21]

As an illustration of the difficulties still attending the commanding general in regard to the secrecy of his plans, it will be interesting to compare the common gossip of this time, throughout Meade's camps, with the actual plans of that general which are now a matter of history. Under the date of November 24th, 1863, this memorandum is found in the corporal's diary: "It is understood by us soldiers that we are to make a move to flank the Johnnies out of Fredericksburg, and make our winter camps along the ridges which they occupied a year ago, obtaining our supplies by

---

21. This abortive advance was not as innocuous as it seemed. On November 25, Lee learned of it and concluded that "General Meade intends to advance." *O.R.*, Vol. 24, Pt. 2, 846.

way of Aquia Creek, and abandon the Orange and Alexandria railroad which we are now using."

Swinton, in his "Campaigns of the Army of the Potomac," says: "It was General Meade's plan to advance on Fredericksburg, and such a move would have saved the morale of the army and the confidence of the country. At this time this general was in a position to successfully make such a movement, but here he was met by previous prescriptions from General Halleck, not to make any change of base. This absurd piece of pedantry prevented what would have been an excellent measure."[22]

General Meade did not make that move, but another instead that was dictated from Washington.[23] It was, like every other move emanating from that source, unsuccessful, while some of the knowing ones of the rank and file recorded another verification of their "I told you soes."

At daylight on the morning of the 26th, the weather having cleared off fine and the mud quickly dried, the army commenced its move on Mine Run for another scrap with the Johnnies. The movements of the Eighteenth are so completely narrated in the corporal's letter to his father, eight days later, that it is transcribed nearly verbatim. The accuracy of his statements, regarding the army as a whole, is a little doubtful in some places, though given as he saw the action from his limited point of view, but the movements of his own regiment are given minutely correct.[24]

> On Thursday morning, your Thanksgiving day in Massachusetts, we started at daylight with five day's rations in our haversacks and marched to the Rapidan, near Ely's Ford where we halted nearly three hours for the pioneers to lay the pontoons. During this delay there was a little artillery firing and cavalry skirmishing on the other side, but nothing of importance to prevent our crossing, and we passed over to a place known as Wycoff's Mills. These were quartz and stamp mills used for extracting gold from the quartz

22. William Swinton's *Campaigns of the Army of the Potomac* (New York, 1866) was an early and provocative (at least to the veterans) history of the Army of the Potomac. Swinton was a former reporter who covered the army throughout the war.

23. Washington authorities did not dictate Meade's next move, but they did limit him to a move using the Orange and Alexandria as his primary supply line and means of communication. See Graham and Skoch, *Mine Run*, 39–41.

24. The following passage is based on Mann's December 4 letter, but it is not a literal quotation from it. When inserting this letter, Mann edited it considerably—altering it for literary flow and inserting some retrospective comments. I have not revised his revisions in this instance, because it amounts to his polished recollection of the events along Mine Run. For those interested in seeing the original text and in comparing the original to this postwar enhancement, see Mann to friends at home, December 4, 1863, Appendix B.

quarries which are extensive about them, and were owned by a Northern man, now quite old, who told me that before the war broke out he had been making money in his operations.²⁵

The march was continued to the edge of the battle ground of Chancellorsville, of last May, where we bivouacked about 10 o'clock in the evening. The next morning we started at sunrise, marched on the plank road toward Fredericksburg for a short distance, then filed to the right upon the plank road leading to Orange Court House. In less than 20 minutes after the move was commenced on this road a small company of rebel cavalry made a dash at our supply train, which was about 600 yards in the rear. They cut out eight of the four-mule teams, drove them down the Fredericksburg road, which we had just left, killed the mules, set fire to the wagons, and captured the drivers. They also gobbled quite a number of stragglers who are always hovering about a supply train. It was a bold dash and all over in 15 minutes, but it delayed our march nearly two hours.

Our forward movement was very slow all the day as the Third Division, which was in the van, was skirmishing over the whole ground in the direction of our movement. At times it was quite brisk, and an occasional cannon shot reached back to our moving column. At three o'clock we emerged from the woods, through which we had been moving all day, and camped in line of battle to the left of the road. The Third Division kept busy with its skirmishing until dark when firing ceased for the night. Thus far the weather had continued cold and pleasant, but was beginning to moderate, and about daylight of the next morning rain commenced and continued until four in the afternoon. It gave us all a wetting that added much to the suffering of the two following days.

We were on the move at daylight, leaving the plank road to the right, by a cross road, and after a two-mile march came out on the turnpike at Robertson's tavern in the Wilderness.²⁶ Here we found that the 3d and 6th Corps had been doing some fighting the day before, and that the enemy had left

25. In the original letter, Mann wrote, "Wycoff's Mill is quite a large establishment. They are used for extracting gold from the gold mines and owned by a Northern man. He was quite an old man and said before the war broke out that he was making money at least there had been some pretty extensive mining operations but of course this war put a stopper upon the works." Map and documentary evidence indicates that Wyckoff's Mill is in fact the well-known "Melville Mine." The owner was John Wyckoff. See Nelson, *Rappahannock and Rapidan Rivers,* 52; Harrison, *Chancellorsville Battle Sites,* 89, and associated references.

26. Sometimes called Robinson's Tavern, this building was a longstanding landmark on the road between Orange and Fredericksburg. It still stands, though it was recently moved to a new location about a quarter-mile back from the Locust Grove crossroads. Its wartime location is now occupied by a convenience store.

our immediate front. We stacked arms and made ourselves as comfortable as possible in our drenched condition. Clearing weather came at four in the afternoon, then we moved our position a hundred yards or more, and bivouacked for the night.

Early the next morning, Sunday the 29th, we moved down the turnpike toward Orange Court House,[27] about two miles, filed to the right and went into line of battle with the whole corps on a ridge of hills. Directly in front of us there was a very decided valley, through which run quite a stream [Mine Run] . . . and across this valley was a similar ridge, though higher, perhaps a mile and half away, and on which, it was plain to be seen, Lee's army was preparing to meet us. This position of the enemy, moreover, was more difficult to approach because the rise was more abrupt and rough.

We could see the rebel army, and noted that it was busy in throwing up earth works and cutting down trees in front of them, taking particular pains to make the falling trees point toward us, thus forming an abatis difficult to penetrate. Here we lay until noon facing each other, not a cannon-shot being fired from either side although hundreds of guns were in easy range, but the skirmishers in the valley between kept up a constant fusilade. It seems that General Meade had decided upon an immediate and general engagement, for we must either fight and win, or retrace our steps quickly to the Rappahannock because our base of supplies was cut completely out, and rations were already alarmingly scarce in our haversacks.

It was supposed that Lee had about two men to our three, but we knew that his were occupying a naturally strong position, already pretty well intrenched and being rapidly strengthened every minute. It was also evident that they were not going to open the fight until they were good and ready, but were well prepared to defend themselves. At this time (noon of the 29th) orders were passed along the lines that we should charge upon the enemy's position at four o'clock, and directions were given to leave our knapsacks behind so as to move in the lightest possible manner. The 20 and 30-pound rifled guns were rumbling into position to render all possible aid, and matters were becoming alarmingly serious.[28]

You people at home, who were never placed in so trying a place, cannot adequately appreciate our feelings, nor can you know the almost despairing, forlorn mental condition of acute suffering that we endured for five mortal hours. It was plainly seen that this position would be more difficult to storm than that of Marye's Heights of a year ago and, although every man about

27. Modern Route 20.
28. Mann consistently overestimates the caliber of Union cannon. Most rifled guns in the army fired ten-pound projectiles; a few fired twenty-pound projectiles. Thirty-pounder rifled guns were rarely used on the battlefield.

me that I knew was sullenly determined to go as far as any officer would lead, we practically knew that no assaulting column could penetrate to that impregnable place. Our brigade was to lead the charge by column of regiments, followed closely by the second and that by the third, on the part of our division.

As the time appointed drew near my comrades grew white, but jaws were setting like so many vises and, for the last half hour, not a word or whisper did I speak or hear. Four o'clock came and went, and still the waiting, dreading ear failed to catch the word "forward." At five o'clock the order was countermanded, and we tried to unstring our nerves by silently rolling ourselves in wet blankets, hoping for the forgetfulness of sleep.

I slept some, maybe two hours about midnight, but the weather was growing extremely cold. The ground was freezing under us and, from the necessities of our own safety, not a spark of fire was allowed. Even the lighting of a pipe must be strictly and carefully hid under the shelter of a blanket. At two the next morning all were silently awakened and orders were communicated in an undertone to "leave knapsacks and prepare for the assault." We crept noiselessly down into the valley under cover of the darkness, thus shortening the distance to the enemy by one-third, where we were massed in a small piece of woods, and lay still as death awaiting further orders.

It was whispered from one to another that an attempt would be made at daylight to storm the heights beyond. The morning dawned colder than the night before it, and I saw men so chilled that they had to be carried to the rear on stretchers. Worse than that, several of the men in this little copse of wood died from the effects of the chill, no doubt hastened by the fatal effects of the cold upon the nervous state that was produced by this suspense of 16 hours. Soon as it was light enough the rebels could be plainly seen from the position where I lay, watching from the heights they occupied—waiting for us to come on.

The first gun was not fired until eight o'clock, then a brisk cannonading followed along the whole line for 20 minutes, though the enemy replied with only a few pieces. Evidently they were reserving and concentrating everything for our expected assault. They must have seen our corps massed in that little bit of woods and, with the guns that could be seen pointing our way, they might have made it terribly hot for our corps, with the chances greatly in favor of throwing us into confusion. But they seemed to be awaiting more game, or felt that the looked-for charge must be repulsed. Our thoroughly chilled condition, when men's teeth were beating the tattoo from the cold, was not conducive to the kind of enthusiasm that was necessary to take us against such odds.

Only an occasional shot from the heights reached us, and I saw but one man injured. He belonged to another regiment, and was occupying a position 25 or 30 yards from where I lay when he was instantly killed in a peculiar manner. The earth had frozen to the depth of two or three inches, and the unexploded shell that did the work struck the ground eight feet or more in front of where he lay, entered under the frozen crust to the depth of 20 inches, passed directly under his body and out of the ground as many feet behind him. The concussion that was communicated by the hard crust, which was slightly heaved by the passage of the shell beneath, tossed him three feet into the air, and he fell dead without a mark upon the body to show the character of the injury.

When the artillery demonstration ceased, the quiet that ensued informed us that Meade had probably changed his plans because no infantry move was made. . . . [He] had . . . wisely concluded that to charge upon this intrenched enemy, under the conditions presented, would have been a gross disregard of a universally accepted military maxim, namely: "Do not make the move that the enemy hopes you will." Not a private in our ranks was so stupid but that he could see the rebels were enthusiastically waiting for us to come on, and hoping that we would. Notice of the countermanded order was received along our front about 8:20, or a minute or two after the cannonading ceased, and that one wise decision of the general commanding gave him a tremendous lift into the respect, veneration, and love of the army he commanded, completely redeeming himself from the opprobrium that the army hung to his name when he allowed Lee to escape from Maryland.[29]

We lay in that little piece of timber all day, with the cold growing colder and the ground freezing deeper. This condition would have been no hardship worth my speaking about if we could have exercised enough to put our blood into circulation, or could have made camp-fires, but it was absolutely

---

29. It was Major General Gouverneur K. Warren, not Meade, who canceled the attack that morning. Warren had charge of the nearly half the army that morning and was charged with conducting the attack across Mine Run. At first light, he rode forward and noted that the Confederates had significantly improved their works during the night. He concluded—probably rightly—that to send the army against such a position would be disastrous. He canceled the attack, inciting in turn the ire of Meade. Meade would eventually calm and would affirm Warren's decision. Indeed, as Mann indicates, the decision not to attack at Mine Run was one of the most popular of the war and elevated Meade's reputation in the army, even though Meade had nothing to do with the cancellation of the attack. One of Meade's staff officers wrote, "I shall always be astonished at the extraordinary courage of General Meade." And a Sixth Corps officer told his wife, "I tell you how it is, Louisa, if Meade ever did a noble act in his life, it was when he concluded not to fight Lee." Graham and Skoch, *Mine Run*, 76–77; Theodore Lyman, *Meade's Headquarters* (Reprint, Salem, N.H., 1987), 58–59; James M. Grenier, Janet L. Coryell, and James R. Smither, eds., *A Surgeon's Civil War: The Letters & Diary of Daniel M. Holt, M.D.* (Kent, Ohio, 1994), 160–61; Hennessy, "I Dread the Spring," in Gallagher, ed., *Wilderness Campaign,* 66–70.

necessary to our own safety that no perceptible movement should be made, while building fires would have given this closely massed corps completely away. Soon as night fairly hung its mantle over us we crept back up the hill to the position of the day before, as silently as an Indian scout goes hunting for his prey.

There the army lay all day Tuesday [December 1], just as willing that the rebels should attack us as they seemed to be for this army to make an assault on their position. But Lee was no greater fool than Meade, and let us severely alone.[30] There was hardly a skirmisher's rifle fired all this day, and after dark the whole army commenced to withdraw from the front of the enemy. Our regiment marched all night, crossed the Rapidan at Germanna Ford, rested two hours at sunrise, then kept on to Stevensburg and bivouacked until the morning of December 3d.

Our rations had given out, and I had been 24 hours without a morsel of food, but during the morning of our arrival at Stevensburg I met a comrade from another regiment, who had not been to the front, who had a small piece of salt port and five hard-tack, and he divided with me. This was all I could get until the midnight following, when we made connections with our supply-trains.

By daylight on the 3d we were on the move, crossing the Rappahannock on pontoons at the station of the same name, then marched up the river to Beverly Ford, where it looks as if the army would pass the winter. Although Mine Run proved to be comparatively a bloodless field, it was the hardest fought battle I ever experienced, and I notice that many of my comrades look as if they were five years older than eight days ago.

---

30. Lee in fact intended to attack the Federals on December 2, but they left their lines before dawn and frustrated Lee's plans. Graham and Skoch, *Mine Run,* 80–81.

TWELVE

THE WILDERNESS

"BEGINNING OF THE END"

In some ways, the year 1863 ended much as it had begun—with the armies sprawled in winter camps, separated by a formidable river (in this case the Rapidan), both with the knowledge that much fighting remained before the great issues of the day were resolved. But in other ways, much had changed between January and December 1863. Gettysburg had clinched the army's confidence—not so much in itself, but in its ability to defeat the Army of Northern Virginia. Much of the turmoil that had characterized and afflicted the Army of the Potomac had abated. McClellan, Porter, and many others bent on using the army as a political machine were gone. The perspective of the men in the ranks had changed, too. Outright enthusiasm had largely vanished, replaced instead with simple determination. As one man wrote, "The war seems to be now the one great job on hand, a steady regular job, in a business reduced to science."[1]

For Thomas Mann, the great issue during the winter of 1863–1864 revolved on his future: should he or should he not reenlist. The enlistments of most of the early-war three-year regiments were to expire in 1864, and the government went to great lengths to entice the veterans to remain in the service. Bounties of up to seven hundred dollars and thirty-day furloughs to units that reenlisted en masse were offered. If not simple reenlistment, Mann had the option of pursuing a commission in one of the new regiments of U.S. Colored Troops then being organized. All winter, he would struggle with the decision, laying out the pros and cons in letters home. In the end, Mann decided not to reenlist or seek a commission. The adventure, he said, was gone, and the "wear of this hard mode of life on my constitution" was too much. Still, Mann asserted, his military experi-

---

1. Letter of Uriah Parmelee, November 21, 1863, Uriah Parmelee Papers, Duke University.

ence had been invaluable. "I would not take thousands of dollars for my past three years experience," he told his parents. And, he wrote, "You will find me very much changed in everything but outside appearance when I come home."[2]

For Thomas Mann, the coming year 1864 seemed to hold one certainty: the end of his service—either due to the end of the war or expiration of his term. It also seemed to hold another certainty: campaigning of unprecedented intensity. In March of 1864, the army rather tepidly greeted Lieutenant General Ulysses S. Grant to the camps around Culpeper and Brandy Station. Grant would not directly command the army (he had command of all Union armies), but he would travel with it, watching over Meade's shoulder. Mann thought well of Grant, but thought well, too, of Grant's opponent. "[Grant] has a far different enemy to cope with than he overcame in his past victories. Gen. Lee's is not a power to be considered lightly." Still, Grant inspired a new bout of optimism: "It would seem that we could now see the beginning of the end of this Cruel War."[3]

Grant would bring with him no magical new strategy, but rather a determination never before seen in Union armies in Virginia. In early May, he would embark on a movement similar to Meade's during the Mine Run Campaign. The Army of the Potomac would cross the Rapidan and force Lee to battle wherever he could be found. Where Grant found Meade was the Wilderness of Spotsylvania—a forsaken land of tangled second growth (over the prior century, much of the area had been timbered to fuel furnaces and build a new plank road leading west from Fredericksburg). Thomas Mann, the Eighteenth Massachusetts, and the Fifth Corps would be among the first to find Lee, and on May 5 would engage in a vicious battle along the Orange Turnpike around a tiny clearing called Saunders Field. Choked with briars and scorched by fires, the Wilderness would make for an especially horrific battlefield. For Thomas Mann, it would be the setting for his final trial as a soldier.

Campaigning for the Army of the Potomac was now finished for the year—until it would be thoroughly reorganized under a new regime, strengthened and recruited, and placed, with the whole military force of

---

2. For discussions of these issues see Mann's letters of January 9 and March 14, 1864, Mann Papers.

3. Mann to members of the lyceum, April 25, 1864, Mann Papers.

the United States, under the command of General Grant. This successful general received his commission on the 9th day of March, 1864, and by May 1st his plan seemed to be matured for a general advance, from all sides, into the enemy's country, and against every armed force that Jefferson Davis could muster. Meantime, Meade's army constructed winter quarters along the Rappahannock and Hazel Rivers, and the men made themselves as comfortable as soldiers could.

The Eighteenth reached its old camp at Beverly Ford before sundown of December 3d, but while the other three regiments of the brigade went into camp, this one was detailed for picket duty. It was sometime after dark before the outposts were satisfactorily placed for the night. Three days later it was relieved by the 22d Massachusetts, and took its position in the line of camps that were to be occupied for the winter. The next day Captain Pray[4] laid out the Eighteenth's camp to a geometrical nicety, and on his plan the exact spot of earth was staked where the sergeant, the corporal, and Dennis [Short] together should build themselves a nondescript habitation to be occupied for five months.[5]

It was not because the rank and file had become more experienced—that the quarters they built for themselves this third winter were more elaborate and comfortable than heretofore—but because those who were of the rank and file then now wore shoulder straps. These new officers had wintered in the bare tents on Hall's Hill and fully appreciated the difference between a cabin that the most ordinary soldier could build for himself, if given the privilege, and the thin, bare, cloth tents that martinetism decreed during raw-recruithood. So, at Beverly Ford, the men were not only permitted but assisted by advice, and the regimental mules, to build substantial log-huts.

The barrack erected by the two non-coms and Dennis was of solid oak and hickory logs. It was 12 feet long by seven wide and four and a half high to the eaves. The shelter tents, previously described, were utilized for a roof, and this thin, light material also allowed sufficient light to filter through it for all practical purposes. Comfortable bunks were constructed for three, and quite an elaborate fireplace and chimney arose from one

---

4. Captain Charles F. Pray enrolled as a sergeant in Company K and rose steadily to the rank of captain. This twenty-nine-year-old bootmaker from Quincy was wounded at Second Manassas and would be killed on June 3, 1864, at Bethesda Church, near Cold Harbor.

5. The camp of the Eighteenth, like most of those of the Fifth Corps, was located on the northeast side of the stream; the vast majority of the army occupied camps on the southwest (toward Culpeper) bank of the river.

side, Virginia fashion, which was topped with an empty pork barrel to eke out its height and favor more draft.[6]

This barrack was an average sample of thousands that rose almost in a night to shelter a city of from 50,000 to 75,000 soldiers who were lying along the aristocratic Rappahannock. Some were better, and others not so good, but all were infinitely better than the army was sheltered in during its first winter of service, and a great improvement over the make-shift huts about Falmouth. The spot occupied by the Eighteenth, on the extreme left of the brigade, 300 yards from the river and ford and almost under the shadow of the Blue Ridge mountains, was one of natural beauty. The view of the Rappahannock for several miles up or down, taking in the junction of the Hazel[7] with it, was like a panorama, with blue mountain ranges for a background. As the old Missionary hymn declared, every prospect pleased, and only the mud was vile.[8]

There is an old axiom that says that "the unexpected always happens." Perhaps such a statement comes as near to the eternal truth as any ancient or modern prophet could prophesy. Anyhow, the two non-coms [Corporal Mann and Sergeant Alderman], who had promised themselves a cosy, comfortable winter; who stood congratulating each other and themselves one day when this log barrack was finished, had not anticipated the afflictions that were soon to follow. As intimated in the last chapter, the chilling effect of the camp-fireless weather at Mine Run produced blood diseases that now began to develop among the men in the form of abscesses, felons, and carbuncles.

The corporal underwent a siege of six weeks, during which he nursed a felon on each hand and a bad, carbuncular sore along side of his nose that shut up one eye for a short period. Part of this time he was seen with both hands swathed in a sling that was prepared by Surgeon Holbrook.[9] But the sergeant came uncomfortably near losing his life through a large abscess that developed near the spine, and that for weeks discharged half a pint of pus every 24 hours. Such a drain upon the vitality, and from so

---

6. Mann noted earlier that Virginians invariably built their chimneys on the outside of the structure, rather than within it.

7. The Hazel River, a major tributary, joined the Rappahannock just north of Beverly's Ford.

8. Mann told his homefolk, "I wish you could all step in here [the hut] and pay us a visit. You would think we were very cosy, and if they only let us remain here two or three months, we promise ourselves good times." Mann to his mother, December 12, 1863, Mann Papers.

9. Surgeon William Holbrook, thirty-eight, from Palmer.

close proximity to the spinal cord, soon reduced him to barely a skeleton and necessitated his removal to the brigade hospital for treatment on January 9th. From thence he was transferred to the Carver general hospital in Washington, and a little later was furloughed to his home in Massachusetts. He was not able to take his place with the regiment again until June. Luckily, the sergeant found powerful friends to assist him out of the hospital's clutches and procure him a furlough to the Berkshire hills, else some one of the National cemeteries would certainly have claimed the remains.[10]

In a letter home January 9, Corporal Tom writes:

> Sergt. Wm. P. Alderman was sent to the Brigade Hospital this morning. He has suffered with a large abscess on the end of his Back Bone for the last month. He has been my chum, and we have rolled in the same blankets together for more than a year—ate out of the same plate and drank from the same cup. He is from Middlefield Mass, and ever since he has been gone I have felt lost and lonesome as could be. Hardly know what to do with myself. Everything seems wrong side up. I don't know whether I have spoken of him before in my letters or not, but he is a man of strong common sense, 25 years of age, and if he has his health, will probably be commissioned before long and I step into his shoes. We have formed a strong friendship for each other and I am in hopes of welcoming him to the Red House [home] before another year, but I fear he has a long tough time before him. His sore runs nearly half a pint of matter every 24 hours and has continued so for the past week.[11]

This absence of the sergeant resulted in moving the corporal up a notch in the scale of promotion, and for three months he was practically the orderly sergeant of the company, filling the place and performing the duties of that non-commissioned officer in a manner all his own. Some weeks later, while

---

10. In a letter written December 18, Alderman delicately described his malady to his siblings as "a sore on my sit down." He suffered mightily: "I don't know what it is but I hope I may never have another. I have suffered everything with it. Could not sleep night or day, sit down, lay down, or stand up with any comfort. The doctor lanced it twice and took from it nearly a pint of matter each time. I have lost 15 to 20 pounds of flesh and feel as [weak] as a cat." Unfortunately for Alderman, his condition would only deteriorate for another month. Alderman to his brother and sister, December 18, 1863, Alderman Papers, FSNMPL.

11. This letter excerpt was not included in the original memoir. It is included here because it is simply one of the most simply eloquent testimonies to the bonds forged between men during this war. Mann to his mother, January 9, 1864, Mann Papers. Incidentally, Alderman would be offered a commission, as Mann predicted, but would refuse it. He returned to the regiment about June 10, a month after Mann had been captured at the Wilderness. Alderman to his brother and sister, June 10, 1864, Alderman Papers, FSNMPL.

the re-enlisted men were enjoying their 30-day furlough, and only eight men were present for duty in the ranks of company "I," the corporal commanded it for more than a month, actually discharging the duties of captain, orderly sergeant, and corporal, all in one person—only receiving, however, corporal's pay for the same.

Extending over a period of from two to four months, the great topic exercising the minds of the rank and file at this time was not exactly the question of "to be or not to be," but whether to re-enlist for the consideration of $900, and 30-day's furlough, or not to re-enlist. Old Massachusetts had another quota to fill, and it was already recognized that one old soldier was worth three ordinary recruits, so heavy inducements were temptingly put before the men whose terms of service were about to expire. . . .

This statement in regard to the value of veterans in comparison with raw recruits, is not a snap one, but was made advisedly, and is corroborated by one of the corporal's letters to his father, in which he gives the following statistics:

> This regiment received 150 recruits as it was about to make the campaign to Antietam. After the battle, less than six weeks after their reception, not more than 50 of them could be found and not one of them was killed or wounded. During August, 1863, we received 200 recruits; these were mostly conscript's substitutes, and four months later only 80 could be found, while but one out of the 200 was injured by a rifle ball. Between 20 and 30 of this last lot deserted, and I am credibly informed that other regiments in our immediate vicinity have fared even worse in regard to the efficiency of their recruits.[12]

In response to the urgings of his brothers, Corporal Tom offered his thoughts on the prospect of re-enlistment.

> The boys [Mann's brothers] seem to wish me "to gain laurels" as a military man. Now since I have been in the service, I have written home as well as I could about our long and severe marches, Battles, etc. . . . I might write

12. Mann, probably knowingly, erred in his assessment of the 1862 recruits—instead subscribing to the almost clichéd disdain of veterans for new recruits. Company I received twelve recruits in 1862. Six would be wounded, one died of disease, two were discharged for disability, one deserted, and one received a dishonorable discharge. The remainder served their terms; indeed, several reenlisted. Of the twenty 1863 enrollees (fourteen of whom were draftees), one was killed, three captured, and two wounded. One of the captured, Private William Moore, enlisted in the Confederate army in December 1864.

for weeks and not begin to give you an iota of an idea of the horrors of a battlefield or the fatigue of a march, exposed to the inclemencies of the weather—rain or shine, mud, ice. A person to have even the remotest shadow of a Battle field must be actually engaged upon one to hear and witness the groans of the dying, the mutilated forms of thousands of your comrades. The whirring and screeching of shells, the whistle of mine balls and the roar and rattle of thousands of firearms.

It all looks well upon paper—the pictures the illustrated papers of the day amuse and gratify thousands of people who have no . . . idea of a Battle. . . . But then if the Battles in which we have been engaged, or [are] likely to be, was all that induced men not to enlist again, I should not hesitate a moment but be only to glad to try three years longer. It is the long, dreary and tiresome marches that wear upon one's health, and the military discipline that one very much dislikes, who is as fond of freedom as myself.

You all very well know my first inducement to become a soldier. It was purely out of love for adventure and the excitement of this kind of life, and you may rest assured that I would reenlist again in a moment if I could not already feel the wear of this hard mode of life upon my constitution. I would not take thousands of dollars for my past three years experience.[13]

Seventeen men re-enlisted from company "I," and 130 from the whole regiment; they were designated as "veteran volunteers." They left these camps in a body on February 25 for Massachusetts, furloughed for 30 days; a happy lot going out, but the returning was not quite so chipper. However, they were indeed the veterans of the Eighteenth, who had weathered nearly three years of rough campaigning, and were worth more than double their number of the new men that could be gathered from the citizenship of Massachusetts at this time. Without that class of men, Grant would have fared worse than he did during the year to come.

A commission was tendered the sergeant [Alderman], which was rightfully his nearly a year earlier, but at this time was refused with thanks. Two months later, when it was decided that the corporal could not be induced to re-enlist, the latter was offered the opportunity of being commissioned in a negro regiment, which was also declined. At this time, and during the spring and summer following, a number of regiments were made up of the hordes of "Contrabands" that had flocked into the Union lines, and it was

13. This passage does not appear in the original memoir. Mann to his mother, January 9, 1864, Mann Papers. In a letter of March 14, 1864, to his friends at home, Mann further reflected, "You will find me very much changed in everything but outside appearance when I come home." Ibid.

deemed desirable to officer them with white men. Such officers were culled from the veteran ranks of the army to a great extent, though the sentiment of the Eighteenth was averse to accepting the proffered honor.

The prejudices entertained by the veterans of the Army of the Potomac, at this time, were very decidedly against the negro race as soldiers. And many of the Massachusetts men who were as violent "abolitionists" in 1861 as the predominating element of the towns to which they belonged, upon closer contact with that race had decidedly changed their opinions of the negro, if not of slavery, in regard to their usefulness as citizens. Besides, it was well understood, by the men who were approached with this tender of a commission in such regiments, that the enemy would make short shift with any who fell into their clutches. In justice to the negro, however, it must be admitted that in many marked instances he made a first-class soldier.

The veteran volunteers returned from their furloughs about the first of April, and by the 15th the strength of company "I" was raised to 45 men through the addition of recruits, the return of the veterans, and a thorough inspection and cleaning out of the brigade and general hospitals. This rigid examination of the various hospitals and convalescent camps found a small army of men who were peremptorily ordered to rejoin their respective regiments. The different provost authorities were equally vigilant in relieving some thousands of enlisted soldiers from various kinds of labor that rightly belonged to civilians . . . and they were returned to the front. Thus the Eighteenth was swelled to about 500 men, and hundreds of other veteran regiments were made to grow in the same manner; and new regiments were added, until the Army of the Potomac again presented a magnificent front of 105,000 men, present for duty, with 274 pieces of artillery.[14]

In spite of this energetic drumming to the front, 60,500 men, whose names were borne upon the rolls, were not effective for duty, a number twice too large, which represents the difference between the 165,500 that Grant was reported as taking into the Wilderness and the number that actually went in.

General Grant made his first visit to this army on March 10th, the day after receiving his commission as Lieutenant General from the hands of

14. Including the Ninth Corps, which would not be technically attached to the army for many weeks, the strength of the forces under Grant and Meade amounted to about 119,000 soldiers. See Gordon C. Rhea, *The Battle of the Wilderness* (Baton Rouge, 1994), 54.

President Lincoln, and on the 26th his headquarters were established at Culpeper. The many changes that were made among the different corps were keenly felt by some of the officers and men, particularly with the old First and Third Corps, which were broken up. The 1st and 2d divisions of the former were assigned to the Fifth Corps, of which General Sykes was relieved from the command, and to which General Warren was assigned in his stead. Colonel Joseph Hayes, who had been in command of the 3d Brigade, was returned to the Eighteenth, and the regiment was changed from the 1st to the 3d Brigade under the command of General Bartlett[15] still, however, in the old 1st Division of the corps and under the command of General Griffin. The Eighteenth's old colonel, Barnes, now brevetted Major General, was sent to take command of a small department that included Norfolk and Portsmouth, Va.[16]

On the 9th of April, the very day one year before the surrender at Appomattox, Grant sent instructions to Meade regarding the latter's movements, in which the following significant sentences occur: "Lee's army will be your objective point. Wherever Lee goes, there you will go also." But the Fifth corps was not moved out of its winter quarters until the morning of May 1st, in obedience to this new order of things. Then, crossing the Rappahannock, the Eighteenth marched to Brandy station and bivouacked until noon of May 3d.[17]

Here it was found that all supplies and material that could not be carried in knapsacks and haversacks, or by a limited number of supply wagons, were being rapidly moved back on the Orange and Alexandria Railroad, toward the latter place, which plainly indicated that this line of communication, as a base of supplies, was to be abandoned—and so it proved. About noon of May 3d, the regiment made another hitch forward and bivouacked for a few hours in the suburbs of Culpeper.[18]

15. Brigadier General Joseph J. Bartlett was, like Griffin, one of only a handful of officers who served with the army from First Manassas to Appomattox. A New Yorker and a lawyer, Bartlett had entered the army with the Twenty-seventh New York and rose from the rank of major to brevet major general. Warner, *Generals in Blue*, 23–24.

16. Meade had contemplated the reorganization of the army for some time. For a complete discussion see John Hennessy, "I Dread the Spring: The Army of the Potomac Prepares for the Overland Campaign," in Gary Gallagher, ed., *The Wilderness Campaign* (Chapel Hill, 1997), 81–86.

17. For Grant's note to Meade see O.R., Vol. 33, 828.

18. A week before departing on the campaign, Corporal Tom described the condition of his army to his family: "There is a vast difference between the state of the army today and what it was a little more than one year ago. Burnside's 'Fredericksburg' and 'Stick in the

The last campaign of the Eighteenth Regiment Massachusetts Volunteers was inaugurated at midnight, the morning of May 4, 1864, when the army moved aggressively forward to meet its old antagonist. Nominally Meade was its commander, but all understood that Grant was at hand and his would be the guiding and presiding genius. His great victories in the West gave him prestige and inspired confidence. This great army moved out across the Rapidan, cutting loose from its winter base of supplies with a fair share of its old-time enthusiasms that only required a show of capable leadership to glow with fever heat. But the redoubtable Grant had reckoned without his host. He was now to meet the ablest commander of modern times, at least the most capable one that the American Continent had produced for nearly a hundred years, and the sequel shows that the campaign that was now on did not progress or terminate as the Union commander expected.

Grant won, but only by using a force that his enemy could not procure, though it must be admitted that his final success was due, in part, to a full equipment of Anglo-Saxon common sense. But it took him several months to learn and cost the price of 70,000 killed and disabled men to teach him the abilities of his antagonist. When he had learned his lesson, he proceeded to trip Lee with that one, all-necessary weapon, namely, three men to the enemy's one. The consummate, masterly generalship of General Robert E. Lee, as displayed through four years of a losing war, is unreservedly acknowledged by every genuine soldier whether fighting for the Union or the Confederacy, and it is no disparagement to General Grant that such is the fact.

As before remarked, however, such reflections belong to the sergeant's "great writers," and if discussed by the rank and file—as they were, nevertheless—it was because they had the right and exercised it, though their opinions, at the time, had no possible influence upon the conduct of the conflict. During this midnight move of May 4th thousands of men who were trudging along in the ranks discussed the question of Grant's ability to cope with Lee in his moves on the battle-field's chess board, but all expressed a readiness, by word or deed, to do their part in his hands, for a fair trial.

Mud' and Hooker's 'Chancellorsville' were then fresh on our minds, and not easily to be forgotten—in fact, the army then was almost in a state of mutiny. During the whole last year we have sustained no defeat, but on the contrary have won the battles of Gettysburg & Rappahannock Station. And tho' General Meade is by no means a brilliant commander, yet he is so cautious that we apprehend no defeat, and therefore entertain a sort of regard for him." Mann to the members of the lyceum, April 25, 1864, Mann Papers.

The Eighteenth moved from Culpeper directly to Germanna Ford, there crossing the Rapidan at seven in the morning, and continuing the march into the heart of a tangled wilderness until the junction of the Germanna Plank Road with the Orange Turnpike was reached at the Wilderness Tavern. Here it bivouacked at three in the afternoon [on May 4], occupying its proper place in the Fifth Corps, which was in the van of the army. By five o'clock on the morning of May 5th, troops were actively moving, but this corps did not start for another hour. The brigade to which the Eighteenth was attached moved by hitches and halts only about two miles before the 3d Division, which was in advance on a cross road leading to Parker's Store, met the enemy as early as seven.[19]

This brought the whole corps to a halt, and skirmishers were pushed out from the several divisions in a number of directions. Griffin's division was deployed into a line of battle across the Orange Turnpike a few hundred yards to the front of its bivouac ground of the night before, which brought the right of the Eighteenth almost on this road, facing to the west. The turnpike ran nearly west, straight as an arrow, and looked like an avenue cut through an interminable forest. About nine o'clock the 1st Michigan, 83d Pennsylvania, and the Eighteenth formed a heavy skirmish line and moved along both sides of the pike for a mile, or more, until a similar advancing line of the rebels was met.[20]

This meeting was not an amicable one for an exchange of shots immediately followed, and one of the latest recruits of company "I," Charley Wilson, immediately fell dead.[21] He was but a 17-year old boy who had already captured the good will of the company by his laughing, boyish manners and ready willingness to do what was required without grum-

---

19. The Pennsylvania Reserves division, commanded by Samuel Wylie Crawford, led the Fifth Corps march along a woods road leading from Wilderness Tavern to Parker's Store, five miles to the southeast. Griffin's division, which included the Eighteenth, was charged with protecting the rear of the Fifth Corps' column near Wilderness Tavern—not moving until the Sixth Corps, coming up from Germanna Ford, relieved it. While Griffin hung back at Wilderness Tavern, he sent skirmishers westward on the Orange Turnpike as a precaution. It was these men, not the Pennsylvanians (as Mann asserted), that first reported the approach of Lee's army from the west. Rhea, *Wilderness*, 95–98.

20. In the original, Mann misidentified the Eighty-third Pennsylvania as the Eighty-third New York—a regiment then serving in another division of the Fifth Corps. O.R., Vol. 36, Pt. 1, 575.

21. Charles H. Wilson, a farmer from Franklin, enlisted on December 18, 1863. Wilson was likely the first infantryman killed in the Overland Campaign and the Battle of the Wilderness. O.R., Vol. 36, Pt. 1, 575.

bling, while "Sherman," who has already been sized up by the sergeant, and who could have been spared without shedding of tears, was no where to be found.[22] From the beginning of this first meeting between the two skirmish lines, which was some after 10 o'clock, the Wilderness was alive with fighting men until after dark. These skirmishing regiments in front of Griffin's division pushed the enemy back half a mile or more, but it was a regular Indian bush-whacking arrangement, the Johnnies firing from behind every tree that was large enough to protect a man's body, then dodging behind another to hide and load—a trick that the Yankees drill-masters had failed to teach.

Over much of this dense forest there were thickets of underbrush sufficient to hide a soldier, or a body of them, 50 yards away, and the enemy had been taught to take advantage of such conditions. Before noon the rebel skirmish line had been greatly strengthened so that instead of one behind a tree there was liable to be two or three, and they began to show a dogged determination not to be pushed back any farther. Meantime, Griffin's division had unslung knapsacks and were following up these advance feelers with a line of battle, and soon after noon the skirmishing regiments were withdrawn into his line. They had found the enemy, though its full strength was not yet ascertained, and this advancing battle front was soon to test it.

Corporal Tom remembers: "The regiment was soon bunched into a solid line of battle; other regiments connected on our right and left and the order to move forward was given. The forward movement was made in as rapid a manner as possible, considering the woods and brush, and the rebel skirmish line fell back as rapidly, though all the time pegging away at us with their muskets. We drove them in upon the main body of Ewell's corps, which was in line of battle half a mile away, to receive us."[23]

This forward movement of Griffin's division was mostly through such an undergrowth of bushes that nothing could be seen of the enemy, or its doings, but the white smoke that belched constantly from behind every pretense of cover. It was a battle of invisibles with invisibles. The afternoon was very hot, for the trees had not yet leaved.[24] The sun was making

22. For an excellent account of this early movement out the Orange Turnpike see Joseph Hayes, Journal extracts, Joshua Chamberlain Papers, Library of Congress.

23. This and other excerpted material about the Wilderness (except the final four paragraphs) are inserted from a postwar article by Mann, "Battle of the Wilderness: Captured By Ewell's Rebel Soldiers in the Midst of Fight," Mann Papers.

24. Mann's memory is faulty here. Most accounts indicate that the leaves were well developed by early May; certainly today Virginia's forests are consistently foliated by May Day.

it decidedly sultry, and there was not a breath of air stirring in these thickets to lift the powder smoke or fan the sweaty, powder-begrimed faces of the contestants. A tremendous and almost continuous roll of musketry was all that could be heard, to the right, to the left, or in the front of this wilderness. Here and there a man toppled over, and the appearance of every soldier within the limited range of vision was grimly ferocious. The appalling death rate that was scoring up was unnoticed at the time because it was covered from the living by the nature of the battle-ground and the thickening smoke.

The division kept its onward movement steadily for two or three hundred yards, while the enemy was as surely giving way to it. By being thus moved slowly enough to allow men to keep in sight of each other, the lines were not seriously disordered, nor were there any important breaks between regiments or brigades. The first mistake was made in ordering a charge. All were ready and anxious to find some way out of the stifling smoke and heat that was accumulating in this tangled forest, and when the order to "charge" was passed along individual regiments started forward on the run. The enemy was easily driven another half mile by this determined, double-quick movement forward, but regiment was becoming more widely separated from regiment, while the men of any single organization were obliged to break into squads to pass around copses of brush that could not be penetrated.[25]

Between 200 and 300 men of the Eighteenth, which managed to keep its autonomy through this half-mile charge, soon found themselves comparatively alone, and were halted by the officers to attempt a connection with something to the right or left. Nothing was seen or heard from the right, while the left seemed to be a hundred yards or more in advance. This movement on the part of the Eighteenth was a concerted one with at least two brigades of the division, and for a short time the firing in its front almost entirely ceased. In the course of another hour, or about four in the afternoon, a connection was made with a portion of the division to the left, but never, during the remainder of the day, to the right, which seemed to be lost on the other side of the turnpike.

In this reformation of the lines, all fell back several hundred yards, then another advance was ordered. While executing it the Eighteenth came in

25. The attack noted here was the most successful of the day for the Union army. Griffin's division drove across Saunders Field and pushed the Confederates back more than a quarter-mile. Mann is entirely correct when he says that the attack lost momentum because of a lack of progress on the right—north of the Orange Turnpike. See Rhea, *The Battle of the Wilderness*, 152–57.

contact with a heavier body of the enemy, as if the Johnnies had been reenforced, and they persistently refused to give any more ground, as if they had found a position that was easily defended. Here the fighting was severe for 15 or 20 minutes—and with no support on the right, which the rebels soon discovered and as quickly availed themselves of by swarming into the break. Already they had developed strength enough for a counter charge, which came from the right and, aided by the thickets of brush and trees, the rebels were soon mixing themselves among the scattered men of this regiment for a hand to hand fight. . . .

Between four and five o'clock in the afternoon, at the point where the Johnnies began to mix with the Yanks and close in from the direction of the unprotected right, the corporal was captured and cared for in a way the rebels had of doing that sort of thing for the next ten months.

> I was leaning against the trunk of a large pine, reloading my musket; the thought of being captured had not entered my mind. But few of my comrades were in my immediate sight, but I knew they were all about me, or supposed I knew, by the flashing of the firing and the orders of the officers. When I raised my musket to fire a hand was reached from the opposite side of the tree, grasped my musket and a commanding voice said: "No more of that you Yank!" A hasty glance showed several butternut-colored soldiers in my immediate vicinity and three or four blue coats who seemed in the same predicament as myself. I was a prisoner of war.
>
> . . . Ewell's line of battle passed on and I was simply within the reb lines, instead of those of the Union. After [they took] my musket and cartridge box I was simply let alone for nearly two hours, and I busied myself in administering to the wounded and the helpless, carrying them water from a swamp hole that was close by, and tearing up blankets to bind wounds and check the flow of blood of the Blue and Gray alike. If I got too near the battle line in my ministrations, I was cautioned to "git back there you Yank!" which was all the attention paid to me till after six o'clock.[26]

Corporal Tom continues:[27]

> While thus wandering around I saw a destructive incident that will not be forgotten while any memory is left. . . . About five o'clock . . . the turnpike was packed as full of rebel reinforcements, coming to the front, as standing

26. Mann was captured on land west of Saunders Field, south of the Orange Turnpike. Those lands are, today, just outside the boundaries of Fredericksburg and Spotsylvania National Military Park.

27. The final four paragraphs quoted here are from Mann's prison memoir, "A Yankee in Andersonville," *Century Monthly Illustrated Magazine,* July 1890, 448. Deleted at the end of the memoir are two unimportant paragraphs simply summarizing the overall tactics and results of the Battle of the Wilderness.

room could be found for. I was standing on the edge of it when [a Union] battery . . . fired two shots, solid ones, skipping along down the turnpike and making two distinct gaps in the solid mass of humanity for a distance of 100 yards or more. Of course the road was instantly cleared by all who were able to leave, but the dead and dying left in the track of those two shots were several hundred. It was the most fearful execution I saw during the whole war from any one battery.[28]

About dark all the scattering prisoners were collected by our captors and marched to General Ewell's headquarters, a little to the rear of his corps [on the Orange Turnpike]. About nine hundred of us were collected in this way, and we found that the most of us had been captured by the celebrated "Stonewall Brigade."

Here I saw General R. E. Lee for the first and only time in my life. He sat upon his horse carelessly, with one knee resting upon the pommel of the saddle. . . . He appeared a middle-sized man, with iron-gray hair and full gray beard, not every closely cut; as fine-looking a specimen of man and soldier as I ever saw. He remarked as we filed past him, "Am sorry to see you in this fix, boys, but you must make the best of it." His tone was kind, and spoken as though he really sympathized with us, as I have no doubt he did.[29]

After dark a guard was detailed to march us to Orange Court House, distant twenty-five miles. We were all exhausted with the day's fighting and heat, and the march before us did not look very promising; for go we must, and that, too, at the point of the bayonet.

Our thoughts upon this lonely, tiresome march were anything but pleasant and comfortable. Only one month more and my term of service would expire. I had been thinking very strongly of the home I had left three years before, and during the whole of that time had not seen it, or even been outside the lines of the Army of the Potomac. Now we were marching the opposite way, toward the rebel prisons—of which we had already heard too much.

---

28. No doubt Mann overestimated the carnage caused by the artillery fire—such destruction by two cannon balls is impossible. But there can be no doubt the spectacle made a deep impression on his memory.

29. Mann also recorded that Lee was smoking a cigar at the time he saw him. Either he was in error, or the officer Mann thought was Lee was someone else. After publishing this recollection in the *Century Magazine,* Confederate veteran E. A. Craighill publicly took Mann to task: "All who knew [Lee] will say this picture is not true to nature," and he concluded, "it is plain he [Mann] never saw General Robert E. Lee." Mann responded by conceding, "It is possible, of course, that I did not see General Lee, but the picture he made sitting upon his horse in the twilight of May 5, 1864, has not been effected from my mind." See E. A. Craighill, "General Lee and the 'Yankee at Andersonville,' " *Century Monthly Illustrated Magazine,* 41: 154–55. It is known, however, that Lee paid a visit to Ewell's headquarters along the Orange Turnpike late on May 5, so it is possible that Mann did indeed see Robert E. Lee.

Epilogue

Long Journey Home

Thomas Mann's memoir ended abruptly with his capture at the Wilderness. The end of his combat service, however, saw the beginning of perhaps his greatest trials. For the next several weeks, Mann endured a meandering trek southward—a journey over roads and in crowded boxcars, punctuated by stays in pens and warehouses in Orange Court House, Lynchburg, and Danville. In mid-May, 1864, buoyed by the hope of exchange, Mann and hundreds of other prisoners from the Wilderness boarded cars again. Southward through North Carolina, through Charlotte, into South Carolina they traveled, passing along the way spur lines that would take them to the Confederacy's coastal cities and, Mann hoped, exchange. But the train passed lines to Wilmington and Charleston, and as it did, Mann's hope to avoid prison faded. Finally, the train approached Macon, Georgia. Through Macon, Mann knew, traveled a line to Savannah—the last of the eastern ports where an exchange of prisoners could take place.

The train continued onward, into the interior of the Confederacy, and Mann braced himself for the reality of being a prisoner of war. At noon on May 20, 1864, Mann's train ground to a halt near a prison in southwestern Georgia. None of the soldiers on board had heard of the place. The Confederates called it Camp Sumter. History would know it as Andersonville. The panorama of the prison stunned Mann—thousands of emaciated soldiers sprawled under makeshift shelters amidst incredible filth. "It required no prophetic powers to convince us that they could never be men again," Mann recalled.

Mann would endure the horrors of Andersonville for four months, crammed into twenty-six acres with as many as thirty-two thousand other men. The experience left him weakened but not debilitated. In September, with the approach of Sherman's army, Mann was among the first load of prisoners evacuated from Andersonville to Charleston, South Carolina. After at least two foiled escape attempts, Mann was taken to the prison at Florence. There fortune would smile on him. The sister of a fellow captive from the Eighteenth, Frank Bonney, lived with a relative near the prison. She would not only provide for Bonney and Mann, but also aid in getting them duty outside the stockade. Finally, the approach of Sherman's army (now moving northward through the Carolinas) brought an end to Mann's prison ordeal. In late February, the Confederates put the prisoners on a train and sent them into Union lines near Wilmington, North Carolina.[1]

Soon after daylight on March 1, 1865 (remembered Mann), "I saw the first free Union soldier in ten long months, in the form of a foraging cavalryman. Our whole train-load cheered him with all the noise we could make, and waved some kind of rag. I never saw a more astonished soldier." Relieved of the need to struggle for life anymore, in the days following his repatriation Mann virtually collapsed. He would spend three weeks largely unconscious in a hospital in Baltimore. At last, he recovered his strength and asked immediately for a furlough. Though still weak and unwell, he received it, and yet another befogged train ride took him to Boston.

On an early spring day in 1865, this veteran soldier—shuffling and emaciated—climbed into a hack for his final wartime ride. Twenty miles over familiar roads, through Dedham, Norwood, Walpole, and Foxboro—towns that had contributed many men to the Eighteenth Massachusetts—Mann rode, looking upon a peaceful civilian landscape that had been entirely foreign to him for nearly four years. Finally the hack, probably unnoticed, rolled into North Wrentham. The Old Soldier, though only twenty-two years old, stepped out and walked the final steps to his house, to the arms of his parents and siblings.

Thomas Mann's wartime adventure-turned-ordeal had come to an end.[2]

1. Frank Bonney to his mother, December 8, 1864, Mann Papers.
2. Mann's prison ordeal and his return home is recounted in his "A Yankee at Andersonville," *Century Monthly Illustrated Magazine*, 40, 447–61, 606–22. The remnants of the Eighteenth Massachusetts, which suffered considerably in the Battle of the Wilderness, continued on until muster-out in early September 1862. The regiment's recruits of 1862 and 1863 were transferred to the Thirty-second Massachusetts (another Fifth Corps regiment). "Sergeant Bill" Alderman's backside boil would not fully heal until early June; he returned to the front until June 10—a month after Mann's capture—declined a commission, and left the service with the rest of the original members of the Eighteenth Massachusetts on September 2, 1864.

Appendix A

A Treatise on Army Mules

We read continuously about the men who marched. We have largely forgotten the thousands of horses and mules that pulled thousands of wagons that followed the men. When an army moved, wagon trains miles long would trail behind or along parallel routes. The engine that made these serpentine machines run was the mule.

Shortly after taking command of the Army of the Potomac, Joseph Hooker experimented with using pack mules to replace the miles of wagon trains that so impeded the army's movement. The experiment failed, and Mann's brief treatise—though it focused on an early war attempt to put mules to work—reveals many of the reasons why.

The difficulties that Virginia mud presented to loaded teams stimulated some bright genius to propose pack mules to convey supplies to the army at the front. It succeeded fairly well among the soldiers of the middle-western part of the country, particularly with those accustomed to the mule in that capacity, but to New Englanders this animal was the embodiment of all that was stupid, obstinate and vicious.

Sergeant G,[1] in attempting to draw a pen picture of the army mule says: "The animal is dun-colored and sad. His countenance is extremely solemn, and in length rivals his ears. The sentimental in his nature is wafted from the ends of his ears, while his humor works out at his heels. His voice is of unusual compass and pitched mostly in the minor key. It has in it the rush of waters, the sighing of winds, the filing of a saw, the grating of slate pen-

---

1. Perhaps Sergeant George W. Thompson, a thirty-six-year-old "straw-worker" from Franklin. Thompson was wounded at the Wilderness and subsequently was listed as a deserter, having left the hospital in November 1864.

cils, and as a whole resembles a clap of thunder drawn through a coarse sieve. When a mule brays he throws up his tail, and not infrequently his heels, in a sort of ecstasy. The step of the army mule is deliberate and indicative of both decision and patience."

These qualities, however, were never exercised on trifling occasions, but showed themselves to the best advantage by his coming to a dead halt when everything else evinced a disposition to move. At such times he seemed to have a monopoly of all the patience in the army.

Before the Eighteenth left Yorktown, the magnificent horses that drew its supply train, and which were a part of its equipment from Massachusetts, were exchanged for mules. The horses were appropriated by the field officers or became a part of the cavalry arm of the army, and the exchange was a good one, as one mule for teaming purposes, under the conditions imposed by Virginia campaigning, was worth four horses. But the experience of the army . . . in obtaining supplies at the front about Yorktown emphasized the necessity of something besides lumbering wagons to depend upon; and it was then the experiment of using pack mules was attempted by this regiment.

A consignment of eight of these hybrids, unsubdued, wild, just as they came from their native ranch somewhere in the great Southwest, was received during the month of April for the Eighteenth to experiment with, as a side amusement while shoveling the rebels out of Yorktown. Sergeant Bill, who was a fairly good judge of horse-flesh and generally calculated to hold the lines over as good a specimen as there was in his country, never could endure a mule. Profanity was considered indispensable in driving this long-eared and nimble-heeled animal, and Bill was not quite equal to that requirement, so his account of it will bear discounting about five percent.

He allowed that there were plenty of boys who knew all about steering an ox-team, and plenty of them who were at home with a horse, but when it came to mules they lacked experience. The average Yankee is strongly imbued with the idea that whatever has been done could be done again, and he could do it; so plenty were found ready and willing to undertake the task of teaching these innocent looking strangers to carry a pack.

But to quote Bill's own words:

> I well remember the morning when the mules were brought out on the parade ground for their first lesson in the service of "Uncle Sam." Volunteers were called for, and any one even down to private number two in the rear

rank, was given an opportunity to mount a mule and begin the show. Of course the boys were all interested, and the whole regiment was out. Our color-bearer, as fine a specimen of vigorous manhood as one could see in the whole army, six feet two in his stockings, with the best of brawn and muscle and pluck to back it up, was the first to offer. He was accepted with a snap, for everybody thought that with "Deck" as first mount that particular mule would give in without a serious struggle.

The first difficulty was to make the mount. When Deck made a vault for its back the mule wasn't there. But by dint of much help by many hands the feat was accomplished at last, and Deck was fairly astride. If the work of mounting had been complicated, the act of dismounting was as simple as possible, being accomplished in "one time and one motion" without a hitch. Result: One color sergeant with one broken leg.

Naturally, the taking of Deck to the hospital had a somewhat dampening effect on the boys. The thing didn't seem so dead easy after all. But, notwithstanding, other men came forward and several of them made their mounts with the same difficulty, and their dismounts with varying degrees of gracefulness, but always with promptness. If there were other casualties of a serious nature, I have forgotten them. Of course there were bruises, but anything less than broken bones didn't count. What was to be done? The mules must be conquered, no matter what happened, and "Jimmy Barnes" was not a man to give up his point.

The "contraband" had already been named by General Butler, before the Eighteenth reached Fortress Monroe, and the cognomen was, as if by an act of magic, shifted from smuggled whiskey to the negroes that were flocking into the lines of the Union army by hundreds. Every officer obtained one or more of these contrabands for body servants, and in one way or another quite a number were scattered around in the camps, ready to do the bidding of anyone who chose to order them about; and it was soon discovered that they knew more about mules than the whole of "Jimmy Barnes' " regiment.

Bill continues: "When it came to dislodging a darkey from its back, these long-eared representatives of unadulterated cussidness found an altogether different condition of things. Rearing, kicking and bucking, with head close to the ground and heels up among the stars, utterly failed to unseat young Sambo. A mule doesn't give it up the first time by any manner of means. As 'stubborn as a mule' is the usual term to express the superlative degree on that line, and though these mules were ridden by the contrabands from time to time, it was evident that there were depths of obstinacy and reserves of meanness that were yet unfathomed."

Colonel Barnes, during his experience with European armies, had seen the donkey used as a pack animal with great efficiency, and why should not the mule, which was very similar though larger and stronger, be made to do likewise, so he persisted and the program was varied from riding to packing. No one knew, experimentally, the scientific way of fixing a pack, though the colonel had seen them placed hundreds of times and essayed to teach the boys, so frequent lessons were given in packing and unpacking, the mules being securely held during the operation. Bill says: "I could detect an expression of sly cunning, a demure look of devilish intelligence in the animal, when these operations were going on, that subsequent events corroborated."

The pack mule, when loaded with a couple of cracker boxes on each side and a lot of camp kettles, shovels, picks, and bundles of tents on top, presents an over-load, top-heavy appearance that is grotesque in the extreme. It was a comical picture, one of frequent occurrence, to see one of these mules capsize on a side hill, roll over upon his back where he was securely held by his load with heels dejectedly dangling in the air, looking like a huge grasshopper. Bill says:

> Nothing in the way of ranks of men, teams, baggage wagons, artillery or what not had any business getting in their way as we moved up the Peninsular on our trial trip with these mules. Ranks broke and men fled before them. They laid down and rolled. They got up and kicked. They bucked and went for the trees whose low-hanging branches helped them to rub off their packs. I remember one whose pack was thicker and higher than his legs were long, and in the process of his many gyrations got completely turned so that the pack was under instead of over his body. Being thicker than his legs were long, he found himself in the position of Abraham Lincoln's stalled ox that could "neither hook one way or kick the other," He could rock forward and touch his front feet to the ground, or rock back and touch his hind feet, and that was all he could do. He could do the "teeter act" all right.

Pack mules did not prove a success and they were soon harnessed into the regulation army wagon, and given over to the darkies as drivers. The value of the mule in the army was very great as it would live and thrive where a horse would starve to death. It was less liable to injury than a horse for a fracas that would kill a horse, or leave it with broken bones, left this hybrid unscathed. Tom tells of seeing a six-mule team, baggage wagon and all, roll down a steep side hill to the bottom of a ravine, a hundred yards, and smashing everything into kindling wood but the mules. When the scene of the accident was reached the mules were found gathered quietly about the debris, uninjured, eating crackers from the broken boxes, and whisking flies with their long ears as unconcernedly as if they had just been led up to their accustomed stalls.

Sergeant G tells of the pranks of one of these pack mules during the siege of Petersburg in 1864; for a part of the army did continue their use.

One night, a mule heavily laden and bristling with shovels, picks, and axes, broke loose from his company, and with a terrible clatter and clamor, went charging into the enemy's lines, undaunted and alone. The enemy, believing they were being charged by cavalry, were in considerable consternation, and hastily formed to resist. They fired in volleys and at will, when the mule, not fancying his reception, wheeled, threw up his heels, brayed, and amid shouts of laughter, came prancing back to his allegiance, unhurt. The boys declared that a braver charge than that of "thet er muel" was seldom made.

Appendix B

Journey to Mine Run

This is the unedited version of Mann's letter describing the Mine Run Campaign. In preparing these memoirs, Mann drew heavily on this and other letters, but often edited them. This letter is included in toto here because it is particularly informative and because the version that appeared in the memoir was edited far more heavily than most of Mann's letter excerpts.

> On Picket Near Beverly Ford Va.
> Dec 4th

Dear Friends at Home

This is the first opportunity I have had for eight or nine days to write a word to anybody and I am going to improve it now. We have received no mail for eight days but are expecting it now every day. Suppose you are aware by reading the papers that the Army of the Potomac has been upon the move for the last few days and before you receive this you will probably hear of the result of our move. But we have had a very severe time and I will give you an outline of our travels and doings.

    The next day after I wrote from our camp near Mountain Run we packed up again and started as I supposed we did before for the White House Landing. Last week Wednesday was very fine and clear so that the mud was considerably well dried and Thursday Thanksgiving about daylight we started with five days rations in the haversacks and marched to the Rap[i]dan near El[y]'s Ford. There we lay for two or three hours while they were laying pontoons. There was a little artil[l]ery firing and cavalry s[k]irmishing across the river but nothing of importance to oppose our crossing and we crossed at a place called WyCoff's Mills and marched to within one mile of our Battleground of Chancellorsville arriving there and camping about 10 o'clock in the evening.

WyCoff's Mills is quite a large establishment. They are used for extracting gold from the gold mines and owned by a Northern man. He was quite an old man and said before the war broke out that he was making money at least there had been some pretty extensive mining operations but of course this war put a stopper upon the works.

I did not have time to examine the Battlefield of Chancellorsville for we started the next morning about sunrise. Marched upon the Plank road towards Fredericksburg for some distance then turned to the right upon another Plank road that leads to Orange C. H. The march was very slow all day for the 3rd Division of this corps were s[k]irmishing all the way and we have only just left the Fredericksburg road when 30 or 40 Rebel Cavalry dashed upon our train that was only one or 200 rods in our rear and captured several of them together with the drivers and team[st]ers driving the teams right down the Fred. road and set fire to them, carrying the men off prisoners = our men, strag[g]lers. Shot several of them and several got shot.

It was a pretty bold dash and all done in fifteen minutes. It delayed us some hour and half when we kept slowly on again the fireing [sic] ahead growing more brisk and finally some cannon shot were fired. About 3 o'clock P.M. we got out of the woods through which we had been marching all day and went into line of battle to the left of the road. There we remained until next morning. There was an old RR there that had been graded and the track never laid. I suppose it was a branch of the Aquia Creek RR to Orange C. H. or Gordonsville. The 3rd Division had done pretty severe s[k]irmishing until after dark when the firing ceased. We received a cannon shot in amongst our regiment but it hurt no one. The weather was beginning to moderate a little and looked like a storm but we did not get it until morning. I slept sound that night but the next morning it commenced to rain and continued until 4 o'clock P.M. At daylight we took a cross road from this Plank Road to the Turnpike marching off to the right about two miles when we came to a place called Robinsons Tavern in the Wilderness. The Rebels had left our front and we captured a few prisoners. At [Robertson's] Tavern the 3rd and 6th Corps had been fighting them the day before and drove them. We hasten across and made our selves as comfortable as possible but we were drenched with rain and mud over shoe. At 4 or 5 o'clock the weather cleared up and we moved our quarters a few rods and slept for the night. Early the next morning Sunday we started down the turnpike towards Orange C. H. went about two miles turned to the right and went into position in line of battle on a ridge in front of the River. In front of us was a kind of valley through which run considerable of a brook. Beyond the brook was another ridge of hills similar to the ones we occupied but higher and more difficult to approach. Perhaps it was *two miles* across this valley but we could plainly see the Rebel Army very busy heaving up earthworks and falling trees to obstruct our passage.

We were now in line of battle the whole of both armies and facing each other with this valley between us our line extending from 3 to 5 miles and the Rebels ditto. There we laid until noon—no cannon fired from either side tho hundreds of them were in position and within range. The s[k]irmishers were in the valley busily engaged all day. We had decided upon a general engagement and that immediately for we must either fight them and conquer or retreat back across the Rap[i]dan. We had only so many days rations and no base of supplies except our teams but communication with Washington entirely cut off. We knew that Lee's army was just two thirds as large as ours and we also knew that the Rebels were in a strong natural and entrenched position and making it stronger every hour. They were not going to open the fight but simply defend themselves. Thus matters stood at noon on Sunday. Then the orders came for us to pack our knapsacks in a pile and be ready and prepared at 4 o'clock P.M. to charge the enemies position. Our large 32 & 20 lb guns were getting into position to help us as much as possible. You can hardly judge of our feelings. Having thoughts of home and loved ones for those 4 long mortal hours. Every man knew that to charge those works was sure death to at least one third our number and that ¼th of the charging party was the greatest number that would ever enter the works alive. The whole corps was to charge at the same time our Brigade the 1st was to lead the charge in front of us while the 2nd and 3rd followed close at our heels. Our whole arti[l]lery was to open the moment we started. Four o'clock came and went and at 5 o'clock we heard the order countermanded and we settled down in quiet for that night.

The weather was extremely cold, ground freezing rapidly. At two o'clock the next morning, Monday we were routed out and the order was repeated "to pack our knapsacks and be ready to charge." We moved silently down into the valley going about ⅓rd the distance to the Rebel works under cover of the darkness and our whole corps was massed in a small piece of wood and there we lay still as death. At 8 o'clock the cannon were to open and we to charge. The morning was as cold as any day last winter so that many of the men were so chilled that they were carried off in stretchers and some even died. When the day broke from where I lay I could plainly see the Rebel works and even their men moving about watching for us to come on. At 8 o'clock the first gun was fired and there was a brisk cannonading for twenty minutes. How intensely we felt every moment you cannot imagine. Not a word or whisper was uttered expecting the order "Attention! Forward Charge."

The Rebels replied to our cannon with perhaps one third of theirs. They were concentrating their energies for our charge. They knew our plan for they could see our corps massed in the little belt of woods and with what cannon they had pointed at us they might have thrown us into disorder making terrible havoc but they were waiting more game or felt that they must repulse our charge or their army was lost. And it certainly would have been for if we could have carried the works in our front "Lees Army" would have been utterly an[n]hilated.

As soon as day light opened we to a man general officers and all declared that to storm the works was impossible. Not but that we might eventually have forced the enemy out of them but $2/3rds$ of our army would have been laid low while Lee's Army would have escaped us for the want of another army to claim a victory.

As I said the can[n]onading lasted 20 minutes. When it ceased every thing was quiet as death again and we were made aware that Meade had ordered the *Charge not to be made*. Think of the load it lifted from our hearts when we learned it. We all blessed Meade for his wisdom and the only fault found with him was that he ever contemplated a charge upon their works. They were stronger than at Fredericksburg last year—twice over.

I cannot describe to you ac[c]urately their works, but can tell you better when I come home.

Every man of us while contemplating the coming *charge* was pale as death but firm and unflinching. We were nearly all "old veterans" and had met death many times but not at such odds. Let some of the men who are quietly enjoying life at home and crying for the news of a fight come and take our place in such a situation for once and it will entirely cure of them of their wish for another fight.

We lay in those works all day. Cold as Greenland! untill dark of Monday night when we silently moved back to our position of Sunday. By this we were aware that we must retreat beyond the Rap[i]dan. There was no fighting Tuesday. Not hardly a s[k]irmisher's gun fired and at night we commenced to withdraw from the enemies front which is a delicate job and I will tell you how it was done in my next letter if you wish.

We marched all night crossed a "Germany Ford" and stopped to rest, two or three miles this side of the ford for about two hours or till sunrise when we marched to Stevensburg and camped until Thursday morning our rations had now given out and I had been 26 hours without a morsal of bread. Our teams had gone a long way ahead to clear the roads for the troops to move rapidly. Thursday morning I met a friend that had a little salt pork & five hardtack he shared with me. From Stevensburg we marched to Rappahannock Station, crossed upon pontoons and came here to Beverly Ford where the Brigade went into camp and our Regiment upon picket where we have now been two days shall probably be relieved the 3rd day.

From Thursday noon I eat nothing untill 12 o'clock at night when our rations came up so that all I could get to eat for over 40 hours was $^{1}/_{4}$th lb raw pork and $2^{1}/_{2}$ hardtack. We now have plenty and today got a ration of soft bread.

It is evident that this army is handled by a master hand and altho we have suffered pretty severely we have met with *no defeat*. Our object was evidently to cross the country to the P[a]munkey River but could not do it and we were very fortunate in getting so safely back. One division of the 1st Corps were left here at Rappahannock Station and they have commenced to demolish the R.R. but on our starting back it was quickly put into running order again.

I should judge from appearances now that we should remain in this v[i]cinity for some time to come perhaps all winter but it is quite certain that if Lee holds his position the other side of the Rap[i]dan we shall not enter when another campaign this winter.

Just before this move the good news from Gen. Grant's Army was read to us in the hope of a telegram from "Stanton" to Gen. Meade. We are all in pretty good spirits tho we have been pretty severely handled.

We received some of the back mail today and I received a letter from Aunt Charlotte and a bundle of four papers from home. I was very glad of them and I suppose there is some one or more letters on the way from home. Dennis received William's letter and is now answering it.

Just this moment another mail has come and I have received Father's and Mother's letter. I have written so much now that I shall not have room to write all I wish upon your letter. I was very glad of it and will answer it in full in a day or two if circumstances permit. Mother[']s it seems was written Thanksgiving evening. About the same time we were "legging it" over the plank road towards the Battle Field of Chancellorsville.

One thing I noticed in the Mass Plowman you sent that gives you a wrong impression of affairs here. It states that "Mead[e]s' Army was ordered to march with 10 days cooked rations." Now our cooked rations throughout the whole army consisted of ¾th lb raw fat pork, one lb or 11 hardtack, a little salt for our fresh beef which was driven by the side of us on the hoof and two spoonfulls each of raw coffee and sugar to each man for one days rations and we took 5 in our haversacks. I wonder if they call them cooked rations?

But I must close this letter hoping to hear from you soon and to be remembered

        As ever Thomas

P.S. Excuse the dirt upon the paper & envelope, for the paper was so long I could not enclose it in my portfolio and in my knapsack it got quite dirty. I commenced this letter last evening but did not mark as I should where I commenced it this morning.

Bibliography

Manuscripts

Alderman, William. Papers. Fredericksburg and Spotsylvania National Military Park Library.
Barnard, George M. Papers. Massachusetts Historical Society.
Barr, George W. Letters. Schoff Collection. Clements Library, University of Michigan.
Berry, John. Diary. *Civil War Times Illustrated* Collection, United States Army Military History Institute.
Gibbon, John. Papers. Historical Society of Pennsylvania.
Guild, Amasa. Scrapbook. Dedham Historical Society.
Hayes, Joseph. Memoirs. Joshua Chamberlain Papers. Library of Congress.
Mann, Thomas H. Papers. Brown University.
Marble, Manton. Papers. Library of Congress.
Parmelee, Uriah. Papers. Duke University.
Partridge. Samuel S. Papers. Fredericksburg and Spotsylvania National Military Park Library.
Porter, Fitz John. Papers. Library of Congress.
Ripley, Josiah. Diary. Library of Congress.
Schurz, Carl. Papers. Library of Congress.
Smith, John L. Papers. Fredericksburg and Spotsylvania National Military Park Library.
Stanton, Edwin. Papers. Library of Congress.
Webb, Alexander S. Papers. Yale University.
Wilkins, John D. Papers. Schoff Collection. Clements Library, University of Michigan.
Woodworth, James R. Papers. Schoff Collection. Clements Library, University of Michigan.

Newspapers

Boston Herald, 1861–65.
Cambridge Chronicle, 1861–65.
Chelsea Telegraph and Pioneer, 1861–65.
Dedham Gazette, 1861–65.
Herkimer County (N.Y.) *Journal*, 1861–65.
Kingston (N.Y.) *Argus*, 1861–65.
Lebanon (Pa.) *Advertiser*, 1861–65.
(Lewiston, Maine) *Daily Evening Journal*, 1861–65.
Norfolk County Journal, 1861–65.
Penn Yan (N.Y.) *Chronicle*, 1861–65.
Rochester Democrat and American, 1861–65.
Rochester Union and Advertiser, 1861–65.
Taunton Daily Gazette, 1861–65.
(Utica) *Oneida Weekly Herald*, 1861–65.

Books

Acken, Gregory P., ed. *Inside the Army of the Potomac: The Civil War Experience of Captain Francis Adams Donaldson*. Harrisburg: 1998.
Alotta, Robert I. *Civil War Justice: Union Army Executions under Lincoln*. Shippensburg: 1989.
Bacarella, Michael. *Lincoln's Foreign Legion: The 39th New York Infantry, the Garibaldi Guard*. Shippensburg: 1996.
Bigelow, John. *Chancellorsville*. Reprint, New York: 1995.
Blight, David W. *When This Cruel War Is Over: The Civil War Letters of Charles Harvey Brewster*. Amherst: 1992.
Bruce, George A. *The Twentieth Regiment of Massachusetts Volunteer Infantry, 1861–1865*. Boston and New York: 1906.
Butler, Benjamin F. *Butler's Book*. Boston: 1892.
Carter, Robert G. *Four Brothers in Blue*. Reprint, Austin: 1978.
Coddington, Edwin. *The Gettysburg Campaign*. Reprint, Morningside: 1979.
Cooling, Benjamin F. *Symbol, Sword, and Shield: Defending Washington during the Civil War*. Reprint, Shippensburg: 1991.
Crouch, Tom D. *The Eagle Aloft: Two Centuries of the Balloon in America*. Washington, D.C.: 1983.
Dana, Charles A. *Recollections of the Civil War*. Reprint, New York: 1963.
Dawes, Rufus. *Service with the Sixth Wisconsin Volunteers*. Marietta, Ohio: 1890.
Dowdey, Clifford. *The Great Plantation: A Profile of Berkeley Hundred and Plantation*. Charles City, Va.: 1967.

Eby, Cecil D., ed. *A Virginia Yankee in the Civil War: The Diaries of David Hunter Strother.* Chapel Hill: 1961.
Eisenschiml, Otto. *The Celebrated Case of Fitz John Porter.* New York: 1950.
Fatout, Paul, ed. *Letters of a Civil War Surgeon.* West Lafayette, Indiana: 1961.
Frye, Dennis E., and John W. Schildt. *Antietam Remembered.* Sharpsburg: 1987.
Gallagher, Gary W., ed. *The Chancellorsville Campaign.* Chapel Hill: 1996.
———. *The Fredericksburg Campaign.* Chapel Hill: 1995.
———. *The Third Day at Gettysburg and Beyond.* Chapel Hill: 1994.
———. *The Wilderness Campaign.* Chapel Hill: 1997.
Gibbon, John. *Personal Recollections of the Civil War.* New York: 1928.
Graham, Martin F., and George F. Skoch. *Mine Run: A Campaign of Lost Opportunities.* Lynchburg: 1987.
Grenier, James M., Janet L. Coryell, and James R. Smither, eds. *A Surgeon's Civil War: The Letters & Diary of Daniel M. Holt, M.D.* Kent, Ohio: 1994.
Harrison, Noel G. *Chancellorsville Battlefield Sites.* Lynchburg: 1990.
———. *Fredericksburg Civil War Sites.* Lynchburg: 1995.
Henderson, William D. *The Road to Bristoe Station.* Lynchburg: 1987.
Hennessy, John J. *Return to Bull Run: The Campaign and Battle of Second Manassas.* New York: 1993.
———. *Second Manassas Battlefield Map Study.* Lynchburg: 1991.
The Hero of Medfield; Containing the Journals and Letters of Allen Alonzo Kingsbury. Boston: 1862.
Hunt, Roger D., and Jack R. Brown. *Brevet Brigadier Generals in Blue.* Gaithersburg: 1990.
Johnson, Allen, ed. *Dictionary of American Biography.* New York: 1928.
Lyman, Theodore. *Meade's Headquarters.* Reprint, Salem, N.H.: 1987.
Massachusetts. Adjutant General. *Massachusetts Soldiers, Sailors and Marines in the Civil War.* 7 vols. Brookline: 1931–1935.
McClellan, George B. *McClellan's Own Story.* New York: 1887.
McClure, A. K. *Abraham Lincoln and Men of War-Times.* Philadelphia: 1892.
McPherson, James A. *For Cause and Comrades: Why Men Fought in the Civil War.* New York: 1997.
Meade, George. *The Life and Letters of George Gordon Meade.* 2 vols. Reprint, Baltimore: 1994.
Michie, Peter S. *The Life and Letters of Emory Upton.* New York: 1885.
Miller, William J., ed., *The Peninsula Campaign of 1862.* Campbell, California: 1995.
Murfin, James V. *The Gleam of Bayonets.* New York: 1965.
Musselman, Homer D. *Stafford County in the Civil War.* Lynchburg: 1995.
Nash, Eugene A. *A History of the Forty-fourth Regiment New York Infantry.* Reprint, Dayton: 1988.
Nelson, Erik F. *Historic Resources Along the Rappahannock and Rapidan Rivers.* Fredericksburg: 1997.

Nevins, Allan, ed. *A Diary of Battle: The Personal Journals of Colonel Charles S. Wainwright, 1861–1865.* New York: 1962.
Norton, Oliver W. *Army Letters, 1861–1865.* Reprint, Dayton: 1990.
Nye, Wilbur S. *Here Come the Rebels.* Reprint, Dayton: 1984.
Parker, John L. *History of the Twenty-second Massachusetts.* Boston: 1887.
Pfanz, Harry W. *Gettysburg: The Second Day.* Chapel Hill: 1987.
Powell, William H. *The Fifth Corps.* Reprint, Dayton: 1984.
Resse, Timothy J. *Sykes' Regular Army Infantry Division, 1861–1864.* Jefferson, N.C.: 1990.
Rhea, Gordon C. *The Battle of the Wilderness.* Baton Rouge: 1994.
Robertson, James I., ed. *The Civil War Letters of General Robert McAllister.* New Brunswick, N.J.: 1965.
Rosenblatt, Emil and Ruth Rosenblatt, eds. *Hard Marching Every Day: The Civil War Letters of Private Wilbur Fisk.* Lawrence, Kansas: 1993.
Schaff, Morris. *The Battle of the Wilderness.* Reprint, Gaithersburg: 1986.
Schouler, William. *A History of Massachusetts in the Civil War.* 2 vols. Boston: 1871.
Scott, Robert Garth, ed. *Fallen Leaves: The Civil War Letters of Major Henry Livermore Abbott.* Kent, Ohio: 1991.
Sears, Stephen W. *Chancellorsville.* New York: 1996.
———. *Landscape Turned Red.* New York: 1983.
———. *To the Gates of Richmond: The Peninsula Campaign.* New York: 1992.
———. *The Young Napoleon.* New York: 1988.
Sears, Stephen W., ed. *For Country, Cause, and Leader: The Civil War Journal of Charles B. Haydon.* New York: 1993.
———. ed. *The Civil War Papers of George B. McClellan.* New York: 1989.
Sedgwick, John. *Correspondence of John Sedgwick, Major General.* New York: 1903.
Siegel, Alan A. *For the Glory of the Union: Myth, Reality, and Media in Civil War New Jersey.* Rutherford, Teaneck, Madison: 1984.
Sparks, David, ed. *Inside Lincoln's Army: The Diary of General Marsena Rudolph Patrick.* New York: 1964.
Stevens, C. A. *Berdan's United States Sharpshooters in the Army of the Potomac.* Reprint, Dayton: 1972.
Sutherland, Daniel E. *Seasons of War: The Ordeal of a Confederate Community, 1861–1865.* New York: 1995.
Trulock, Alice Rains. *In the Hands of Providence: Joshua L. Chamberlain and the American Civil War.* Chapel Hill: 1992.
Warner, Ezra. *Generals in Blue.* Baton Rouge: 1964.
Weld, Stephen M. *War Diaries and Letters of Stephen Minot Weld.* Reprint, Boston: 1978.

Wheeler, William. *Letters of William Wheeler of the Class of 1855,* Y.C. n.p.: n.d.
Wiley, Bell I. *The Life of Billy Yank.* Reprint, New York: 1971. See especially 75–76. For more commentary see "From Captain Weidman," *Lebanon* (Pa.) *Advertiser,* August 6, 1862.
Woodward, Evan M. *Our Campaigns.* Philadelphia: 1865.
Wormley, Katherine Prescott. *The Other Side of War: With the Army of the Potomac.* Boston: 1889.

Articles and Dissertations

Chamberlain, Joshua L. "My Story of Fredericksburg." *Cosmopolitan,* 1912, 148–59.
Craighill, E. A. "General Lee and the 'Yankee at Andersonville.' " *Century Monthly Illustrated Magazine,* 41, 154–55.
"Doctor T. H. Mann Dies in Conn." *Milford Daily Journal,* March 3, 1916.
Everson, Erastus W. "Forward Against Marye's Heights: The Last Onslaught at Fredericksburg—A Line of Dead Heroes." *Philadelphia Weekly Times,* March 4, 1882.
"Fitchburg: What Postmaster Mann Has Done for the Service." *Boston Herald,* October 16, 1898.
Gabler, Henry. "The Fitz John Porter Case: Politics and Military Justice." Ph.D. dissertation, City University of New York, 1979.
Gallagher, Gary W. "Brandy Station: The Civil War's Bloodiest Arena of Mounted Combat." *Blue and Gray Magazine,* October 1990, 9–22, 44–53.
Guild, Amasa. "The Eighteenth Massachusetts Regiment Volunteer Infantry in the Rebellion . . ." *Dedham Historical Register,* 13 (1902): 98–105; 14 (1903): 2–11, 48–55, 75–83, 108–17.
Hall, Clark B. "Season of Change: The Winter Encampment of the Army of the Potomac, December 1, 1863–May 4, 1864." *Blue and Gray Magazine,* April 1991, 8–22, 48–62.
Hammond, Mary Acton, ed. " 'Dear Mollie': Letters of Edward A. Acton to His Wife, 1862." *Pennsylvania Magazine of History and Biography,* 89:1 (January 1965).
Hopper, Gordon E. "Dr. Thomas Mann, One of Milford Daily News Founders." *Milford Daily News,* June 4, 1994.
Mann, Thomas H. "A Yankee at Andersonville." *Century Monthly Illustrated Magazine,* 40, 447–61, 606–22.
Milano, Anthony J., ed. "Letters from the Harvard Regiments," in *Civil War: The Magazine of the Civil War Society.* Vol. 13.
Ogden, James. "Prelude to Battle: Burnside and Fredericksburg, November 1862." *Morningside Notes, An Occasional Publication of Morningside Bookshop,* Catalogue 23. Dayton: n.d., 3–12.

Woodward, Daniel, ed. "The Civil War of a Pennsylvania Trooper." *Pennsylvania Magazine of History and Biography*, 87 (1963).

Government Documents

Martindale, John H. Court of Inquiry. Record Group 153, Court Martial Case File KK298, National Archives.

United States Congress. *Report of the Joint Committee on the Conduct of the War, Senate Reports, No. 8, No. 108.* 2 vols. Washington, D.C.: 1863.

United States Congress. *Senate Executive Document 37; Proceedings and Report of the Board of Army Officers in the Case of Fitz John Porter.* 4 vols. Washington, D.C.: 1879.

United States War Department. *Official Records of the War of the Rebellion.* 128 vols. Washington, D.C., 1880–1891.

Index

Abolition and abolitionists, xii, 96, 141, 160, 186
African Americans, xii, xiii, 174–75; Mann's comments upon, 63, 106, 141
Albany, New York, xiv
Alderman, William S. ("Sergeant Bill"), xv, xvi, xviii, 2, 7, 11, 12, 33 n, 45, 60, 68, 73, 83, 124, 138, 181, 227–28, 230; quotations from, 25–26, 28, 34–35, 39–40, 61, 75–76, 80–81, 86, 113 n, 126, 160, 186, 200–01, 202, 215–16, 228 n, 242–44
Aldie, Virginia, 167, 172
Aldie Gap, 169
Alexandria, Virginia, 22, 24, 31, 47
Alfred, George, 33
Anderson, Richard H., 156 n
Andersonville, xv, xvi, 12, 239–40
Andrew, John (governor), 4
Antietam, Battle of, 95–96, 101–02, 143, 152
Antietam Creek, 189
Aqueduct Bridge, 22, 23 n, 98
Aquia Landing, 87, 89, 114, 218
Arlington House, 22–23
Army of Northern Virginia, 85, 152, 224
Army of the Potomac, 28, 38, 43–44, 96–97, 129, 171, 187, 192, 194, 231, 232–33 n; and emancipation, xi–xii, 108, 166–67
Ashby's Gap, 170

Auburn, Virginia, 210
Averell, William Woods, 40 n, 129 n
Ayres, Romeyn B., 169 n, 193

Bailey's Crossroads review, 20, 39–40
Baker, Fisher, 10, 12, 94 n, 113, 187–88
Balloons, 70–71
Baltimore, 98, 99
Baltimore and Ohio Railroad, 18
Banks Ford, 156
Barnes, James, 9, 10, 16, 37, 41, 47, 50, 65, 67, 72–73, 79, 86, 97, 111–12, 115–18, 120–23, 129, 143, 156, 232, 244; described, 2, 10, 11; at Gettysburg, 176, 178–79
Bartlett, Joseph J., 232
Bartlett, William Francis, 4 n
Baseball, 41, 165
Batchelor, Lindsay, xvii
Battles and Leaders of the Civil War, xv
Bealeton Station, 211
Beaver Dam Creek, Battle of, 72–73
Berdan, Hiram, 54 n
Berdan's Sharpshooters, 54, 55
Berkeley Plantation, 78. *See also* Harrison's Landing
Beverly Ford, 197–98, 206, 223, 226
Blackford, Mr., 106
Blackford's Ford, 102–04
Blenker's Division, 31
Bly, Ezra, 33

Bonney, Frank, 240
Boonsboro, Maryland, 189
Boston and Providence Railroad, 14
Boston Herald, xiv
Botts, John Minor, 196–97
Brandy Station, 206, 225; battle of, 168 n
Bristoe Station, 210; battle of, 204, 208
Broad Run, 207
Brooks, W. T. H., 136 n
Brown, John, 110–11.
Bugbee, Samuel, 109–10.
Bullock Farm (Chancellorsville), 159 n
Bull Run, 24, 112, 169, 209
Bull Run, First Battle of. *See* Manassas, First Battle of
Bull Run, Second Battle of. *See* Manassas, Second Battle of
Burkittsville, Maryland, 190
Burnside, Ambrose E., 108–09, 113, 114–15, 123, 127–29, 130–31, 134, 136, 143, 152
Butler, Benjamin F., 18
Butterfield, Daniel, 35 n, 130 n, 137

"California Joe," 55–56, *See also* Head, Truman
Capitol Hill, 18, 24
Carver General Hospital, 228
Catlett Station, 169, 207
Cavalry, 137–38
Cemetery Hill, 175
Centreville, Virginia, 24, 46 n, 96, 167, 169, 207–08
Century Magazine, xv
Chain Bridge, 22, 23
Chamberlain, Joshua L., 123 n, 176
Chancellorsville, Virginia, 151 n, 153, 155, 156 n, 157–58, 219; battle of, 150–51, 153, 155–63, 171
Chantilly, Battle of, 96
Charles City Court House, 82
Charleston, South Carolina, 240
Chickahominy River, 52, 59, 65 n, 67, 69, 81–82, 87
Civilians, impact of the war upon, 27, 43–44, 74–75, 111–12, 196–99
Claflin, George H., 210–11

Cleveland, Grover, xiv
Cochrane, John, 136 n
Coggin's Point, 82–84
Commissary Department, 11
Committee on the Conduct of the War, 140, 164
Comte de Paris, 38–39
Copperheads, xiii, 128, 166–67, 193–94
Cornwallis, Lord, 50
Corps badges, 137
Craighill, E. A., 238 n
Crawford, Samuel W., 179 n, 234 n
Culpeper, Virginia, 205, 206, 225, 232
Culpeper County, Virginia, xiv, 196–97, 204
Culp's Hill, 175

Davis, Henry, 29–30, 37
Dedham, Massachusetts, xi, 3
Desertion, 136
Devil's Den, 175–76, 179
Dogan Ridge (Manassas), 90–91
Draftees and the draft, 187, 199–201, 215–16
Draft Riots, 192–93
Drinking, 5, 8, 30–32
D'Utassy, Frederick, 31

Earthworks, 52
Edson, Charles F., 110
Edward's Ferry, 172
Elizabethport Ferry, 18
Eltham's Landing, 63
Ely's Ford, 151 n, 153, 218–19, 246
Emancipation, xii–xiii, 44
Emancipation Proclamation, xii, 107, 108, 141–42
Emmittsburg, 189
Equipment, 17, 72, 105
Execution, of deserters, 187, 201–03

Fairfax Court House, Virginia, 24, 46 n, 96, 208
Fair Oaks, Battle of, 59, 68–69
Fall's Church, Virginia, 25, 46 n
Falmouth, Virginia, 114, 130 n, 141, 163, 165, 167, 227

INDEX

Ferrerro, Edward, 136 n
Ferry Farm, 119 n
Fitchburg, Massachusetts, xiv
Fitchburg *Evening Mail,* xiv
Folaney, John, 201–03
Forrest, Frederick D., 5 n, 109 n
Fort Corcoran, 20, 22–23, 36, 97, 99
Fort Donelson, x, xi,
Fortress Monroe, 44, 47, 49, 87
Foxboro, Massachusetts, 4
Franklin, Massachusetts, 4
Franklin, William B., 136 n
Frederick, Maryland, 98, 100, 173, 189
Fredericksburg, Virginia, 65 n, 85, 89, 90, 109, 114–15, 118–24, 128, 150; battle of, 8, 115, 118–27, 142–43, 152

Gaines, William, 65 n
Gaines's Mill, 65, 69; battle of, 73, 79, 87, 101
Gainesville, Virginia, 210
Georgetown, 98
Germanna Ford, 153, 223, 234
Germanna Plank Road, 234
Gettysburg, Battle of, 8, 172 n, 175–89, 224
Glee Club, Eighteenth Massachusetts, 32–35
Grant, Ulysses S., 45, 225–26, 231–33
Griffin, Charles, 103, 109, 156, 234–35
Grove Church, 167–69
Groveton Woods (Manassas), 92 n
Gum Springs, Virginia, 169

Halleck, Henry W., 87, 101, 171
Hall's Hill, 20, 23, 24, 29, 31, 35, 68, 97, 226
Hampton, Virginia, 47–48, 49, 51
Hancock, Winfield Scott, 63, 183, 185
Hanover, Pennsylvania, 173 n
Hanover Court House, Battle of, 59, 66, 67
Harper's Ferry, 24, 110–11
Harrison, Benjamin, 78 n
Harrison, Noel G., xvii
Harrison, William Henry, 78 n, 80
Harrison's Landing, 35, 60, 79, 80, 87, 89
Hartwood Church, 116–18, 134, 151, 153, 167
Hay, John, 95

Hayes, Joseph P., 9–10, 171, 188, 192, 232
Hays, Harry (Confederate general), 213
Hazel River, 226, 227
Head, Truman, 55 n
Heintzelman, Samuel P., 63
Hemenway, William W., 180, 182
Hennessy, Caroline, xvii
Henry Hill, 91
Hewins, William G., 158
Hill, Ambrose Powell, 105
Holbrook, William (surgeon), 227–28
Holmes, Oliver Wendell, 4 n
Hooker, Joseph, 36, 38 n, 63, 114, 127–28, 136–38, 143 n, 150–52, 156, 164–65, 171
Hunt, Henry J., 184–85
Hunting Creek (Run), 155

Ingraham, Timothy, 9, 86

Jackson, Thomas J. "Stonewall," 71–72, 158
James River, 48, 79, 87
John Brooks (steamer), 76
Johnson, George, 116
Johnston, Joseph E., 68–69 n, 85
Jordan, Hartley, 12–13

Kearny, Phillip, 96
Keedysville, Maryland, 190
Kelly's Ford, 138 n, 150, 151 n, 153, 168, 216
Key Bridge, 23 n
Keyes, Erasmus, 63
Kingsbury, Amos Alonzo, 57–58
Krick, Robert E. L., xvii
Kuhn, George, 201–03

Lae, Emil, 201–03
Laird, William, 122
Lee, Robert E., 22, 59, 74, 85, 95, 102, 111 n, 114–15, 136, 152, 160, 166–67, 170–71, 204, 209, 220, 223, 233, 238
Leesburg, Virginia, 98 n, 172
Libertytown, Maryland, 173
Lick Run, 156 n
Lincoln, Abraham, xii, 20, 45 n, 81, 85, 87

n, 107, 136, 195; at Bailey's Crossroads review, 39–40; Antietam visit, 106; and Emancipation Proclamation, 108, 141–42; Stafford County visit, 143
Little Round Top, 175–76, 181–82
Long Bridge, 21, 22, 31
Longstreet, James, 63 n
Lorello, Daniel, xvii
Lovettsville, Virginia, 190
Lowe, Thaddeus S. C., 70–71

Magruder, John B., 49
Maine Regiments: Second, 21, 23, 104, 122, 164 n; Sixth, 214; Twentieth, 97
Maintien, George, 12, 13, 33
Malvern Hill, Battle of, 78, 79
Manassas, First Battle of, 7
Manassas, Second Battle of, xvii, 8, 22 n, 89–95, 101, 109
Manassas Gap, 191–92
Manassas Gap Railroad, 210
Manassas Junction, 24, 44–47, 89, 169, 208
Mann, Henry, xvii
Mann, Levi (father), xi
Mann, Lydia (mother), xi
Mann, William, xvii
Martindale, John H., 21–22, 33–36, 37 n, 79
Marye's Heights, 120–125, 130, 152, 155, 220
Maryland Campaign, 95–105
Massachusetts regiments: Third Battery, 159; Ninth Battery, 179 n; Second, 110; Sixth, 99; Eighteenth, 1–240; Twentieth, 4 n, 31 n; Twenty-second, 21, 23, 53, 61 n, 79, 103, 104, 122, 165, 211, 226; Fifty-fourth, 14 n
Mattaponi River, 63
McAvoy, Frederick, 33, 93
McCall, George, 73
McCallum, Gilbert, 210, 212
McClellan, George B., xi–xii, xiv, 21, 24 n, 31, 36, 69, 70, 74 n–75 n, 90 n, 95–96, 108, 128, 143, 150, 164, 224; views upon, 38–39, 43–44, 84, 85, 134, 136, 141, 186–87, 194–95; at Bailey's Crossroads review, 39–40; and Siege of Yorktown, 45; return to army, 96–97; and Antietam Campaign, 97, 101–02, 105; relieved of command, 113; rumored to be reinstated, 171–72
McDowell, Irvin, 66, 67
McGinnis, John, 5 n, 8, 25, 112, 173–75, 199, 212
Meade, George G., 130, 143 n, 151, 159, 171, 173 n, 187–88, 204–05, 209, 217–18, 220, 222–23, 225, 232 n, 233
Mechanicsville, Battle of, 72–73
Mechanicsville, Virginia, 59
Medfield, Massachusetts, 4
Medway, Massachusetts, 4
Melville Mine (Wyckoff's Mill), 218–19
Michigan regiments: First, 21, 93 n, 94 n, 104, 122, 205, 211, 234; Fourth, 103
Middleboro, Massachusetts, 4, 86
Middleburg, Virginia, 112, 167, 170
Middlefield, Massachusetts, 228
Middletown, Maryland, 100, 189
Milford, Massachusetts, xiv
Milford Daily News, xiv
Mine Run Campaign, xvi, 204, 217–23, 225, 246–51
Monocacy River, 172
Morell, George, 24, 65, 105, 108–09
Mount Vernon, 47
Mountain Run, 246
Mud march, 1863, 19, 127, 130–36, 152
Mules, 241–45
Munson's Hill, 23, 39–40

Neponset River, 14
New Baltimore, Virginia, 210
Newport News, Virginia, 87, 89
Newspapers, 38
Newton, John, 136 n
New York City, 16, 18, 192–93
New York regiments: Twelfth, 93 n, 94; Thirteenth, 21, 23, 93 n, 94 n, 104; Seventeenth, 72; Twenty-fifth, 21, 23, 122, 155; Thirtieth, 93n; Thirty-ninth, 31
Norfolk, Massachusetts. *See* North Wrentham
Norfolk, Virginia, 48

North Wrentham, Massachusetts, x, xiii, 240

Old Point Comfort, 47, 48, 78
Orange and Alexandria Railroad, 205, 207 n, 210, 212, 218, 232
Orange Court House, 219, 220, 238
Orange Plank Road, 156 n
Orange Turnpike, 155, 156 n, 234, 238
O'Reilly, Frank, xvii

Pamunkey River, 63, 64, 73, 76
Parker's Store, 234
Parrott, Robert G., 159 n
Parrott rifle, 159, 182
Patrick, Marsena, 195 n
Pennsylvania Avenue, 18–19
Pennsylvania regiments: Sixth Cavalry, 73, 80–81; Eighty-third, 234; 118th, 97, 103–04, 122, 140, 201–02, 211–212; 139th, 209 n
Pennsylvania Reserves, 73, 179–80, 234 n
Phillipe, Louis, 38–39
Picket duty, 25–27, 139–40
Pickett's Charge, 182–84
Pleasonton, Alfred, 168 n
Plymouth, Massachusetts, 4
Poker, 42
Pontoon bridges, 119, 163, 172, 218–19
Pope, John, 85, 90 n, 95, 113
Poquosian Creek, 49
Porter, Fitz John, xii, 21, 32, 36, 37 n, 61–62, 64–65, 70–71, 79, 108, 113, 224; characterized, 24 n; views of, 43–44; and Second Manassas, 90 n, 95–96
Portsmouth, Virginia, 48
Potomac River, 22, 44, 47, 87, 95, 102–04, 111, 172, 189–90
Powhite Creek, 65 n
Pray, Charles F., 226
Prim y Prats, Juan, 69

Rainese, John, 201–03
Rains, Gabriel, 61 n
Rapidan River, 46, 150, 151 n, 152, 153, 155, 218, 225
Rappahannock River, 46, 85, 89, 115, 129–30, 134, 139, 150, 152, 153, 161–63, 186, 204–05, 226–27
Rappahannock Station, 89 n, 250; battle of, 204, 211–14
Ray, George A., 210
Readville, xi, 2, 4 n, 9, 14–16
Reenlistment, xiii, xiv, 224–25, 229–31
Regimental bands, 16–17 n
Revere, Paul J., 4n
Rhode Island troops: First Cavalry, 169
Richmond, Fredericksburg, and Potomac Railroad, 87 n
Richmond, Virginia, 44, 59, 66, 67, 71
Roberts, Otis C., 214
Robertson's Tavern, 219, 247
Rockville, Maryland, 98–100
Russell, David A., 213

Salem Church, 161 n
Saunders Field, 236 n, 237 n
Schoolhouse Branch (Manassas), 92 n
Schurz, Carl, 38 n
Sedgwick, John, 160–61, 195 n, 214
Seven Days Battles, 59–60, 71, 142–43, 152
Seven Pines, Battle of, 59, 69
Sharpe, George H., 138 n
Shenandoah River, 111
Shenandoah Valley, 111
Shepherdstown Ford, Battle of, 102–04, 109, 152, 155
Sherman, Gilbert, 215 n
Shiloh, Battle of, x
Short, Dennis, 8, 98–100, 226
Sickles, Daniel E., 175–76
Simmons, Isaac R., 157
Skinner, Zenas, 93
Slavery, x, xii, 186
Smith, Frank, 8
Smith, William F., 136 n
Snicker's Gap, 112
Snickersville, Virginia, 111, 190
Snow, James, 8, 11
Soule, Preston, 12, 68, 80
South Mountain, 100–01, 189
Stafford County, Virginia, 151
Stevensburg, 223, 250
Stoneman, George, 72–73, 79, 138, 168 n

Stonington, Massachusetts, 16
Straggling, 98–100, 173–75
Stratton House (Fredericksburg), 122 n
Stuart, J. E. B., 138
Sturgis, Samuel, 136 n
Sumner, Charles (senator), 38 n
Sutlers, 75
Sykes, George, 65, 155, 169, 171, 173 n, 232

Tents, 41
Thomas, Steven, 86
Thompson, George W., 192
Thoroughfare Gap, 169
Tift, Ransom, 13–14
Tobacco, 65–66
"Touch the Elbow" (song), 33–35
Training, 5, 7–16

Unfinished railroad (Manassas), 86, 91–95, 209
Uniforms, 5, 39 n
United States Colored Troops, views upon, 141, 224–25, 230–31
United States Ford, 151 n, 153, 155, 162
United States troops, Regulars: Battery D, Fifth Artillery, 103, 182 n
Upton's Hill, 23

Vincent, Strong, 176
Volunteer soldiers, ix, 1, 2–4
Vanderbilt (steamer), 76

Wainwright, Charles, 137 n
Walpole, Massachusetts, 4
Walter, Charles, 201–03
Wappings Heights, Battle of, 191–92

Warren, Gouverneur K., 36, 137, 222 n, 232
Warrenton, Virginia, 112, 192, 207, 210
Warrenton Junction, 89
Warwick River, 49, 51
Washington, D.C., x, 2, 18–19, 31, 96
Washington, George, 47
Washington, Martha Custis, 59, 74
Westminster, Maryland, 173
Weston, George F., 213
Westover Mansion, 35, 80
West Point, Virginia, 63
White, William B., 176
White House Landing, 60, 73–74
Wilderness, Battle of, xvi, xvii, 216, 225, 233–38
Wilderness Tavern, 234
Williamsburg, Battle of, 63, 152
Williamsburg, Virginia, 87
Williamsport, Maryland, operations before, 189–90
Wilson, Charles H., 234
Wilson, Henry (senator), 21
Winter quarters, 40–41, 115–16, 129, 165, 217, 226–28
Women, soldiers' interaction with, 28–30
Woonsocket, Rhode Island, xiv
Wrentham, Massachusetts, 1
Wrentham Lyceum, xi, xiii
Wyckoff's (Wycoff's) Mill, 218–19, 247

Yellow Chapel. *See* Hartwood Church
York River, 49, 51, 63, 78
Yorktown, Virginia, 11, 49, 62, 87, 242; advance upon, 50–51; siege of, 44, 51–58, 152; evacuation of, 58, 60

Zoan Church, 156 n